The **Rough Guide** to

# Vienna

written and researched by

## Rob Humphreys

ROUGH
GUIDES

www.roughguides.com

# Contents

**The Secession**
colour section
following p.112

**Coffee and cakes**
colour section
following p.208

SCHAUFLER-PLATZ

Hofburg  JOSEFS-PLATZ

**Colour maps** following
p.296

Introduction to

# Vienna

**Most visitors to Vienna have a vivid image of the city in mind: a monumental vision of Habsburg palaces, trotting white horses, old ladies in fur coats and mountains of fat cream cakes. And they're unlikely to be disappointed. Vienna positively feeds off imperial nostalgia – High Baroque churches and aristocratic piles pepper the old town, or Innere Stadt; monumental projects from the late nineteenth century line the Ringstrasse; and postcards of the Emperor Franz-Josef and his beautiful wife "Sisi" still sell by the sackful.**

 Just as compelling as the old Habsburg stand-bys are the wonderful **Jugendstil** and early modernist buildings, products of fin-de-siècle Vienna, when the city emerged as one of Europe's great cultural centres. This was the era of Freud, Klimt, Schiele, Mahler and Schnitzler, when the city's famous **coffeehouses** were filled with intellectuals from every corner of the empire. In a sense, this was Vienna's golden age, after which all has been in decline: with the end of the empire in 1918, the city was reduced from a metropolis of over two million, capital of a vast empire of fifty million, to one of little more than one and a half million, federal capital of a small country of just eight million souls.

Given the city's twentieth-century history, it's hardly surprising that the Viennese are as keen as anyone to continue plugging the good old days. This is a place, not unlike Berlin, which has had the misfortune of serving as a weather vane of European history. Modern anti-Semitism as a politically viable force was invented here, in front of Hitler's very eyes, in the first decade of the century. It was the assassination of an arrogant Austrian archduke that started World War I, while the battles between Left and Right fought out in the streets of Vienna mirrored those in Berlin in the 1930s. The weekend Hitler enjoyed his greatest electoral victory in the Reichstag was the moment the Austrians themselves invented Austro-fascism. In 1938, the country became the first "victim" of Nazi expansion, greeting the Führer with delirious enthusiasm. And after the war, for a decade, Vienna was divided, like Berlin, into French, American, British and Soviet sectors.

While the visual scars from this turbulent history are few and far between – even Hitler's sinister concrete Flaktürme are confined to the suburbs – the destruction of the city's once enormous Jewish community is a wound that has proved harder to heal. Vienna's Jewish intellectuals and capitalists were the driving force behind much of the city's fin-de-siècle culture. Little surprise then, that the city has since struggled to live up to its glorious past. After the war Vienna lost its cosmopolitan character and found itself stuck in a monocultural straightjacket. Since the end of the Cold War, however, this has begun to change, with the arrival of a second wave of immigrants from the former provinces of the old empire. How Vienna will learn to accept its new, multicultural identity remains to be seen.

Nevertheless, Vienna remains an inspiring city to visit, with one of the world's greatest art collections in the **Kunsthistorisches Museum**, world-class

▲ Mozart souvenirs

orchestras, and a superb architectural heritage. It's also an eminently civilized place, clean, safe (for the most part) and peopled by courteous citizens who do their best to live up to their reputation for *Gemütlichkeit* or "cosiness". And despite its ageing population, it's also a city with a small, but lively, nightlife of cool cafés, clubs and drinking holes. Even Vienna's traditional restaurants, long famous for quantity over quality, have begun to overhaul their methods of cooking and presentation, although these are supplemented by a wonderful residue of reassuringly old-fashioned *Kaffeehäuser*, where the fin-de-siècle city is lovingly preserved in aspic.

# What to see

For all its grandiosity, Vienna is surprisingly compact: the centre is just a kilometre across at its broadest point, and you can travel from one side of the city to the other by public transport in less than thirty minutes. This means you can get to see a lot in a relatively short space of time.

The most obvious place to start is in Vienna's central district, the old medieval town or **Innere Stadt** (literally the "inner town"). Retaining much of its labyrinthine street layout, it remains the main commercial district, packed with shops, cafés and restaurants. The chief sight here is Stephansdom, Vienna's landmark cathedral and its finest Gothic edifice, standing at the district's pedestrianized centre. Tucked into the southwest corner of the Innere Stadt is the **Hofburg**, the former imperial palace and seat of the Habsburgs, now home to a whole host of museums.

When the old fortifications surrounding the Innere Stadt were torn down in 1857, they were gradually replaced by a showpiece boulevard called the **Ringstrasse**. It is this irregular pentagon-shaped thoroughfare that, along with the Danube Canal, encloses the Innere Stadt. Nowadays the Ringstrasse is used and abused by traffic as a ring road, though it's still punctuated with the most grandiose public

▲ Kaffeehaus

buildings of late-imperial Vienna: the parliament, town hall, opera house and university and several museums, including the city's fabulous cultural complex, the **MuseumsQuartier**, and the **Kunsthistorisches Museum**, home to one of the world's finest art collections.

## Public transport

If there's one thing that every visitor would like to take home from Vienna, it's the public transport system, which is among the most efficient in the world. The U-Bahn is clean and constantly expanding, the trams are silent and smooth, and, even more remarkably, the buses run on schedule, to a timetable. Imagine: you go to a bus stop, look up the time of the next bus, and it arrives when it says it will. Simple, you might think, but just a dream for many of the world's urban commuters.

The most stylish of the **U-Bahn** lines is the ultra-modern U3; the most aesthetically pleasing the U6, which has lots of original Jugendstil stations designed by Otto Wagner. On the **trams**, take the #1 or #2 for a free tour of the Ringstrasse (see p.86). Best of all, though, is **bus #2a**, which winds its way through the impossibly narrow streets of the Innere Stadt and finally through the courtyards of the Hofburg itself. For the privilege of using this system, the Viennese pay just €14 a week, less than half of what commuters in London have to spend. And the whole system runs on trust. At least once a month, you're likely to be stopped by an inspector, and with the fines high and the ticket prices low, you'd be a fool to get caught.

▲ Fiaker

Beyond the Ringstrasse lie Vienna's seven inner suburbs, the **Vorstädte**, whose outer boundary is comprised of the traffic-clogged *Gürtel* (literally "belt") or ring road. If you're travelling on any kind of budget, you're likely to find yourself staying somewhere out in the Vorstädte. The highlight here is the **Belvedere**, to the south of the Innere Stadt, where you can see a wealth of paintings by Austria's trio of modern artists: Gustav Klimt, Egon Schiele and Oskar Kokoschka.

Although the **Danube** is crucial to Vienna's identity, most visitors see very little of the river, whose main arm flows through the outer suburbs northeast of the city centre. In fact, east of the Danube Canal, only the **Prater**, with its famous Ferris wheel and funfair, is essential viewing.

There's little reason, either, to venture beyond the *Gürtel* into the outer suburbs, except to visit **Schönbrunn**, the Habsburgs' former summer residence, a masterpiece of Rococo excess and an absolute must if only for the wonderful gardens. The hilly woodland paths of the **Wienerwald**, on the northwestern edge of the city, have been a popular rural retreat for the Viennese since the days of Beethoven and Schubert, who gained inspiration from their vine-backed slopes. Both composers now lie – along with thousands of other Viennese – at the opposite end of the city, in the far southeast corner, in the city's fascinating **Zentralfriedhof** (Central Cemetery).

# When to go

L ying at the centre of Europe, Vienna experiences the extremes of temperature typical of a continental climate, with hot summers and correspondingly cold winters. In terms of weather, therefore, late spring and early autumn are by far the best times to visit. There are other reasons, too, to avoid July and August in particular, as this is when many of the city's theatres and concert halls close down. Sure, there's enough cultural activity to keep the tourists amused, but the Viennese tend to get the hell out. In contrast, Christmas and New Year are peak season in Vienna. Not only does the city look great in the snow – and you can be sure that the Viennese are very efficient about keeping the paths clear – but also the ball season, known as *Fasching*, gets under way, along with the glittering Christmas markets and, of course, the world-famous New Year's Day concert.

## Average temperatures and rainfall

|  | Jan | Feb | Mar | Apr | May | Jun | Jul | Aug | Sep | Oct | Nov | Dec |
|---|---|---|---|---|---|---|---|---|---|---|---|---|
| **Vienna** | | | | | | | | | | | | |
| Max/Min (ºC) | 1/-4 | 3/-3 | 8/-1 | 15/6 | 19/10 | 23/14 | 25/15 | 24/15 | 20/11 | 14/7 | 7/3 | 3/-1 |
| Rainfall (mm) | 39 | 44 | 44 | 45 | 70 | 67 | 84 | 72 | 42 | 56 | 52 | 45 |

# 20

## things not to miss

*It's not possible to see everything that Vienna has to offer on a short trip – and we don't suggest you try. What follows is therefore a subjective selection of the city's highlights, from the showpiece museums and churches to its relaxed cafés, tranquil parks and appealing day-trip destinations – all arranged in five colour-coded categories to help you find the very best things to see, do and experience. All entries have a page reference to take you straight into the guide, where you can find out more.*

**01 Tram round the Ringstrasse** Page **86** • For a free sightseeing tour of the Ringstrasse, just hop on tram #1 and then #2 and start reading Chapter 3.

## 02 Museums-Quartier

Page **96** • Vienna's newest arts complex houses an orgy of works by Schiele, the city's chief modern art museum, and a host of funky cafés and bars.

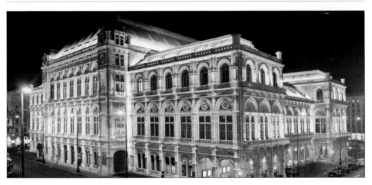

## 03 Opera
Page **100** • Vienna boasts one of the world's top opera houses, and also one of its most democratic, with standing-room tickets for as little as €2.50.

## 04 Prater
Page **151** • With its iconic Ferris wheel and old-fashioned funfair, the Prater is probably the best reason to venture east of the Danube Canal.

**05 Schatzkammer** Page **74** •
The imperial family may have gone, but their hoard of crown jewels is full of absolute gems.

**06 Trześniewski** Page **208** •
Minimalist snack bar, presided over by formidable assistants, serving tiny *Brötchen* washed down with a *Pfiff* – a city institution.

**07 Zentralfriedhof** Page **190** • One of the world's most awesome municipal cemeteries, with over two and a half million corpses, including Beethoven, Schubert, Brahms, Schönberg and the entire Strauss family.

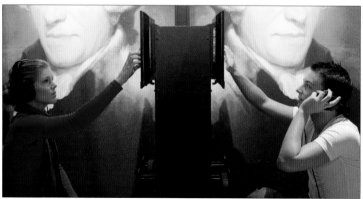

**08 Haus der Musik** Page **51** • The museum of the conservative Vienna Philharmonic is one of the city's most innovative, with lots of interactive musical fun and games.

**09** **Karlskirche** Page **104** • Quite simply the most spectacular Baroque church in the capital, inside and out.

**10** **Fiakers** Page **27** • In a place so steeped in nostalgia, it would be churlish not to have a ride in a Fiaker.

**11** **Kaffeehäuser** Page **206** and *Coffee and cakes* **colour section** • With their tuxedoed waiters, calorific cakes, copious newspapers and unhurried air, Vienna's *Kaffeehäuser* are the city's most important and enduring social institutions.

**13** **Kirche am Steinhof** Page **180** • Otto Wagner's Jugendstil masterpiece is a magnificent domed church built for the inmates of the local psychiatric hospital.

**12** **The Third Man** Page **106** • This classic black-and-white film was shot amid the rubble of postwar Vienna – it's shown every weekend in one of the city's cinemas, guided tours take place weekly and there's even a museum.

**14 Secession** Page **103** • This remarkable Jugendstil art gallery still puts on contemporary art shows, as well as preserving Klimt's original fresco from the 1902 exhibition.

**16 Naschmarkt** Page **107** • Genuinely multiethnic outdoor food market, with a great flea market on Saturdays.

**15 Heurigen** Page **222** • Sitting in an orchard surrounded by vineyards, overlooking the city, sipping the local wine, is one of the pleasures of a Viennese summer.

**17 Schönbrunn** Page **161** • By far the most magnificent of the Habsburgs' many palaces, Schönbrunn also boasts the most wonderful gardens, woods, fountains, mazes, hothouses and zoo.

**19 Belvedere** Page **130** • Twin Baroque palaces separated by formal gardens and a great collection of works by Klimt, Schiele and Kokoschka.

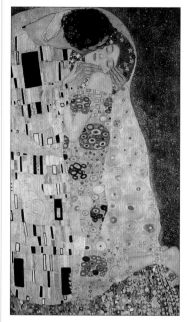

**18 Kunsthistorisches Museum** Page **114** • A spectacular late nineteenth-century building housing one of the world's greatest art collections, famous above all for its Brueghels.

**20 Stephansdom** Page **42** • The undisputed heart of Vienna, the city's cathedral features some superb medieval craftsmanship, extensive catacombs and a couple of great viewpoints from its twin towers.

# Basics

# Basics

# Getting there

Unless you're coming from a neighbouring European country, the quickest way to get to Vienna is by plane. The city receives direct flights from just about every European capital; flight time from London is just over two hours. There are also one or two nonstop flights from North America, though you'll get a much wider choice – and often lower fares – if you fly via London or another European gateway.

With most airlines, how much you pay depends on how far in advance you book and how much demand there is during that period – the earlier you book, the cheaper the prices.

Another option, if you're travelling from Britain or elsewhere in Europe, is to go by train, bus or car. These usually take considerably longer than a plane and may not work out that much cheaper, but are undoubtedly better for the environment.

## Flights from Britain and Ireland

You can fly to Vienna direct **from London and Dublin**. The most competitive fares are with the budget airlines, though the national airlines, British Airways (BA) and Austrian Airlines, have had to slash their prices accordingly. If you book far enough in advance or can be flexible about dates, you can find return fares from London to Vienna for as little as £50 (taxes included). From Ireland, return airfares start at around €120 return from Dublin. Of course, if you don't book early, prices can skyrocket. Routes can change – and airlines go under – with little notice, so check airport and airline websites for the latest.

## Flights from the US and Canada

Austrian Airlines is the only airline to offer nonstop flights **from North America** to Vienna all year round. You'll get a much wider choice of flights and prices, though, if you opt for an indirect flight and one or two changes of plane, allowing you to depart from any number of North American cities and travel via one of the major gateways.

Flying time from the east coast to Vienna is about nine hours. **Fares** depend very much on the flexibility of the ticket and on availability; a New York–Vienna return costs $700 and upwards, a Toronto–Vienna return Can$1000 and upwards.

## Flights from Australia and New Zealand

Flight time **from Australia and New Zealand** to Vienna is more than twenty hours, depending on routes and transfer times. There's a wide range of routes, with those touching down in Southeast Asia the quickest and cheapest on average. Given the length of the journey, you might be better off including a night's stopover in your itinerary, and indeed some airlines include one in the price of the flight.

The cheapest direct scheduled flights to London can usually be found on one of the Asian airlines. Average **return fares** (including taxes) from eastern gateways to London are Aus$1500–2000 in low season, Aus$2000–2500 in high season. Fares from Perth or Darwin cost around Aus$200 less. You'll then need to add Aus$100–200 onto all these for the connecting flight to Vienna. Return fares from Auckland to London range between NZ$2000 and NZ$3000 depending on the season, route and carrier.

## Trains

You can travel from London to Vienna overnight in around twenty hours. Fares start at around £180 return but depend on the route you take and how far in advance you book your ticket.

To reach Vienna **by train**, first take the Eurostar from London St Pancras to

## Five steps to a better kind of travel

At Rough Guides we are passionately committed to travel. We feel strongly that only through travelling do we truly come to understand the world we live in and the people we share it with. But the extraordinary growth in tourism has also damaged some places irreparably, and of course **climate change** is exacerbated by most forms of transport, especially flying. This means that now more than ever it's important to **travel thoughtfully** and **responsibly**. At Rough Guides we feel there are several main areas in which you can make a difference:

• Consider what you're contributing to the **local economy**, and how much the services you use do the same.

• Consider the **environment** on holiday as well as at home. Try to patronize businesses that take account of this.

• Travel with a purpose, not just to tick off experiences. Consider **spending longer** in a place, and getting to know it and its people.

• Consider **alternatives to flying**, travelling instead by train or bus or boat where possible.

• Make your trips **"climate neutral"** via a reputable carbon-offset scheme. All Rough Guide flights are offset, and every year we donate money to a variety of charities devoted to combating the effects of climate change.

Brussels. From there, the most direct, and usually the cheapest, route is via **Cologne (Köln)**, from which there's an overnight service to Vienna.

Although you can crash out on the seats, it makes sense to book a **couchette**, which costs an extra £15 one way in a six-berth compartment, rising to £25 in a three-berth compartment. Couchettes are mixed-sex and allow little privacy; for a bit more comfort, you can book a bed in a single-sex two-berth sleeper for around £50.

**Fares** for continental rail travel have become much more flexible; shop around for the best deal, rather than taking the first offer you get. Tickets are usually valid for two months and allow as many stopovers as you want on the specified route. If you're travelling with one or more companions, you may be eligible for a further discount.

The cheapest way to book tickets is usually **online**, but you may have to use several websites to get the best deals. For more details, visit the superb website Ⓦwww.seat61.com.

### Buses

One of the cheapest ways to get to Vienna is **by bus**. Eurolines runs a direct service from London's Victoria Coach Station more or less daily throughout the year. Coaches tend to set off in the morning, arriving in Erdberg

U-Bahn station roughly 23 hours later. The journey is bearable (just about), with short breaks every three to four hours, but only really worth it if you've left it too late to find a budget flight. Advance fares can be as cheap as £85 return; under-26s and over-60s are eligible for further discounts.

### Driving

With two or more passengers, **driving to Vienna** can work out relatively inexpensive. However, it is not the most relaxing option, unless you enjoy pounding along the motorway systems of Europe for the best part of a day and a night.

**Eurotunnel** operates a 24-hour train service carrying vehicles plus passengers from Folkestone to Calais. At peak times, services run every ten minutes, with the journey lasting 35 minutes. Off-peak fares in high season start at £150 return (passengers included). The alternative is to catch one of the **ferries** between Dover and Calais, Boulogne or Dunkirk, or between Ramsgate and Ostend. Prices vary enormously but if you book in advance, summer fares can be as little as £70 return per carload. Journey times are usually around ninety minutes. If you're travelling from north of London, however, it might be worth taking a longer ferry journey from Rosyth, Newcastle, Hull or Harwich.

Once you've made it onto the continent, you face something in the region of **1200km of driving**. For Vienna, the most direct route from Ostend or Calais is via Brussels, Liège (Luik), Cologne (Köln), Frankfurt and Nuremberg (Nürnberg). It costs nothing to drive on motorways in Belgium and Germany, but to go on an Austrian autobahn, you must buy and display a sticker or *Vignette* (available at border crossings and petrol stations); the cheapest version, valid for ten days, costs €7.90. If you're travelling by car you'll need proof of ownership or a letter from the owner giving you permission to drive the vehicle. You also need a country identification sticker, a red warning triangle in case you break down, a first-aid kit (all are compulsory in Austria), and a "Green Card" for third-party insurance cover at the very least.

## Airlines, Agents and Operators

### Airlines

Aer Lingus ⓦ www.aerlingus.com
Air Canada ⓦ www.aircanada.com
Air New Zealand ⓦ www.airnewzealand.com
Air Transat ⓦ www.airtransat.com
American Airlines ⓦ www.aa.com
Asiana Airlines ⓦ www.flyasiana.com
Austrian Airlines ⓦ www.austrian.com
bmi ⓦ www.flybmi.com
British Airways ⓦ www.ba.com
Cathay Pacific ⓦ www.cathaypacific.com
Continental Airlines ⓦ www.continental.com
Delta ⓦ www.delta.com
easyJet ⓦ www.easyjet.com
Gulf Air ⓦ www.gulfair.com
KLM ⓦ www.klm.com
Lauda Air ⓦ www.laudaair.com
Lufthansa ⓦ www.lufthansa.com
Malaysia Airlines ⓦ www.malaysiaairlines.com
Qantas ⓦ www.qantas.com
Royal Brunei ⓦ www.bruneiair.com
Singapore Airlines ⓦ www.singaporeair.com
Thai Airways ⓦ www.thaiair.com
United Airlines ⓦ www.united.com
Virgin Atlantic ⓦ www.virgin-atlantic.com

### Agents and operators

North South Travel ⓦ www.northsouthtravel .co.uk. Friendly, competitive travel agency, offering discounted fares worldwide. Profits are used to support projects in the developing world, especially the promotion of sustainable tourism.
STA ⓦ www.statravel.com. Worldwide specialists in independent travel; also student IDs, travel insurance, car rental, rail passes, and more. Good discounts for students and under-26s.
Trailfinders ⓦ www.trailfinders.com. One of the best-informed and most efficient agents for independent travellers.

### Rail contacts

Deutsche Bahn ☎ 0871/880 8066 (Mon–Fri 9am–5pm), ⓦ www.bahn.com. Competitive discounted fares for any journey from London across Europe, with very reasonable prices for journeys passing through Germany.
European Rail ☎ 020/7387 0444 (Mon–Fri 9am–5pm), ⓦ www.europeanrail.com. Rail specialist that consistently offers competitive prices on international rail tickets from anywhere in the UK.
Eurostar ☎ 08705/186 186 (Mon–Fri 8am–7pm, Sat & Sun 9am–5pm), ⓦ www.eurostar.com. Latest fares and youth discounts (plus online booking) on the Eurostar service, plus competitive add-on fares from the rest of the UK.
Man in Seat 61 ⓦ www.seat61.com. The world's finest train website, full of incredibly useful tips and links for rail travel anywhere in the world.
National Rail ☎ 0845/748 4950 (24hr), ⓦ www .nationalrail.co.uk. First stop for details of all train travel within the UK – fares, passes, train times and delays due to engineering works.
Rail Europe ☎ 08705/848 848 (Mon–Fri 9am–7pm, Sat 9am–6pm), ⓦ www.raileurope .co.uk. SNCF-owned information and ticket agent for all European passes and journeys from London. They also have an office at 1 Regent St, London SW1 (Mon–Fri 10am–6pm, Sat 10am–4pm).
TrainsEurope ☎ 0871/700 7722 (Mon–Fri 9am–5.30pm), ⓦ www.trainseurope.co.uk. Agent specializing in discounted international rail travel.

### Bus contacts

Eurolines UK ☎ 0871/781 8177, ⓦ www.eurolines .co.uk; Ireland ☎ 01/836 6111, ⓦ www.buseireann .ie. Tickets can also be purchased from any National Express or Bus Éireann agent.

### Ferry contacts

To find the cheapest fares across the Channel, check out ⓦ www.ferrysmart.co.uk
DFDS Seaways ☎ 0871/522 9955, ⓦ www .dfdseaways.co.uk. Newcastle to Amsterdam.

**Eurotunnel** ☎0844/335 3535, ⓦwww.eurotunnel .com. Folkestone to Calais through the tunnel.
**LD Lines Network** UK ☎0800/917 1201, ⓦwww .ldlines.co.uk. Newhoven to Dieppe and Ramsgate to Ostend.
**Norfolkline** ☎020/8127 8303, ⓦwww .norfolkline-ferries.co.uk. Dover to Dunkirk and Rosyth (near Edinburgh) to Zeebrugge.

**P&O Stena Line** ☎0871/664 5645, ⓦwww .poferries.com. Dover to Calais and Hull to Rotterdam and Zeebrugge.
**SeaFrance** ☎0871/423 7119, ⓦwww.seafrance .com. Dover to Calais.
**Stena Line** ☎0844/770 7070, ⓦwww.stenaline .co.uk. Harwich to the Hook of Holland.

# Arrival

Vienna is a surprisingly compact city, with a population of just one and a half million. Its airport lies just over 20km southeast of the city centre, with fast connections to get you into town. The international train stations and main bus terminal are linked to the centre by the fast and efficient U-Bahn (metro) system.

## By air

Vienna's clean and efficient airport, **Flughafen Wien-Schwechat** (☎7007, ⓦwww.vienna airport.com), has a supermarket open daily until late, and a half-decent selection of bars and restaurants. There are two main terminals (1 & 2), with a new terminal, SKYLINK, due to open in 2012.

**CAT**, the City Airport Train, runs 20km to the city centre (daily 5.30am–11.30pm; ⓦwww.cityairporttrain.com). Tickets cost €10 (€9 online), and trains leave every thirty minutes, taking sixteen minutes to reach the City Air Terminal at Wien-Mitte (U-Bahn Landstrasse/Wien Mitte). Alternatively, you can catch **S-Bahn** line S7 (daily 4.30am– midnight) which runs between Wolfsthal and Wien Floridsdorf, calling at the airport en route; the service runs every thirty minutes, with the trip from the airport to Wien-Mitte or Wien-Nord (U-Bahn Praterstern) taking thirty minutes. This is the cheapest way to get into town, costing €3.60 one way; however, if you plan to do a bit of travelling when you first arrive, you'll save some money if you ask for a travel pass (*Netzkarte*) for the central zone (see opposite) at the same time.

**Vienna Airport Lines buses** from the airport to Schwedenplatz leave every thirty minutes (daily 4.30am–11.30pm), taking around twenty minutes to reach the city centre, and costing €7. Buses also run every thirty minutes to the Westbahnhof (see below).

If you're taking a **taxi** to the centre, opt for an airport taxi rather than a standard one; if you go to C&K Airport Service (☎444 44), for example, they will charge around €30 one way.

## By train, bus and boat

Arriving in Vienna by train from the west, you'll end up at the **Westbahnhof**, five U-Bahn stops west of Stephansplatz in the city centre on the U3 line. Through trains and trains from east of Vienna currently terminate at **Wien-Meidling (U-Bahn Meidling-Philadelphiabrücke)**, southwest of the city centre, but will eventually stop at the new main train station, **Wien-Haupt- bahnhof** (ⓦwww.hauptbahnhof-wien.at), south of the city centre, which will be opera- tional from 2013 onwards, with a final completion date of 2015. Of Vienna's other stations, **Franz-Josefs-Bahnhof**, in the northern suburb of Alsergrund, serves as an arrival point for services from Lower Austria and the odd train from Prague (take tram #D or #1 into town), while **Wien-Nord** (U-Bahn Praterstern), in Leopoldstadt, is used exclu- sively by local and regional trains, including the S-Bahn to the airport. For more on trains to Vienna, see p.19.

Vienna has no main bus station, so your arrival point by **bus** will depend on which company you're travelling with. Eurolines long-distance buses currently arrive at Erdberg U-Bahn, on the southeastern edge of the centre.

In the unlikely event of your arriving on one of the **DDSG boat services** (ⓦwww.ddsg-blue-danube.at) from Bratislava, or further up the Danube, you'll find yourself disembarking at the Schiffahrtszentrum by the Reichsbrücke, some way northeast of the city centre; the nearest station (U-Bahn Vorgartenstrasse) is five minutes' walk away, one block west of Mexikoplatz.

# City transport

Although Vienna's city centre is best explored on foot, to cover larger distances you'll need to use the extremely efficient city transport system known as the *Wiener Linien* (ⓦwww.wienerlinien.at). The trams and buses are punctual and the rapidly expanding U-Bahn (metro) is clean, very quick, and very reasonably priced too.

## Tickets and passes

A single-journey **ticket** (*Fahrschein* or *Einzelfahrschein*), standard for all forms of public transport, costs €1.80 from machines and ticket booths (*Vorverkauf*) at major tram junctions and U-Bahn stations, and also from tobacconists (*Tabak-Trafik*). When you enter the U-Bahn, or board a tram or bus, you must punch (*entwerten*) your ticket in one of the blue machines. You can then make one journey, during which you can change buses, trams or U-Bahn lines as many times as you like, without punching your ticket again, as long as you proceed in a logical direction without any "breaks".

If you don't get it together to buy a ticket before boarding a tram or bus, you can buy one for €2.20 from the machines beside the driver – these need not be punched. Tickets for kids aged 6 to 15 cost €0.90 (€1.10 on board); under-6s travel free, and under-16s

travel free on Sundays, public holidays and during school holidays (pick up a calendar at a *Wiener Linien* information office).

If you plan to make more than two journeys a day, invest in a **travel pass** or *Netzkarte*, which allows travel on all trams, buses, U- and S-Bahn trains within the city limits. Machines and booths at all U-Bahn stations sell a 24-hour *Stundenticket* (€5.70), a 48-hour *Stundenticket* (€10), and a 72-hour *Stundenticket* (€13.60); when buying your ticket from a machine, select the central zone or *Kernzone* (*Zone 100*), which covers all of Vienna. You must punch your single *Netzkarte* at the start of your first journey – your 24 or 72 hours begins from that point. The Vienna Card/*Wien-Karte* (€18.50) gives discounts at local attractions as well as being a 72-hour *Netzkarte* (see opposite for more details). The *Wiener Einkaufskarte* (€4.60) is a daily travel pass

### Travel information offices

There are *Wiener Linien* **information offices** at the following U-Bahn stations: Stephansplatz, Karlsplatz, Praterstern and Westbahnhof (all Mon–Fri 6.30am–6.30pm, Sat & Sun 8.30am–4pm); Floridsdorf, Philadelphiabrücke, Schottentor and Landstrasse (all Mon–Fri 6.30am–6.30pm).

valid between 8am and 8pm, aimed at shoppers and not available on Sunday.

Another option is a four-journey **strip ticket** or *Streifenkarte* (€7.20). The card can be used by one or more people – simply punch one strip on the card for each person in the group. To do this you must fold the card over before inserting it in the blue machines, starting with strip 1. Even more useful is the **8-day ticket**, or *8-Tage-Klimakarte* (€28.80), which works like the strip ticket, but is valid for eight (not necessarily consecutive) days' travel, calculated in 24-hour periods. It can be used by one person for eight days, two people for four, and so on.

If you're staying in Vienna longer than three days, it may be worth buying a **weekly card** or *Wochenkarte* (€14), available only from coded ticket machines or ticket offices at U-Bahn stations. The pass runs from 9am Monday to 9am the following Monday so there's no need to punch the ticket; it's transferable in the sense that it can be passed to another person for them to use, though two people travelling together need two separate tickets). The **monthly ticket** or *Monatskarte* (€49.50), which runs for a calendar month, works in much the same way.

The Viennese being a law-abiding bunch, there are few **ticket inspectors** (*Kontrolleur*), but if you are caught without a valid ticket or pass – known by the politically incorrect term *schwarzfahren* (black travelling) – you'll be handed an on-the-spot fine of €70 (plus €2.20 for a ticket).

## U-Bahn

Vienna's **U-Bahn**, which opened in 1978, boasts five lines (U1–4 and U6), and is by far the fastest way to get around the city. Trains run from between 5am and 6am until between midnight and 1am (the times of the first and last trains are posted at each station). Not all U-Bahn lines are underground: the U4 and U6 lines run partly on the old overground Stadtbahn created in the 1890s, and both lines retain some of their original stations and bridges designed by Otto Wagner. Each line is colour-coded (U1 is purple, U2 red and so on); to figure out which platform you want, look out for the name of the end station in the direction you wish to travel. A U2 extension, from Aspernstrasse to Aspern should be completed by 2013, and a U1 extension from Reumannplatz to Rothneusiedl by 2015.

## Trams and buses

Vienna has one of the largest **tram** systems in the world, with 28 routes crisscrossing the capital. Electric trams – *Strassenbahn* or *Bim* (after the noise of the bell) as they're known locally – were introduced in 1897 and most still sport the traditional white-and-red livery. After the U-Bahn, trams are the fastest and most efficient way to get around, running every five to ten minutes, depending on the time of day. They're pretty punctual, though some lines don't run on weekends or late at night, so be sure to check the timetables posted at every stop (*Haltestelle*). The final destination of the tram is also indicated by a small sign above the timetable itself.

**Buses** (*Autobusse*) tend to ply the narrow backstreets and the outer suburbs; despite having to battle with the traffic, they're equally punctual. In the heart of the Innere Stadt, where there are no trams and only two U-Bahn stations, there are several very **useful bus services** (Mon–Sat only): #1A, which winds its way from Schottentor to Stubentor; #2A from Schwedenplatz through the Hofburg to U-Bahn Neubaugasse; and #3A from Schottenring to Schwarzenbergplatz. Bus #13A is another useful route as it wends its way north–south and vice versa through the fourth to the eighth districts of the Vorstädte.

## Vienna Card (Wien-Karte)

The much-touted **Vienna Card** (*Wien-Karte*) costs €18.50, lasts for 72 hours and is perfect if you're on a flying visit to the city. Not only does it give you free travel on the city transport system (worth €13.60 in itself), it also gives discounts of around 10–20 percent (occasionally more) on most of the city's sights, opera tickets, shops and even taxis. For more information, visit ⓦwww.wienkarte.at.

## S-Bahn

The **S-Bahn**, or *Schnellbahn* to give it its full name, is of most use to Viennese commuters. However, it's also the cheapest way to get to and from the airport, and is useful if you're staying out in the suburbs. S-Bahn trains are less frequent than U-Bahn trains – running every fifteen to thirty minutes – and are strictly timetabled. The double-decker rolling stock, known as the *Wiesel* (weasel), is air-conditioned and a pleasure to ride on.

## Taxis and faxis

**Taxis** are plentiful and fairly reliable, with the minimum charge around €2, plus €1 if you've gone to a taxi rank and €2 if you've called one by phone, followed by an extra €1 or so per kilometre or couple of minutes. You can't flag down a taxi, but you can catch a cab at one of the taxi ranks around town, or phone ☎31 300, 40 100 or 60 160. You can, however, hail a bicycle taxi, known as a **faxi** (☎0699/120 05 624, ⓦwww.faxi.at), which costs €2.50 per kilometre.

## Guided tours and walks

Vienna Sightseeing Tours (ⓦwww.viennasightseeing.at) runs various **bus tours** around the city and surrounding districts. The standard city tour (daily: April–Oct 9.45am, 10.45am & 2.45pm; Nov–March 9.45am & 2pm; €39) takes around three hours, though only the summer 10.45am tour and winter 2pm tours have English commentary. They also run a **hop-on hop-off bus** (daily: April–Oct every 30min 10am–5pm; July & Aug every 15min 10am–7pm; Nov–March hourly 10am–4pm), with running commentary in English and German; tickets cost €20 for a day-ticket.

Alternatively, you can jump aboard Vienna's yellow-liveried **Ring-Tram** (daily 10am–6pm), which sets off from Schwedenplatz and circumnavigates the Ringstrasse every thirty minutes, with optional multi-lingual headphone commentary. Tickets cost €6 for a Ring Tour, €9 for a 24-hour hop-on, hop-off ticket, or €14 for a 24-hour ticket that includes a *Netzkarte* for the rest of the city's public transport system (see p.23). If you don't want the commentary, save your euros by hopping on a westbound **tram** #1 at Schwedenplatz, and changing to tram #2 outside Oper, which will allow you to circumnavigate the Ringstrasse anticlockwise.

Most appealing are the **walking tours** organized by Vienna's official tourist guides – you'll find details, such as whether the tours are in German or English, in the monthly *Wiener Spaziergänge* leaflet from the tourist office (ⓦwww.wienguide.at). These cover a relatively small area in much greater detail, mixing historical facts with juicy anecdotes in the company of a local specialist. Subjects covered range from Jugendstil (Art Nouveau) architecture to Jewish Vienna, and the regular Third Man tour (see p.106). With the exception of the latter, tours cost around €14 and last between one and a half and two hours. Simply turn up at the meeting point specified.

Another option are **bicycle tours** in German and English run by Pedal Power (May–Sept daily 10am & 2.30pm; ⓦwww.pedalpower.at); tours set off from outside the Oper, cost €26 and last around three hours.

The main company running **boat trips** on the Danube is the DDSG (ⓦwww.ddsg-blue-danube.at). Its **Grand Danube Rover Cruise** (April–Oct 2–4 daily) departs from the Danube Canal beside Schwedenplatz, goes through a lock and calls at the Reichsbrücke on the Danube itself, so you can embark and disembark at either stop. A one-way ticket between the two points costs €16 (1hr 30min), a return costs €22 (3hr). Vienna doesn't look its best from the canal or the river, but you will get to see Hundertwasser's Fernwärme or paper incinerator, Otto Wagner's weir and lock at Nussdorf, the Millenniumstower, and, on the way back, the Prater and the Buddhist temple – you can even choose to go on a Hundertwasser-designed boat, MS *Vinobona*.

## All-night transport

In the wee small hours, you can catch a **NightLine night bus**. These run every thirty minutes from 12.30am to 5am; all 22 routes pass through Schwedenplatz at some point. Tickets are the same as for all other forms of transport, and travel passes are valid. On Friday and Saturday nights the U-Bahn runs throughout the night at fifteen-minute intervals.

### Bicycles, cars and Fiaker

Despite the fact that **cycling** isn't very popular in Vienna, the city has introduced a system of free bike rental called Citybike (Ⓦ www.citybikewien.at). Equipped with a credit card (or with a CityBike Tourist Card, which costs €2), you can pick up (or drop off) one of the bikes (*Fahrräder*) from over fifty different locations. The bikes are free for the first hour, €1 for the second hour, another €2 for the third and €4 for every hour thereafter. The bike stations are closed in winter, whenever the weather's bad. Between April and October, you can also rent state-owned bicycles cheaply (€10–15 a day) from Westbahnhof, Wien-Nord and Floridsdorf train stations, and return the bikes to a different station. For other bike rental firms, see Ⓦ www.wien.gv.at. Bicycles can be taken on the U- and S-Bahn from Monday to Friday between 9am and 3pm and after 6.30pm, and from 9am on Saturdays and Sundays. You must buy a half-price ticket for your bike.

**Cars** are really not necessary for getting around Vienna. If, however, you arrive in the city by car and need to park, it's as well to know the **parking restrictions** in a blue zone (*Blauzone*), or short-term parking zone (*Kurzparkzone*), which will be marked by a "beginning" (*Anfang*) and an end (*Ende*). In general, the maximum length of stay in the first district (Altstadt or Innere Stadt) is ninety minutes (Mon–Fri 9am–7pm, Sat as indicated on sign); in the second to ninth districts (inner suburbs or Vorstädte), and in the twentieth district, you can park for up to two hours (Mon–Fri 9am–8pm, Sat as indicated on sign). On Sundays it's a free-for-all. However, check the signs before parking, as exact restrictions do vary. If there's no pay-and-display machine, you'll need to buy a 30-, 60- or 90-minute parking voucher (*Parkschein*) from a tobacconist or post office, and fill it in before displaying it.

An expensive Viennese indulgence is a ride in a soft-top horse-drawn carriage or **Fiaker**, driven by bowler-hatted, multilingual coachmen who will happily give you a guided tour; there are *Fiaker* ranks at Stephansplatz, Heldenplatz, Michaelerplatz and Albertinaplatz. It's best to settle on the price and duration of your ride beforehand; the going rate is €50 for twenty minutes, or €70 for forty minutes, but it's worth haggling.

# The media

You'll find the full range of foreign newspapers at kiosks dotted around the city centre. They're generally a day old, though one that you can buy on the day of issue is the European edition of *The Guardian*. Similarly, the *International Herald Tribune* is widely available the same day, and contains a useful distilled English version of the *Frankfurter Allgemeine Zeitung*. The weekly English-language newspaper *Austria Today* is available at most newsstands, and gives a fairly dull rundown of Austrian news, plus a few listings. *Ether* is a free monthly magazine for English-speaking expats.

## Newspapers and magazines

Heavily subsidized by the state, the **Austrian press** is for the most part conservative and pretty uninspiring. Nearly half of newspaper readers read the populist *Kronen Zeitung* tabloid, commonly known as the *Krone*, while plenty of the rest read the slightly more centrist tabloid, *Kurier*. Of the qualities, *Der Standard*, printed on pink paper, is centre-left while the rather straight-laced *Die Presse* is centre-right. One peculiarly Austrian phenomenon is the bags of newspapers you'll find hung from lampposts. Law-abiding citizens take one and put their money in the slot provided.

Vienna boasts a good weekly **listings** tabloid, *Falter* (Ⓦ www.falter.at), which is lively, politicized and critical, and comes out on Wednesday. Even if your German isn't great, you should be able to decipher the pull-out *Wienprogramm & Lexicon* section, which contains the week's listings. Most of the headings are self-explanatory, but it's just as well to know that Musik-E covers classical music, while Musik-U is for pop, jazz and folk. The national dailies also have limited listings of what's on in Vienna.

Nearly all cafés and bars and, in particular, the traditional Viennese coffeehouses, have a wide selection of newspapers and magazines for patrons to browse through, occasionally even English-language ones.

## Television and radio

Austrian **television** is unlikely to win any international awards for cutting-edge programming or presentation. There are two main state-run channels: ORF 1 and ORF 2 (which has regional programmes), plus a state-run sports channel ORF Sport Plus and TW1, a more magazine-style state-run digital channel; the chief commercial channel is ATV, whose programming is mostly imported.

Many Austrians tune into German channels such as ARD and ZDF for a bit of variety, and of course a lot of hotels and pensions have satellite TV, which means you should be able to tune in to BBC World News or CNN.

The state-run **radio** channels all feature a lot of chattering, though Ö1 (87.8/92FM) offers some decent classical music, in addition to news in English during the 8am *Morgenjournal*. The state-run FM4 (103.8FM) plays alternative music, with hourly news and weather (and much of the daytime programming) in English. The **BBC World Service** (Ⓦ www.bbc.co.uk/worldservice) broadcasts in English on 100.8FM in Vienna, though you can also receive it on short wave. Also available on short wave is Radio Austria International, which broadcasts Austrian news in English.

# Festivals

Vienna has such a vast number of festivals and events throughout the year that it's hard to turn up without coinciding with at least one. Below are some of the highlights.

**New Year's Day Concert (Neujahrskonzert)** Ⓦ www.wienerphilharmoniker.at. The Vienna Philharmonic's world-famous, schmaltzy Strauss-fest is broadcast live around the world from the Musikverein (and beamed live onto a large screen on the front of the Rathaus).

**Fasching ends** Ⓦ www.ballkalender.info. Vienna's ball season reaches its climax during the Carnival season, with the most famous ball of the lot, the Opernball, taking place on the **Thursday before Ash Wednesday** and the beginning of Lent.

**International Accordion Festival** Ⓦ www .akkordeonfestival.at. This vibrant festival pulls in groups from the US to the Balkans and is held over the course of four weeks from **late February to late March**.

**Osterklang** Ⓦ www.theater-an-der-wien.at. This **Easter** music festival, held at the Theater-an-der-Wien, is devoted to ecclesiastical music from Baroque to contemporary.

**Vienna City Marathon** Ⓦ www.vienna-marathon .com. On a Sunday in **April**, the Vienna Marathon starts at the Reichsbrücke by the UNO City and finishes with a circuit of the Ring.

**Frühlingsfestival** Ⓦ www.musikverein.at. Spring classical music festival, held at the Musikverein, with the focus on Austrian composers.

**Wiener Festwochen** Ⓦ www.festwochen.or.at. The city's main cultural festival runs from **mid-May until mid-June** and features opera, music and theatre from all over the world. It kicks off with a free concert in front of the Rathaus.

**Donauinselfest** Ⓦ www.donauinselfest.at. The Donauinselfest is a free open-air pop festival held on the Donauinsel on a weekend in **June** and sponsored by the Social Democrats (SPÖ).

**JazzFestWien** Ⓦ www.viennajazz.org. The two-week jazz festival takes place across the city's jazz clubs and other live-music venues in **late June and early July**.

**ImPulsTanz** Ⓦ www.impulstanz.com. International dance festival from **mid-July to mid-August**, showcasing every genre of contemporary dance.

**Viennale** Ⓦ www.viennale.at. The city's film festival, the Viennale, takes place over two weeks at the **end of October**.

**All Saints' Day (Allerheiligen)** On All Saints' Day **(November 1)** huge numbers of Viennese head for the city's cemeteries, in particular the Zentralfriedhof, to pay their respects to the dead.

**Wien Modern** Ⓦ www.wienmodern.at. A festival of contemporary classical music, held in **November** at the Konzerthaus.

**Ball season** Ⓦ www.ballkalender.info. November 11 marks the official beginning of the ball season, which lasts **until Ash Wednesday** (and beyond), though the balls don't really get going until after New Year.

**Christkindlmarkt** Ⓦ www.christkindlmarkt.at. From the **end of November to Christmas Eve**, there's a Christkindlmarkt, selling Glühwein (mulled wine) and lots of tacky Christmas gifts, in front of the Rathaus. Smaller versions are laid out in Spittelberg, Freyung, Schönbrunn and a few other venues across the city.

# Travel essentials

## Addresses

When writing **addresses**, the Viennese write the district number first, followed by the street name, and then the house number; most residential addresses also include an apartment number, separated from the house number by a slash. For example: 9, Löblichgasse 11/14, denotes Flat 14 at no. 11 Löblichgasse in the ninth district. We have used this system throughout the book. Sometimes you'll find addresses preceded by the postal code rather than the district, often with an "A" (for Austria) hyphenated to the beginning. For example: A-1010 Wien for the first district, A-1020 for the second, A-1220 for the 22nd, and so on. Lastly, there are a few common abbreviations to be aware of, including: –str. for –strasse, –g. for –gasse, and –pl. for –platz.

## Children

**Children** are generally neither seen nor heard in Vienna. You won't see too many of them in the cafés and restaurants around town; hotels and pensions tend to be slightly more accommodating. For visitors with kids, Schönbrunn (see p.171) is a must, as it harbours the Tiergarten (Zoo), Palmenhaus (Palm House), Wüstenhaus (Desert House) and Irrgarten (Maze). Closer to the centre

there are the Schmetterlinghaus (Butterfly House) in the Hofburg (see p.85), and the aviary and aquarium of Haus des Meeres (see p.140). The Prater (see p.154) can also be fun, and most children love to ride on the trams. Museums that might appeal to small kids include the Strassenbahnmuseum (Tram Museum) described on p.139, the Kindermuseum in the MuseumsQuartier (see p.96). Older kids might get more from the Technisches Museum (see p.179), the militaria at the Heeresgeschichtliches Museum (see p.137) or the brilliant hands-on Haus der Musik (see p.51).

## Costs

Although Vienna is by no means a budget destination, it is not quite as **expensive** as people imagine. It's true that coffee and cake at a traditional coffeehouse will cost you dear, but eating out costs less than in many EU countries, and rooms in the city's pensions and hotels are only moderately expensive. That said, Austria is one of the wealthiest countries in the world, and if you have the money, Vienna has plenty of luxury shops, hotels and restaurants ready to relieve you of it. After you've paid for your own room, count on a minimum of €30 a day, which will buy you breakfast, a takeaway lunch, a budget

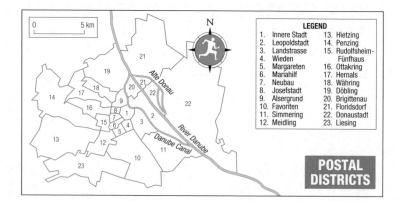

| LEGEND | |
|---|---|
| 1. Innere Stadt | 13. Hietzing |
| 2. Leopoldstadt | 14. Penzing |
| 3. Landstrasse | 15. Rudolfsheim- |
| 4. Wieden | Fünfhaus |
| 5. Margareten | 16. Ottakring |
| 6. Mariahilf | 17. Hernals |
| 7. Neubau | 18. Währing |
| 8. Josefstadt | 19. Döbling |
| 9. Alsergrund | 20. Brigittenau |
| 10. Favoriten | 21. Floridsdorf |
| 11. Simmering | 22. Donaustadt |
| 12. Meidling | 23. Liesing |

**POSTAL DISTRICTS**

dinner and a beer or coffee, but not much else. Eating sit-down meals twice a day, visiting museums and drinking more beer and coffee (especially coffee) will cost you more like €60 a day; if you want to go to the opera or a club, then you could easily double that figure.

## Crime and personal safety

Vienna is pretty **safe** compared to many capital cities. The Viennese themselves are a law-abiding lot, almost obsessively so. Old ladies walk their dogs in the city's parks late at night, and no one jaywalks. That said, crime does, of course, exist in Vienna as elsewhere and is on the rise, so it's as well to take the usual precautions.

Large sections of the Gürtel ring road double as a red-light district, and are best avoided. The Karlsplatz underpass and the Stadtpark both have dubious reputations, as do the major train stations, particularly after dark. Even so, none of these places are, strictly speaking, no-go areas.

Almost all problems encountered by tourists in Vienna are to do with petty crime. Reporting thefts to the police is straightforward, though it takes some time to wade through the bureaucracy. The Austrian **police** (*Polizei*) – distinguishable by their dark blue uniforms and white peaked caps, with a red-and-gold band – are armed, and are usually civil. It's important to carry ID with you at all times, ideally your passport, or at least a driving licence. Making photocopies of your passport and tickets is a very sensible precaution.

The main central police station (*Polizeiin-spektionen*) can be found at 1, Deutsch-meisterplatz 3 (U-Bahn Schottenring).

## Discounts

Most sights and some cinemas and theatres in Vienna offer **concessions** for senior citizens, the unemployed, full-time students and children under 16, with under-5s being admitted free almost everywhere – proof of eligibility will be required in most cases. Once obtained, **youth/student ID cards** soon pay for themselves in savings. Full-time students are eligible for the International Student Identity Card or ISIC (ⓦwww.isic.org), which

entitles the bearer to special air, rail and bus fares, and discounts at museums, theatres and other attractions. The card costs around £9/$22. If you're not a student, but you are 25 or younger, you can get an International Youth Travel Card, or IYTC, which costs the same and carries the same benefits.

## Electricity

The standard voltage is continental 220 volts AC. Most European appliances should work as long as you have an adaptor for continental-style two-pin round plugs. North Americans will need this plus a transformer.

## Embassies and consulates

**Australia** 4, Mattiellistrasse 2–4 ☎506 740, ⓦwww.australia.embassy.gov.au; U-Bahn Karlsplatz.
**Canada** 1, Laurenzerberg 2 ☎531 38-3000, ⓦwww.canadainternational.gc.ca; U-Bahn Schwedenplatz.
**Ireland** 1, Fifth Floor, Rotenturmstrasse 16–18 repetition ☎715 4246, ⓦwww.embassyofireland .at; U-Bahn Schwedenplatz.
**South Africa** 19, Sandgasse 33 10 ☎320 6493, ⓦwww.dirco.gov.za/vienna; tram #38.
**UK** 3, Jaurèsgasse 10 ☎716 13-5333, ⓦukinaustria.fco.gov.uk; tram #71.
**US** 9, Boltzmanngasse 16 ☎313 39-0, ⓦwww .usembassy.at; tram #5, #33, #37, #38, #40, #41 or #42.

## Emergencies

**Fire** ☎122
**Police** ☎133
**Ambulance** ☎144

## Entry requirements

Citizens of the US, Canada, Australia, New Zealand and all European countries (except Albania, Belarus, Bosnia, Macedonia, Montenegro, Russia, Serbia and Ukraine) do not require an **entry visa** for Austria. EU citizens need only a national identity card and can stay for as long as they want, but those who plan to stay permanently should register with the local police. Citizens of the US, Canada, New Zealand and Australia require a passport, and can stay up to three months. Visa requirements do change, however; it's always advisable to check the current situation before leaving home.

## Health

On production of a passport everyone is entitled to free emergency hospital treatment. The main **A&E department** (*Unfall* is an "accident") is in the gargantuan Allgemeines Krankenhaus (AKH), 9, Währinger Gürtel 18–20 (☎404 00-0, ⓦwww.akhwien .at; U-Bahn Michelbeuern-AKH). If it's a child that's ill, though, it's best to head for Sankt Anna Kinderspital 9, Kinderspitalgasse 6 (☎401 70, ⓦwww.stanna.at; U-Bahn Alser Strasse). On production of a **European Health Insurance** Card (EHIC), you can visit the doctor free of charge – phone ☎513 95 95 to find an English-speaking doctor. Most pharmacies (*Apotheken*) are open Monday to Friday 8am to noon and 2pm to 6pm, Saturdays 8am to noon; all of them should have directions to the nearest 24-hour pharmacy posted in the window.

## Insurance

Even though EU health care privileges apply, you should get **travel insurance** against theft, loss and illness or injury. Non-EU citizens should check whether they are already covered before buying a new policy. If you need to take out insurance, you might consider the travel insurance offered by Rough Guides (see below).

## Internet and wi-fi

With any luck the hotel or hostel you're staying at will have **internet access**. Otherwise, you can get online at many of Vienna's cafés and bars, several of which have free **wi-fi**, known locally as **WLAN**: try congenial cafés such as *Café Museum* (see p.209), *Café Prückel* (see p.210) or *Café Stein* (see p.213) or check out ⓦwww .freewlan.at. For details of how to get your laptop online when abroad, check out the useful website ⓦwww.kropla.com.

## Laundry

There are no coin-operated **launderettes** in the Innere Stadt; the nearest one is at 9, Nussdorferstrasse 80 (U-Bahn Nussdorfer Strasse). Alternatively, you can have your clothes washed at one of the city's central dry-cleaners such as Gisela-Putzerei, 1, Rauhensteingasse 1 (U-Bahn Stephansplatz).

## Left luggage

The main train stations all have €2 coin-operated **lockers** (*Schliessfächer*); the airport and smaller stations have left-luggage counters (*Gepäckaufbewahrung*).

## Lost property

The city's chief **lost property** office is the Zentrale Fundbüro, 3, Am Modenapark 1–2 (☎4000-8091; U-Bahn Stadtpark). If the item was lost on public transport, call ☎7909 188; if it was lost on Austrian Railways, phone ☎58 00 22-222.

## Mail

Vienna's main **post office** (*Hauptpostamt*) is at Fleischmarkt 19, A-1010, just off Schwedenplatz (Mon–Fri 7am–10pm, Sat & Sun 9am–10pm; ☎0577 677-1010, ⓦpost.at). The post offices in the Westbahnhof (Mon–Fri 7am–8pm, Sat & Sun 9am–8pm) and Franz-Josef-Bahnhof (Mon–Fri 7am–8pm, Sat & Sun 9am–2pm) are also open late. All other post offices – identified by a yellow sign saying *Postamt* – have regular opening

### Rough Guides travel insurance

Rough Guides has teamed up with WorldNomads.com to offer great **travel insurance** deals. Policies are available to residents of over 150 countries, with cover for a wide range of **adventure sports**, 24hr emergency assistance, high levels of medical and evacuation cover, and a stream of **travel safety information**. Roughguides.com users can take advantage of their policies online 24/7, from anywhere in the world – even if you're already travelling. And since plans often change when you're on the road, you can extend your policy and even claim online. Roughguides.com users who buy travel insurance with WorldNomads.com can also leave a positive footprint and donate to a community development project. For more information go to ⓦwww.roughguides.com/shop.

hours (Mon–Fri 8am–noon & 2–6pm), with the main ones eschewing their lunch break and opening on Saturdays, 8am to 10am.

Outbound air mail (*Flugpost*) from Austria usually takes three or four days to reach the UK, about five days to reach the US, and a week to ten days to Australia and New Zealand. Stamps (*Briefmarken*) for postcards within the EU are obtainable from tobacconists (*Tabak*), but for anything more complicated or further afield, you'll probably have to go to a post office, where they like to weigh everything.

Poste restante (*Postlagernd*) letters can be sent to any post office, if you know the address. At the main post office (see above) go to the counter marked *Postlagernde Sendungen*. Mail should be addressed using this term rather than "poste restante"; it will be held for thirty days (remember to take your passport when going to collect it).

## Maps

The maps in this guide, and the **free city plans** you can pick up from tourist offices and hotels, should be sufficient to help you find your way around. For something more durable, the best maps are by Freytag & Berndt, who produce a range of plans of the city, marked with bus and tram routes. The 1:20,000 spiral-bound *Buchplan Wien* map is the most comprehensive. Alternatively, Falkplan produces a fold-out map, with a good large-scale section of the Innere Stadt.

## Money

Austria's currency is the **euro** (€), which is divided into 100 cents. There are seven euro notes – in denominations of 500, 200, 100, 50, 20, 10 and 5 euros, each a different colour and size – and eight different coin denominations, including 2 and 1 euros, then 50, 20, 10, 5, 2 and 1 cents. Euro coins feature a common EU design on one face, but different country-specific designs on the other. No matter what the design, all euro coins and notes can be used in the following EU states: Austria, Belgium, Cyprus, Estonia Finland, France, Germany, Greece, Ireland, Italy, Luxembourg, Malta, the Netherlands, Portugal, Slovakia, Slovenia and Spain.

There are **ATMs** all over Vienna, from which you should be able to take out cash using either a debit or credit card. Banks tend to give the best rates and charge the lowest commission when it comes to changing money and travellers' cheques; most are open Monday to Friday 8am to 12.30pm and 1.30 to 3pm, with late closing on Thursdays at 5.30pm.

## Opening hours

Shops are allowed to open Monday to Friday 6am to 7.30pm, Saturday 6am to 6pm, with late shopping usually on Thursdays. Some still close at lunchtimes and on Saturday afternoons, and all are shut on Sundays. The only exceptions to this rule, apart from pharmacists and a few bakeries, are the shops in the main train stations and the airport, which are open late and at weekends. Those in search of cigarettes after hours will find cigarette machines outside most state-run tobacconists (*Tabak*). Cafés, bars and restaurants tend to stay open much longer. The traditional **coffeehouses** in particular often open as early as 7am and continue until or after 11pm, and the trendier cafés stay open until 2am and later. Formal **restaurants** tend to open at lunch and dinner, but close in between. Most places where you can drink and eat have a weekly closing day or *Ruhetag*.

## Phones

Austrian **phone booths** are easy enough to spot and to use, with instructions in four languages (including English). The dialling tone is a short pulse followed by a long one; the ringing tone is long and regular; engaged is short and rapid. At the time of going to press the minimum charge is 50 cents, but you're likely to need much more to make even a **local call**, since telephone calls are still quite expensive despite the recent deregulation.

Viennese **telephone numbers** within the city vary in length. One further peculiarity is those numbers that include a hyphen. It's not always necessary to dial the numbers after the hyphen, especially if it's a zero, which simply signals the system has **direct dial extension numbers** (*Durchwahlen*). If you know the extension you want, or it's

## Useful telephone numbers

### Phoning Vienna from abroad
**From Australia and New Zealand** ☎0011 + 43 + 1
**From Britain and Ireland** ☎00 + 43 + 1
**From North America** ☎011 + 43 + 1
Note that the Vienna city code is 01 – if you see the old phone code, 0222, just replace it with 01.

### Phoning abroad from Vienna
Note that the initial zero is omitted from the area code when dialling the UK, Ireland, Australia and New Zealand from abroad.
**Australia** ☎00 + 61 + city code
**New Zealand** ☎00 + 64 + city code
**Republic of Ireland** ☎00 + 353 + city code
**UK** ☎00 + 44 + city code
**US and Canada** ☎00 + 1 + area code

### Information
**Directory enquiries & operator** ☎11 88 77
You can also view the Vienna telephone directory and Yellow Pages online at
Ⓦwww.herold.at

given as part of the number, then you may dial it immediately after the main number.

You can make an **international call** from any phone, though it's easier to do so with a **phone card** (*Telefonkarte*) rather than from a coin-operated phone. Best value are prepaid phone cards, which will give you much longer call time and can be used from any public or private phone. Simply call the toll-free access number and then punch in the PIN given on the card.

If you're taking your **mobile/cell phone** (known as a *Handy* in German) with you, check with your service provider whether your phone will work abroad and what the call charges will be. Mobiles bought for use in Europe, Australia and New Zealand should work fine, though a mobile bought for use in the US is unlikely to work unless it's a tri-band phone.

### Public holidays

On the national **public holidays** listed below, banks and shops will be closed all, or most of, the day. Museums and galleries will, somewhat confusingly, either be closed or open for free. Note, too, that the city's museums are always free on May 17 (International Museum Day) and October 26 (National Day). During the school summer holidays – July and August – you'll find Vienna quieter than usual, with many theatres and other businesses closed for all or some of the period.

January 1 Neujahr
January 6 Epiphany/Heilige Drei Könige
Good Friday Karfreitag
Easter Monday Ostermontag
May 1 Labour Day/Tag der Arbeit
Ascension Day 6th Thurs after Easter/Christi Himmelfahrt
Whit Monday 6th Mon after Easter/Pfingstmontag
Corpus Christi 2nd Thurs after Whitsuntide/Fronleichnam
August 15 Assumption Day/Mariä Himmelfahrt
October 26 National Day/Nationalfeiertag
November 1 All Saints' Day/Allerheiligen
November 15 Feast Day of St Leopold
December 8 Immaculate Conception/Mariä Empfängnis
December 24 Heiliger Abend
December 25 Weihnachtstag
December 26 Stefanitag
New Year's Eve Silvester

### Soccer

Soccer is second only to alpine skiing as the nation's most popular sport. Austria's premier league is the *Bundesliga*, in which ten teams play each other twice at home and twice away. The **season** runs from mid-July to early December and then February to May, with most games played on Saturday evenings;

tickets are easy to buy on the day and cost around €20. Vienna and Austria's top soccer team, **FK Austria Wien** (ⓦwww.fk-austria.at), play at the 13,400-capacity **Franz-Horr-Stadion** on Fischhofgasse in Favoriten (tram #67 two stops from U-Bahn Reumannplatz); their nickname is *Die Veilchen* (The Violets) after their fetching strip. Their main rivals are **SK Rapid Wien** (ⓦwww.skrapid.at), known as *Die Grün-Weissen* (The Green-Whites) who play at the 18,500-capacity **Gerhard Hanappi Stadion** on Keisslergasse in Hütteldorf (U-Bahn Hütteldorf) pro. Big international games are played at the 50,000-plus-capacity **Ernst-Happel-Stadion** in the Prater (U-Bahn Stadion), for more on which see p.155.

## Swimming pools

The **Amalienbad**, 10, Reumannplatz 23 (U-Bahn Reumannplatz), has a wonderful Art Deco interior, particularly the sauna. The **Angelibad**, 21, An der oberen Alten Donau (U-Bahn Neue Donau), is an open-air riverside swimming place. **Jörgerbad**, 17, Jörgerstrasse 42–44 (tram #43), is also very beautiful inside, while **Krapfenwaldlbad**, 19, Krapfenwaldgasse 65–73 (bus #38A), is a swish, stylish 1920s outdoor pool up in the foothills of the Wienerwald (May–Sept) with great views; so too the **Schafbergbad**, 18, Josef-Redl-Gasse 2 (bus #42B).

## Time

Austria is normally one hour ahead of the UK and Ireland, six hours ahead of EST and nine hours ahead of PST. Clocks go forward in spring and back again some time in autumn – the exact date changes from year to year.

## Tipping

**Tipping** is expected in the more upmarket hotels, taxis, and in most cafés, bars and restaurants, usually up to the nearest five or ten euros depending on how much you've spent and how good the service was. In more expensive restaurants, you'll find the bill arrives with a fifteen-percent service charge already tacked on to the total.

## Tourist information

The main **tourist office** of the Vienna Tourist Board or *Wien Tourismus* is behind the opera house on Albertinaplatz at the corner of Maysedergasse (daily 9am–7pm; ☎24 555, ⓦwww.vienna.info). The staff should be able to answer most enquiries, and will happily hand out a free map of the city, with all the bus routes, tram lines and metro stations marked on, plus all the opening times of the various museums and galleries.

Ask also for the tourist board's monthly *Programm* for opera, concert and theatre schedules, upcoming exhibitions, and the monthly goings-on at the state museums. Anyone under 26 might prefer to try the youth-oriented tourist office, *wienXtra*, at 1, Babenbergerstrasse 1 (Mon–Wed 2–7pm, Thurs–Sat 1–6pm; ⓦwww.wienxtra.at), on the corner of the Ringstrasse. There are also **information desks** at the airport (daily 8.30am–9pm) and at the Westbahnhof (daily 7am–10pm).

For the most comprehensive and critical **listings**, you need the weekly tabloid *Falter* (see p.28).

## Travellers with disabilities

As in most EU countries, regulations in Austria require public buildings to be wheelchair-friendly (*Rollstuhlfreundlich*). As a result Vienna is becoming gradually more **accessible** for travellers with special needs.

Wheelchair access to hotels is by no means universal, however, and is more likely in upmarket establishments than in inexpensive places.

Access to the country's **public transport** system is improving and hassle-free if you plan your trip and contact the relevant train station several days in advance.

As for **urban transport** in Vienna, almost all U-Bahn stations are now fully equipped with lifts, escalators and a guidance system for the blind – call ☎7909-100 for the latest information. Low-floor trams now operate on nearly all routes – a wheelchair symbol flashes to let passengers know when the next low-floor tram will arrive. All buses in Vienna "kneel" to let people on and off, and have retractable ramps for wheelchair users. For a clearer picture, get the English-language leaflet *Accessible Vienna* from the Vienna tourist board (see above) before you set off. This describes the level of access to U-Bahn stations, hotels and many tourist sights, and contains lots of other useful information.

## Websites

**About Vienna** Ⓦ www.aboutvienna.org. Lots of useful information about the city's sights, culture and cuisine, plus up-to-date listings.

**Austria – general information** Ⓦ www.tiscover .com. Tourist site for booking accommodation, including self-catering and campsites, flights and car rental online. Updated regularly so it can tell you what's happening in Vienna over the next few weeks or months.

**Ex-pat Vienna** Ⓦ www.virtualvienna.net or www .vienna-expats.net. There are several expat websites to choose from, which post up news, listings and great tips for living in the city plus forums for discussing issues.

**Vienna City Hall** Ⓦ www.wien.gv.at. The city-council website has lots of information in German, plus a very useful search engine that will find any address in the city for you on a map – click on Stadtplan and write in the street name.

**Vienna Life** Ⓦ www.vienna-life.com. Light-hearted website about all things Viennese, from the Ultravox song to the Congress, plus an online guide of hotels, bars, shops, museums and galleries, with reviews.

**Vienna Tourist Board** Ⓦ www.wien.info. The official Vienna tourist board's English/German website, with information on everything from secondhand bookshops to late-night eating options and art exhibitions. You can also book hotel accommodation online.

**Wiener Zeitung** Ⓦ www.wienerzeitung.at. Website of the official Vienna city authorities' newspaper. The English version gives you lots of news and tourist information and has plenty of useful links.

# The City

# The City

# The Innere Stadt

V ienna's first district – the **Innere Stadt** (Inner City) or Altstadt (Old City) – has been the heart of the city since the Romans founded **Vindobona** on the banks of the Danube in 15 BC. It was here, too, that the Babenberg dukes built their power base in the twelfth century, and later, the Habsburgs established the Hofburg (covered in Chapter Two) as their imperial residence. Consequently, unlike the older quarters in many European cities, the Innere Stadt remained the chief place of residence for the city's aristocracy throughout the Baroque period and beyond, and its narrow, cobbled lanes remained the unlikely addresses of dukes and duchesses, princes and ambassadors. In fact, the city occupied the same space from the thirteenth century until the zigzag fortifications, which had twice protected the city against the Turks, were finally taken down in the mid-nineteenth century.

The focus of the Innere Stadt – and the one thing on every tourist itinerary – is the city's magnificent Gothic cathedral, **Stephansdom**, whose single soaring spire also acts as a useful geographical landmark. Close by are the chief pedestrianized shopping streets of **Kärntnerstrasse**, **Graben** and **Kohlmarkt**, which grow progressively more exclusive the nearer you get to the Hofburg. There's a steady ebb and flow of folk along these streets at most times of the day, but the **Kaisergruft**, the last resting place of the Habsburgs, just off Kärntnerstrasse, is the only other sight that attracts large numbers of visitors. Head off into the rest of the Innere Stadt, with its baffling medieval layout, hidden courtyards and passageways, and you'll soon lose the crowds. Even though it holds most of the city's finest Baroque churches and palaces, the dearth of premier-league sights puts many off the scent.

## Stephansplatz and around

The geographical and spiritual heart of the Innere Stadt is **Stephansplatz**, a pedestrianized square occupied by the hoary Gothic bulk of the city cathedral. This square hasn't always been so central – the first church built here lay outside the city walls, and the square itself was a graveyard until 1732. Nowadays, though, it's one of the best places to watch Vienna's streetlife, from the benign young slackers who lounge around on the benches by the U-Bahn, to the beleaguered folk in eighteenth-century costumes, wearily flogging tickets for classical concerts. The other whiff of heritage is the smell of horse dung that wafts across the square from the *Fiaker* lined up along the north wall of the cathedral.

Apart from the cathedral, the square's most dominant feature is the **Haas Haus**, a strikingly modern, tinted-glass-and-polished-stone building that, understandably,

39

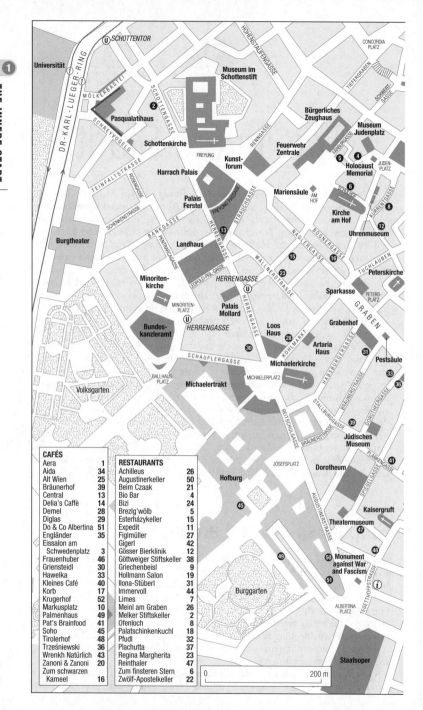

**CAFÉS**

| | |
|---|---|
| Aera | 1 |
| Aida | 34 |
| Alt Wien | 25 |
| Bräunerhof | 39 |
| Central | 13 |
| Delia's Caffè | 14 |
| Demel | 28 |
| Diglas | 29 |
| Do & Co Albertina | 51 |
| Engländer | 35 |
| Eissalon am Schwedenplatz | 3 |
| Frauenhuber | 46 |
| Griensteidl | 30 |
| Hawelka | 33 |
| Kleines Café | 40 |
| Korb | 17 |
| Krugerhof | 52 |
| Markusplatz | 10 |
| Palmenhaus | 49 |
| Pat's Brainfood | 41 |
| Soho | 45 |
| Tirolerhof | 48 |
| Trześniewski | 36 |
| Wrenkh Natürlich | 43 |
| Zanoni & Zanoni | 20 |
| Zum schwarzen Kameel | 16 |

**RESTAURANTS**

| | |
|---|---|
| Achilleus | 26 |
| Augustinerkeller | 50 |
| Beim Czaak | 21 |
| Bio Bar | 4 |
| Bizi | 24 |
| Brezlg'wölb | 5 |
| Esterházykeller | 15 |
| Expedit | 11 |
| Figlmüller | 27 |
| Gigerl | 42 |
| Gösser Bierklinik | 12 |
| Göttweiger Stiftskeller | 38 |
| Griechenbeisl | 9 |
| Hollmann Salon | 19 |
| Ilona-Stüberl | 31 |
| Immervoll | 44 |
| Limes | 7 |
| Meinl am Graben | 26 |
| Melker Stiftskeller | 2 |
| Ofenloch | 8 |
| Palatschinkenkuchl | 18 |
| Pfudl | 32 |
| Plachutta | 37 |
| Regina Margherita | 23 |
| Reinthaler | 47 |
| Zum finsteren Stern | 6 |
| Zwölf-Aposteller | 22 |

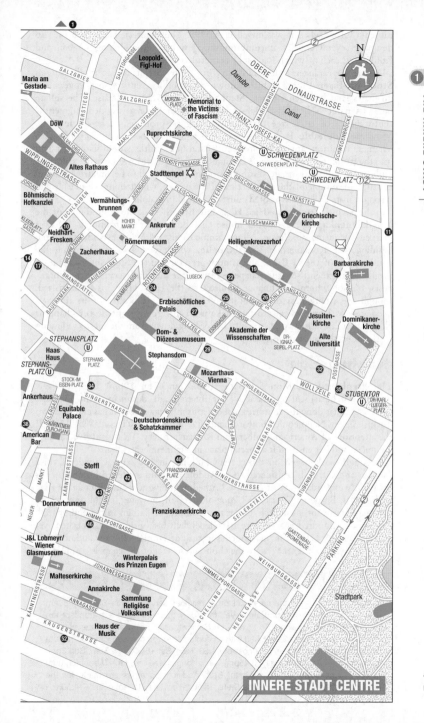

**INNERE STADT CENTRE**

caused a furore when it was unveiled in 1990. The architect, Hans Hollein, also designed several equally uncompromising jewellery stores along Graben and Kohlmarkt, each of which is a minor masterpiece (see p.52).

Despite appearances, Haas Haus isn't in fact on Stephansplatz at all, but on **Stock-im-Eisen-Platz**, a little-known geographical entity that covers the no-man's-land between Graben, Stephansplatz and Kärntnerstrasse. The square takes its name – literally "stick-in-iron" – from the nail-studded, sixteenth-century slice of larch tree that stands in a glass-protected niche set into the grandiose **Equitable Palace** on the corner of Kärntnerstrasse. According to Viennese tradition, apprentice locksmiths and blacksmiths would hammer a nail into the trunk for good luck. The Equitable building itself is well worth exploring: built in the 1890s, its ornate vestibule (originally designed to be a metro entrance) is a superb example of the architecture of the period, with lashings of marble and wrought iron, and a glass-roofed courtyard faced in majolica tiles.

In the paving between the Haas Haus and the cathedral, the ground plan of the **Magdalenenkapelle**, a charnel house that burnt to the ground in 1781, is marked out in red sandstone. Almost immediately below it lies another church building, the Romanesque **Virgilkapelle**, which was discovered during the construction of the U-Bahn, and is now preserved in the Stephansplatz station itself. The thirteenth-century chapel – at one time the family crypt of the Chran-nests, one of whom was finance minister to the Habsburgs – is little visited, though the strangeness of its location and the simple beauty of its recesses, decorated with red wheel crosses, make it an intriguing sight. If the chapel is closed, you can satisfy your curiosity by looking down from the metro's viewing platform by the information office.

## Stephansdom

The **Stephansdom** (Mon–Sat 6am–10pm, Sun 7am–10pm; free; Ⓦ www .stephanskirche.at) still towers above the Innere Stadt, dominating the Viennese skyline as it has done for centuries. An obvious military target, it has endured two Turkish sieges, Napoleonic bombardment, and in the latter stages of World War II the attentions of American bombers and Russian artillery. That it survived at all is a miracle, and has ensured it a special place in Viennese hearts.

Although work began on the current building in 1304, the cathedral's chief founder and patron is considered to be Rudolf IV, who modelled his designs for the greatly expanded nave on St Vitus Cathedral in Prague, being built at the time by his rival, Emperor Charles IV. Poor old Rudolf, however, could only secure collegiate status for his church, under the bishopric of Passau. In the end, it took more than a hundred years before an independent bishopric was established; yet another century before the final touches were added to the exterior; and not until the early twentieth century were the choir and several of the chapels completed.

### Visiting Stephansdom

Visitors can only enter the nave outside of religious services (Mon–Sat 9–11.30am & 1–4.30pm, Sun 1–4.30pm), and even then only the north aisle and transept are accessible without paying. To have a proper look at anything else in the nave or choir, you have to pay €3, or €4.90 with an audioguide. You can also join a 30-minute **guided tour** (Domführung) at a cost of €4.50 (Mon–Sat 10.30am & 3pm, Sun 3pm; English tours April–Oct daily 3.45pm), or a longer evening tour (Abendführung) at 7pm (June–Sept only; 1hr 30min; €10). Additional charges are made for the catacombs, the Pummerin and the Steffl – a ticket covering the lot costs €14.50.

## The exterior

The cathedral's steeply pitched **roof** has been decorated with multicoloured tiles forming giant chevrons since 1490, and is said to be modelled on a Saracen carpet. The double-headed imperial eagle on the south side dates from 1831, while the north holds the emblems of the City of Vienna and the Second Republic and the date 1950, marking when the roof was retiled after the war.

The cathedral's most magnificent **exterior** feature, the sublime **Südturm** (south tower) – ironically nicknamed **"Steffl"** (Little Stephen) by locals – soars to a height of 137m. To reach the top, it's a blind scramble up 343 steps, accessible from outside the cathedral (daily 9am–5.30pm; €3.50). The planned Nordturm (north tower), or Adlerturm (Eagle Tower), was to have been built along similar lines, but fell victim to cost-cutting in the build-up to the first

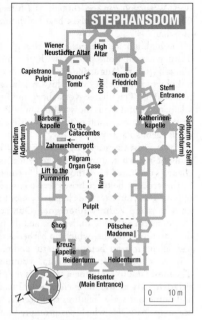

Turkish siege of 1529; its half-built stump eventually received a diminutive copper cupola in 1556. The north tower is accessible from inside the cathedral; the views from the top aren't as good, but there is a lift. You also get to see the cathedral's **Pummerin** or "Boomer" (daily: July & Aug 8.15am–6pm; Sept–June 8.15am–4.30pm; €4.50), only rung on special occasions. The current bell is a postwar rehash of the twenty-ton original, cast from a Turkish cannon captured during the 1683 siege.

The main entrance to the cathedral is via the **Riesentor** (Giants' Gates), a rare survivor from the cathedral's twelfth-century predecessor. Two robust Romanesque towers, peppered with crockets and known as the **Heidentürme** (Pagans' Towers), flank the Riesentor. Note, too, the O5 inscription, the symbol of the Austrian resistance (see p.260) to the left of the main door. The thirteenth-century sculpted figures around the main portal are also worth inspecting, especially the devilish creatures to the left below the apostles, though the iron railings and the ebb and flow of visitors make them hard to appreciate.

## The interior

The first thing that strikes you as you enter the gloomy, high-vaulted **interior** of the cathedral is that, despite the tourists, Stephansdom is still very much a place of worship. At peak times, it can be difficult to get a seat in the area immediately to your right, facing the **Pötscher Madonna**, a painting that sits below a delicate late-Gothic baldachin. Legend has it that the Madonna wept tears from her unusually large eyes and was responsible for the Habsburg victory at the Battle of Zenta against the Turks in 1697.

The leader of the imperial troops at Zenta, Prince Eugène of Savoy, is buried in the **Kreuzkapelle**, off the north aisle – all except his heart, which, it is thought, was transported to Turin, the city he liberated in 1706. Sadly, the chapel is usually shut behind a heavy iron grille, so you can't see the prince's tomb on the south wall. What you can see, though, is a fifteenth-century crucifix, whose statue of Christ sports a shaggy black beard of human hair – according to legend, it's still growing.

The highlight of the cathedral, though, is without doubt the early sixteenth-century carved stone **pulpit**, with portraits of the four fathers of the Christian Church (saints Augustine, Gregory, Jerome and Ambrose), sculpted by an unknown artist, who carved his own image peering from a window below the pulpit stairs. The filigree work above and below the staircase is masterly, as are the salamanders and toads (now behind ugly Perspex barriers), symbolizing good and evil, pursuing one another up the banister, and culminating in a barking dog who keeps them all at bay.

If you want to escape the crowds, head for the **Barbarakapelle**, in the north transept, which features hanging pendants, stamped with heraldic bosses. The chapel is dedicated to all those killed in concentration camps, and the small triangle in the crucifix below Christ's feet contains ashes from Auschwitz. On the wall opposite, as you leave the chapel, look out for a half-torso of Christ in suffering, known as the **Zahnwehherrgott** (Our Lord of the Toothache). According to Viennese legend, three students coined the nickname and were immediately struck down with toothache, which no barber-surgeon could cure, until the young men had fallen prostrate before the statue and prayed for forgiveness.

To view the rest of the cathedral, you must pay an entrance fee (see box, p.42). The most famous monument within is the glorious red marble **Tomb of Emperor Friedrich III**, in the south choir aisle. In among the 240 statues, 32 coats of arms and numerous scaly creatures that decorate the tomb is the emperor's mysterious acronym, AEIOU, which has prompted numerous interpretations, ranging from the obvious *Austria Erit In Orbe Ultima* ("Austria will be the last in the world"), to the ingenious *Aquila Electa Iovis Omnia Vincit* ("The chosen eagle conquers all things"). Friedrich himself revealed the German version to be *Alles Erdreich Ist Österreich Untertan* ("The whole world is subject to Austria"), though some wags put forward the more appropriate *Aller Erst Ist Österreich Verloren* ("In the first place, Austria is lost"), since Friedrich had great difficulty keeping hold of Upper and Lower Austria and was in fact driven out of Vienna by the Hungarian king Matthias Corvinus in 1485.

It's worth popping into the **Katharinenkapelle**, in the south transept, to see the chapel's beautiful baptismal font, made in 1481. Its marble base features the four apostles; the niches of the basin are decorated with the twelve disciples, Christ and St Stephan; and the wooden lid, shaped like a church spire, is smothered with sculpted scenes. Up above, there's a wonderful ceiling boss of St Catherine with her wheel and sword, on the end of a drooping pendant.

In the north choir aisle, the winged **Wiener Neustädter Altar**, a richly gilded masterpiece of late-Gothic art, dates from the mid-fifteenth century, but was only brought to the cathedral in 1883. If the altar's wings are closed, only four rows of saints will be depicted; when open, they reveal up to 72 saints. At the centre of the altar are the Madonna and Child, the Birth of Christ, the Adoration of the Magi, the Coronation of Mary and the latter's death, all sculpted in high relief out of wood. Below the altar to the left lies the **Donor's Tomb**, adorned with sandstone effigies of Rudolf IV and his wife, Catherine of Bohemia (they're actually buried in the catacombs), which would originally have been richly gilded and peppered with precious stones.

## The catacombs

A stairway in the north transept leads down into the **catacombs** or *Katakomben* (guided tours only: every 15–30min Mon–Sat 10–11.30am & 1.30–4.30pm,

Sun 1.30–4.30pm; €4.50), which, initially at least, are a bit disappointing, having been over-restored in the 1960s. Rudolf IV and his wife are buried here, along with other early Habsburgs, plus sundry priests, bishops and archbishops. Rudolf himself, who during his seven-year reign managed to found both the cathedral and the university, died aged 26 in Milan in 1365. He was carried back to Vienna sewn into a cowhide to preserve his body. Last of all, a small chamber lined with cages is filled with bronze caskets containing the entrails of the later Habsburgs. Their bodies are buried in the Kaisergruft (see p.48), their hearts in the Augustinerkirche (see p.81).

From the bottom of the stairs, you enter the damp, dimly lit labyrinth of eighteenth-century catacombs. Closed in 1783 after the stench became too overpowering, they have been left more or less untouched since. Around sixteen thousand locals are buried here, their bones piled high in more than thirty rooms; the final chamber holds a particularly macabre pile left over from a medieval plague pit. You exit from the catacombs via a secret staircase that deposits you outside the cathedral, by the place where Mozart's body was blessed before being buried in St Marxer Friedhof (see p.139). At the very northeastern corner of the cathedral, near the catacombs exit, is the **Capistrano Pulpit**, originally the cathedral's main interior pulpit. It was from here that the Venetian priest, St Johannes of Capistrano, preached his sermons against the Turks during the fifteenth century; the extravagant sunburst and statue of St Francis trampling on a Turk are Baroque additions.

## Dommuseum

The former Cistercian abbey of Zwettlhof, on the north side of Stephansplatz, houses the **Dommuseum** (Tues–Sat 10am–5pm; €7; Ⓦ www.dommuseum.at), containing a mishmash of the cathedral's most valuable treasures and artwork on the first floor (access through the passageway at Stephansplatz 6). In amongst it all, there are some arresting medieval sculptures in wood – St Dionysius (aka Denis) carrying his severed head to his place of burial (in 3D relief), St Aegydius (aka Giles) looking rather sadly at the arrow stuck through his hand – and some High Baroque (not to say high kitsch) pieces, like the shrine of the Madonna, whose cloak opens up to reveal God (forming the main part of her body) with a host of worshippers' faces tucked inside her cloak. The highlight, though, is the fourteenth-century stained-glass window of an angel from the Stephansdom. The dimly lit treasury is stuffed with monstrances and macabre reliquaries, including St Leopold's hipbone, a piece of the Virgin Mary's belt and a smidgen of holy blood.

## Schatzkammer des Deutschen Ordens

An even more bizarre ecclesiastical treasure-trove, belonging to the Teutonic Knights, can be seen at the **Schatzkammer des Deutschen Ordens** (May–Oct Tues, Thurs & Sat 10am–noon, Wed & Fri 3–5pm; €4; Ⓦ www.deutscher-orden .at), spread over five rooms on the second floor of the Deutschordenshaus; enter from Singerstrasse 7, one block south of Stephansplatz, and ask for the information booklet in English. One of the three main military-religious orders to emerge during the Crusades in the twelfth century, the Teutonic Knights are now a purely charitable organisation, with their headquarters in Vienna.

The treasury's varied collection, assembled by seven centuries of **Grand Masters** (*Hochmeister*), ranges from the mundane – seals, coins and crosses in room 1 – to the peculiar, particularly well represented in room 2. Note the red coral salt-cellar tree hung with fossilized sharks' teeth – thought to be adders' tongues and therefore able to detect poisoned food – and a series of vessels made from coconut shells. One Goan specimen has silver mountings, complete with tiger-shell spoons sporting wonky silver handles, while another in chinoiserie style has a wonderful "swizzle stick". Also in this room is the most amazing table clock, smothered in a garland of silver-gilded leaves studded with garnets and turquoise. Room 3 holds further bizarre exhibits from the **Kunstkammer**, collected by the Grand Master Archduke Maximilian III, like the three bezoars – "a concretion found in the stomach of Persian wild goats" – to which the Persians attributed great healing powers, and a coral pendant depicting Jonah reclining on the tongue of a diminutive whale. The Order's military past is represented by such exotic arms and armour as a wiggly sixteenth-century Sumatran dagger with a handle carved out of rhino horn into the shape of the Buddha, with sapphire eyes and ruby eyebrows.

Before you leave, pop inside the **sala terrena** (which looks like a gazebo) on the ground floor, to admire the Baroque trompe l'oeil murals of flowers, birds, statues and carousing gods; the room is now used for concerts of Mozart by performers clad in period garb. The building's misshapen cobbled **courtyard** is a peaceful spot festooned with ivy and flower boxes, where Brahms spent the best part of two years in 1863–65, though inevitably it's Mozart who gets the plaque for his brief sojourn here in the spring of 1781. After the likes of the *sala terrena*, the Order's **Deutschordenskirche**, next door, appears relatively modest. Despite centuries of remodelling, the church retains its Gothic origins. Decorated with the Order's numerous coats of arms, it features a superb sixteenth-century Flemish winged altarpiece depicting the Passion.

## Mozarthaus Vienna

The **Mozarthaus Vienna** (daily 10am–8pm; €9; ⓦ www.mozarthausvienna.at) lies immediately east of the cathedral (pass through the *Durchhaus* at Stephansplatz 5a and enter at Domgasse 5). Here, on the first floor, Mozart, Constanze and their son, Karl Thomas, lived for three years, during which the composer enjoyed his greatest success. This was Mozart's swankiest accommodation in Vienna; he even had his own billiards room and space for visitors. The composer Johann Nepomuk Hummel stayed here as Mozart's live-in pupil for two and a half years; Josef Haydn was a regular visitor, opining that Mozart was "the greatest composer that I know in person or by name".

Sadly, however, despite all the history, the museum is a bit disappointing. A lift whisks you to the third floor, so you have to wade through two floors of manuscript facsimiles and portraits before you reach the apartment itself. Only one of Mozart's rooms actually retains the original decor of marble and stucco (the Camesina family, who owned the property, were stucco artists), and there are none of Mozart's personal effects and precious little atmosphere. Nevertheless, the building has a lovely courtyard, the views along Blutgasse are great, and there's the chance to hear recordings of Mozart's music.

# Kärntnerstrasse

As its name suggests, **Kärntnerstrasse** lies along the old road from Vienna to the Austrian province of Carinthia (Kärntner). Once home to the city's luxury retail trade, it's still a favourite street for promenading and window-shopping, even though many of the shops are simply chains. One shop that recalls the days of old

**Wolfgang Amadeus Mozart** (1756–91) moved to Vienna in March 1781, after a summons from his employer, the irascible Archbishop of Salzburg, Count Colloredo, who was visiting his sick father in the city. Within three months Mozart had resigned from his post as court organist to the archbishop – or "arch-oaf" (*Erzlimmel*), as he called him – causing a rift with his overbearing father, who was assistant Kapellmeister in Salzburg. The relationship was further strained when Mozart, against his father's wishes, moved in with the all-female Weber family, and grew particularly attached to one of the daughters, **Constanze**. In August 1782, Mozart eventually married the 19-year-old Constanze in the Stephansdom. Their union appears to have been happy, despite most biographers' misogynist attacks on Constanze as unworthy of his genius. Mozart himself hated to be parted from her, if his letters – "I kiss and squeeze you 1,095,060,437,082 times" – and the fact that he rarely left her side, are anything to go by.

After giving many concerts as conductor and pianist, Mozart turned his hand to **opera**, enjoying his greatest success in July 1782 with what is now his least-known operatic work, *Die Entführung aus dem Serail* (The Escape from the Harem). It was after hearing *Die Entführung* for the first time that Emperor Josef II is alleged to have said: "Too beautiful for our ears, and an awful lot of notes, dear Mozart", to which Mozart replied, "No more notes than necessary, Your Majesty!" Such tales have led to a popular belief that Mozart and Josef were constantly feuding over artistic debates: in his letters, however, Mozart's criticisms of the notoriously stingy emperor were on purely financial matters.

Mozart's next opera, *Le Nozze di Figaro* (The Marriage of Figaro), was premiered in May 1786 to a decidedly mixed reception, running for just nine performances. This was partly because its subject matter, in which a lecherous count is prevented from seducing a servant girl by an alliance between the serving classes and his own long-suffering wife, was controversial – as a play it had already been banned in Paris and Vienna. Josef II obviously liked it, however, inviting the cast to give a special performance at his summer residence at Laxenburg. And Figaro's subversive overtones went down a storm in Prague, where Mozart premiered two later operas, *Don Giovanni* and *La Clemenza di Tito* (The Clemency of Tito), both of which were written in Vienna.

Mozart's **final work** was his *Requiem*, commissioned anonymously by an "unknown messenger" in the last year of the composer's life. Only after Mozart's death did the patron's identity become known: it was the recently widowed Count Franz Walsegg-Stuppach, who wished to pass the composition off as his own. In the end it became Mozart's own requiem, since it was still unfinished when he died during the night of December 4–5, 1791, after suffering rheumatic fever for two weeks. Few biographers have forgiven Constanze for not attending the **funeral service** at Stephansdom; some, however, assert that she was too distraught to show up. She has also been criticized for having the *Requiem* completed by one of Mozart's pupils, Sussmayr, so as to get the final payment – though this seems fair enough for a widow left with their two remaining children to raise (and apparently Mozart had suggested this course of action on his deathbed).

Yet more anecdotes surround the generally accepted rivalry with the Kapellmeister **Antonio Salieri**, though this, too, has been overplayed. Salieri was exclusively an opera composer, while Mozart, at least until 1786, was known chiefly as an instrumental composer and virtuoso pianist. Some went as far as to suggest that Salieri himself poisoned Mozart, an allegation strenuously denied by Salieri on his deathbed years later, but to no avail: Alexander Pushkin dramatized it, Nicolai Rimsky-Korsakov made it into an opera, and most famously *Amadeus*, Peter Shaffer's play on the subject, was made into an Oscar-winning film by Miloš Forman. For the story of how Mozart ended up in a pauper's grave, see p.139.

is **J. & L. Lobmeyr** (Ⓦwww.lobmeyr.at), at no. 26; besides flogging expensive glass and crystal to designs by Adolf Loos and Josef Hoffmann for the Wiener Werkstätte (see p.112), it also houses the **Wiener Glasmuseum** (Mon–Fri 10am–7pm, Sat 10am–6pm; free). Stairs at the back lead to the second-floor balcony, where wonderful, mostly antique, exhibits include an incredible range of chandeliers, culminating in a copy of the 1960s chandelier that graces the New York Metropolitan Opera House.

Directly opposite Lobmeyr stands the **Malteserkirche**, its imposing Neoclassical entrance forming a misleading introduction to what is basically a simple, single-nave Gothic church. Inside, however, there's a splendid Neoclassical monument to Jean de la Valette, Grand Master of the Knights of Malta, who in 1565, as depicted in the monument's frieze, defended the island from the Turks – two of whose moustachioed brethren hold up the monument. Kärntnerstrasse continues south past the Staatsoper (see p.100), across the Ringstrasse to Karlsplatz (see p.102).

# Neuer Markt and Kaisergruft

One block west of Kärntnerstrasse, the open space of **Neuer Markt**, formerly the city's medieval flour market, now rather shamefully serves as a car park. The centrepiece of the square is the Providentia fountain, better known as the **Donnerbrunnen**, after its Baroque sculptor Georg Raphael Donner. The nudity of the figures perched on the edge of the fountain – they represent the four Austrian tributaries of the Danube: the Enns, March, Ybbs and Traun – was deemed too risqué by Empress Maria Theresia, who had the lead statues removed in 1770 to be melted down and made into cannons. They were returned unharmed in 1801, and in 1873 replaced by bronze copies: the young male figure of Traun, in particular, depicted on the point of catching a fish with his trident, clearly showed rather too much buttock for contemporary tastes, hence the judiciously placed fig leaf.

## Kaisergruft

The buildings that surround the square are fairly undistinguished, including the **Kapuzinerkirche**. This dour church is nonetheless one of Vienna's premier sights, for since 1633, its crypt – the **Kaisergruft** (daily 10am–6pm; €5) – has been the unlikely resting place of the Habsburgs. They chose the Capuchins (an offshoot of the Franciscans) as a gesture of modesty; to underscore the point, an elaborate ceremony was enacted at each Habsburg funeral. As the funeral cortege approached the church, the prior would ask "Who seeks entry here?" The grand master of the

### Meissl und Schadn

Emperor Franz-Josef was famous for eating *Tafelspitz* (boiled rump of beef) for lunch every day. His courtiers, naturally, followed suit and one of the best places to sample the dish was the legendary **Meissl und Schadn** restaurant on Neuer Markt, which regularly offered more than 25 varieties of *Tafelspitz*. The restaurant was also the scene of imperial Vienna's most famous **political assassination**. On October 21, 1916, Prime Minister **Count Karl von Stürgkh** was shot dead, while enjoying his after-dinner cigar, by fellow diner **Friedrich Adler**. The assassin, son of the leader of the Social Democrats, Viktor Adler, was appalled by the slaughter of the war, and incensed by Stürgkh's refusal to reconvene parliament. Adler was sentenced to life imprisonment, but later released in an act of clemency by Emperor Karl I, and went on to outlive *Meissl und Schadn* itself, which was destroyed in the air raids of World War II.

court would reply "I am His Majesty Emperor of Austria, King of Hungary." The prior would then maintain "I know him not, who seeks entry?" "I am Emperor, Apostolic King of Hungary, King of Bohemia, Dalmatia, Croatia, Slavonia, Galicia, Lodomeria, Illyria, Jerusalem, Archduke of Austria, Grand-Prince of Transylvania, Grand Duke of Tuscany and Krakow, Duke of Lorraine, Salzburg, Styria, Carinthia and Carniola." The prior would insist "I know him not, who seeks entry here?" At this the grand master would kneel, saying "A humble sinner, who begs God's mercy" – only then would the coffin be allowed in.

The Kaisergruft is entered from a doorway to the left of the church. Notices demand *Silentium!* – don't let them kid you, this place is a tourist attraction above all else. Inside, though the crypt is neither gloomy nor in any sense Gothic, it is, nevertheless, an intriguing insight into the Habsburgs' fascination with death.

To follow the tombs in chronological order, turn right immediately as you enter the crypt, and head for the small **Founders' Vault** on the right at the far end; here you'll find Matthias and his wife, Anna, who founded the Kaisergruft, and whose bodies were transferred here in 1633 (a decade or so after their deaths). Back by the main entrance are four monster Baroque pewter sarcophagi. Those of Leopold I and Josef I were designed by Johann Lucas von Hildebrandt, the latter sporting ghoulish skulls in full armour below, and with bat wings above. Those of Karl VI and his wife are utterly "his'n'hers" designs by Rococo artist **Balthasar Ferdinand Moll**: his sits on lions, with toothy skulls sporting crowns at each corner; hers sits on eagles, with women in mourning veils at each corner.

The main focus and highlight of the crypt is the nearby **Maria Theresia Vault**, almost entirely taken up with Moll's obscenely large double tomb for the empress and her husband, Franz Stephan. Over three metres high and wide, six metres long, and smothered in Rococo decorations, it depicts the imperial couple sitting up in bed, as if indignantly accusing one another of snoring. Immediately below their feet lies the simple copper coffin of their son, **Josef II**, to whom such pomposity was anathema. It was he who instigated the idea of a reusable coffin, and issued a decree enforcing its use in all funerals – not surprisingly, given the Viennese obsession with elaborate send-offs, the emperor was eventually forced to back down. Several more of Maria Theresia's sixteen children lie in the shadow of their mother, in ornate Rococo coffins, as does the only non-Habsburg among the crypt's 143 coffins, Karoline Fuchs-Mollard, the empress's governess.

After the Maria Theresia Vault it's all downhill architecturally. The **Franz Vault** contains only the fairly plain tombs of Franz II and his four wives. Ferdinand I and his wife share the **Ferdinand Vault** with 37 others, though they're all buried in niches in the wall. At the far end of the crypt, the gloomy postwar bunker of the **New Vault** features jazzy, concrete, zigzag vaulting. Star corpses here include Maximilian I, Emperor of Mexico, assassinated there in 1867, and Marie Louise, Napoleon's second wife. Their son, the Duke of Reichstadt or "L'Aiglon" (see p.171), who died of consumption at the age of 21, was also buried here until 1940, when Hitler had his remains transferred to Paris as a gesture of goodwill.

Finally, there's the **Franz-Josef Vault**, the emperor's sarcophagus, permanently strewn with fresh flowers. Even more revered, though, is his wife, **Empress Elisabeth**, assassinated in 1898, whose tomb is draped in Hungarian wreaths and colours. On the other side of the emperor is the coffin of their eldest son, Crown Prince Rudolf, who committed suicide in 1889.

The **Gruftkapelle** beyond contains the Kaisergruft's most recent arrival, the **Empress Zita**, who died in 1989 in exile in Switzerland, and was buried here with imperial pomp and circumstance. In the corner is a bust of her dashing, bemedalled husband, the **Emperor Karl** I, who was deposed in 1918, and is buried on the island of Madeira, where he died of pneumonia in 1922.

## On Mozart's trail

It's almost as hard to avoid images of Mozart in Vienna – on chocolate boxes, on liqueur bottles, on tourist brochures, on flyers for concerts – as it is in his home town of Salzburg. For, as described on p.47, Mozart spent the last decade of his life here, during which he composed almost all of his most famous works. He moved thirteen times, for assorted reasons, not least because he never managed to secure a permanent full-time posting, and thus was always on the point of leaving the city. Today the streets of the Innere Stadt are littered with **plaques** marking his various addresses, though in fact, only one – the Mozarthaus – still stands, and is now a museum to the composer. The following is a chronological list of all his known Viennese residences:

**Singerstrasse 7**. On his arrival in March 1781, Mozart stayed here with the Archbishop of Salzburg in the House of the Teutonic Knights.

**Petersplatz 11**. In May, Mozart rented a room from the Weber family, but had to move out in early September, due to rumours about his liaison with one of the daughters, Constanze.

**Graben 17**. After leaving the Webers, he moved round the corner to lodge with the Arnsteins, the city's most privileged Jewish family.

**Wipplingerstrasse 19**. Following the success of his opera *Die Entführung aus dem Serail*, Mozart moved here in July 1782, to be joined, after their marriage in August, by Constanze.

**Wipplingerstrasse 14**. In December 1782, the Mozarts moved down the street to a house belonging to a wealthy, converted Jew, Baron Wetzlar, where they lived in two rooms on the fourth floor.

**Kohlmarkt 7**. Three months later, in February 1783, Mozart moved again, as a favour to Wetzlar, who needed the rooms. Wetzlar waived the back rent, paid for the move, and paid for the Kohlmarkt lodgings.

**Judenplatz 3**. In April 1783, Mozart moved into "good accommodations", where his first child, Raimund Leopold, was born (his wife's cries during labour are alluded to in the second movement of his D minor String Quartet).

**Graben 29**. In January 1784, the Mozarts moved to the Trattnerhof, one of the most famous addresses in all Vienna at the time, owned by the wealthy publisher, Johann Thomas von Trattner, whose second wife, Maria Theresia, was one of Mozart's first pupils.

**Schulerstrasse 8**. In September 1784, the Mozarts moved into the Camesina House, behind Stephansdom (now the Mozarthaus; see p.46).

**Landstrasse Hauptstrasse 75–77**. In April 1787, the Mozarts moved out of the Innere Stadt into a garden apartment in the third district of Landstrasse – here he composed *Eine kleine Nachtmusik*.

**Tuchlauben 27**. In December 1787, landlord problems forced them to move to the corner of Schultergasse and Tuchlauben.

**Währingerstrasse 26**. In June 1788, due to financial difficulties, the Mozarts moved again. Mozart's financial crisis was partly precipitated by the Turkish threat – 1788 was known as the *Türkenjahr* – and later compounded by the French Revolution.

**Judenplatz 4**. They kept this address from January 1789 for almost two years. It was here that their fifth child died and Constanze's illness began – an ulcerated leg with fears of infection, which brought further financial worries, as she had to move temporarily to Baden to take the cure.

**Rauhensteingasse 8**. Mozart's last move – his thirteenth address – took place in September 1791, when it appears that he had largely overcome his money problems. During their time here the couple's sixth child, Franz Xaver, was born, Mozart wrote *La Clemenza di Tito and Die Zauberflöte*, and spent his last days working on his *Requiem*. The plot is now occupied by the Steffl department store.

There's yet more musical tomfoole[ry]
Opera, where you can create your ow[n]
percussive at the Rhythm Tree, an[d]
computer-bank of sounds at the end.

# Graben and Kohlm[arkt]

The prime shopping streets of Graben[...]
that Kärntnerstrasse has lost. Their sh[...]
as if the Empire lives on, and sport th[e]
*königlich* (Imperial and Royal) – the Au[...]
Her Majesty the Queen" flaunted by t[...]
these old-fashioned stores are several[...]
jewellers produced by the doyen of m[...]

## Graben

**Graben** – its name translates as "dit[ch]
Roman camp. Filled in during the thi[...]
widened at the start of the nineteenth [...]
date. The most conspicuous monume[nt]
Column), or Dreifaltigkeitssäule (Tri[nity]
towering, amorphous mass of swirlin[g]
and shields, all covered in a cobweb of[...]
side of the column, below the kneel[...]
gleefully plunge a flaming torch into[...]

### Designer shops

By no means all the shops at street lev[el]
stuck in the Habsburg era; several [...]
design. First off, there's the **Knize** tai[lor]
marble facade was designed by **Ado[lf]**
work, it combines a love of rich ma[...]
ornamentation. The ground-floor sale[...]
panelled fitting room upstairs is uncha[nged]
Loos facade can be seen at Kohlmarkt[...]
Despite his name (and rumours to th[...]
underground toilets on Graben, which[...]
 After World War II, **Hans Hollein**, of [...]
Loos had left off. The first real shot ac[...]
tecture was his **Retti** candle shop (no[...]
the 1960s, the doorway of its smooth [...]
Then, in the early 1970s, he gave the [...]
26, a polished marble facade spliced [...]
into the door frame. Clearly enamou[red]
design another Schullin branch at Ko[...]
more subtle interplay of shapes and [...]
slender wooden columns support a [...]
portholes serve as showcases, and br[...]

[th]e 1679 plague, similar monuments were
[ini]tiative of the Jesuits, as much to celebrate
[...], and for that matter the Turkish "plague".
[co]unter-Reformation.

[...]brandt-designed **Bartolotti-Partenfeld**
[...]theergasse, survive of the Baroque era on
[...]ing buildings are early works by Otto
[...]stil architecture: the 1895 **Ankerhaus**, at
[...]Spiegelgasse and Dorotheergasse, and the
[...]arble loggia forms the most eye-catching
[...]nkerhaus to see a wrought-iron-and-glass
[...]agner's own purpose-built studio.

[...]sse is a classic post-Napoleonic, or Bieder-
[...] as a savings bank for the burgeoning
[...]n the facade), and in its severe, unadorned
[...]icially sanctioned style of the Metternich
[...] acting as a visual symbol of the latter's
[...]g the entrance to the flagship store of
[...] Harrods food hall, a cluster of naked
[...]far end of the street serve as an uninten-
[...] as a red-light district, which stretch back

[...]g a little square of its own, is the **Peter-**
[...]lebrandt in 1708, and without doubt the
[...]The confines of space within which he had
[...]n-towered church is dominated by its great
[...]ithin, the dome's fresco of *The Assumption*
[...]ttmayr is difficult to discern, but still adds
[...]rics, created by the lashings of salmon pink
[...]yed throughout. Note the richly-coloured
[...]loaks turn into stucco as they overlap the
[...]l the fabulous cupola painting in the choir
[...]al designers, a group of early eighteenth-
[...]lized in trompe l'oeil. The lavish gilded
[...]he most dramatic work of art is the silver
[...]o Mattielli, opposite, depicting St John of
[...]rles Bridge by some nasty-looking Czech
[...]rb directing the proceedings. Also worth
[...]pew ends, which sprout a trio of cherubic
[...]d skeletons from the catacombs in Rome,
[...]pelle and the Kapelle der Heilige Familie.
[...]under of the Opus Dei movement, José
[...]e in the Peterskirche.

[...]ben, the most rewarding is **Dorotheer-**
[...]nstitutions. The first two face each other
[...]ian, nicotine-stained *Café Hawelka* (see
[...]ch bar, *Trzesniewski*, opposite (see p.208).

Further up on the left is the *Hotel Graben*, where, from 1914 until his death in 1919, the poet Peter Altenberg was a permanent guest.

### Jüdisches Museum

Vienna's intriguing **Jüdisches Museum** (daily except Sat 10am–6pm; €6.50; Ⓦ www.jmw.at) is halfway up Dorotheergasse in the Palais Eskeles at no. 11. The city was home to the world's first Jewish Museum, founded in 1896 but forcibly closed by the Nazis in 1938; not until 1989 was it finally re-established. Lavishly refurbished, it boasts an excellent bookshop and the *Teitelbaum Café*.

On the **ground floor**, head for the covered courtyard (now a lecture hall), dominated by a giant glass cabinet display of Judaica by artist Nancy Spero. The prophetic nature of its etched quotations from the Torah and other sources is revealed on the walls, peppered with photographic images from Jewish culture and history. On the whole, though, the curators have rejected the usual static display cabinets and newsreel photos of past atrocities. Instead, the excellent temporary exhibitions on the first floor focus on celebrating Viennese Jewish life and culture, past and present.

Special exhibitions occupy part of the **second floor**, which also contains a permanent display of 21 free-standing glass panels imprinted with holograms – ranging from the knob of Theodor Herzl's walking stick to a short clip capturing an everyday instance of anti-Semitism from 1911. These ghostly images, accompanied by judicious soundbites (in German and English) on Zionism, assimilation and other key issues, pithily trace the history of Vienna's Jewry, juxtaposing the enormous achievements of the city's Jews – from Gustav Mahler to Billy Wilder – with its justified reputation as a hotbed of anti-Semitism.

Taking something of a different tack, the **third floor** contains the *Schaudepot* or storage depot. The displays of Hanukkah candelabra and other ritual objects, located in large movable glass cabinets, are deliberately haphazard – they constitute all that is left of the pre-1938 Jewish Museum and the community it served, and include many items literally pulled from the embers of the city's synagogues, torched during *Kristallnacht* (see p.259).

### Dorotheum

Further on, beyond the Jüdisches Museum, stands the institution from which the street gets its name. The **Dorotheum** (Mon–Fri 9am–6pm, Sat 9am–5pm; Ⓦ www.dorotheum.com) is the city's premier auction house, founded in 1707, at Emperor Josef I's request, as a pawnshop for the rich – the euphemism for those who had fallen on hard times was "going to visit Aunt Dorothy". At the daily auctions nowadays, almost anything is up for sale, from second-rate artworks, which go for a song, to Jugendstil furniture and minor works by the likes of Klimt and Schiele, for which you need to take out a mortgage.

Don't be intimidated by the plush interior – anyone can walk in and view the goods free of charge. In the Glashof, on the ground floor, there are even fixed-priced goods for sale over the counter, from Hoffmann chairs to utter tat. The grandest showroom is the main auction hall on the first floor with its high ceiling and second-floor balcony. There's another fixed-price shop for fine art on the second floor, along with an excellent café.

# Kohlmarkt

Although the line of the old Roman moat continues down the narrow street of Naglergasse, most shoppers and strollers turn left at the end of Graben up **Kohlmarkt**, site of the old wood and charcoal market. The most striking aspect of this street is the perfectly framed vista of the Michaelertor, its green dome marking the main entrance to the Hofburg from the Innere Stadt. Before you head up Kohlmarkt, though, be sure to look up at the roof of the building on the corner, whose copper cupola is topped by a splendid Hussar, once used to advertise a shop.

Even more than Graben, Kohlmarkt is the city's last bastion of luxury retailing, perhaps best expressed by **Demel**, a very "k.u.k." establishment, which still advertises itself as the imperial and royal confectioners. Established in 1786 as *Zuckerbäckerei* to the Habsburgs, its very famous and opulent *Kaffee-Konditorei*, dating from 1888, is at no. 14 (see p.207). Another Viennese institution is the **Artaria Haus**, a Jugendstil building set back from the street at no. 9, and faced in marble by Max Fabiani in 1901, the bolted slabs on the first floor anticipating Wagner's Postsparkasse (see p.113). The bookshop of the master mapmakers, Freytag & Berndt, occupies the ground floor, while Artaria & Co itself, publishers of musical ditties by the likes of Haydn, Mozart and Beethoven, is situated on the first floor.

# Michaelerplatz to the Mölker Bastei

**Michaelerplatz**, the square at the top of Kohlmarkt, is the Hofburg's backdoor. Like nearby **Herrengasse** ("Lords' Lane") and **Minoritenplatz**, it has thanks to its proximity to the royal court long been a high-prestige address. Once upon a time, every single house here was the town palace of some aristocratic family or another; most now serve as ministries and embassies, so this can be a lifeless quarter, especially at the weekend. Nevertheless, both Michaelerplatz and Minoritenplatz are showpiece squares, and Herrengasse is worth exploring, if only for the Palais Ferstel, which houses the famous *Café Central* (see p.56) and Vienna's most opulent nineteenth-century shopping arcade, which brings you out onto the triangular square of **Freyung**, home to some fine exhibition galleries.

## Michaelerplatz

**Michaelerplatz** is dominated on one side by the exuberant arc of the neo-Baroque Michaelertrakt, begun in the 1720s by Fischer von Erlach's son, but only completed in the 1890s. Its curving balustrade is peppered with a lively parade of eagles, giant urns and trophies, while the gate's archways are framed by gargantuan statues of Hercules, and, at either end, fountains overburdened with yet more ungainly statuary: to the right, imperial land power; to the left, imperial naval power – though both were in short supply when the works were erected in 1897. The centre of the square is occupied by a collection of archeological remains that lie exposed in a designer concrete trench (another of Hollein's works); most of what you see, however, are heating ducts dating only from the nineteenth century – hardly heart-stopping stuff.

Much more intriguing is the **Looshaus** (Mon–Fri 8am–6pm), on the corner of Kohlmarkt and Herrengasse, which caused an uproar when it was built in 1909–11 by Adolf Loos. Franz-Josef despised this "house without eyebrows" – in other words lacking the sculpted pediments that sit above the windows of most Viennese buildings. Work was temporarily halted due to the protests, and only allowed to continue after Loos agreed to add bronze flower-boxes (to be filled with flora all year round). Today, it's hard to see what all the fuss was about: the rippling green marble columns that frame the main entrance look inoffensive enough. The original occupants, Loos's own tailors, Goldman & Salatsch, went bankrupt in

1925, but the current owners, Raiffeisenbank, have their name displayed in simple gilt letters across the upper facade, just as Loos originally instructed Goldman & Salatsch. The bank holds regular exhibitions in the foyer, so feel free to walk in.

The next block along from the Loos Haus is taken up by the altogether more conventional late-nineteenth-century Palais Herberstein, erected on the site of the **Café Griensteidl**, demolished in 1897. Reconstructed and reopened on the ground floor in 1990, the *Griensteidl* was, in its day, the preferred meeting place of the *Jung-Wien* (Young Vienna) literary circle, most notably Arthur Schnitzler, Hermann Bahr and Hugo von Hofmannsthal. The journalist Karl Kraus, another regular, wrote his most famous diatribe, *The Demolished Literature*, against the *Jung-Wien* circle, shortly after the destruction of the café, suggesting that the movement "would soon expire for lack of a foyer". Instead, the *Jung-Wien* posse simply moved down Herrengasse to the *Café Central* (see below), much to the annoyance of Kraus himself, who was a regular there, too.

The oldest building on Michaelerplatz, and the source of its name, is the **Michaelerkirche** (daily 7am–10pm; free; ⓦ www.michaelerkirche.at), first built in the thirteenth century, though the Neoclassical facade, added in 1792, somewhat obscures this fact. Inside, the church retains its plain Gothic origins, but sculptor Lorenzo Mattielli's *Fall of Angels* steals the show: a Rococo cloudburst of cherubs and angels rendered in alabaster, tumbling from the ceiling above the high altar. The gilded organ – the largest Baroque organ in Vienna – is very fine, and there are regular recitals. The church boasts an enormous **crypt** (April–Oct Mon–Sat guided tours 11.30am & 1.30pm; Nov–March by appointment ☎522 80 00; €5), containing hundreds of well-preserved mummified corpses, some still expensively turned out and even bewigged, among them the librettist of Mozart's opera *La Clemenza di Tito*, Pietro Metastasio.

## Herrengasse

**Herrengasse** was the preferred address of the nobility from the time the Habsburgs moved into the Hofburg until the fall of the dynasty in 1918. Its name dates from the sixteenth century, when the Diet of Lower Austria (*Niederösterreich*) built its regional headquarters or **Landhaus**, which still stands at no. 13. It was here at the Landhaus that the Viennese **1848 revolution** began on March 13. A large crowd of students, artisans and workers gathered outside the building demanding, among other things, freedom of the press and the resignation of the arch-conservative Prince Metternich. At one o'clock in the afternoon, soldiers fired into the crowd, killing several people and sparking off a mass uprising in the city. Metternich resigned and fled the city the next day, disguised, so the story goes, as a washer-woman. Emperor Ferdinand was another political casualty, abdicating in favour of Franz-Josef, but the revolt was eventually crushed on October 31.

Two doors up from the Landhaus, at no. 9, the **Palais Mollard** is a Baroque palace that now houses two museums run by the Nationalbibliothek: the Globen-museum and the Esperantomuseum (see p.80). Opposite the Landhaus, the grandiose Italianate **Palais Ferstel** was built in the Ringstrasse style by Heinrich Ferstel in 1860 for the Austro-Hungarian National Bank. It also housed the Stock Exchange until 1877, but more importantly it has long been home to Vienna's most famous *Kaffeehaus*, **Café Central**, restored in 1986 primarily as a tourist attraction, albeit a very beautiful one. At the turn of the last century, the café's distinctive Gothic vaults were *the* meeting place of the city's intellectuals, harbouring not only the literary lights of the *Jung-Wien* movement, but also the first generation of Austrian Socialists: Karl Renner, Viktor Adler and Otto Bauer. The latter were occasional chess adversaries of Leon Trotsky, who whiled away several years here before World War I. Other famous patrons of that era include Tito, Freud, Hitler, Lenin and, between the wars, the Vienna Circle of logical positivists. At the entrance sits a life-sized papier-mâché model of the moustachioed poet **Peter Altenberg**, another fin-de-siècle regular.

Further up Herrengasse, past the café, is the entrance to the **Freyung Passage** – built in the 1860s as part of the Palais Ferstel – an eminently civilized, lovingly restored shopping arcade, which links Herrengasse with Freyung (see p.58). The focus of this elegant marble passage is a glass-roofed, hexagonal atrium, with a fountain crowned by a statue of the *Donaunixen* (Danube Mermaid), whose trickling water echoes down the arcade.

## The Redl affair

Without doubt the greatest scandal to hit the Habsburgs in their twilight years was the infamous affair of **Colonel Alfred Redl**, who committed suicide in the early hours of May 25, 1913. Not only had the head of counter-intelligence in the imperial army been uncovered as a **Russian spy**, but he had been blackmailed into it because of his homosexuality.

For some time, the Austrian military had been concerned about the leaking of classified information to the Russians. Then, early in April 1913, a letter was discovered to one "Nikon Nizetas", containing a considerable sum of money and the names and addresses of known safe houses. Sent to the main post office in Vienna, it had remained unclaimed. **Austrian counter-intelligence** decided to send an incriminating duplicate letter, and wait for someone to pick it up. For six weeks, two agents sat in the building opposite waiting for a clerk in the post office to ring the bell that had been specially installed to warn them of the arrival of "Nikon Nizetas".

When the bell finally rang at 5.55pm on May 24, one agent was having a pee, and the other was in the canteen. By the time they reached the street, they had missed their man, but they managed to take down the cab number. As the two men stood around considering their next move, the self-same cab miraculously reappeared outside the post office. Fortuitously discovering that "Nizetas" had left the felt sheath for his dagger in the back of the cab, they eventually retraced him to the **Hotel Klomser**, in the Palais Battyány, Bankgasse 2. The agents were shocked to find that the man who answered to Nizetas's description was one of their own superiors, Colonel Redl, who had just returned to the hotel. The agents handed the sheath to the concierge and waited to see if Redl would reclaim it. Caught off-guard as he left the hotel, Redl accepted the sheath from the receptionist, and then realizing what he had done, took flight. After a brief chase through the Innere Stadt, Redl gave himself up. He was handed a loaded revolver and told to go to his hotel room and do the honourable thing.

The whole affair would have been successfully hushed up – suicide among the upper echelons was very common – had it not been for the locksmith who was called in to break into Redl's Prague flat. The place was decked out like a camp boudoir with pink whips on the wall and women's dresses in the cupboard. Unfortunately for the authorities, the locksmith in question was supposed to be playing football with investigative journalist **Egon Erwin Kisch**. When he told Kisch why he hadn't turned up, Kisch sent the story to a Berlin newspaper, and on May 29, the War Ministry was forced to admit the real reasons behind Redl's suicide. Redl's lover, Lieutenant Stefan Hromodka, on whom he had spent a small fortune, was sentenced to three months' hard labour (he later married, had several children and lived for another fifty years). Kisch became a popular hero overnight; the best table in the *Café Central* was reserved for him on all his visits to Vienna. The Redl affair served as the plot for John Osborne's 1965 play *A Patriot for Me* and the subject of the 1985 film *Colonel Redl* by István Szabó.

# Minoritenplatz

On the opposite side of Herrengasse, hidden around the back of the Hofburg, **Minoritenplatz** is a peaceful, cobbled square entirely surrounded by the Baroque former palaces of the nobility, now transformed into ministries and embassies.

At its centre is the fourteenth-century **Minoritenkirche**, whose stunted octagonal tower is one of the landmarks of the Innere Stadt (the top was knocked off by the Turks during the 1529 siege). The main entrance boasts probably the best-preserved Gothic portal in Vienna, with a tripartite tympanum depicting the Crucifixion. Inside, the church is impressively lofty, but the real highlight here is Giacomo Raffaelli's copy of Leonardo da Vinci's *The Last Supper*, on the north wall – only close inspection reveals it to be a mosaic, so minuscule are the polished mosaic pieces. The work was actually commissioned in 1806 by Napoleon, who planned to substitute it for the original in Milan, taking the latter back to Paris. By the time it was finished, however, Napoleon had fallen from power and Emperor Franz I bought it instead, hoping in vain to install it in the Belvedere. Only in 1847 did the Austrians manage to bring it back to Vienna and install it here.

On the south side of the square is a magnificent palace built for Emperor Karl VI by Hildebrandt as the Court Chancery, and now the **Bundeskanzleramt** (Federal Chancery), home of the Austrian Chancellor and the Foreign Ministry, whose main entrance opens onto **Ballhausplatz**. Prince Metternich presided over the numerous meetings of the Congress of Vienna here in 1814–15 (see p.249), and here too, in the Chancellor's office, the Austro-fascist leader Engelbert Dollfuss was assassinated during the abortive Nazi putsch of July 25, 1934. Dollfuss was shot in the mêlée after 154 members of the outlawed SS entered the building; his demands for a doctor and a priest fell on deaf ears, and he died after two and a half hours.

# Freyung

The aforementioned Freyung Passage from Herrengasse brings you out onto **Freyung** itself, a misshapen square centred on the Austria-Brunnen, unveiled in 1846 with bronze nymphs representing Austria and the key rivers in the Habsburg Empire at the time: the Danube, Po, Elbe and Vistula. In medieval times Freyung was a popular spot for public executions, while it hosted open-air theatre performances during its annual Christkindlmarkt during the eighteenth and nineteenth centuries. Freyung boasts a **market** once more, this time selling organic produce (Fri & Sat) and in the run-up to Christmas, there's a small Christkindlmarkt.

## Schottenstift

Freyung derives its name – meaning "Sanctuary" – from the **Schottenstift** (Monastery of the Scots), which dominates the north side of the square, and where fugitives could claim asylum in medieval times. The monastery was founded in 1155 by the Babenberg Duke Heinrich Jasomirgott, though the Benedictine monks invited over were, most probably, Irish and not Scottish. They were eventually expelled, having shocked Viennese society by "trading in furs, initiating wild dances and starting games of ball". The monastery's glory days may be over, but its highly respected Schottengymnasium, founded in 1807, remains one of the country's most prestigious boys' schools. Beyond the ornate Baroque plasterwork and faux marble, the **Schottenkirche** retains just a few reminders of its Romanesque origins in its southern choir chapel.

To view the former monastery's impressive art collection, in the **Museum im Schottenstift** (Thurs–Sat 11am–5pm; €5; ⓦ www.schottenstift.at), buy a ticket from the *Klosterladen* (monastery shop) beside the church, then take the stairs to the first floor. The walls are covered with mostly seventeenth- and eighteenth-century Dutch and German still lifes and landscapes. The prize exhibit, though, is the fifteenth-century winged altarpiece, which used to reside in the Schottenkirche. Thirteen of its original sixteen panels survive: one side depicts scenes from the life of the Virgin; the reverse side (originally shown only at Easter) tells the story of the Passion. The vivid use of colour, the plasticity of the faces, and the daring stab at perspective mark this out as a masterpiece of late-Gothic art. Interestingly, the story is given a local setting: the Visitation of the Virgin Mary to Elizabeth takes place in Spiegelgasse, and the town of Krems is portrayed in the picture of Christ carrying the cross, while medieval Vienna forms the backdrop for the Flight to Egypt.

## Mölker Bastei

The **Mölker Bastei**, one of the few remaining sections of the old zigzag fortifications that once surrounded the Innere Stadt, can be found up the sloping cobbled lane of Schreyvogelgasse, west of Freyung. This spot should be familiar to fans of the movie *The Third Man*, for it's in the doorway of no. 8 that Harry Lime (played by Orson Welles) appears for the first time.

High up on the Mölker Bastei itself, at no. 8, is the **Pasqualatihaus** (Tues–Sun 10am–1pm & 2–6pm; €2; free on first Sun of month; ⓦ www.wienmuseum.at), where Beethoven lived on and off from 1804 onwards (he stayed at more than thirty addresses during his 35 years in Vienna). Herr Pasqualati wisely left the flat below empty so Beethoven could make as much noise as he wanted. The apartment is one of three museums dedicated to Beethoven in Vienna, though as usual, there's no indication of how the place looked at the time he lived there. Perhaps this is just as well – according to one visitor it was "the darkest, most disorderly place imaginable… under the piano (I do not exaggerate) an unemptied chamber pot… chairs… covered with plates bearing the remains of last night's supper". Instead, you're left to admire Ludwig's gilded salt and pepper pots and battered tin sugar container, and listen to some of his music.

# Am Hof to Hoher Markt

Several beguiling alleyways are hidden deep within the part of the Innere Stadt that lies between **Am Hof** and **Hoher Markt**. This was the heart of the Roman military camp of Vindobona and later where the Babenbergs established their royal court, with the city's medieval Jewish ghetto close by. Few reminders of those days remain above ground but you can find out more about Vindobona at the excellent **Römermuseum** on Hoher Markt, and more about the medieval ghetto at the **Museum Judenplatz**, the site of Rachel Whiteread's controversial **Holocaust memorial**.

## Am Hof

**Am Hof** is the largest square in the Innere Stadt, an attractive, tranquil spot, marred only by the surface protrusions of its underground car park. The name – *Hof* means both "royal court" and "courtyard" – dates from medieval times, when this was the headquarters of the Babenbergs, who lorded it over Vienna until the Habsburgs took the reins in 1273. The jousting tournaments, religious plays and public executions have long gone, and the centrepiece is now the rather forbidding, matt black **Mariensäule** (Marian Column), erected by Emperor Ferdinand III as a thank-you to the Virgin for deliverance from the Protestant Swedish forces in the Thirty Years' War. At the base of the column, blackened cherubic angels in full armour wrestle with a dragon, lion, serpent and basilisk, representing hunger, war, heresy and the plague.

Dominating the square is the **Kirche am Hof**, from whose balcony the end of the Holy Roman Empire was declared in 1806, on the orders of Napoleon. The church's vast Baroque facade, topped by a host of angels, belies the fact that this is, for the most part, a fourteenth-century Gothic structure. Inside, it's a hotpotch, with the Gothic Carmelite church struggling to get out from under the Jesuits' rather crude later Baroque additions. Corinthian capitals are glued onto the main pillars, and the aisles have been turned into a series of side chapels, with stuck-on stucco porticos – only the coved and coffered ceiling of the choir succeeds aesthetically. The adjoining former Jesuit seminary became the imperial war ministry, and thus a prime target during the 1848 revolution. On October 6, the mob stormed the building, dragged out the War Minister, Count Latour, and strung him up from a nearby lamppost. Three railway workers were later hanged for the offence.

Another architectural illusion stands opposite the church: the palatial facade of no. 7–9 conceals the city's **Feuerwehr Zentrale** (Central Fire Station), where the engines are hidden behind the series of double doors. The firemen originally kept their equipment next door at no. 10 in the former **Bürgerliches Zeughaus** (Civic Armoury), suitably decorated with a panoply, several trophies and a double-headed eagle, and crowned by a spectacular cluster of figures holding up a gilded globe.

### Off Am Hof

If you pass under the archway by the Kirche am Hof, and head down **Schulhof**, you can see the church's Gothic origins clearly in its tall lancet windows and buttresses. Watchmakers continue to ply their trade from tiny lock-ups between the buttresses at the back, while opposite stands the Baroque Palais Obizzi, home to the world's oldest clock museum, the **Uhrenmuseum** (Tues–Sun 10am–6pm; €4; free first Sun of month; @www.wienmuseum.at), ranged over three floors of Schulhof 2. Founded in 1917, its conservative displays fail to bring the collection alive. Nevertheless, you'll find every kind of time-measuring device, from sophisticated seventeenth-century grandfather clocks to pocket sundials. Other unusual exhibits include the world's smallest pendulum clock, which fits inside a thimble, and a wide array of eighteenth-century *Zwiebeluhren*, literally "onion clocks", set within cases shaped like fruit, musical instruments and the like.

## Judenplatz

Two distinct alleyways lead north from Schulhof to one of Vienna's prettiest little squares, **Judenplatz**, dominated by Rachel Whiteread's mausoleum-like **Holocaust-Mahnmal** (Holocaust Memorial). Smothered in row upon row of concrete casts of books like an inside-out library, the bunker-like memorial deliberately jars with its surroundings; a chilling A to Z of Nazi death camps is inscribed into its low plinth.

As the name suggests, Judenplatz was originally home to the city's **medieval Jewish ghetto**, dating back to the twelfth century. The smoke-blackened foundations of its chief synagogue – burnt to the ground in 1421 – and a few modest finds, can now be viewed in the **Museum Judenplatz** (Mon–Thurs & Sun 10am–6pm, Fri 10am–2pm; €4; @www.jmw.at), entered at no. 8. Medieval Jewish life in Vienna is depicted in a short video with an English audioguide, and an interactive multimedia exhibition.

Nine tenths of what the world celebrated as Viennese culture of the nineteenth century was a culture promoted, nurtured or in some cases even created by Viennese Jewry.

Stefan Zweig, *The World of Yesterday*, 1942

Most Jews have mixed feelings about Vienna: the city that nurtured the talents of Jewish geniuses such as Sigmund Freud, Gustav Mahler and Ludwig Wittgenstein also has a justifiable reputation as a hotbed of **anti-Semitism**. The city where the father of Zionism, Theodor Herzl, spent much of his adult life (see p.184) is also seen by many as the cradle of the Holocaust, where Hitler spent five years honing his hatred; where in 1986, Kurt Waldheim was elected president, despite (or possibly even thanks to) rumours that he had participated in Nazi atrocities in the Balkans; and where, in 2000, the extreme right-wing FPÖ, led by Jörg Haider, helped form a coalition government.

Jews have lived in Vienna on and off for something like a thousand years. When the medieval community was **expelled** in 1420, all the two hundred or so who remained were burned at the stake. In the seventeenth century, Emperor Ferdinand II established a walled **ghetto** east of the Danube (see p.152), but with the Counter-Reformation at its height, Emperor Leopold I expelled the community once again in 1670. Vienna suffered financially from the expulsion, and with the Turks at its gates, a small number of Jewish financiers and merchants, hastily granted the status of *Hofjuden* or "**Court Jews**", were permitted to resettle. The most famous was Samuel Oppenheimer, chief supplier to the imperial army under Leopold I. Despite their elevated status, the position of the Court Jews was precarious. Not until Josef II's 1781 Toleranzpatent could they take up posts in the civil service and other professions, and build their own synagogue. At the same time, the Toleranzpatent began the process of assimilation, compelling Jews to take German names and restricting the use of Yiddish and Hebrew.

After the 1848 revolution, when only around two thousand Jews were living in Vienna, all official restrictions on Jews were finally abolished. In the next sixty years, thousands arrived from the Habsburg provinces of Bohemia, Moravia and Galicia; most settled, initially at least, in **Leopoldstadt**. By 1910, there were approximately 180,000 Jews in the city – almost ten percent of the population, and more than in any other German-speaking city. While the majority were far from well-off, a minority formed a disproportionately large contingent in high-profile professions like banking, medicine, journalism and the arts. The Rothschilds ranked among the richest families in the empire; virtually the entire staff on the liberal newspapers *Neue Freie Presse* and the *Wiener Tagblatt* was Jewish; the majority of the city's doctors were Jews, as were most of the leading figures in the **Austrian Socialist Party**. Other prominent Viennese Jews included the **writers** Arthur Schnitzler, Robert Musil, Stefan Zweig and Josef Roth, and the **composers** Arnold Schönberg, Alban Berg and the Strauss family.

Those Gentiles who found themselves sinking into poverty after the stock market crash of 1873 desperately needed a scapegoat. They eagerly latched onto anti-Semitism, promoted by the Christian Social Party under Karl Lueger, Vienna's populist mayor from 1897 to 1910. Perversely, this virulent anti-Semitism helped to save more Jews from the Nazis than in more tolerant places, since thousands had already fled the country before the 1938 **Anschluss**. Humiliations instigated by the Nazis – such as making Jews clean toilets with prayer shawls, or forcing them to chew the grass of the Prater like cows – and enjoyed by voyeuristic locals, meant that by 1941 a total of 120,000 Viennese Jews had escaped. Those that remained, however, were trapped, and some 65,000 died in the **Holocaust**. Right now, the community of around seven thousand is enjoying something of a **renaissance**, much of it centred once again in Leopoldstadt, maintaining a dozen synagogues and several schools across the city.

Ironically, Judenplatz already has a much older memorial commemorating the pogrom of 1421, known as the Wiener Geserah, and clearly visible on the oldest house on the square, **Zum grossen Jordan** (The Great Jordan), at no. 2. However, in this case, the inscription, beside a sixteenth-century relief of the Baptism of Christ, celebrates the slaughter, when the Jews were driven out of Vienna. Those Jews lucky enough to escape fled to Hungary; the rest were burned at the stake, or – to avoid that fate – killed by the chief rabbi, who then committed suicide himself. The Latin inscription reads: "By baptism in the River Jordan bodies are cleansed from disease and evil, so all secret sinfulness takes flight. Thus the flame rising furiously through the whole city in 1421 purged the terrible crimes of the Hebrew dogs. As the world was once purged by the flood, so this time it was purged by fire."

The square's Jewish associations are also recalled by the statue of the writer **Gotthold Ephraim Lessing** (1729–81), striding forward in a great trench coat. Lessing, a theology graduate, was a key figure in the eighteenth-century German Enlightenment, who pleaded for tolerance towards the Jews. Erected in 1935, the statue proved too much for the Nazis, who had it destroyed; after the war, the sculptor Siegfried Charoux made a new model, but it wasn't returned to its original spot until 1982.

The most elaborate building on the square is Fischer von Erlach's **Böhmische Hofkanzlei** (Bohemian Court Chancery), with a monumental Baroque facade that continues halfway down Jordangasse. What you see on Judenplatz is only the side of the building, whose lavish main portal actually looks out onto Wipplinger-strasse. The Austrians ruled over the Czechs from 1627 to 1918 from here; it now houses Austria's supreme Constitutional and Administrative courts.

## Altes Rathaus

Across busy Wipplingerstrasse from the Böhmische Hofkanzlei, the **Altes Rathaus** (Old Town Hall) is a dour-looking Baroque palace that served as the city's town hall until 1885 (when the huge Ringstrasse Rathaus was finished; see p.92). No one knows where the city's original town hall stood, but by the fourteenth century one was located near what's now the oldest part of the Altes Rathaus. The **Salvatorkapelle**, a Gothic chapel founded as the town hall chapel, is today hidden away at the opposite end of the courtyard from the fountain. A strange little building, much altered over the centuries, its most handsome feature is its ornate Renaissance portal, flanked by richly carved columns and visible only from Salvatorgasse.

The main courtyard of the complex is undistinguished but for Donner's wonderful **Andromeda Brunnen** from 1741, which depicts the Greek myth in lead relief. Sculpted in full relief and left at the mercy of a sea monster to appease the gods, Andromeda looks unfeasibly calm as Perseus, in very low relief, descends from afar on a winged horse to do away with the beast, which meanwhile spouts water noisily from its mouth into the basin below.

On the north side of the main courtyard, the highly informative **DöW** or **Documentation Centre of the Austrian Resistance** (Mon–Wed & Fri 9am–5pm, Thurs 9am–7pm; free; Ⓦ www.doew.at), explores the history of Austrian antifascist resistance. Besides an excellent summary of the political upheavals of the interwar republic, from the rise of Austro-fascism to the war itself, there's a comprehensive catalogue of the atrocities of the Holocaust. Despite the high level of popular support for the Nazis, the Austrian resistance remained extremely active throughout the war; 2700 of its members were executed, and thousands more murdered by the Gestapo. In addition to the photographs, newsreel and text, one or two artefacts bring the displays to life: resistance pamphlets, a partisan outfit and items from Mauthausen concentration camp.

## Maria am Gestade

More compelling by far than the Salvatorkapelle, the Gothic church of **Maria am Gestade**, up Salvatorgasse, is topped by an elaborate filigree spire prickling with crockets and pinnacles, symbolizing the Virgin's heavenly crown – lit from within after dark, it's a stunning sight. With its drooping, beast-infested pendants and gilded mosaics, the stone canopy of the slender west facade is also worth admiring, ideally from the steep steps leading up from Tiefergraben. "Am Gestade" means "by the riverbank" – Tiefergraben used to be a minor tributary of the Danube, and the church was founded to serve bargees.

The unusual interior – the nave is darker and narrower than the choir and set slightly askew – is a product of the church's cramped site, lying as it does on the very edge of the old medieval town. That said, much of what you see is the result of nineteenth-century restoration, as the church caught fire in 1809 when it was used by the Napoleonic forces as an arms depot. The remains of Vienna's little-known patron saint, **Clemens Maria Hofbauer** (1751–1820), can be seen in a gilded reliquary in a side chapel, set within a jazzy, modern marble table beneath some rare medieval stained glass. As well as being a trained baker, and a Redemptorist missionary, Hofbauer was also responsible for the welfare of the city's Czech community, which peaked at over 100,000, and which the church continues to serve today.

## Hoher Markt and around

An unremarkable square surrounded by dour postwar buildings and packed with parked cars, **Hoher Markt** has two redeeming features. The first is its centrepiece, Fischer von Erlach's **Vermählungsbrunnen** (Marriage Fountain), depicting the marriage of Mary and Joseph by the High Priest, for which there is no biblical evidence and few iconographical precedents. Even more remarkable is the ornate bronze baldachin and gilded sunburst with a dove flying out of it, held aloft by Corinthian columns with gilded rams'-head urn handles (which light up at night), under which the trio shelter. The second – the real reason folk come here – is the glorious Jugendstil **Ankeruhr**, a gilded clock designed by Franz Matsch in 1914, which spans two buildings on the north side of the square. Each hour, a gilded cut-out figure, representing a key player in Vienna's history, shuffles across the dial of the clock; at noon, the entire set of twelve figures (whose identities are revealed on a street-level plaque) slowly stagger across to a ten-minute medley of mournful organ music.

Despite appearances, Hoher Markt is Vienna's oldest square. This was the heart of **Vindobona**, the Roman military camp established on the border of the empire around 15 BC to house a legion of around six thousand soldiers. To learn more about Vienna's Roman past, visit the **Römermuseum** (Tues–Sun 9am–6pm; €4, free on first Sun of month; Ⓦwww.wienmuseum.at), on the south side of the square. The remains of two large houses, with underfloor and wall heating, can be examined, while local finds range from tweezers and small altars to a stone manhole cover and part of a relief from a coffin.

Prime among other sights worth seeking out in the streets around Hoher Markt are the secular medieval frescoes or **Neidhart-Fresken** at Tuchlauben 19 (Tues–Sun 10am–1pm & 2–6pm; €2, free on first Sun of month; Ⓦwww.wienmuseum .at). Executed around 1400, but only rediscovered in 1979, the wall paintings are patchy but jolly; some illustrate the stories of the *Minnesinger* (aristocratic minstrel) Neidhart von Reuenthal, others depict a snowball fight, a ball game, dancing and general medieval merriment.

Round the corner in Brandstätte, a rather more recent architectural highlight, the **Zacherlhaus**, was built by the Slovene Josip Plečnik in 1905. The exterior is all grim, grey granite, relieved only by the ranks of Atlantes holding up the cornice and by the winged figure of the Archangel Michael above the ground floor, but it's the building's lens-shaped stairwell, hidden away at no. 2–4 Wildpretmarkt, that makes its way into the Secession coffee-table books and postcards. Once you've made it down the black marble corridor, and sneaked past the janitor, you can admire the weird and wonderful lamps, whose twisted bronze stands, topped by lighted globes, punctuate each floor of the wood-panelled stairwell.

# Around the Ruprechtskirche

During the 1980s, the bars and clubs that sprouted up in the area around Ruprechtskirche helped drag Vienna's nightlife out of the doldrums. The area became fondly known as the "Bermuda Dreieck" or **Bermuda Triangle**; while it's no longer the Zeitgeist, there are still a hefty number of bars hereabouts, particularly along Seitenstettengasse and Rabensteig. During the day, however, it's all pretty quiet, disturbed only by the few tourists who come to appreciate the narrow cobbled streets and the two main sights: the **Ruprechtskirche**, Vienna's oldest church, and the **Stadttempel**, the only synagogue in the entire city to survive *Kristallnacht*.

## Stadttempel (Synagogue)

Ironically, it was the building restrictions in force when the **Stadttempel** (Mon & Thurs guided tours 11.30am & 2pm; €3; bring ID; Ⓦ www.jmw.at) was built, in 1826, that enabled it to be the only synagogue to survive the Nazi period. Under Josef II, synagogues had to be concealed from the street, so from the outside you get no hint of what lies behind 2–4 Seitenstettengasse. Despite its hidden location, it still suffered damage on *Kristallnacht* in 1938, but has since been lavishly restored. Designed top to bottom by Biedermeier architect Josef Kornhäusel, it's a perfect example of the restrained architecture of the period, its top-lit, sky-blue oval dome dotted with golden stars and supported by yellow Ionic pillars that frame the surrounding two-tiered gallery. The presence of armed police outside on Seitenstettengasse is a sad consequence of the terrorist attack on the Stadttempel that killed two people in 1981; the continuing vandalism of Jewish property in Austria; and, of course, the controversial policies of the Israeli government.

## Ruprechtskirche and around

Around the corner from the Stadttempel on Ruprechtsplatz, the plain, stout architecture of the ivy-covered **Ruprechtskirche** attests to its venerable age. Originally built as long ago as the eighth century, the current building dates partly from the twelfth century, though it has been much altered and expanded. Inside, the vivid reds and blues of the modern stained glass are somewhat overwhelming, detracting from the uniquely intimate ambience. Mass is still said here, and the space is also frequently used for art exhibitions.

From beside the Ruprechtskirche, steps lead down to **Morzinplatz** by the Danube Canal, a notorious address during the Nazi period. On the west side of the square stood the *Hotel Metropol*, erected by a rich Jewish family to cope with the influx of visitors to the city's 1873 exhibition, but taken over by the Gestapo in 1938 to serve as their headquarters. Thousands were tortured here before the building was razed to the ground towards the end of the war. The plot is now occupied by the Leopold-Figl-Hof, named after the country's postwar Foreign Minister, who passed through the *Metropol* en route to Dachau. A **Monument to the Victims of Fascism** showing a prisoner surrounded by granite boulders from Mauthausen concentration camp was erected in front of the apartments in 1985. There's also a permanent **Memorial to the Victims in the Austrian Resistance Movement** (Mon 2–5pm, Thurs & Fri 9am–noon & 2–5pm; free) around the back, on Salztorgasse, where detainees were bundled in for interrogation.

# East of Rotenturmstrasse

**East of Rotenturmstrasse**, which stretches from Stephansplatz to Schweden-platz, Vienna's intricate, medieval streetplan continues. It's this, more than any specific sight, which makes a wander in this quarter rewarding, though four churches, varying from High Baroque to neo-Byzantine, provide a focus. Inciden-tally, the red tower that gave Rotenturmstrasse its name – it was actually a red-and-white chequered city gate – has long since disappeared.

## Fleischmarkt and Postgasse

**Fleischmarkt**, the old meat market, straddles Rotenturmstrasse east as far as Postgasse. Greek merchants settled here in the eighteenth century and, following the 1781 Toleranzpatent (see p.77), built their own Greek Orthodox church on Griechengasse. The only inkling that there's a church here is from the cupola and pediment, which face onto Hafnersteig. On Fleischmarkt itself, though, there's another more imposing stripy, red-brick **Griechische Kirche**, redesigned in mock-Byzantine style in 1861 by Ringstrasse architect Theophil Hansen, its decorative castellations glistening with gilt. Opening hours are erratic, and you may not be able to get past the gloomy, arcaded vestibule – ideally, try on a Sunday – to see the candle-lit interior, pungent with incense and richly decorated with icons, gilded frescoes and a giant iconostasis. Next door to the church, at no. 11, is the popular inn *Griechenbeisl* (see p.217), a Viennese institution for more than five centuries; patronized by the Greeks, by textile merchants from Reichenberg (Liberec) in Bohemia, and by the likes of Beethoven, Brahms, Schubert and Strauss. Inevitably, it milks the connections.

Turn right into Postgasse at the end of Fleischmarkt to reach another neo-Byzantine edifice, the Ukrainian Greek-Catholic **Barbarakirche**, a much lighter confection, with a pistachio-and-apricot-coloured facade. Peek inside at the pale-pink-and-blue nave to see its Rococo iconostasis, studded with medal-lion-style icons. Far more imposing, though, is the Italianate facade of the **Dominikanerkirche**, further south along Postgasse; the vast interior is an orgy of early Baroque stucco and frescoes, rebuilt in the 1630s following damage in the first Turkish siege.

# Dr-Ignaz-Seipel-Platz and Heiligenkreuzerhof

One block west of Postgasse along Bäckerstrasse lies **Dr-Ignaz-Seipel-Platz**, named after the leader of the Christian Socialists, who became the country's chancellor in 1922. Son of a cab driver, a trained priest, and, ironically, one-time professor of moral theology, Seipel was one of the city's most vociferous anti-Semites, who openly flirted with re-ghettoizing the Jews. Given the eventual fate of Austria's Jews, this rather attractive little square might have been better left as Universitäts Platz, since its east side is still taken up by the **Alte Universität** (Old University), founded by Rudolf IV in 1365, and thus the second oldest (after Prague's) in the German-speaking world. The current barracks-like building dates from the seventeenth century when, along with many leading educational institutions, it was handed over to the Jesuits.

By the eighteenth century, the university had outgrown its original premises. A more fanciful Baroque extension – now the **Akademie der Wissenschaften** (Academy of Sciences) – was built on the opposite side of the square. Its barrel-vaulted Freskenraum, decorated with frescoes by Franz Maulbertsch, is occasionally open to the public in summer for exhibitions (Mon–Fri 10.30am–5.30pm). **Josef Haydn** made his last public appearance here at the premiere of his oratorio *Die Schöpfung* on his seventy-sixth birthday in 1808. This was the occasion when Haydn – commonly known, even during his lifetime, as "Papa Joe" – is alleged to have laid his hands on the kneeling Beethoven, saying "What I have started, you shall finish."

Next door to the university, the rigidly flat facade of the **Jesuitenkirche** (also known as the Universitätskirche) rises in two giant tiers that tower over the square. Begun in 1627 at the peak of the Jesuits' power, the church smacks of the Counter-Reformation and is among the most awesome Baroque churches in Vienna. Striking features include the gargantuan red-and-green barley-sugar spiral columns;, the exquisitely carved inlaid pews; the richly gilded pulpit; and Andrea Pozzo's clever trompe-l'oeil dome – the illusion only works from the back of the church; walk towards the altar and the "dome" is revealed as a sham.

Behind the Jesuitenkirche runs the picturesque cobbled lane of **Schönlaterngasse** (Beautiful Lantern Lane); a copy of the ornate lamp immortalized in its name juts out of the wall of no. 6. Opposite, at no. 7, stands the **Basilikenhaus**, where the dreaded basilisk – the half-toad, half-cock king of the serpents – was supposedly discovered in 1212 at the bottom of a well. The canny baker's apprentice who volunteered to go down and capture the beast took a mirror with him, and the basilisk, seeing its own reflection, turned to stone – you can view a sculpture of the creature in a niche on the facade.

A gateway next door leads into one of Vienna's hidden gems, the **Heiligenkreuzerhof**, the secret inner courtyard that's owned by the Cistercian abbey of Heiligenkreuz, southwest of Vienna. A perfectly preserved slice of eighteenth-century Vienna, the courtyard is used for a weekly craft market on Sunday mornings. To visit the courtyard's winsome **Bernardikapelle** – a favourite venue for posh weddings – ring the bell of the *Hauswart* (caretaker), or call ☎512 58 96.

# The Hofburg

His gaze wandered up high walls and he saw an island – gray, self-contained, and armed – lying there while the city's speed rushed blindly past it.

Robert Musil, *A Man without Qualities*

Enmeshed in the southwest corner of the Innere Stadt, the **Hofburg** (Court Palace) is a hotchpotch of a place, with no natural centre, no symmetry and no obvious main entrance. Its name is synonymous with the Habsburgs, the dynasty that, at one time, ruled a vast multinational empire, stretching the length and breadth of Europe. Nowadays, apart from the tiny proportion retained as the seat of the Austrian president, the palace has been taken over by various state organizations, museums and, even more prosaically, a conference centre.

Seven centuries of architecture lie within the sprawling complex, much of it hidden behind anodyne, Baroque facades. Part of the reason for the palace's complicated ground plan was the unwritten rule among the Habsburgs that no ruler should use the rooms of his or her predecessor. Oddly enough, the most attention-grabbing wing of the palace, the vast Neue Burg, is a white elephant, only completed in 1913, and never, in fact, occupied by the Habsburgs.

Despite its plummet in status, two of Vienna's most famous attractions keep the Hofburg at the top of visitors' agendas: the **Wiener Sängerknaben** (Vienna Boys' Choir), who perform regularly in the Hofburgkapelle, and the **Spanische Reitschule** (Spanish Riding School), who trot their stuff in the Winterreitschule. The real reasons to visit the Hofburg, though, are the **Schatzkammer** (Imperial Treasury), with its superb collection of crown jewels, and the **Prunksaal**, Fischer von Erlach's richly decorated Baroque library. Also here are the **Kaiserappartements**, where the Emperor Franz-Josef I (1848–1916) and his wife Elisabeth lived and worked – her life is the subject of the palace's popular **Sisi Museum**. The palace also boasts several excellent museums and galleries: the **Albertina**, home to the world's greatest graphics collections, several departments of the Kunsthistorisches Museum, housed within the Neue Burg – the **Hofjagd- und Rüstkammer** (Court Hunting and Arms Collection), the **Sammlung alter Musikinstrumente** (Collection of Early Musical Instruments) and the **Ephesos Museum** (Ephesus Museum) – the **Museum für Völkerkunde** (Museum of Ethnology), and the **Schmetterlinghaus** (Butterfly House), part of the Burggarten.

## The Hofburg in history

Otakar II, King of Bohemia and Duke of Austria, erected the first fortress around 1275. Three years later, the first of the Habsburgs, **Rudolf I** (1273–91), defeated and killed Otakar in battle, and expanded and strengthened the place. His

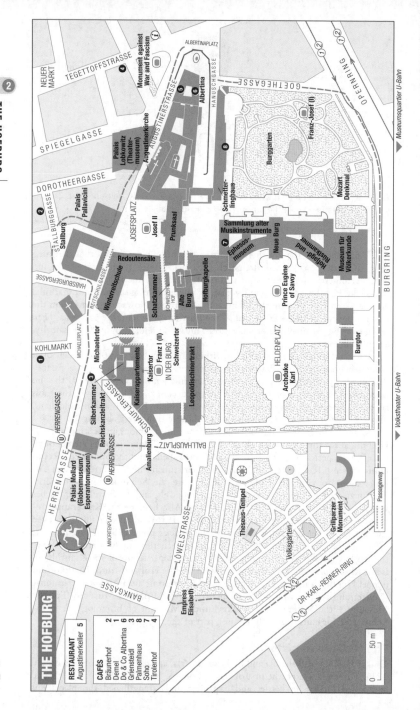

**THE HOFBURG**

**RESTAURANT**
Augustinerkeller 5

**CAFÉS**
Bräunerhof 2
Demel 1
Do & Co Albertina 6
Griensteidl 3
Palmenhaus 8
Soho 7
Tirolerhof 4

NEUER
MARKT

TEGETTHOFFSTRASSE

ALBERTINAPLATZ

Monument against
War and Fascism

SPIEGELGASSE

Palais
Lobkowitz
(Theater-
museum)

Augustinerkirche

GOETHEGASSE

Albertina

HANUSCHGASSE

DOROTHEERGASSE

Palais
Pallavicini

Franz-Josef (I)

Burggarten

STALLBURGGASSE

Stallburg

JOSEFSPLATZ

Josef II

Prunksaal

Schmetter-
linghaus

Mozart
Denkmal

HABSBURGERGASSE

Redoutensäle

Sammlung alter
Musikinstrumente

Museum für
Völkerkunde

BURGRING

Winterreitschule

Schatzkammer

Hofburgkapelle

SCHWEIZER
HOF

Ephesus-
museum

Alte Burg

Neue Burg

KOHLMARKT

Michaelertor

Franz I (II)

Prince Eugène
of Savoy

MICHAELERPLATZ

Kaisertor

IN DER BURG

Schweizertor

Kaiserappartements

HELDENPLATZ

Silberkammer

Leopoldinertrakt

Burgtor

HERRENGASSE

Reichskanzleitrakt

Archduke
Karl

Amalienburg

BALLHAUSPLATZ

Palais Mollard
(Globenmuseum/
Esperantomuseum)

HERRENGASSE

MINORITENPLATZ

LÖWELSTRASSE

Theseus-
Tempel

Passageway

BANKGASSE

Volksgarten

Grillparzer
Monument

Empress
Elisabeth

DR.-KARL-RENNER-RING

OPERNRING

▼ Museumsquartier U-Bahn

▼ Volkstheater U-Bahn

▼ Burgtheater U-Bahn

N

0    50 m

successor, Albrecht I (1291–1308), added a chapel, but only when **Ferdinand I** (1556–64) decided to make Vienna the Habsburgs' main base did the Hofburg become established as the chief dynastic seat.

Although the palace was protected by the city walls until 1857, the Habsburgs left nothing to chance after **Friedrich III** (1440–93) and his family were besieged in 1462 by the angry Viennese, and later by the Hungarian king Mathias Corvinus, during which they had to eat the pets – and the vultures who landed on the roof – in order to survive. Subsequent generations quit the palace (taking the imperial treasury with them) long before the enemy arrived. In 1683, with the Turks at the gates of Vienna, **Leopold I** (1657–1705) left in such haste, one eye-witness reported "the doors of the palace were left wide open". The same happened in 1805 and 1809, when Napoleon and his troops passed through, and in 1848, when the court fled, leaving the revolutionaries free to convene in the Winterreitschule.

After the downfall of the Habsburgs, the palace became more or less a state-run concern. Only one wing, the Leopoldischinertrakt, is retained for affairs of state, and is home to the **Bundespräsident** (Ⓦ www.hofburg.at). Otherwise, the Hofburg is a relaxing place to wander round, mercifully free of officious types telling you to refrain from sitting on the steps and the like, and you can walk through the courtyards at any time of day or night – there's even a bus service (#2a) that runs right through the palace.

# In der Burg

The largest of the Hofburg's enclosed courtyards, **In der Burg**, is the one that sees the most human traffic. It was once a much livelier place, the venue for the daily changing of the guard under the Habsburgs, and, in the Middle Ages, the scene of tournaments, military parades and executions. At the centre is an overblown monument to the **Emperor Franz**, dressed, appropriately enough, in a Roman toga, since as well as being (as Franz I, after 1804) the first Austrian emperor, he was (as Franz II, until 1806) the last Holy Roman Emperor. Erected in the 1840s, the monument was a culmination of the patriotic cult of "Franz the Good", victor over Napoleon and host of the Congress of Vienna. Franz fever took off as soon as the emperor breathed his last in 1835, when aristocratic ladies fought over the feathers from the pillow on his deathbed.

The south side of the courtyard is occupied by the vast range of the **Leopold-ischinertrakt** (Leopold Wing), with its lime-green pilasters. Built by, and named after, Leopold I, and later occupied by Empress Maria Theresia, it is now closed to the public, as part of the president's official residence. Opposite, the **Reichskanzleitrakt** (State Chancellery Wing), a giant, cream-coloured, Baroque confection, was built by a combination of Hildebrandt and the Fischer

②

von Erlachs. Taking its name from the bureaucrats of the Holy Roman Empire, who resided here until 1806, it now houses the Kaiserappartements (see below). The two wings are joined at the west end by the sixteenth-century **Amalienburg**, built for Emperor Rudolf II, though he preferred Prague to Vienna. It takes its present name from Amalia, the widow of Josef I, who lived here until her death in 1742. Though essentially a Renaissance building, it sports a dinky little Baroque bell tower and weather vane, not to mention a sundial, a clock and a gilded globe that shows the current phase of the moon. The rooms now open to the public date from the time of Empress Elisabeth, who died in 1898, and Emperor Karl I (1916–18).

## Kaiserappartements

The **Kaiserappartements** (daily 9am–5.30pm; July & Aug 9am–6pm; €9.90; ⓦwww.hofburg-wien.at) have always been a bit disappointing. Unlike Schön brunn, virtually every room is decorated in the same style – dowdy, creamy-white walls and ceilings with gilded detailing, parquet flooring and red furnishings. The decor is a legacy of the last imperial occupant, the **Emperor Franz-Josef**, who was notoriously frugal in his daily life. For opulence, you need to head out to Schönbrunn (see p.161).

To make up for this, the palace has created a **Sisi Museum**, a hagiographical exhibition on Franz-Josef's wife, Empress Elisabeth, whose cosseted life was pretty miserable, whose demise was violent and unexpected, and who has had an almost cultish following among Austrians ever since a 1950s trilogy of romantic films, starring Romy Schneider as the empress.

### Silberkammer

Before heading upstairs to the imperial apartments, you're ushered into the ground-floor **Silberkammer** (Silver Collection) – not to be confused with the Schatzkammer (see p.74), where the crown jewels are displayed. Whereas the latter has universal appeal, the Silberkammer is more of an acquired taste. The exhibition begins with room after room of cake and jelly moulds, kitchen utensils, bed linen, crockery, silver cutlery and candelabra. Also on display are the chests for moving all this gear from palace to palace, several original imperial menus and napkins folded (to a secret formula) to look like birds. More unusual still are the silverware used by Empress Elisabeth on her many sea voyages, the dolphin service made for the empress's villa in Corfu and the Hungarian earthenware service made for her private dairy at Schönbrunn. The star exhibit, the early nineteenth-century monster Milanese table-centrepiece in gilded bronze, stretches for more than ten metres in a covered courtyard along a table strewn with classical figures and gilded bronze-and-crystal urns. In addition, don't miss the stone jugs and salvers, with which the emperor and empress washed the feet of 24 ordinary men and women (dressed as pilgrims) every year on Maundy Thursday – pictures close by depict the event, though Elisabeth, who only had to wash the feet of the oldest woman, usually opted out altogether (meaning all the women missed out on the ceremony). Elsewhere, there are fine examples of Sèvres, Minton and Meissen porcelain, plus an impressive collection of Japanese and Chinese porcelain.

### Sisi Museum

Upstairs, you enter the **Sisi Museum**, which explores (and exploits) the myth surrounding Empress Elisabeth, whose death mask kicks things off. Next follows a corridor filled with Sisi memorabilia, including photos of the monuments to Elisabeth that were erected throughout the empire, and – best of all – film clips of her various celluloid incarnations. Further on, there's a delightfully kitsch collection of half-life-sized plaster statues of the imperial couple through the decades – like a complete set of imperial garden gnomes.

In one room, you'll find Franz Xavier Winterhalter's famous portrait of the empress, aged 28, décolletée, dressed in her star gown, with **jewelled stars** in her

## Empress Elisabeth (1837–98)

**Empress Elisabeth** – or Sisi as she was, and still is, affectionately known – was born into the eccentric Wittelsbach dynasty that produced the likes of her cousin "Mad" King Ludwig II of Bavaria. She enjoyed a carefree, sheltered upbringing, until she became engaged to Emperor **Franz-Josef I** – another cousin – at the age of just fifteen, after an entirely public, two-day courtship. While devoted to his new bride, Franz-Josef was in thrall to his mother, the Archduchess Sophie, who had their children removed from Elisabeth's care as soon as they were born. Later, Elisabeth advised her daughter, "Marriage is an absurd institution. At the age of fifteen you are sold, you make a vow you do not understand, and you regret for thirty years or more that you cannot break it."

By 1860, having dutifully produced a male heir, Elisabeth developed a psycho-somatic illness, and fled to Madeira for six months. She spent much of the rest of her lonely life **travelling around Europe**, under the pseudonym of **Countess Hohenembs**. She crisscrossed the continent, never staying in one place for long, and went on interminable cruises (she had an anchor tattooed on her shoulder) on her imperial steamer *Miramar*, alarming her companions by asking to be tied down on deck during storms. She sought solace in fencing, hiking and riding – she was reckoned to be one of the finest horsewomen in Europe – in the preservation of her beauty, and in writing poetry.

Although Elisabeth won admiration with her beauty, at the time most Viennese resented her frequent absences from the capital, and were appalled at her **pro-Hungarian** sentiments. Fluent in Hungarian – she even wrote letters to the rest of the family in Hungarian – she was instrumental in the political compromise with Hungary in 1867. After a brief reconciliation between the imperial couple, which resulted in the birth of Marie Valerie, the only child to whom Elisabeth was ever close, Sisi and Franz-Josef remained irrevocably estranged. She even encouraged Franz-Josef to get a mistress, introducing him to the actress Katharina Schratt, "very much as a woman might put flowers into a room she felt to be dreary", as biographer Rebecca West put it.

After her cousin, King Ludwig, and her only son, **Crown Prince Rudolf**, committed suicide within a few years of each other, she became convinced that she too was mentally unstable. From then on, she dressed only in black, and carried a mourning fan which she used to hide the wrinkles that were beginning to appear on her face. As she herself put it, "When we cannot be happy in the way that we desire there is nothing for it but to fall in love with our sorrows."

Notwithstanding her mental and physical state, few would have predicted her final demise. On September 10, 1898, the empress was assassinated by an Italian anarchist, **Luigi Luccheni**, on Lake Geneva. A local newspaper had unwisely announced the arrival of the empress, who was travelling incognito. As she was about to board a steamer to go to tea with Baroness Rothschild, Luccheni rushed up and stabbed her in the heart with a sharpened file. Like the empress, Luccheni had also been wandering aimlessly around Europe, in his case looking for someone famous to kill. He planned to assassinate the Duke of Orléans, but when he failed to arrive in Geneva, resolved to attack the Austrian empress instead. Her martyrdom has ensured that the myth and mystery surrounding her life remain as compelling as ever, long after her death.

hair, plus replicas of those very stars and several other sets of the empress's jewellery. Displayed next door are her comprehensive dental hygiene set; the mourning fan, painted by her daughter Marie Valerie, behind which she used to hide; and a reconstruction of her opulent personal railway carriage saloon. Her apotheosis, though, occurs in the shrine-like room, where a Sisi mannequin stands bathed in dark-green light surrounded by the sound of seagulls and inspired by a line from one of her poems "*Eine Möwe bin ich von keinen Land*" (I am a seagull from no land). In the final room, still sporting its original forensic label from the trial in Geneva, is the **murder weapon**: a three-sided metal file with a wooden handle.

## Franz-Josef's apartments

Following the Sisi Museum, you enter **Franz-Josef's apartments**. Despite being a field marshal, the emperor almost invariably dressed in a simple lieutenant's uniform. His eating habits were equally spartan: a breakfast of coffee, *Semmel* (bread roll) and a slice of ham (except during Lent) was followed by a lunch of

### Emperor Franz-Josef I (1848–1916)

**Emperor Franz-Josef I** was Europe's longest-serving monarch in his day, and Austria's most popular. His 68-year reign was the most sustained period of stability the country had ever known, and a stark contrast with what followed. Like his grandfather, Franz I – "Franz the Good" (see p.69) – he was a legend in his own lifetime, and, thanks to the Viennese love of nostalgia, the myth continues today. As historian William Johnston wrote, "Franz-Josef I symbolized more than he achieved." His aversion to innovation was legendary, epitomized by his addiction to the **Spanish court ceremonial**. At dinner, guests could only begin to eat when the emperor did, and had to cease at the moment the emperor finished each course. Franz-Josef being a very fast eater, his guests rarely enjoyed more than a few mouthfuls. Such dinners were also very silent, as no one was permitted to speak unless spoken to by the emperor – and he was more intent on eating. On his sickbed, during a particularly severe illness, though he could barely speak, he is said to have reprimanded the doctor who had been hastily summoned: "Go home and dress correctly." "Lord, this court is stuffy," remarked Edward VII, when in Vienna while Prince of Wales.

Despite the pomp and protocol that surrounded him, Franz-Josef was a simple man. When the first official census was conducted in Austria, he famously wrote down his occupation as "self-employed civil servant". Indeed, his dedication to his job was legendary: he woke at 3.30am (occasionally 4am), washed in cold water and would be at his desk by 5am. He preferred to take his meals at his desk and, towards the end of his life, liked to be in bed by 8.30pm. He had no great love of the arts – "I go to the opera as a sacrifice to my country," he once wrote to his mistress. His only passions were hunting and mountain climbing, and his annual holiday was invariably taken in **Bad Ischl**, in the Salzkammergut.

Franz-Josef's personal life was something of a disaster. He was in awe of his powerful mother, the Archduchess Sophie, who arranged and then proceeded to sabotage his marriage to his cousin Elisabeth (see p.71). Despite his estrangement from Elisabeth – she spent as little time as possible in his company – Franz-Josef remained dedicated to her all his life. Meanwhile, for over thirty years, he conducted an affair with the Burgtheater actress **Katharina Schratt**. Matters outside the bedroom were no better. His brother Maximilian was executed in Mexico in 1867, his only son Rudolf committed suicide in 1887, and his wife was assassinated in 1898. On the morning of November 20, 1916, at the age of 86, Franz-Josef rose at 3.30am for the very last time. His last words to his valet that night were: "Tomorrow morning, half past three".

*Tafelspitz* (boiled rump). He distrusted telephones, cars and electricity, and his only concession to modern life was his use of the telegraph. Twice a week, the emperor would stand behind the high desk in the **Audience Room** and receive the hoi polloi, who were required to come in uniform, tail-coat or national costume. According to court etiquette, visitors had to bow three times at the beginning and at the end of the audience, backing out of the room so as not to display their derrières to the emperor.

Passing swiftly through the pale turquoise Conference Room, where the emperor used to consult his ministers, you come to the **Emperor Franz-Josef's Study**. Here, seated at his rosewood desk, the emperor would give each official document, however trivial, his close attention before signing it, thus earning himself the nickname, "the first bureaucrat of the empire". Pride of place over the desk was always given to Winterhalter's portrait of Empress Elisabeth, décolletée, hair down and ready for bed, though the version you see here is, in fact, a copy. A hidden door leads into a cramped room that was occupied by the emperor's personal valets. Franz-Josef is said to have gone through valets "like candles", literally wearing them out with his early-morning routine.

The **Emperor's Bedroom** features the simple iron bedstead in which he slept under a camelskin cover. The delights of a modern washbasin were alien to the ascetic emperor, hence the foldaway toilet set. Only at the insistence of Elisabeth did Franz-Josef agree to install lavatories in the Hofburg; he himself preferred to use a bedpan. Moving through the Large Salon, you reach the **Small Salon**, now a memorial room to Franz-Josef's ill-fated brother, Maximilian, Emperor of Mexico, and his ambitious wife, Charlotte, daughter of the king of the Belgians, whose portraits hang here. The bust is of the Austrian naval hero Tegethoff, who defeated the Italians at the Battle of Lissa in 1866, and was later entrusted with bringing back Maximilian's body to Vienna from Mexico, after his assassination in 1867.

## Elisabeth's apartments

The empress's suite of rooms in the Amalienburg adjoins the Small Salon. Originally kitted out for the imperial newlyweds in 1854, these rooms were used exclusively by Elisabeth after the couple's estrangement – if Franz-Josef wanted to enter, he had to ring the bell behind the curtains in the Small Salon. Even so, the empress considered the Hofburg "a prison fortress", and spent as little time as possible here. Any feminine touches there might have been have long since disappeared – in any case, the empress slept on a simple fold-away iron bed (painted to imitate walnut), which you can now see in the **Empress's Living Room and Bedroom**.

Significantly, the paintings in the **Empress's Dressing and Exercise Room** are not of the imperial family – most of whom she despised – but of her Bavarian family and her beloved horses and dogs. Here you get to see the gymnastic equipment on which the empress exercised daily, a practice considered highly unorthodox at the time. She even had wooden rings screwed into the panelling above the doorway. Elisabeth was obsessed with her beauty, which required full-time maintenance. She was in the habit of rising at 5am, often plunging into a cold bath, followed by gym and a massage. Elisabeth took three hours to dress, partly because of her hair, which reached down to her heels; washing it in cognac and egg took up an entire day. To maintain the 50cm waistline she boasted until the day she died, the empress would lace herself so tightly she was frequently short of breath.

After the last few rooms, of minor interest only, you exit onto **Ballhausplatz**, at the far western end of the Hofburg.

# Alte Burg

The **Alte Burg** (Old Palace) lies at the very heart of the Hofburg, where the first fortress was built in 1275. A small section of the old moat, and the original drawbridge mechanism, survives by the main entrance, known as the **Schweizertor** (Swiss Gate) after the Swiss mercenaries who guarded it under Maria Theresia. The gateway itself, with its maroon-and-grey-banded columns and gilded relief, was erected in 1552 under Ferdinand I; above it, a gilded inscription lists his innumerable kingdoms, ending with the glorious "ZC", meaning "etc". Stairs on the right of the main courtyard – known as the **Schweizerhof** (Swiss Courtyard) – climb to the Hofburgkapelle, where the Vienna Boys' Choir performs Mass every Sunday (see p.76). Below is the entrance to the world-famous Schatzkammer, home to the Habsburgs' most precious treasures.

## Schatzkammer

Of all the museums in the Hofburg, the imperial **Schatzkammer** (daily except Tues 10am–6pm; €12; ⓦwww.khm.at) is far and away the most rewarding. Here you can see some of the finest medieval craftsmanship and jewellery in Europe, including the imperial regalia and relics of the Holy Roman Empire, the Habsburgs' own crown jewels, and countless reliquaries and robes, goldwork and silverware. Much of it was collected by Ferdinand I for his *Kunstkammer*, and from his reign onwards, the collection became a sort of unofficial safety-deposit box for the Habsburgs. Under Karl VI, the treasury was gathered together and stored on the ground floor of the Alte Burg; the original iron door displayed at the entrance is dated 1712. Labelling is in German only, so consider hiring an audioguide (€3).

### Insignia and mementoes of the Habsburgs

From the fifteenth century onwards, with only a brief caesura, the Habsburgs ruled as Holy Roman Emperors. In 1804, Franz II pre-empted the dissolution of the Holy Roman Empire by two years, declaring himself Franz I, Emperor of Austria, and using the stunning golden **Crown of Rudolf II**, studded with diamonds, rubies, pearls and, at the very top, a huge sapphire, as the Austrian imperial crown. The crown now forms the centrepiece of room 2; like the accompanying orb and a sceptre carved from a narwhal's tusk, it was made in Prague in the seventeenth century. For Franz I's coronation as King of Hungary in 1830, he commissioned a glorious gold-embroidered ermine burgundy cloak, with an ermine collar and a long train, now displayed in room 3 alongside some lovely velvet hats for knights, sporting huge ostrich feathers.

The sequence of rooms goes slightly awry at this point, so pass quickly through room 9, and turn left into room 5, where the mother of all cots resides: an overwrought, silver-gilt cradle with silk and velvet trimmings, made in 1811 by the City of Paris for Napoleon's son – known variously as the **Duke of Reichstadt** or "King of Rome" – by his second wife, Marie Louise, daughter of Emperor Franz I. The poor boy must have had nightmares from the golden eagle that hovers over the cot, and it comes as no surprise that this sickly, sensitive child died young (see p.171). Also displayed here are mementoes of Franz-Josef's ill-fated brother, Emperor Maximilian of Mexico, including his Mexican gold sceptre and chain of state.

Passing swiftly through the beautiful baptismal robes and vessels in room 6 – some were embroidered by Maria Theresia herself for her grandchildren – you enter room 7, which contains the remnants of the **Habsburgs' private jewellery** (most was spirited out of the country on the orders of Emperor Karl I in the last few weeks of World War I). Some serious stones are on display here, including a Colombian emerald the size of a fist, carved into a rather ugly salt cellar in Prague in 1641, and the huge garnet, "La Bella", which forms the centre of a double-headed eagle, along with an amethyst and an opal set in enamel (both considered as valuable as diamonds at the time). Another remarkable treasure is the solid gold **Turkish crown of István Bocskai**, the rebel King of Hungary, from 1605, inlaid with pearls and precious stones. More difficult to spot are the few pieces of Empress Elisabeth's jewellery, looking a bit upstaged among such illustrious company. Finally, before you leave, don't miss the golden rosebush presented by the pope to Franz I's wife, a traditional papal gift on the fourth Sunday in Lent to "the most worthy person".

Room 8 contains the so-called "**inalienable heirlooms**", two pieces collected by Ferdinand I, which the Habsburgs were keen to hold onto: a giant fourth-century agate dish, stolen from Constantinople in 1204 and thought at the time to be the Holy Grail, and a 2.43m-long narwhal's tusk, originally believed to have come from a unicorn and thus be a sacred symbol of Christ.

## Geistliche Schatzkammer

At this point, you come to the five rooms (I–V) devoted to the **Geistliche Schatzkammer** (Sacred Treasury). These hold a bewildering array of ecclesiastical robes, golden goblets, crystal crosses, jade candlesticks, huge monstrances and reliquaries. In room IV, where the star reliquary purports to contain the nail that pierced the right hand of Christ, there's also a monstrance boasting a fragment of the cross, and one of only three pieces of St Veronica's *sudarium* or veil to be authenticated by the Vatican. Among macabre items in room IV is a small seventeenth-century ebony-framed glass cabinet, filled with miniature skeletons partying round the glittering red-and-gold tomb of Ferdinand III, commissioned by his son, Leopold I.

## Insignia of the Holy Roman Empire

Backtracking through the Sacred Treasury and rooms 6 and 5, you'll reach room 9. Here, you'll find the late medieval **crown jewels and regalia of the Electoral Prince of Bohemia**, including matching gold lamé cloak, gloves and hat. As the Holy Roman Emperor was automatically also King of Bohemia from the fourteenth century onwards, someone had to stand in for the latter during the imperial coronation. Still more ancient royal insignia are displayed in room 10, which found their way into Habsburg hands via the Hohenstaufen dynasty. Striking items include the snazzy red silk stockings of William the Conqueror, and the red silk mantle decorated with Kufic inscriptions worn by Roger II when he was crowned King of Sicily in the twelfth century.

The highlight of the entire collection is the **crown jewels of the Holy Roman Empire** in room 11, traditionally kept in Nuremberg, but brought to Vienna in 1796 and retained by the Habsburgs after the empire was abolished in 1806. The Nazis took them back to Nuremberg in 1938, but the Americans returned them in 1945. The centrepiece is the octagonal **imperial crown** itself, a superb piece of Byzantine jewellery, smothered with pearls, large precious stones and enamel plaques. Although legend has it that the crown was used in the coronation of Charlemagne in 800, it dates back only to Otto I in 962. Similarly encrusted with jewels are the eleventh-century imperial cross, the twelfth-century imperial orb, and the very venerable ninth-century **Purse of St Stephen**, which belonged to Charlemagne himself and, so the story goes, contained earth soaked in the blood of the first Christian martyr.

Also on display in room 11 is the legendary **Holy Lance** (aka the Spear of Destiny), with which Longinus, a Roman centurion, pierced the side of Christ on the cross; the central pin at the end of the lance is supposed to be a nail from the cross. The lance, which probably dates from the seventh century, was alleged to have magic powers. The young Hitler is supposed to have had a mystical revelation in front of this exhibit, which changed the course of his life (and therefore of twentieth-century history). Whatever the truth, Hitler had the lance taken to Nuremberg after the Anschluss, and it was only returned after the war, by General Patton.

Many of the **imperial relics** in Room 12 were donated to the treasury by Emperor Karl IV, a serious relic freak. What you see is a mere *soupçon* of the original collection of more than two hundred relics (he apparently even stole one from the pope). There's a tooth from John the Baptist, a bit of the tablecloth from the Last Supper, a bone from the arm of St Anne, a chip of wood from Christ's manger, and even a small piece of his bib.

### The Burgundian treasures

The last four rooms (13–16) of the Schatzkammer contain the substantial dowry that came into Habsburg hands in 1477, when Emperor Maximilian I married the only daughter and heiress of the Duke of Burgundy. By so doing, Maximilian also became Grand Master of the **Order of the Golden Fleece**, an exclusive order of chivalry founded in 1430, whose insignia are displayed here: heavy mantles embroidered with gold thread, a collar of golden links from which the "fleece" would hang, and the ram emblem, worn by the knights at all times. The Grand Master was responsible for replacing any collars that were lost in battle; to his financial embarrassment, Maximilian had to pay for four golden collars that vanished in hand-to-hand fighting during the Battle of Guinegate in 1479. The Habsburgs remain Grand Masters of the Order, which still exists today. The final room contains an amazing collection of fifteenth-century gold-embroidered Mass robes covered in portraits of saints.

## Hofburgkapelle

The **Hofburgkapelle** (Jan–June & mid-Sept to Dec Mon–Thurs 11am–3pm, Fri 11am–1pm; €1.50; Ⓦ www.hofburgkapelle.at), up the stairs above the entrance to the Schatzkammer, was built in the late 1440s by Emperor Friedrich III. Despite numerous alterations over the centuries, the interior retains its stellar vaulting, its carved ceiling bosses, and its fifteenth-century polychrome statues protected by Gothic canopies. The chief point of visiting is to hear Mass performed by the Hofmusikkapelle, made up of members of the Wiener Sängerknaben, or **Vienna Boys' Choir** (Ⓦ www.wsk.at), accompanied by musicians from the Wiener Philharmoniker and singers from the Staatsoper.

Founded in 1498 by Emperor Maximilian I, the choir used to perform for the imperial family; famous Sängerknaben have included Schubert and Haydn. The choir went under with the Habsburgs, but was revived in 1924 and, dressed in ludicrous sailors' uniforms and caps (fashionable in the 1920s), is now a major Austrian export. There are, in fact, four choirs, who rotate jobs, the most important of which is to tour the world. The easiest way to hear them is to go to Sunday Mass at the Hofburgka-pelle at 9.15am (Jan–June & mid-Sept to Dec). **Tickets** can be bought in person (Fri 11am–1pm & 3–5pm; €5–29; standing room is free), or booked in advance by fax or email (Ⓕ 533 99 27-75, Ⓔ whmk@chello.at) and picked up on Friday or before Mass on Sunday. The boys remain out of sight up in the organ loft; the only time you get a proper look at them is when they give an encore at the end of the service, and then get their photos taken in the courtyard outside.

# Josefsplatz and around

Without doubt one of the most imposing squares in Vienna, **Josefsplatz** is lined on three sides by the blank, brilliant-white Baroque facades of the Hofburg. The square started out as the churchyard of the **Augustinerkirche** (now masked by the south wing of the Augustinertrakt), and later served as the training ground for the **Spanische Reitschule** (now housed to the north). It's appropriate then, that the central spot is occupied by an equestrian statue of the emperor Josef II – rather surprisingly, the first-ever public statue of a Habsburg when it was unveiled in 1807.

## Emperor Josef II (1780–90)

If any one Habsburg embodied the spirit of the Enlightenment it was **Emperor Josef II**. Born in 1741, the eldest son of Empress Maria Theresia, Josef was groomed for his role from an early age. After the death of his father, Franz Stephan, in 1765, his mother appointed him co-regent with her, and from 1780 he ruled in his own right. His reforming zeal surpassed that of all his predecessors put together – he published an estimated 6000 decrees and 11,000 new laws.

Josef's most famous reform, the **1781 Toleranzpatent**, allowed freedom of worship for non-Catholics, and lifted many restrictions on Jews. In addition, he expelled the Jesuit order, and closed down four hundred monasteries. Such policies incurred the wrath of the established church, but Josef himself was a devout Catholic – his aim was to reduce the power of the Church in secular life, and thus give him and his officials a much freer hand. Other decrees had more altruistic motives: aristocratic privilege before the law was abolished, with miscreant counts made to sweep the streets as punishment much as commoners had for centuries. His most popular measures included opening the royal gardens of the Prater and Augarten in Vienna to the public, and the court opera house to non-aristocratic patrons.

During his reign, the royal household was stripped of its former grandeur, and court ceremony virtually disappeared – he abolished imperial birthdays and gala-days, forty of which were observed annually. He dressed simply, drove through the streets in a two-seater carriage and was often seen on foot with the people. On becoming regent, he handed over his personal inheritance to the state treasury and demanded that his brother Leopold do the same, much to the latter's disgust. He lived for most of the time in a small outbuilding in the **Augarten** (see p.158), boarding up much of the Hofburg and Schönbrunn.

Despite his liberal policies, Josef was something of a despot – "everything for the people, and nothing through the people" was his catchphrase – who listened to no advice, and whose invasions of his subjects' privacy did not endear him to them. He forbade the wearing of corsets, on health grounds; the superstitious practice of ringing church bells to ward off lightning; the dressing of saintly images in real clothes; and even the baking of honeycakes (which he considered bad for the digestion). Most famously, he banned coffins, because of a shortage of wood, insisting corpses should be taken to the cemetery in **reusable coffins**, and buried in linen sacks to hasten decomposition.

Though Josef clearly loved his first wife, **Isabella of Parma**, she had eyes only for his sister, Maria Christina. Isabella died of smallpox in 1763, having given birth to two daughters, neither of whom survived to adulthood. Josef's second marriage, to **Maria Josepha of Bavaria**, was no love match. "Her figure is short, thick-set, and without a vestige of charm. Her face is covered with spots and pimples. Her teeth are horrible," he confided to a friend on first setting eyes on her. He treated her abysmally, and it was a release for her when she too died of smallpox in 1767. The emperor failed to attend the funeral, never remarried, took no mistresses, and lived as a bachelor until his death of tuberculosis at the age of just 48.

It's Josef who lends his name to the square, which he opened to the public by tearing down the wall that enclosed it within the Hofburg.

The attic storey of the central wing bristles with marble statuary and urns: the sculptural group above the main entrance features Minerva, goddess of wisdom, trampling Ignorance and Hunger with her four-horse chariot; on either side Atlantes struggle to contain a cluster of scientific instruments and two giant gilded globes from tumbling onto the cobbles below.

The north wing on Josefsplatz houses the **Redoutensäle**, originally the court theatre, but remodelled in the 1740s as a ballroom and banqueting hall. Mozart and Beethoven both conducted performances of their own works here, and the rooms became the traditional venue for the annual Hofball, held in February under the Habsburgs at the high point of the *Fasching* (carnival or ball season). Anthony Trollope's mother Fanny, who attended a masked ball here in 1836 at which over four thousand were said to be present, thought "the press was almost intolerable, and the dust raised by it such as quite to destroy the beauty and effect of this very magnificent room".

## Winterreitschule and Stallburg

Performances of the Spanische Reitschule take place regularly in the splendid Baroque **Winterreitschule** (Winter Riding School), on the west side of Josefsplatz. Purpose-built by Josef Emanuel Fischer von Erlach in 1735, the 55m-long **Reitsaal** is surrounded by a two-tiered spectators' gallery (with notoriously bad sightlines) held up by 46 Composite columns. The former imperial box at one end features an equestrian portrait of Emperor Karl VI, to which all the riders raise their hats on entering.

### Spanische Reitschule

The Habsburgs' world-famous **Spanische Reitschule** (Spanish Riding School) has its origins with Archduke Karl, brother of Maximilian II, who established several studs at Lipizza, northeast of Trieste (now the Slovene town of Lipica), in the 1570s. By cross-breeding Spanish, Arab and Berber horses, the studs created the Lipizzaner strain, which subsequently supplied the Habsburgs with all their cavalry and show horses. After World War I, the stud was moved to **Piber** in western Styria.

Since the early nineteenth century, only **silver-white stallions** have been used; at birth Lipizzaner foals can be any shade of brown to grey, but their coats turn white when they are four years old. Starting to learn dressage steps at age 7, they gradually progress to the aerial exercises for which they are famous, and can live to the ripe old age of 32. The highlight of the **dressage** is the *Capriole*, where the horse leaps into the air and tucks up all four of its legs. The riders wear period costume: black boots that reach above the knee, white buckskin jodhpurs, double-breasted brown tail coats, white gloves and a black bicorn hat.

The Spanish Riding School is such an intrinsic part of Vienna's **Habsburg heritage industry**, it's difficult not to feel a certain revulsion for the whole charade. That said, to witness the Lipizzaners' equestrian ballet is an unforgettable, if faintly ridiculous, experience; certainly those with any interest in horses will feel compelled to see at least a rehearsal. As Edward Crankshaw famously remarked more than half a century ago:

"The cabrioling of the pure white Lipizzaners is, by all our standards, the absolute of uselessness. The horses, fine, beautiful, and strong, are utterly divorced from all natural movement, living their lives in an atmosphere of unreality with every step laid down for them and no chance whatsoever of a moment's deviation. And so it was with the nineteenth-century Habsburgs."

It was in these unlikely surroundings that Austria's first democratically elected assembly met in July 1848, and voted to abolish serfdom (the court having fled to Innsbruck). The horses are kept in the **Stallburg** (stables), an arcaded Renaissance palace, on the other side of Reitschulgasse, originally conceived in 1559 by Emperor Ferdinand I as a private residence for his son, Maximilian. When Maximilian became emperor, however, he converted the building into the imperial stables.

You can glimpse the horses as they are taken over to (and brought back from) the Winterreitschule for their morning exercise, but for a closer look, it's best to watch a **training session** (*Morgenarbeit*; Jan–July & mid-Aug to Dec Tues–Sat 10am–12.30pm; €12). To avoid the queues, turn up after 11am, when it's usually easy enough to get in as folk soon get bored. Buy tickets either at the **visitor centre** (Tues–Sat 9am–4pm) under the Michaelertor, or from the box office on Josefsplatz on the morning of the training session (9am–noon). You can also sign up for an hour-long **guided tour** of the Winter and Summer Riding Schools and the Stallburg (check for exact timings, but usually daily 2, 3 or 4pm; €16). For **performances** (*Vorführungen*), it's best to book online in advance (March–June & Sept–Dec Sat and/or Sun 11am; seats €47–173; standing-room €23–31; Ⓦ www.srs.at).

# Nationalbibliothek

Spread out across the Hofburg, the **Nationalbibliothek** (Ⓦ www.onb.ac.at) is Austria's largest working library, home to millions of books. For visitors, its ornate Baroque Prunksaal on Josefsplatz is the main attraction, but you can also visit various offshoots: the Globenmuseum, Esperantomuseum and Papyrusmuseum.

## Prunksaal

If the Karlskirche (see p.104) is Johann Bernhard Fischer von Erlach's sacred masterpiece, then the **Prunksaal** or State Hall (Tues, Wed & Fri–Sun 10am–6pm, Thurs 10am–9pm; €7), is his most stunning secular work. Stretching the full length of the first floor of the central wing on Josefsplatz, it's by far the largest Baroque library in Europe; started in 1723, the year of Fischer's death, it was finished off by his son, Josef Emanuel. Access is via the staircase in the southwest corner of the square.

Entering the **library**, you're immediately struck by its sheer size: nearly 80m in length and 30m in height at its peak. Not an architect to be accused of understatement, Fischer von Erlach achieve his desired effect by an overdose of elements: massive marble pillars and pilasters, topped by gilded capitals, gilded wood-panelled bookcases, carved balconies accessed by spiral staircases, and from floor to ceiling, thousands of leather-bound books, including the 15,000-volume personal library of Prince Eugène of Savoy.

The space is divided into two quasi-transepts by a transverse oval dome, underneath which stands a statue of Emperor Karl VI, one of sixteen marble statues of Spanish and Austrian Habsburg rulers executed by the unlikely-named Strudel brothers, Peter and Paul. Directly above you (and Karl) is Daniel Gran's magnificent, colourful **fresco**, with the winged figure of Fame holding a rather misshapen pyramid. The emperor himself appears on a medallion just below Fame, flanked by Hercules and Apollo. Other celestial groups include a model of the library heading Karl's way – in case you miss it, the woman depicted as Austrian magnanimity is pointing to it. At the lowest level, Gran has painted trompe-l'oeil balconies, on which figures hold scholarly discussions.

## Esperantomuseum

Several of the Nationalbibliothek's collections have been moved to the **Palais Mollard**, a short stroll away from the Hofburg at Herrengasse 9. Here, on the ground floor, the **Esperantomuseum** (Tues–Sun 10am–6pm, Thurs until 9pm; €3) is a fascinating and totally unexpected little exhibition with captions in German, Esperanto and English.

Dr Esperanto (meaning "Hopeful One") was the pseudonym used by Polish optician **Dr Ludvik Zamenhof** when he invented his artificial language in 1887 – you can hear the man himself reading a passage in Esperanto. Zamenhof was a Jew who hailed from Bialystok, where Polish, Russian, Yiddish and German were all spoken. He saw Esperanto as an easy-to-learn, worldwide *lingua franca*. Esperanto certainly carries less ideological baggage than English, but it's a deeply Eurocentric language. Rooted in Latin-based Romance languages, it's plain sailing for an Italian, but virtually impenetrable at first sight for, say, an Egyptian. Although it never caught on in the way its creator originally hoped, there are now more than 100,000 Esperanto-speakers worldwide.

As well as giving you a quick rundown on how Esperanto works, the museum also contains sections on other **planned languages** such as Interlingua (a kind of grammarless Latin); neo-Slavic, designed to replace the seven or so Slav languages that plagued the Austro-Hungarian Empire; and Solresol, a musical language. There's even a chance to hear Hamlet's famous "To be or not to be" soliloquy spoken in Klingon.

## Globenmuseum

The first floor of Palais Mollard, Herrengasse 9, is occupied by the state-of-the-art **Globenmuseum** (Tues–Sun 10am–6pm, Thurs until 9pm; €5). Founded in the 1940s by Robert Haardt, the man who invented the rolling globe without a fixed axis, it's the largest such museum in the world. The collection begins with a copy of the world's oldest terrestrial globe, a depiction of the Europeans' pre-Columbus world from 1492 by Martin Behaim of Nuremberg (where the original is kept). Two beautifully executed giant globes come from late seventeenth-century Venice, one terrestrial and one celestial; the latter is covered in the most wonderful pictorial representations of the constellations. Other highlights include a globe pair by Mercator, the first to depict rhumb-lines crossing the meridians at the same angle. Look out, too, for the giant early inflatable globe from 1831, and the unusual planetary globes of Venus and Mars.

## Papyrusmuseum

The Nationalbibliothek's **Papyrusmuseum** (Tues, Wed & Fri–Sun 10am–6pm, Thurs 10am–9pm; €3) is located near the main reading room in the Neue Burg (see p.82); turn left as you approach the library turnstiles and descend to the basement. What you see is but a minuscule selection of its 100,000 or more papyri. Most of the labelling is in German, but some English is scattered about. Among sample texts in numerous ancient tongues from Hebrew to Aramaic are receipts, snippets of literature, aphorisms, magic spells, lists and tax accounts. Quirkier items include a fourth-century BC Greek recipe for toothpaste, Arabic advice from the ninth century on how to mix a laxative, and the marriage and divorce contracts of a couple who tied the knot and went their separate ways all in the space of a year (158 AD). The oldest written papyrus is the vast Book of the Dead in the end cabinet, executed in 1500 BC and smothered in hieroglyphics.

# Augustinerkirche

Hidden behind the south wing of Josefsplatz, the **Augustinerkirche** (Ⓦwww .augustinerkirche.at) is one of the oldest parts of the Hofburg, dating back as far as the 1330s. Built for the monks of the adjacent Augustinian monastery, the church was adopted as the court parish church in 1634. It was the scene of several notable Habsburg weddings, including those of Maria Theresia and Franz Stephan, Franz-Josef and Elisabeth, Crown Prince Rudolf and Stephanie, and the proxy marriage of the Archduchess Maria Louisa to Napoleon in 1810 (his stand-in was the Archduke Karl, who had been defeated by the French emperor at Deutsch-Wagram the previous year).

Inside, the church retains its lofty quadripartite Gothic vaulting. The chief attraction is Antonio Canova's Neoclassical **Christinendenkmal** in the right-hand aisle, a lavish memorial to Maria Christina, favourite daughter of Maria Theresia, erected in 1805 by her husband, Albert, Duke of Saxony-Teschen. A motley procession of marble mourners heads up the steps for the open door of the pyramidal tomb, while a winged spirit and a sad lion embrace on the other side, and another winged genius holds aloft the Duchess's medallion. They'd be disappointed if they ever got inside, though, for she's actually buried in the Kaisergruft. Canova's pupils were so taken with the mausoleum that they adapted the design for Canova's own mausoleum in Venice's Frari church.

The church also boasts a richly gilded Rococo organ, on which Anton Bruckner composed, and gave the premiere of, his *Mass no. 3 in F minor* in 1872. That musical tradition lives on; a full orchestra accompanies Sunday morning Mass. After Mass, you can get a guided tour of the church's Lorettokapelle (€2.50), containing the imperial **Herzgruft** (Heart Crypt), where 54 silver urns, arranged neatly on two semicircular shelves, contain the hearts of the later Habsburgs. If you ask nicely, the priest will also show you the neighbouring **Georgskapelle**, in the centre of which lies the empty marble tomb of Emperor Leopold II. Balthasar Ferdinand Moll's gilded wall tomb for Count Leopold Daun, on the far wall, is even more extravagant, and includes a relief of the 1757 Battle of Kolín in which Daun trounced the Prussians. Also buried here is Maria Theresia's faithful physician, Gerhard van Swieten, who saw her successfully through fifteen pregnancies.

# Albertina

South of the Augustinerkirche, the **Albertina** (daily 10am–6pm, Wed until 9pm; €9.50; Ⓦwww.albertina.at) is a mishmash of a building that occupies the southernmost bastion of the Hofburg. The entrance is from the vast raised terrace, which overlooks the back of the Staatsoper and is surmounted by a grand equestrian statue of Archduke Albrecht, who vanquished the Italians at the Battle of Custozza, one of the few bright moments in the otherwise disastrous Austro-Prussian War of 1866.

Founded by (and named after) Albert, Duke of Saxony-Teschen, in 1768, the Albertina boasts one of the world's largest collections of **graphic arts**: fifty thousand drawings, etchings and watercolours, and more than a million and a half printed works. It owns some 43 drawings by Raphael, 70 by Rembrandt, 145 by Dürer – more than any other gallery – and 150 by Schiele, plus many more by the likes of Leonardo da Vinci, Michelangelo, Rubens, Bosch, Bruegel, Cézanne, Picasso, Matisse, Klimt and Kokoschka.

With such a vast archive at its disposal, the Albertina stages outstanding changing exhibitions of graphics, devoted to one artist, period or theme. Besides its temporary galleries, the Albertina has a few **Prunkräume**, palatial Neoclassical rooms designed by Josef Kornhäusel, which feature lashings of gilding, quality parquet flooring, top-notch chandeliers and colourful silk-lined walls. Only a couple of rooms, like the Goldkabinett and the Marmorsaal, stand out – more interesting are works on show, from Michelangelo to Klimt, which give an idea of the depth and range of the collection. If you're flagging, the *Do & Co Albertina* **café** is a great place to stop, with a lovely summer terrace overlooking the Palmenhaus and Burggarten (see p.209).

# Neue Burg

The last wing of the Hofburg to be built – completed in 1913 – was the **Neue Burg**, a piece of pure bombast crafted in heavy neo-Renaissance style by Gottfried Semper and Karl von Haseauer. Semper originally planned to create a vast *Kaiserforum* by enclosing Heldenplatz with another new palatial wing mirroring the Neue Burg, and linking both wings to the nearby *Hofmuseen* via a pair of triumphal arches spanning the Ringstrasse – in the end, only the southern arc of the Neue Burg got built.

**Heldenplatz** (Heroes' Square) thus remains a wide, slightly meaningless, expanse, which nonetheless affords a great view across to the Rathaus and Parliament buildings on the Ringstrasse (see p.86). The square takes its name from Anton Fernkorn's two nineteenth-century equestrian statues, whose generals appear to be marshalling the surrounding parked cars into battle. The one of Archduke Karl, who defeated Napoleon at Aspern in 1809 (and then lost to him at Deutsch-Wagram shortly afterwards) depicts the horse cleverly balanced on its hind legs. Fernkorn failed to pull off this unique trick with the statue of Prince Eugène of Savoy, and had to resort to using the horse's tail for extra stability.

The Neue Burg itself is now home to the Nationalbibliothek's main reading room, the Papyrusmuseum (see p.80), plus several other museums. For the Viennese, though, it's forever etched in the memory as the scene of Hitler's victorious return to Vienna on **March 15, 1938**, when thousands gathered here to celebrate the Anschluss. "To say that the crowds which greeted him… were delirious with joy is an understatement," observed eye-witness George Clare before he fled the country. Hitler appeared on the central balcony of the Neue Burg and declared: "As Führer and Chancellor of the German nation and the German Reich I hereby announce to German history that my homeland has entered the German Reich."

To the west of Heldenplatz, the **Burgtor** cuts something of a pathetic figure as the official entrance to the Hofburg. Built into the walls in the 1820s – to commemorate the 1813 Battle of Leipzig, when the Austrians defeated Napoleon – it is the city's only surviving gateway. However, stripped of its accompanying walls, its classical lines and modest scale are at odds with everything around it. It was converted by the Austro-fascists in the 1930s to serve as Vienna's chief memorial to the fallen soldiers of World War I.

## Neue Burg museums

A single ticket (Wed–Sun 10am–6pm; €12; ⓦ www.khm.at) covers three museums in the **Neue Burg**: the Hofjagd- und Rüstkammer (Court Hunting and Arms Collection), the Sammlung alter Musikinstrumente (Collection of Early Musical Instruments), and the Ephesos (Ephesus) Museum. No English information is provided for those museums, so it's a good idea to pick up a free audioguide. The Museum für Völkerkunde (Museum of Ethnology) has its own separate entrance and requires a separate ticket (see p.84).

## Hofjagd- und Rüstkammer

The **Hofjagd- und Rüstkammer** or Waffensammlung (Weaponry Collection) boasts one of the world's finest assemblages of armour – what follows is just an overview. Most items date from the fifteenth to the seventeenth century; for the arms and armour of the later imperial army, head for the Arsenal (see p.137).

To the right of Saal I, there's a splendid array of **jousting equipment** made for the knights of Emperor Maximilian I (1493–1519). To minimize the death rate among competitors, whose necks were particularly vulnerable, the helmets were attached to the armour. The High Renaissance **costume armour** in Saal III was for show only, its design deliberately imitating then-fashionable clothes: puffy sleeves, decorative bands inlaid with gilded silver, and slightly comical pleated skirts. It's hard to imagine going to a wedding in the suit made for Albrecht of Brandenburg in 1526, with its huge pleated skirt, beetle-crusher shoes and grotesque helmet with wings and a beak.

Saal IV holds some fabulous sixteenth-century **Milanese armour**, including numerous shields depicting heroic exploits, and a cuirass with a cap complete with naturalistic ears and curly hair. The obsessive collector Archduke Ferdinand of Tyrol (1529–95) ordered the bank-breaking **Adlergarnitur** (Eagle Armour) in Saal V, with its exquisite gilded garniture. Equally resplendent is the blue-gold suit of armour made for Emperor Maximilian II (1564–76), with vertical gold bands in imitation of contemporary Spanish court dress. The superb **gold rapier** here, with its gilded cast-iron hilt, belonged to Ferdinand's brother, Maximilian II. Check out, too, the ghoulish Turkish masks in the side gallery, ordered for a jousting tournament in the 1550s.

Saal VI features great Ottoman arms and armour – sabres, jewel-studded daggers, horse plumes, bows and the like – taken as spoils during the sixteenth-century wars against the Turks. Yet more richly decorated suits of armour fill Saal VII, including the **Rosenblattgarnitur** (rose-petal armour) ordered by Maximilian II for the tournament held in Vienna in 1571 to celebrate his brother Karl's wedding; equally fancy suits, known as the **Flechtbandgarnitur** (interwoven armour), were created for his two sons, Rudolf and Ernst. There's more Milanese craftsmanship in Saal VIII, including a rapier whose hilt features numerous Moors' heads.

## Sammlung alter Musikinstrumente

Archduke Ferdinand of Tyrol is again responsible for many of the rare pieces in the collection of **early musical instruments**, designed to be admired for their artistry rather than the sound they produced. As well as hearing some on the audioguide, you can actually play one or two replicas, marked with a green dot.

Starting chronologically in Saal IX, the collection features, in Saal X, a unique set of sixteenth-century **dragon-shaped shawms** from Ferdinand's Kunstkammer. In Saal XI, you'll find a vertically strung **clavicytherium** richly inlaid with ivory, ebony, tortoiseshell and mother-of-pearl – it was played by Emperor Leopold I himself, who was a musician and composer in his own right. Also on display are the miniature instruments he had made as toys for his kids, and an ivory-backed lute from 1580, which Ferdinand himself used to play.

In Saal XII, check out the hurdy-gurdy, the thin, portable and very elaborate dance master's violin and the rare tangent piano, a precursor of today's pianoforte.

There's also an extraordinarily lifelike beeswax bust of Josef Haydn, sporting a wig of real human hair. The **tortoiseshell violin**, decorated with gold and ivory, in Saal XIII, was bought by Maria Theresia; like many such showpieces, it's totally unsuitable for playing. Also in this room is a set of six ornate gilded silver trumpets used in the Hofmusikkapelle until the end of the nineteenth century. The far corner holds an early nineteenth-century **glass harmonica,** of the kind invented by American statesman Benjamin Franklin.

Next door the ornate **Marble Hall** (Saal XIV) is still occasionally used as a concert venue. Eye-catching exhibits in Saal XV include a crystal flute and several portable instruments, including a string instrument that doubled as a walking stick. On the way out, there's a harmonium designed to play Schönberg's twelve half-tones, a self-portrait of the artist-composer, and a zither that belonged to Anton Karas.

### Ephesos Museum

From 1866 until a ban on the export of antiquities from Turkey stopped the flow early last century, Austrian archeologists made off with a lot of first-class relics from the ancient city of Ephesus, on the coast of Asia Minor. Not until 1978 was the loot finally publicly displayed in the **Ephesos Museum**, occupying one half of the Neue Burg's monumental staircase.

The most significant find, the impressive forty-metre-long **Parthian Frieze**, was sculpted in high relief around the second century AD, shortly after the Roman victory in the Parthian Wars. The relief ran round the base of a pantheon in honour of Lucius Verus, Roman co-emperor, along with his adoptive brother, Marcus Aurelius. The adoption of the brothers by Antoninus Pius (himself adopted by Emperor Hadrian) is depicted at the end of the corridor on the right, followed by battle scenes from the campaign, and finally Lucius Verus's apotheosis on the far left of the corridor (he was deified on his death in 169 AD).

Other notable finds include one side of the Octagon, a burial chamber with Corinthian columns, an Amazon from the **Temple of Artemis** – one of the Seven Wonders of the Ancient World – and a Roman bronze copy of a classical Greek sculpture depicting an athlete cleaning sand from his hands with a scraping iron. You can also see a vast wooden model of Ephesus (and lots of text in German on the excavations), and a model of the Temple of Artemis. Finally, there's a selection of minor finds from the Sanctuary of the Great Gods on the Aegean island of Samothrace, excavated in the 1870s by Austrian archeologists.

### Museum für Völkerkunde

In the section of the Neue Burg nearest the Ring, the **Museum für Völkerkunde** (daily except Tues 10am–6pm; €8; ⓦ www.ethno-museum.ac.at), houses a bewildering array of secular and religious artefacts from around the world. The single most-prized item is the stunning sixteenth-century gilded **Aztec feather headdress**, believed for many years to have belonged to Emperor Moctezuma II (Montezuma), and given by Hernán Cortés, the Spanish conquistador, to Emperor Karl V. The museum also owns artefacts brought back from Captain Cook's expeditions, snapped up at auction in 1806 by Emperor Franz I.

Large-scale ethnographic exhibitions are staged regularly, and there are even a few permanent galleries. The chief one open currently, on the first floor, is devoted to **South Asia and Southeast Asia**. Its dimly-lit rooms are filled with fascinating items ranging from stone Buddhas from the second century AD to wooden seated figures used by Len Dong practitioners of today. There's a great collection of Vietnamese water puppets and a video of them performing; a whole cabinet on the cult of Communist leader Ho Chi Minh; and a fabulous pantheon of seated and garlanded deities, surrounded by party lights and used until recently by a spiritual healer in Thailand.

## Volksgarten

Forming a large triangular wedge to the northwest of Heldenplatz, the **Volksgarten** (daily: April–Oct 8am–10pm; Nov–March 8am–8pm; free) opened in 1820 on the site of the old Burgbastei (palace bastions), blown up by Napoleon's troops in 1809. Appropriately enough, it was laid out as a formal French garden, and quickly became a favourite resort of the nobility – especially the "Aristocratic Corner", for which an entry fee had to be paid. When the rest of the fortifications were torn down in 1857, the garden was extended, and it remained an upper-crust haunt long after that.

Its focal point now is the Doric **Theseus-Tempel** – a replica of the Theseion in Athens – erected in the 1820s. Commissioned by Napoleon to house *Theseus and the Minotaur* by Antonio Canova, it's been more or less permanently closed since the statue was transferred to the newly opened Kunsthistorisches Museum in 1890. Plans in the 1930s by Carl Moll and Josef Hoffmann to turn the temple into a pantheon of Austria's musicians sadly came to nothing, and the building remains unused for the most part. In the garden's far northern corner, a seated statue of **Empress Elisabeth** presides over a melancholic sunken garden of remembrance. The opposite corner shelters an equally imposing monument to **Franz Grillparzer** (1791–1872), the poet and playwright, seated before a marble backdrop with reliefs illustrating his plays.

## Burggarten and Schmetterlinghaus

The **Burggarten** (daily: April–Oct 6am–10pm; Nov–March 6.30am–7pm; free), like the Volksgarten, came into being fortuitously after Napoleon blew up the bastions around the Hofburg. Unlike the Volksgarten, however, it was landscaped in the informal English style, and retained as a private garden for the Habsburgs until 1918. It now lies hidden behind the giant Neue Burg, though its entrance off the Ringstrasse is announced grandly enough by the marble **Mozart Denkmal** by Viktor Tilgner. Unveiled on Augustinerplatz in 1896 and moved here in 1953, the plinth features frolicking cherubs, two reliefs from *Don Giovanni*, as well as representations of the composer's father and sister, with whom he used to tour Europe as a *Wunderkind*.

Elsewhere, in the shrubbery, there's an equestrian statue by Balthasar Ferdinand Moll of Franz Stephan, Maria Theresia's husband, which has come down in the world since the bastion it used to adorn was blown up, and a rather downcast statue of **Franz-Josef** in his customary military garb. Incredibly, despite the omnipresence of the latter's image during his long reign – the emperor's portrait hung in millions of households across the empire – and the great trade in memorabilia since then, there was no public statue of Franz-Josef in Vienna until this one was erected by private individuals in 1957.

On the far side of the garden, the elegant glass **Palmenhaus** was designed by Friedrich Ohmann in Jugendstil around 1900. The left-hand section provides a suitably steamy environment for the colourful tropical butterflies, moths, birds and bats of the **Schmetterlinghaus** (April–Oct Mon–Fri 10am–4.45pm, Sat & Sun 10am–6.15pm; Nov–March daily 10am–3.45pm; €5; Ⓦ www.schmetterlinghaus .at) – such is the heat that you'll do well to take more than half an hour. The much larger middle section of the Palmenhaus has been converted into a very swish, palmy **café** (see p.210).

# The Ringstrasse

From morning until late at night, I ran from one object of interest to another, but it was always the buildings that held my primary interest. For hours I could stand in front of the Opera, for hours I could gaze at the Parliament; the whole Ringstrasse seemed to me like an enchantment out of The Thousand and One Nights.

Adolf Hitler, *Mein Kampf*

On Christmas Eve 1857, Emperor Franz-Josef I announced the demolition of the zigzag fortifications around the old town and the building of a **Ringstrasse**, a horseshoe of imperial boulevards to be laid out on the former *glacis* (the sloping open ground between the walls and the suburbs). Vienna had been confined within its medieval walls since the 1683 Turkish siege – now, with the Ottoman threat receding, the Habsburgs could create a boulevard befitting an imperial capital. Twelve major public buildings were set down along its course between 1860 and 1890 – among them an opera house and theatre, two museums, a parliament building, a university and a town hall – all at no cost to the taxpayer. By the end of World War I, though, the Habsburgs were no more: as Edward Crankshaw wrote, "[the Ringstrasse] was designed as the crown of the Empire, but it turned out to be a tomb".

Today Vienna's Ringstrasse looks pretty much as it did in the last days of the Habsburgs, studded with key landmarks. The monumental public institutions remain the chief sights, in particular the two monster museums – the **Naturhistorisches** and **Kunsthistorisches** (covered in Chapter Four) – and the **Staatsoper**. Countless other cultural institutions occupy prime positions on or just off the

---

### Exploring the Ringstrasse

Plagued by heavy traffic, the Ringstrasse is not much fun to stroll along nowadays. In addition, the boulevard's sheer size – 5km from end to end – and its uneven distribution of sights precludes exploration on foot. You can however appreciate the scale of the Ring by **tram**. The Ring-Tram (daily 10am–6pm every 30min) makes a full circuit in a clockwise direction from Schwedenplatz; aimed at tourists, with tickets costing €6, it has headphone commentary in various languages. A cheaper alternative is take a regular tram #1 from Schwedenplatz to Oper, which covers the western half of the Ringstrasse, and tram #2, which continues back to Schwedenplatz.

From the trams, only Karlsplatz lies entirely hidden from view. Each section of the Ring is **individually named** (eg Schottenring, Dr-Karl-Lueger-Ring, etc); the following account works **anti-clockwise** from the Ring's most northerly point, at Schottenring U-Bahn, to the final segment of Stubenring, where the boulevard once more rejoins the Danube Canal.

Ring, most notably the city's chief cultural complex, the **MuseumsQuartier,** plus the glorious Jugendstil **Secession** building and Vienna's most imposing Baroque church, the **Karlskirche**, both on Karlsplatz.

### Ringstrasse architecture and history

Unlike the rest of Vienna, the Ringstrasse was built on an epic scale, its width designed to facilitate the mobilization of cannons in the event of revolution. Memories of 1848 were still fresh in the minds of the military, and it's no coincidence that among the first buildings to be completed were the two **barracks** at either end of the Ring. However, within a decade of the 1857 imperial decree, Austria had changed from an undiluted autocracy to a constitutional monarchy. As a result, the emphasis of the Ringstrasse shifted, too, from an imperial showpiece to an expression of liberal values, with a **town hall** among its landmarks.

While the nobility, ensconced in Baroque palaces in the old town, tended to look down on the Ringstrasse as a place of residence, the wealthy **bourgeoisie** were happy to snap up buildings, which, designed to ape the aristocratic *palais*, were in reality little more than glorified apartment blocks or *Zinspalais* (rented palaces). It was a popular deceit, as even the modernist architect Adolf Loos, who dubbed Ringstrasse Vienna's "Potemkinstadt", had to admit: "Viennese landlords were delighted with the idea of owning a mansion and the tenants were equally pleased to be able to live in one."

From its earliest days, the Ring was a **fashionable** place to hang out, particularly around the new opera house, where every stratum of society would take part in the daily afternoon promenade. In April 1879, at the emperor's **silver wedding** celebrations, hundreds of thousands of Viennese, including the imperial family, watched as tens of thousands took part in a choreographed and costumed procession. The artist Hans Makart led the ensemble, dressed as Rubens in black velvet, and mounted on a white horse.

Later, it became a popular spot for **demonstrations**. The largest took place in November 1905, when 250,000 workers marched silently along the Ring to demand universal suffrage. Similar crowds lined the Ring to greet Hitler on his triumphal entry into the city after the Anschluss of April 1938 – and again in 1945 when Karl Renner appeared at the Rathaus to proclaim the restoration of the Austrian Republic.

Unfortunately, with the advent of the motor car, the Ring has become little more than a public racing track. The great institutions remain, along with their attendant cafés, but in between, airline offices, fast-food outlets and travel agents predominate. It's still a favourite spot for political rallies, but the only mass gathering that regularly takes place here is for the last lap of the annual Vienna marathon.

## Rossauer-Kaserne and the Börse

Erected in 1955 at the northern apex of the Ring, the **Ringturm** is one of the few high-rise buildings in central Vienna, acting as a marker (or so its architects like to think) for the start of the Ringstrasse. A more distinguished building, on the opposite side of the Ring, is the **Rossauer-Kaserne**, a fanciful, red-brick barracks, built in the late 1860s. One of the first constructions on the Ring, occupying three blocks, it originally formed a strategic and architectural pendant to the barracks on Stubenring. The crenellated complex, with its mock-Gothic turrets and machicolations, is now home to the Ministry of Military Affairs and Sport, and is best viewed across **Deutschmeisterplatz**, which features a giant militaristic monument to an infantry regiment, topped by a flag-wielding bronze soldier.

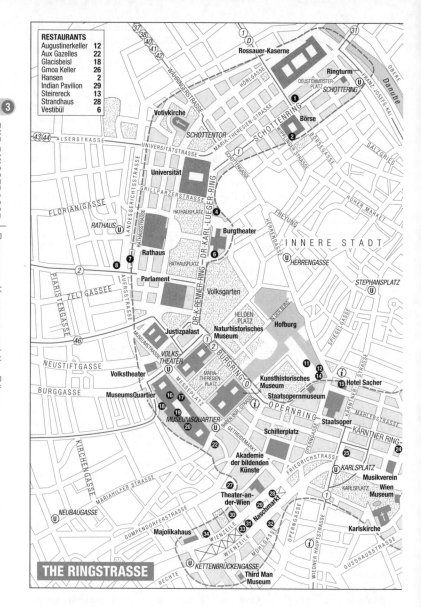

RESTAURANTS
| | |
|---|---|
| Augustinerkeller | 12 |
| Aux Gazelles | 22 |
| Glacisbeisl | 18 |
| Gmoa Keller | 26 |
| Hansen | 2 |
| Indian Pavilion | 29 |
| Steirereck | 13 |
| Strandhaus | 28 |
| Vestibül | 6 |

THE RINGSTRASSE

The key public building on Schottenring is the former **Börse** (Stock Exchange), designed in the 1870s by the Danish architect Theophil Hansen, a pioneer of the historicist architecture that characterizes the Ringstrasse. Here, Hansen chose to ape the Italian Renaissance – viz the arches, rooftop battlements and corner towers – in a style popularized with the construction of the opera house a decade earlier. The main hall was partially destroyed by fire in 1956, so you don't miss anything by viewing the building from the tram.

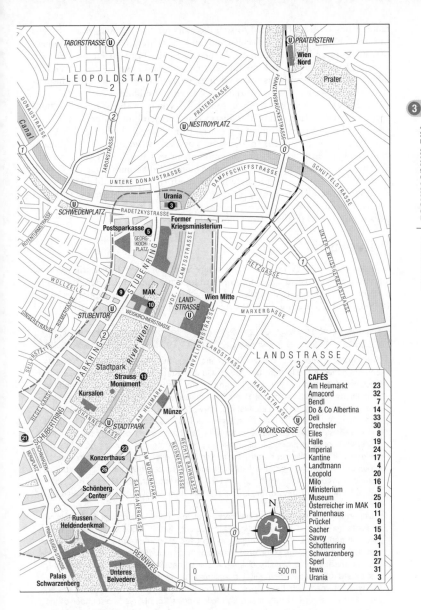

| CAFÉS | |
|---|---|
| Am Heumarkt | 23 |
| Amacord | 32 |
| Bendl | 7 |
| Do & Co Albertina | 14 |
| Deli | 33 |
| Drechsler | 30 |
| Eiles | 8 |
| Halle | 19 |
| Imperial | 24 |
| Kantine | 17 |
| Landtmann | 4 |
| Leopold | 20 |
| Milo | 16 |
| Ministerium | 5 |
| Museum | 25 |
| Österreicher im MAK | 10 |
| Palmenhaus | 11 |
| Prückel | 9 |
| Sacher | 15 |
| Savoy | 34 |
| Schottenring | 1 |
| Schwarzenberg | 21 |
| Sperl | 27 |
| tewa | 31 |
| Urania | 3 |

## Votivkirche

The first public building on the Ringstrasse – begun in 1854, even before the emperor had ordered the demolition of the city ramparts – was the vast **Votivkirche** (Tues–Sat 9am–1pm & 4–6pm, Sun 9am–1pm; free; Ⓦwww .votivkirche.at), designed by the Vienna-born architect Heinrich Ferstel in the style of the great Gothic cathedrals. Erected opposite the spot where a Hungarian tailor, János Libényi, had tried to stab the emperor the previous year – he was thwarted only by the emperor's collar and cap – the church was to be "a monument of patriotism and of devotion of the people to the Imperial House". Forever associated with the old order – the Church and the Crown – the Votivkirche differed from the later Ringstrasse buildings, which derived much of their inspiration from the liberal ideology of the newly ascendant middle class.

For all its size, there is something spiritually lacking in the Votivkirche. Built partly to serve the large influx of soldiers to the capital following the 1848 revolution, the church has no natural parishioners. Its interior, badly damaged in World War II, is gloomy, save for its colourful postwar stained glass, and it remains underused and little visited. The one monument worth a look is the sixteenth-century marble tomb of Count Salm, who commanded Vienna during the Turkish siege of 1529 – it's in the baptistry by the south transept. The highlight of the church's **museum** (Tues–Fri 4–6pm, Sun 10am–1pm; €3.90), up in the triforium – access from the north aisle – is the Antwerp Altar, a superb full-relief, polychrome gilded triptych, from the 1460s.

## Universität

Founded by Rudolf IV in 1365 in the Innere Stadt, Vienna's **Universität** (Ⓦ www .univie.ac.at) had to campaign long and hard to secure a prominent Ringstrasse site, owing to its radical past. Vienna's students had been enthusiastic supporters of the 1848 revolution, forming their own Academic Legion, manning the barricades and

### Pornography at the Universität

The biggest scandal in the Universität's history was the **"Faculty Paintings"**, murals commissioned in 1894 from the painter **Gustav Klimt** for the university's Grosser Festsaal. Klimt had already completed murals for the Burgtheater (1886–88) and the Kunsthistorisches Museum (1891), and the university no doubt expected more of the same. However, by the time the first picture, *Philosophy*, was unveiled in 1900, Klimt had broken with Vienna's main independent artists' association and helped to found the rebellious Secession. More importantly, he had moved a long way from the university's original proposal for a painting to illustrate the triumph of light over darkness. It was this, as much as anything else, which caused 87 professors to protest. The painting's tangled mass of naked, confused humanity – "a victory of darkness over all" in the words of one critic – was not what the Ministry of Culture and Education had had in mind. The scandal drew 34,000 onlookers to see the painting in just two months.

Unperturbed, Klimt exhibited the second of the murals, *Medicine*, the following year, its naked and diseased figures provoking further abuse. Questions were asked in parliament, where the artist was accused of "pornography" and "perverted excess". In 1905, having completed the last of the trio, *Jurisprudence*, Klimt resigned the commission. The Ministry claimed it still owned the paintings, and were only persuaded otherwise when Klimt threatened the removal men with a gun. The fee was returned with the help of the industrialist August Lederer, who received *Philosophy* in return. Klimt's friend and fellow artist Kolo Moser, co-founder of the Secession, purchased the other two. All three were placed in **Schloss Immendorf** in the Salzkammergut for safe-keeping during World War II, but were destroyed in a fire started by retreating SS troops on May 5, 1945. Copies of the murals can be seen in the university's **Grosser Festsaal** (if it's not being used); pick up an **audioguide** from the concierge, or join a **guided tour** (Sat 10.30am in German & 11.30am in English; €5).

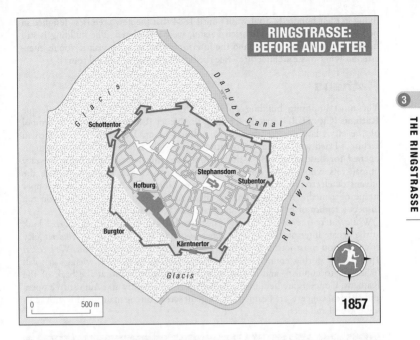

# RINGSTRASSE: BEFORE AND AFTER

Danube Canal

Glacis

Schottentor

Stephansdom

Hofburg

Stubentor

River Wien

Burgtor

Kärntnertor

Glacis

N

0    500 m

1857

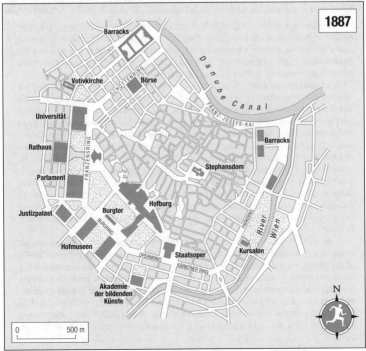

1887

Barracks

Danube Canal

Votivkirche    Börse

SCHOTTENRING

FRANZ-JOSEFS-KAI

Universität

Rathaus

Barracks

FRANZENSRING

Parlament

Stephansdom

Justizpalast

Hofburg

Burgtor

BURGRING

RING

Hofmuseen

OPERNRING    Staatsoper

Kursalon

River Wien

KÄRNTNER RING

Akademie
der bildenden
Künste

N

0    500 m

dying in their hundreds. So it wasn't until 1884 that the new premises, designed in neo-Renaissance style by Heinrich Ferstel, were completed. The building is still used today by the university, and the interior is well worth a visit if you're interested in Ringstrasse architecture – see the box for details of guided tours.

## Rathaus

The most imposing building on the entire Ringstrasse is the cathedralesque **Rathaus** (City Hall) – strictly speaking the Neues Rathaus – a powerful symbol of the city's late nineteenth-century political clout. Designed by the German architect Friedrich Schmidt in imitation of Brussels' Hôtel de Ville, the Rathaus opened for business in 1884, though one can only feel sympathy for the city bureaucrats who had to work in its gloomy neo-Gothic chambers before the advent of electricity. Its central tower, over 100m high, is topped by a copper statue of a medieval knight, known affectionately as the *Rathausmann*; you can inspect a replica of him at close quarters in the Rathauspark below.

While you're free to walk through the town hall's seven courtyards, to get a look at the ornate interior, home to the *Bürgermeister* (mayor) and the *Gemeinderat* (city council), you must join a 45-minute **guided tour** in German (Mon, Wed & Fri 1pm except during council sessions or holidays; free; Ⓦwww.wien.gv.at); call ☎525 50 to confirm, and assemble at the Stadtinformation at the back of the Rathaus. Concerts are held in the Arkadenhof, and in July and August free opera and classical concerts are beamed onto a giant screen on the main façade, with stalls selling food and beer.

### Karl Lueger (1844–1910)

**Karl Lueger**, mayor from 1897 to 1910, is by far the most infamous Viennese *Bürger- meister* – the nearby section of the Ring is named after him. Brought up by his widowed mother, who ran a tobacco shop, Karl made it to the city's most prestigious private school, the Theresianum, as a day scholar, and subsequently became a lawyer before entering politics as a left-wing Democrat in 1870.

His elegant appearance, impeccable manners and skilful oratory earned him the nickname *"der schöne Karl"* (handsome Karl), but his reputation is tarnished by the **anti-Semitic rhetoric** he adopted during the 1880s. In 1890, he made a speech in the Reichsrat suggesting that the city's Jews should be put on a ship, sent out to sea and sunk. In 1893, he formed the **Christian Social Party** (Christlichsoziale Partei), whose blend of municipal socialism, Catholicism and anti-Semitism proved irresist- ible to the Viennese petite bourgeoisie, in which Lueger had his roots. However, his election as mayor in 1895 was followed by two years of deadlock as Emperor Franz- Josef refused to ratify his taking office, wary of his popularity and anti-Semitism. Once in power, Lueger toned down the latter, resorting to it when he needed to maintain his popular appeal, and dropping it when he needed the cooperation of the city's wealthy Jewish financiers – hence his catchphrase, *"Wer a Jud is bestimm' i"* ("I decide who is a Jew").

In his thirteen years as mayor, Lueger laid the foundations for the **municipal socialism** that was established by the Social Democratic Workers' Party (SDAP) in the 1920s. He was responsible for much of the infrastructure the Viennese enjoy today: he piped in water from Styria, built gas works, created a green belt around the city, made provisions for cheap burials, built schools and old people's homes, enlarged the parks, and electrified the tram and subway network. His funeral in 1910 was the largest the city had ever seen, with more than 200,000 lining the streets, among them one of Lueger's biggest fans, the young, out-of-work artist, Adolf Hitler.

In the month leading up to Christmas, when the city's most famous **Christ-kindlmarkt** (mid-Nov to Christmas; ⓦ www.christkindlmarkt.at) takes place, the area in front of the Rathaus is crowded with stalls selling candy, decorations and traditional wooden toys. Folk flock here after work to drink hot *Glühwein* and *Punsch* to ward off the cold. In the New Year, this same area is turned into a giant outdoor ice-skating rink (daily noon–11pm).

# Burgtheater

Directly opposite the Rathaus, the **Burgtheater** (ⓦ www.burgtheater.at) seems modest by comparison – until you realize that the sole function of the theatre's two vast wings is to house monumental staircases leading to the grand boxes. In practical terms, though, the design by Gottfried Semper and Karl Hasenauer was none too successful. Less than a decade after the opening night in 1888 the theatre had to close in order to revamp the acoustics, which were dreadful, and to modify the seating, some of which allowed no view of the stage at all. The theatre was Badly gutted by fire in April 1945, so only the staircase wings still boast their sumptuous decor, including ceiling paintings by Franz Matsch and Gustav Klimt. To see these, the theatre lays on fifty-minute **guided tours** (Jan–June & Sept–Dec daily 3pm; €5.50), with weekend tours in English (Fri–Sun).

# Parlament

South of the Rathaus, the Neoclassical **Parlament** (ⓦ www.parlament.gv.at) was erercted in 1883, one of five major Ringstrasse buildings by the Danish architect Theophil Hansen. From street level, it's difficult to see past the giant Corinthian portico and its accompanying wings and pavilions. Stand back, though, and it becomes clear that the huge main body of the building – home to the lower house or *Nationalrat* (National Council), and upper house or *Bundesrat* (Federal Council), of the Austrian parliament – is mostly hidden behind the projecting facade. The interior, with its atrium of fluted columns, is well worth a visit; there are **guided tours** in German and English (mid-July to mid-Sept Mon–Sat hourly 11am–4pm; mid-Sept to mid-July Mon–Thurs 11am & hourly 2–4pm, Fri 11am & hourly 1–4pm, Sat hourly 11am–4pm; €4), except when parliament is in session.

The building's main **pediment frieze** shows Emperor Franz-Josef I granting the seventeen peoples of the empire a deeply undemocratic constitution. For the most part, however, Hansen plumped for classical antiquity rather than contemporary politics, with Roman horse-tamers and seated historians punctuating the two ramps. Between the ramps stands a gargantuan **statue of Athene**, goddess of wisdom, sporting a natty gilded plume in her helmet and presiding over a fountain served by four writhing mermen, representing the Danube, Inn, Elbe and Moldau. The attic of the main building, meanwhile, is peppered with 76 classical statues, 66 reliefs and four bronze chariot groups – these are best viewed from the sides of the building, where you'll find porticos held up by **caryatids** modelled on the Erechtheion on the Acropolis.

In its first fifty years, the parliament had a somewhat chequered history. Initially, the building served as the *Reichsrat* (Imperial Council) for the Austrian half of the empire, a body deadlocked by nationalist factions of Croats, Czechs, Poles, Romanians, Slovenes and Germans. The nadir came in 1897 when the Polish count Kasimir **Badeni** attempted to introduce his language ordinances, which would put Czech on an equal footing with German in the Czech Lands. Conservatives and German-Nationals organized an "Obstruction Concert", with whistles, sleigh bells, harmonicas, cowbells, gongs, toy trumpets, hunting horns and snare drums.

During the din, one member delivered a twelve-hour filibuster that ended at 8.45am the next morning. Following the Badeni debacle, the emperor bypassed parliament and ruled through the bureaucracy, until the introduction of universal male suffrage in 1907. Parliament was again prorogued shortly before World War I and didn't reconvene until after Franz-Josef's death.

On November 12, 1918, the *Reichsrat* held its last session, during which the Austrian republic – known officially as **Deutsch-Österreich** (German-Austria) – was declared from the ramps before parliament. The Babenberg colours of the new Austria, red-white-red, were hoisted on the tall masts either side of Athene; also present were the Pan-German nationalist students with their black-red-gold banners, and the Communist-dominated 41st battalion of the *Volkswehr* known as the *Rote Garde* (Red Guard). The latter tore up the Pan-German banners, and also removed the white from the Austrian banners, leaving red rags flying. Shots were fired, the *Rote Garde* tried to storm the parliament building; two people were killed and 45 injured. Five months later, there were more revolutionary rumblings as a posse of Communists, spurred on by the recently established Soviet republics in Bavaria and Hungary, broke in and set fire to the parliament building. In the street fighting that followed, five policemen and a woman were killed.

On the Ides of March, 1934, democracy was put on hold indefinitely as the Austro-fascists ordered police to block the entrance to the building to prevent parliamentary members from assembling. On seizing power, one of the Austro-fascists' first acts was to remove the **Monument of the Republic**, erected south of the parliament building after World War I, and featuring the busts of Socialist politicians Jakob Reumann, Viktor Adler and Ferdinand Hanusch. Strangely, the monument wasn't destroyed, but simply put into storage (rather like Austrian democracy itself), and returned to its rightful place after World War II.

## Burgring

On the other side of **Burgring** from the Hofburg stand the two so-called *Hofmuseen* (court museums), opened to the public in the late nineteenth century. The **Kunsthistorisches Museum** (History of Art Museum), housing one of the world's top art collections, is covered in detail in Chapter Four; the **Naturhistorisches Museum** (Natural History Museum) is described below. Designed in pompous neo-Renaissance style, with giant copper-domed cupolas and colossal wings, they are the work of Karl Hasenauer, and, as such, virtual mirror images of each other. The overall plan was thought up by the great Dresden architect, Gottfried Semper, who envisaged a monumental *Kaiserforum*, linking the museums to the Neue Burg via a pair of triumphal arches spanning

### The burning of the Justizpalast

Set back slightly from the Ring, the **Justizpalast** is an impressive neo-Renaissance monster of a building that holds a special place in Austrian history. On July 15, 1927, the day after three right-wing activists were acquitted of murdering a Socialist man and boy, a spontaneous demonstration of several thousand workers descended on and set fire to the Justizpalast. Chaos ensued, with mounted and armed police charging the crowd, and police reinforcements shooting live ammunition, leaving eighty-odd people dead, and up to one thousand wounded. The Socialists promptly called a general strike, which was deftly crushed by the heavily armed *Heimwehr*, the right-wing militia, who acted as strike breakers, and civil war was put off for a few more years.

the Ringstrasse. The project was interrupted by World War I, and then binned altogether after the fall of the Habsburgs.

Today, the museums remain cut off from the Hofburg by the traffic roaring round the Ring. They stare blankly at one another across **Maria-Theresien-Platz**, a formal garden peppered with topiary and centred on a gargantuan monument to Empress Maria Theresia. She presides over four of her generals (on horseback), and three of her advisers, plus her doctor (standing), who guided her through sixteen successful pregnancies. If you stand between the two big museums with your back to the Hofburg, you will find yourself looking at the **MuseumsQuartier** or **MQ**, Vienna's cultural complex, hidden away in the former imperial stables, built in the eighteenth century by Johann Bernhard Fischer von Erlach.

# Naturhistorisches Museum

In many ways very little has changed at the **Naturhistorisches Museum** (daily except Tues 9am–6.30pm, Wed 9am–9pm; €10; ⓦ www.nhm-wien.ac.at) since it opened in 1889. Whereas most European cities have tried to pep up their natural history collections with animatronic dinosaurs, ecological concerns and the like, the hard sell has pretty much passed Vienna by. Many of the display cabinets are more than a century old, the dim panes of glass almost pre-industrial, and the stuffed animals within having succumbed to a uniform, musty, grey hue. Even now places as distant as Illyria (the eastern Adriatic coast) and Galicia (part of present-day Poland and Ukraine) are described as part of Austria. That said, as a museum of museums, the Naturhistorisches is fascinating and, of course, the building itself is a visual feast.

An exception to the above is the **Vivarium**, immediately to the left as you enter: a tropical aquarium, vivarium and aviary featuring everything from clown fish and snakes to terrapins and Australian goldfinches. The upper ground floor (*Hochparterre*) kicks off with five rooms of **minerals** (I–V) in the east wing, among them some impressive slabs of green malachite, a giant fluorescent red ammonite and a huge chunk of transparent quartz. Polished marble tiles are accompanied by the names of buildings within the old Empire that feature the materials. More interesting is the penultimate room (IV), which contains various objects made from precious and semiprecious stones, including a bouquet made with 761 semiprecious stones and 2102 diamonds, given as a (morning-after) wedding gift by Maria Theresia to Franz Stephan. The final room contains Franz Stephan's very own orrery and several **meteorites**, the biggest of which is a 909kg monster found in Australia in 1884.

The paleontology section (VI–X) starts in room X – a huge hall decorated with caryatids struggling with weird, evolutionary beasts – where you can find a diplodocus skeleton, complete with fossilized dino-poo. Many of the **fossils** in room IX originate from the ocean bed of the Miocene Sea (which is where Vienna was fifteen million years ago). Look out for the beautiful giant palm-leaf fossils, the giant skeleton of a "small" deinothere (a kind of prehistoric elephant), and, in room VII, the fossil of a Megarachne, the world's largest-ever spider, which grew to 50cm in diameter in the high-oxygen carboniferous tropical swamps of 320 million years ago.

The prehistoric section begins in room XI with the **Venus of Willendorf**, the museum's most famous exhibit due to its age and its exaggerated sexuality. A stout, limestone figure with drooping breasts and swollen vulva, this fertility symbol stands just 11cm high, but is something like 25,000 years old, and is dramatically displayed in its own darkened chamber.

The west wing includes finds from the prehistoric Beaker folk and various implements, jewellery and arms from Iron Age burial tombs at **Hallstatt** in the

Salzkammergut. There's some impressive Thracian silver jewellery, a reconstructed gilded funereal chariot from the Iron Age, and a staggering collection of human skulls. The Kindersaal, beyond, is one of the museum's few concessions to modernization, though this tired playroom, built in the 1970s, isn't going to impress kids brought up on interactive, hands-on displays.

Zoology occupies the entire top floor except the first room (XXI), which contains a 3D **panopticon** through which you can take a peek at natural wonders of the world (including bits of the museum itself). The exhaustive **zoology** displays progress from starfish, corals and seashells in the east wing, through butterflies, spiders and frogs, to a bevy of bears, big cats and monkeys in the west. Some may find the pickled fish and lizards, the jars of snakes and reptiles, and the dissected frog more than they can stomach, but young kids will undoubtedly enjoy it. There's a little light historical relief in room XXIX, where you can see two stuffed eagles caught by Crown Prince Rudolf, just nine days before his suicide.

## MuseumsQuartier

Hidden behind the plain but vast facade of the former imperial stables, the **MuseumsQuartier** (ⓦ www.mqw.at), which opened in 2001, is home to a bewildering array of **galleries and museums**, performance and arts spaces, as well as great cafés and restaurants. The paler of the two cubes that dominate the MQ's central courtyard or *Haupthof* houses the **Leopold Museum**, the most popular attraction here, containing the world's largest collection of works by Egon Schiele. Less universally popular is **MUMOK**, the darker cube, the city's chief gallery of modern art. Overall, however, the MQ has succeeded in carving out a respectably trendy niche for itself on Vienna's crowded cultural map.

The two major permanent displays are described below, but various temporary exhibition spaces are also worth exploring. The central former winter riding school is now used by **Kunsthalle Wien** (daily 10am–7pm, Thurs 10am–9pm; €11.50; ⓦ www.kunsthallewien.at), the city's top contemporary art gallery, as well as providing a modern dance performance space for **Tanzquartier Wien** (ⓦ www.tqw.at).

In the westernmost courtyard (Hof 7), the **Architekturzentrum Wien** (daily 10am–7pm; €7; ⓦ www.azw.at), houses a one-room permanent exhibition on Austrian architecture from the Ringstrasse and Secession through to Rotes Wien and the odd postwar gem, as well as hosting excellent temporary exhibitions. Adjacent is the **designforumMQ** (Wed–Fri 10am–6pm, Sat & Sun 11am–6pm; €4; ⓦ www.designforum.at), with exhibitions on product design and advertising.

Last but not least, the **ZOOM Kindermuseum** in Hof 2 (Mon–Fri 8.30am–5pm, Sat & Sun 10am–5.30pm; €3–5; ☏ 524 79 08, ⓦ www.kindermuseum.at), is

---

### Visiting the MuseumsQuartier

The courtyards of the **MuseumsQuartier** are open 24 hours a day, and several cafés and bars remain open until the early hours. Each sight has its own opening times and entrance fees, though various combined tickets are available; the Duo Ticket (€17) gets you into the two main sights, the Leopold Museum and MUMOK, while the Kombi Ticket (€25), covers the Leopold Museum, MUMOK, the Kunsthalle Wien and the Architekturzentrum Wien. The nearest U-Bahn stations are Museumsquartier and Volkstheater.

a real hands-on treat for kids. The introductory section is an enjoyable interactive exhibition for kids aged 6 to 12, exploring everything from sculpture to astronomy; in the ZOOM Studio, children can get stuck into some serious artistic endeavours. Those with younger kids should head straight for ZOOM Ocean, which is basically an indoor marine-themed play area, while older kids from 8 to 14 can try their hand at animation and music making in ZOOM Lab. The staff all speak English so language shouldn't be an issue, but you really need to book a few days in advance – numbers are restricted and visits are timed.

If you've got kids, it's as well to know about the nearby **Kinderinfo** office (Tues–Thurs 2–7pm, Fri–Sun 10am–5pm), which has an indoor play area with a slide and free internet access for older children.

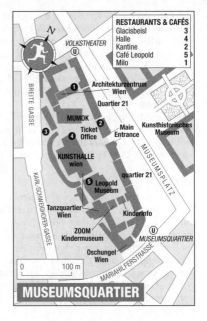

Also in this courtyard, **Dschungel Wien** (Mon–Fri 2.30–6.30pm Sat & Sun 4.30–6.30pm; €7.50; Ⓦ www.dschungelwien.at), puts on theatre performances and workshops for young people.

## Leopold Museum

The light limestone cube of the **Leopold Museum** (daily except Tues 10am–7pm, Fri 10am–9pm; €10; Ⓦ www.leopoldmuseum.org) houses the private collection of Rudolf Leopold, an ophthalmologist who became an obsessive art collector. Leopold was particularly keen on the works of Egon Schiele, which he picked up for next to nothing in the 1950s, but which eventually got him so heavily in debt that he had to strike a deal with the Austrian state: they wrote off his tax bill and built a museum, and he allowed his remarkable collection to be shown to the public.

The museum's major works by **Egon Schiele** (1890–1918) are permanently displayed on the ground floor (O), including the famous (and much reproduced) *Reclining Woman*. The hypocritical Habsburg establishment that had imprisoned him for "immorality" and "seduction" is the target in *Cardinal and Nun* and *The Hermits*, a double-portrait of Schiele and Klimt dressed in monks' habits from around the same period. There are several flat, autumnal townscapes inspired by Schiele's brief sojourn in his mother's Bohemian hometown, Český Krumlov (Krumau), and several frankly disturbing, morbid depictions of motherhood: *Blind Mother*, *Dead Mother* and *Mother with Two Children II*.

On the top floor (O4), Wien 1900 features more Schiele plus several works by **Gustav Klimt** (1862–1918), from early superrealistic canvases such as *Blind Man* to the dreamy, square-framed landscapes that Klimt knocked off in his summer holidays on the Attersee. The most important work in the collection, however, is *Death and Life*, in which the colourful jumble of humanity seems oblivious to Death with his little red cudgel. A whole room is devoted to the little-known **Richard Gerstl** (1883–1908), whose works were never exhibited during his brief life. His nude self-portrait from the year of his suicide is as uncompromising and honest as his almost Christ-like *Self-Portrait Against a Blue Background*, from a few years earlier, is striking and unusual. Alongside these are works by Schiele's contemporaries Kolo Moser, Carl Moll and Adolf Loos – everything from oil paintings to stained-glass designs, furniture and glasswork. Look out, too, for the emerald-green, fairytale-like *Dolomite Landscape* (1913) by **Oskar Kokoschka**, and the depictions of the hardships of peasant life and World War I by **Albin Egger-Lienz** (1868–1926).

On the third floor (O3), you'll find a whole range of superb **Expressionist** and Fauvist works by the likes of Kupka, Kirchner, Vlaminck, Jawlensky and Emil Nolde, plus lesser-known works from the interwar period – all are on long-term loan from the Thyssen-Bornemisza private collection.

## MUMOK

Built to house the city's chief permanent collection of modern art, the dark grey basalt cube of the **Museum moderner Kunst Stiftung Ludwig Wien**, better known as **MUMOK** (Tues–Sun 10am–6pm, Thurs 10am–9pm; €9; Ⓦwww .mumok.at), is an intimidating building from the outside. Inside, things don't get much better: the layout is confusing – you enter at level 4 – and the lack of natural light depressing. Still, if you like your art conceptual, MUMOK owns some great stuff, and though much of it remains hidden in the vaults, enough is put on show to keep you amused. The entrance fee lets you look at the (more or less) permanent displays described below, plus the three or four temporary exhibitions.

### Gustav Mahler (1860–1911)

While Mahler's symphonies are now firmly established in the concert repertoire, not that long ago his music was only rarely performed. In his lifetime Mahler was much better known as a conductor. Born to a Jewish family in Bohemia, he studied at the **Vienna Conservatory** before spending the next decade as a jobbing *Kapellmeister* at provincial theatres in the Prussian and Habsburg empires. At the age of 28, the ambitious Mahler got his big break when he landed the job at the Royal Hungarian Opera in Budapest. Ten years later, in 1897, following an entirely mercenary conversion to Roman Catholicism, he reached his "final goal" and became director of Vienna's Imperial Opera House.

Mahler's ten years in charge of the Oper were stormy to say the least. He instituted a totally new regime, banning claques (opera stars' paid supporters), insisting that the lights of the auditorium be dimmed during performances, and allowing latecomers entry only after the overture or between acts. In his behaviour towards performers he was something of a tyrant, hiring and firing with abandon and earning himself the nickname of *Korporal vom Tag* (Duty Corporal) for his demanding work schedules and his bluntness. "Is music meant to be so serious?" the emperor is alleged to have said when hearing of these innovations, "I thought it was meant to make people happy."

The music critics were divided, many praising his painstaking attention to detail, others lambasting him for reworking other composers' scores. Needless to say, the anti-Semitic press had a field day, subjecting Mahler to racist jibes, objecting to his "Jew-boy antics on the podium", and caricaturing his eccentric appearance. The gossip columnists were also kept busy, especially when, in 1902, Mahler married **Alma Schindler**, the strikingly beautiful stepdaughter of Carl Moll, the Secession artist, and, at 22, a woman almost half his age. Mahler's views on marriage were rigidly bourgeois: she was to give up her composing. "You must become 'what I

In the basement (level 1), the **Wiener Aktionismus** archive tells the story of the city's very own extremely violent performance-art movement that spilled blood and guts (literally) all over Vienna in the 1960s. On level 3 you'll find much more familiar stuff: **Pop Art** by Warhol and Lichtenstein, one of César's ubiquitous crushed cars, a Klein blue painting, a small wrapped object from Christo's early years, a smashed-up piano by Nam June Paik, Robert Rauschenberg's "neo-dada" cardboard collages, and John Chamberlain's anti-consumerist scrap-metal sculptures, to name but a few. And don't miss **Yoko Ono**'s *Painting to Hammer a Nail*, which the artist exhibited in London in 1966. It was at the opening that Yoko first met John Lennon. She asked him for five shillings to hammer an imaginary nail into the painting; he said he'd give her an imaginary five shillings for the imaginary nail. Instant Karma.

## Around Oper

The human flow around **Oper** (the city's opera house or Staatsoper) – much of it heading into the seedy Opernpassage, which stretches south as far as Karlsplatz (see p.102) – makes this the busiest section of the Ringstrasse. In the late nineteenth century, this crossroads became known as the "Sirk Ecke", after the once-fashionable *Sirk Café*. The nearby Kärntner Ring, which runs down to Schwarzenbergplatz, became the Viennese Corso, where, according to one contemporary French visitor, "every branch of society from the great world, to the *demi-monde*, to the 'quarter world', as well as the world of diplomacy and the court" promenaded in the afternoon. Nowadays most people prefer to stroll along Kärntnerstrasse rather than battle with the roaring Ringstrasse traffic.

need' if we are to be happy together, ie my wife, not my colleague," he wrote to her. Not surprisingly, the marriage proved extremely difficult for both parties.

Ten years at the Oper took its toll: "Other theatre directors look after themselves and wear out the theatre. I look after the theatre and wear out myself," he wrote to a friend. Towards the end of 1907, Mahler pinned a farewell note to the opera house notice board, saying "I meant well, I aimed high … In the heat of the moment, neither you nor I have been spared wounds, or errors." The previous summer, at the Mahlers' private villa by the Wörthersee in Carinthia, their elder daughter, Maria (Putzi), had died of scarlet fever, and Mahler himself had been diagnosed as having a heart valve defect. It was time to move on. By signing up with the **New York Metropolitan Opera**, Mahler simultaneously doubled his income and reduced his workload. However, the increased travelling and the strain it imposed on his marriage and health proved too much.

By 1910, Alma had begun an affair with the modernist architect Walter Gropius, and Mahler, in desperation, travelled to Holland to consult Freud. Mahler blamed himself (probably rightly so) for selfishness, and attempted to make amends, showering Alma with affection and encouraging her to compose again. As it turned out, though, Mahler didn't have long to live. In New York he was diagnosed as having subacute bacterial endocarditis, and the family travelled back to Vienna for the last time. Crowds gathered outside the sanatorium, the press issued daily bulletins from the bedside of "der Mahler". He died during a thunderstorm (just like Beethoven), and his last word is alleged to have been "Mozart!" According to his wishes, his tombstone in **Grinzinger Friedhof** (see p.187), designed by Josef Hoffmann, has nothing but "Mahler" written on it. "Any who come to look for me will know who I was", he explained, "and the rest do not need to know"

## Staatsoper

That the **Staatsoper** (Ⓦ www.wiener-staatsoper.at) was the first public building
to be completed on the Ringstrasse – opening in May 1869 with a performance
of Mozart's *Don Giovanni* – is an indication of its importance in Viennese society.
Designed in Italian Renaissance style – even the Austrians deferred to Italy as the
home of opera – it has a suitably grandiose exterior, with a fine loggia beneath
which the audience could draw up in their carriages. However, compared with
the other monumental edifices on the Ringstrasse the opera house sits low. This
was the most common criticism of the building when it was completed, and
when Emperor Franz-Josef was heard to concur with his aides on this issue, one
of the architects, Eduard van der Nüll, hanged himself. Van der Nüll's grief-
stricken friend and collaborator on the project, August Siccardsburg, died two
months later of a heart attack. Neither architect lived to witness the first night.
Thereafter Franz-Josef always chose the safe riposte "*Es war sehr schön, es hat mir
sehr gefreut*" (It was very beautiful, I enjoyed it very much) whenever he was asked
his official opinion.

The Staatsoper caught fire during an air raid on March 12, 1945, and the rebuilt
auditorium is now pretty undistinguished. Prestigious past directors include Gustav
Mahler, Richard Strauss, Herbert von Karajan and Claudio Abbado, though each
had a notoriously difficult relationship with the opera house. As the name suggests,
the Staatsoper still receives massive state subsidy, and hundreds of cheap *Stehplätze*
(standing-room tickets) are sold each day on a first-come-first-served basis (see
p.228). This is probably the best way to visit the opera house, but you can also go
on one of the daily 40-minute **guided tours** in English (times posted up on east
side; €6.50). Your ticket also covers entrance to the **Staatsopernmuseum** (Tues–
Sun 10am–6pm; €3), around the corner at Goethegasse 1, a large round room
containing a photo gallery of the stars who have graced the opera's stage since it
reopened in 1955.

## Behind the Staatsoper

All Vienna's top three hotels – the *Sacher*, the *Bristol* and the *Imperial* – are within a
stone's throw of the opera house. The most famous of the trio, behind the
Staatsoper, is the **Hotel Sacher**, built in the 1870s on the site of the old
Kärntnertor Theater, where Beethoven's ninth symphony premiered in 1824.
Founded by Eduard Sacher, the hotel became the aristocrats' favourite knocking
shop, particularly after 1892 when it was run by Eduard's widow, the legendary,
cigar-smoking Anna Sacher, until her death in 1930. Perhaps the most famous
incident to take place here was when Archduke Franz Ferdinand's younger
brother, Otto, appeared in the hotel lobby naked except for his sword and the
Order of the Golden Fleece around his neck, though this is also where John and
Yoko first introduced "bagism" to the world, in 1969. On a more banal note, the
*Sacher*'s continuing popularity rests on its famous *Sachertorte* invented by Eduard's
father, Franz, who was Prince Metternich's chef. The cake is, of course, available
all over Vienna, but the *Sacher* claims that no one else has the true recipe.

On an old bomb site, to the north of the *Sacher*, stands Alfred Hrdlicka's
**Monument against War and Fascism**. Made up of several separated statues, the
monument makes no direct mention of the Holocaust, but includes instead a
crouching Jew scrubbing the pavement, recalling the days following the Anschluss,
when some of the city's Jews were forced to clean up anti-Nazi slogans with
scrubbing brushes dipped in acid. Many Jews, however, consider the image
degrading, among them Simon Wiesenthal, who successfully campaigned for a
Holocaust memorial to be erected in Judenplatz (see p.60).

# Akademie der bildenden Künste

Set back from the Ring, the **Akademie der bildenden Künste** (Tues–Sun 10am–6pm; €5; ⓦ www.akademiegalerie.at) – Academy of Fine Arts – occupies an imposing neo-Renaissance building by Theophil Hansen on Schillerplatz, southwest of the Staatsoper. The Academy was founded in 1692, and its main purpose continues to be teaching, but the school also houses a small, much-overlooked study collection. To see the paintings, follow the signs to the **Gemäldegalerie**: turn right after the porter's lodge, up four flights of stairs to the first floor, then right again to the end of the corridor. The **Aula** – straight ahead as you pass through the main entrance – is also worth a glimpse, both for its decor and for the regular, wacky student installations.

While the Academy's collection is tiny compared to the Kunsthistorisches Museum, it does have one or two superb works, including one star attraction: *The Last Judgement* triptych by **Hieronymus Bosch** (c.1450–1516), the only Bosch triptych outside Spain. The action in the left panel, *Paradise*, is a taster for the central panel, the *Last Judgement* itself, most of which is taken up with strange half-animal devil figures busy torturing sinners in imaginatively horrible ways; the right panel, *Hell*, looks even less fun. Overall, the possibility of salvation seems

## Hitler in Vienna

Although he was born and grew up in Upper Austria, **Adolf Hitler** (1890–1945) spent five and a half formative years in Vienna. He arrived in the city aged just 17, hoping to enrol at the **Academy of Fine Arts**. However, though he passed the entrance exam, his portfolio, mostly architectural sketches of Linz, was rejected as "inadequate". Saying nothing about his failure to his family, he stayed in Vienna for a whole year, living fairly comfortably off his father's inheritance and, following the death of his mother, his orphan's pension. In September 1908, Hitler tried once more to get into the Academy: this time he failed the entrance exam. These two rejections hit hard, and still rankled two years on, as he wrote to a friend, "Do you know – without any arrogance – I still believe that the world lost a great deal by my not being able to go to the academy and learn the craft of painting. Or did fate reserve me to some other purpose?"

Very little is known about Hitler's time in Vienna, though he spent a good three years in a men's hostel in the eastern district of **Brigittenau**, abutting Leopoldstadt, where he sold his mediocre paintings mostly to Jewish frame dealers. The evidence is scanty, but Hitler appears to have worked for brief periods as a snow shoveller at the Westbahnhof (and elsewhere), and as a painter and decorator at the Kunsthistorisches Museum. He even auditioned for a part in the chorus at the Theater-an-der-Wien, but was rejected when he couldn't produce the right clothes for the part.

Some sources claim that Hitler contracted some minor sexually transmitted disease, possibly from a Jewish prostitute, while in the city, hence his obsession with syphilis and prostitution – both of which he rails against at length in *Mein Kampf*. Other accounts portray Hitler as some kind of proto-hippy, with beard and long hair, practising yoga and tripping on mescaline. Again, there's no concrete evidence, though Hitler was certainly **homeless** in the winter of 1909, after which he became increasingly unkempt, wearing his beard and hair long.

For much of his stay in Vienna, Hitler was a **draft dodger** – something he neglects to mention in *Mein Kampf* – since he should have signed up in 1909. By the end of 1912 he was liable to a year in prison and a large fine; this was what eventually led him to flee to Germany in 1913. After a 25-year gap, Hitler returned to Vienna under rather different circumstances in March 1938, following the Anschluss. He stayed at the *Hotel Imperial* on the Ringstrasse, gave a speech to the multitude from the Neue Burg on Heldenplatz and, within 24 hours, was on a plane back to Germany.

painfully slim, with only a lucky few having made it to the small corner of the painting given over to heaven.

Displayed in the same room are two works by Lucas Cranach the Elder: *Lucretia*, a classic Cranach nude, and his moralistic-erotic *Ill-Matched Couple*. The Academy's Italian works are fairly disappointing, apart from **Botticelli**'s *Madonna Tondo*, and Titian's *Tarquin and Lucretia*, a late work replete with loose brushwork and brooding, autumnal colours. In the same room as the last two, look out for Murillo's sentimental *Two Boys Playing Dice*.

Flemish and Dutch paintings make up the core of the collection, with an early **Rembrandt** portrait of a young woman in a black dress, a self-portrait by Van Dyck aged just 14, preparatory studies for the Jesuit church frescoes in Antwerp (and lots of nudes) by Rubens, plus works by Jordaens, Ruisdael, Hoogstraten and David Teniers the Younger. After Bosch, though, the other outstanding master-piece is the *Family Group in a Courtyard* by **Pieter de Hooch** (1629–84), with its sublime tranquillity and clever play on perspective.

Also on display are several Venetian views by Guardi, Biedermeier paintings by Waldmüller (who taught at the Academy), and a much-reproduced portrait of Maria Theresia by her official court painter, Martin van Meytens. The final room holds a brief selection of twentieth-century Austrian art, including works by Hundertwasser, Fritz Wotruba and Herbert Boeckl.

## Karlsplatz

Overlooked by the city's most awesome Baroque church and the gilded Secession building, as well as several other key Ringstrasse institutions, **Karlsplatz** should be one of Vienna's showpiece squares. Instead, the western half is little more than a vast traffic interchange, with pedestrians relegated to a set of seedy subways that stretch north as far as the opera house. The problem is that there's never been any

grand, overall plan at Karlsplatz – the Naschmarkt was held here until the 1890s, and when it moved to the nearby Wienzeile, the heart was ripped out of the square. The city council provided a site for the Secession, but the avenue that should have connected it with the Karlskirche never materialized. As a result, it's actually impossible to stand back and admire the Secession building without seriously endangering your life.

## Secession

In 1898, Joseph Maria Olbrich completed one of the most original Jugendstil buildings in Vienna, the headquarters for the art movement known as the **Secession** (Tues–Sun 10am–6pm, Thurs until 8pm; €8.50; Ⓦ www.secession.at). Though the dome of gilded bronze laurel leaves is the most startling feature – the Viennese dubbed it the "golden cabbage" – all the building's decorative details are worth closer inspection. On the side, three wise owls emerge from the rendering, while the main entrance is adorned with a trio of gorgons, a pair of salamanders and copious gilded foliage; above is the group's credo, "For every age its art; for art its freedom", replaced after being removed by the Nazis. Don't miss the tortoises at the feet of the ornamental bowls, Georg Klimt's bronze doors with snake handles, and Arthur Strasser's bronze statue of an overweight Mark Anthony on a chariot drawn by panthers (originally displayed at the group's fourth exhibition in 1899).

The main hall upstairs continues to stage contemporary art installations, while downstairs in the basement Gustav Klimt's **Beethovenfries** is on permanent display. The frieze was intended to last only for the duration of the group's fourteenth exhibition held in 1902. In the end, it was preserved, but not shown to the public again until 1986. The centrepiece of the exhibition, a heroic nude statue of Beethoven by the German sculptor Max Klinger, is now in the entrance of Leipzig's Neues Gewandhaus, with an incomplete copy in the Wien Museum. For the opening of the exhibition, Gustav Mahler conducted his own orchestration of the fourth movement of Beethoven's ninth symphony. Auguste Rodin deemed Klimt's frieze "tragic and divine", but most visitors were appalled by the whole exhibition, with its bare concrete chambers designed by Josef Hoffmann, and it proved a financial disaster.

With much of the mural consisting of huge blank spaces framed by floating maidens, Klimt's frieze looks strangely half finished. In between are three heavily painted sections: *Longing for Happiness*, where the weak, represented by three naked emaciated figures, appeal to a knight in golden armour; *Hostile Forces*, featuring a slightly comical giant ape with a serpent's tail and wings, and his three daughters, the gorgons, backed up by the figures of Disease, Madness and Death, and surrounded by decorative sperm and ovaries; and finally *Ode to Joy*, which culminates in an embracing couple, offering, in Schiller's words, *Diesen Kuss der ganzen Welt!* (this kiss to all the world). An excellent leaflet in English (available from the ticket desk) explains the symbolism in greater detail; Klimt's preparatory sketches are also on display.

## Resselpark

The central section of Karlsplatz is the leafy **Resselpark**, named for Josef Ressel (1793–1857), Czech inventor of the screw propellor. Despite thinking up the device ten years before John Ericsson, Ressel was prevented from experimenting with it by the Habsburg bureaucracy, and thus remains little known. His statue stands close to that of another hapless innovator, the tailor Josef Madersperger, who invented a sewing machine in 1815, but died penniless because no Austrian would market it. Johannes Brahms, who died in 1897 at Karlgasse 4, now part of the nearby Technische Universität, is also represented.

Resselpark is chiefly remarkable for the **Otto Wagner Pavillon Karlsplatz** (April–Oct Tues–Sun 10–6pm; €2), a duo of entrances to the old Stadtbahn, originally erected in 1899 on Akademiestrasse but moved here in the 1960s. Wagner broke with his usual design here, partly in deference to the presence of the nearby Karlskirche, adding gold trimmings and a sunflower motif. The green, wrought-iron framework, common to all his Stadtbahn stations, forms an essential part of the overall design, framing a series of thin marble slabs and creating a lovely, curving, central canopy. Today, one pavilion houses a **café** during the summer, while the other has an **exhibition** on Otto Wagner; both have retained some of their original interior decor.

## Musikverein

On the north side of Karlsplatz, the **Musikverein** (ⓌWwww.musikverein.at), Vienna's number one concert hall, was designed by the ubiquitous Theophil Hansen in the 1860s. The classical terracotta exterior apes the opera house with its front loggia, but you really need to attend a concert in the Grosser Saal to appreciate its unbeatable acoustics and the sumptuous decor with its parade of gilded caryatids. Home to the world-famous **Vienna Philharmonic** (Ⓦwww .wienerphilharmoniker.at), the Musikverein's most prestigious event is the annual schmaltzy Neujahrskonzert on New Year's Day, a tradition started under the Nazis in 1939, and one which is now transmitted live around the world to an estimated 1.3 billion viewers (it's also beamed live onto a large screen on the front of the Rathaus).

The concert hall itself also has a rich musical history, as the place where the composer **Arnold Schönberg** and his followers unleashed atonal music – Schönberg preferred to call it "the emancipation of dissonance" – on an unsuspecting and unready Viennese public. The worst disturbance took place on March 31, 1913, at a concert conducted by Schönberg, during which two of Alban Berg's *Altenberg Lieder*, songs based on the *bon mots* scribbled on the back of postcards by poet Peter Altenberg, were premiered. Programmes were used as missiles, blows were exchanged and the concert had to be abandoned after an ambulance was sent for. Schönberg, of all people, later complained that Berg's *Altenberg Lieder* were "so brief as to exclude the possibility of extended thematic development". Berg was mortified and the *Lieder* remained unheard and unpublished until seventeen years after his death in 1935.

## Karlskirche

Rising majestically above everything around it, the **Karlskirche** (Mon–Sat 9am–12.30pm & 1–6pm, Sun noon–5.45pm; €6; Ⓦwww.karlskirche.at) is, without doubt, the city's finest Baroque church. A huge Italianate dome with a Neoclassical portico, flanked by two giant pillars modelled on Trajan's Column, and, just for good measure, a couple of hefty Baroque side towers, it's an eclectic and rather self-conscious mixture of styles, built to impress. Even surrounded by the mess that is Karlsplatz, the church is an awesome sight – particularly at night when it's bathed in light and reflected in the lake – and must have been even more so when there was nothing between it and the Hofburg except the open space of the *glacis*.

The story goes that **Emperor Karl VI** vowed to build a church during the plague of 1713. Architect Johann Bernhard Fischer von Erlach won the competition to design the building; his son, Johann Michael, completed the job in 1737. The church is actually dedicated to the sixteenth-century saint, **Carlo Borromeo**, canonized for his ministrations during the famine and plague in Milan in 1576. However, the fact that the emperor and saint shared the same name no doubt played a part in Karl VI's choice, conveniently glorifying both at the same time. The Karlskirche's dual nature – votive and imperial – is nowhere more evident than with the columns: imperial symbols, whose reliefs, rather than portraying Emperor Trajan's campaigns (as on the originals), illustrate Borromeo's life. To emphasize the point, the columns are topped by giant gilded Habsburg eagles, and, above the lanterns, the imperial crown.

Your entry fee includes an **English audioguide**, which can be useful for orientating yourself. Thanks to the windows and lantern in the oval dome, the interior is surprisingly sparse and light, allowing a much better appreciation of **Johann Michael Rottmayr**'s vast fresco than you get of the artist's work in the Peterskirche (see p.53). The subject is the apotheosis of Carlo Borromeo, along with a bit of Counter-Reformation Luther-bashing – note the angel setting fire to the German's Bible and the depiction of Luther in cahoots with the devil. Everything else in the church finds it rather hard to compete with the sublime beauty of the dome, though Fischer von Erlach's sunburst above the main altar is definitely worth a closer look. Interwoven with the golden rays are stucco clouds and cherubs accompanying St Carlo as he ascends into heaven. The small **Museo Borromeo** upstairs contains the saint's vestments, including his terrific cardinal's hat, golden mitre and red pontifical shoes.

## Wien Museum Karlsplatz

Housed in an unprepossessing modernist block to the side of the Karlskirche, the **Wien Museum** (Tues–Sun 9am–6pm; €4; ⓦwww.wienmuseum.at) puts on excellent temporary exhibitions on the city's social and political history. In addition, the permanent collection covers the city's 2000-year history at a brisk trot, contains period rooms preserved wholesale from the city's lost buildings, and boasts a pretty good fin-de-siècle section, which alone more than justifies a visit, with paintings by Klimt, Schiele and their contemporaries, an interior by Adolf Loos, and several cabinets of Wiener Werkstätte pieces.

The **Roman and Gothic** section, on the ground floor, is – like much of the museum – a ragbag assortment. The largest Roman relic is the tomb of a cavalryman who died in Vindobona (Vienna) in 96 AD. There's a fifteenth-century gilded leather helmet – one of several hung on the wall – topped with a female figure whose arms are in the process of being swallowed by a giant fish, and the Albertinischer Plan, the oldest map of the city, from 1421. The most interesting pieces here, though, are the stained-glass windows and sandstone statues salvaged from the Stephansdom after World War II bomb damage, and the wonderfully beastly gargoyles from the Minoritenkirche.

The museum also owns a welter of paintings, including minor works by the key artists of the **Baroque** period in the former empire: Paul Troger, Johann Michael Rottmayr and Franz Anton Maulbertsch, plus a fine portrait of a dapper young art collector by Angelika Kaufmann. You can also view a smattering of spoils from the city's two Turkish sieges in 1529 and 1683: a vast red silk banner, Turkish horse plumes sporting crescent moons, several swashbuckling sabres, and an ornate tent lantern. Before you head upstairs be sure to take a look at the model of Vienna, which shows the city shortly before the old zigzag fortifications were torn down in 1857.

At the top of the stairs, turn left into the **Biedermeier** section (1815–48), commemorating an era that marked a return to simple, bourgeois values after the excesses of the Baroque period. There's a room in the "Pompeii style" from a now demolished old town palace where the wealthy Geymüller family entertained poet and playwright Franz Grillparzer, whose musty living quarters are lovingly preserved further on. Numerous mawkish Biedermeier paintings surround Grillparzer's room, epitomized by Ferdinand Georg Waldmüller's sentimental depictions of rural folk and flattering portraits of the bourgeoisie.

## Fin-de-siècle Vienna

Moving on through the modest collection of 1848 revolutionary memorabilia, you come to two paintings by **Hans Makart**, who was lionized by the Viennese in his day, but has since been eclipsed by his more famous pupil, **Gustav Klimt**. Don't miss either the wonderful mother-of-pearl studded chair, designed by **Otto Wagner**, and presented to the Mayor of Vienna, Karl Lueger, in 1904, on his sixtieth birthday, or Josef Engelhart's emblematic *Im Sophiensaal*, which captures perfectly the loose sexuality of Viennese café life.

The centrepiece of this section, though, is another model of Vienna, this time from after the construction of the great Ringstrasse buildings of the late nineteenth century, accompanied by before-and-after photos. To the side is a living/dining room designed in 1903 by modernist architect **Adolf Loos** for his first marital home on nearby Bösendorferstrasse. Despite his diatribes against ornament of any kind, Loos loved rich materials – marble, mahogany and brass – and created for himself a typically plush *gemütlich* interior.

Beyond Loos's room are works of art from Vienna's artistic golden age, including Max Klinger's nude statue of Beethoven, which formed the centrepiece of the Secession exhibition of 1902 (see colour section), albeit without its coloured marble drapery and seat. Max Kurzweil's striking portrait of a *Woman in Yellow*, lounging luxuriantly on a sofa, is a classic fin-de-siècle painting. Several of **Gustav Klimt**'s works can be found here, too, including his *Pallas Athene* from 1898, marking his first extensive use of gold, which was to become a hallmark of his work, and, elsewhere, the portrait of his lover, Emilie Flöge, in a dress of her own design.

The museum also owns a handful of excellent works by **Egon Schiele**, from an idiosyncratically distraught study of sunflowers from 1909 to the harrowing *Blind Mother II*. The fondly painted view of the artist's bedroom in Neulengbach – a clear homage to Van Gogh – was executed shortly before his brief imprisonment

---

## The Third Man

Filmed on location during the postwar period when Vienna was divided (like Berlin) between the four Allied powers, **The Third Man** (directed by Carol Reed in 1949) is a British *film noir* classic that's without a doubt the city's most famous contribution to cinematic history. The stark, black-and-white, expressionist cinematography, the haunting theme tune and seedy bombed-out locations perfectly captured the fatigued, defeated atmosphere of the city at the beginning of the Cold War.

Since the early 1980s, *The Third Man* has been shown every Friday and Saturday at the Burgkino, Opernring 19, and the film's continuing popularity has spawned a mini tourist industry all of its own. You can visit several key locations freely, including Josefsplatz, the Zentralfriedhof, and the Prater. To check out the sewers, however, join one of the regular **Third Man Tours** (Mon & Fri 4pm; 2hr 30min; €17; Ⓦwww .viennawalks.com), conducted in German and English.

Film buffs should also head for the **Third Man Museum** (Tues 6–8pm; Sat 2–6pm; €7.50; Ⓦwww.3mpc.net), a couple of blocks south of the Naschmarkt at Pressgasse 25. This private collection includes photos and news clippings from the period, as well as posters, stills and reviews of the film, plus you get to see a two-minute clip from an old 1930s projector to whet your appetite. There's even a mock-up of the Gartenhaus from the Heuriger, run by Anton Karas (who wrote and performed the film's zither theme tune), and the chance to hear more than three hundred different versions of the tune.

on a charge of "displaying an erotic drawing in a room open to children". The characteristically angular portraits of the art critic and collector Arthur Roessler and his wife Ida – loyal friends and patrons throughout Schiele's life – are among the artist's earliest commissioned portrait oils. Also of note are **Richard Gerstl**'s nervous self-portrait from 1905 and his portrait of Arnold Schönberg, with whose wife Gerstl had a disastrous affair, the termination of which led to his suicide. Schönberg's own portrayal of fellow composer Alban Berg hangs close by, as does his portrait of his daughter.

## Naschmarkt and around

By all accounts, the River Wien, which used to wend its way across Karlsplatz, was an unsavoury stretch of water: "This black and vilely-smelling ditch is a foul blot upon the beauty and neatness of this lovely city, and must certainly produce a miasma extremely prejudicial to health," noted Anthony Trollope's mother, Fanny, in the early nineteenth century. So it no doubt came as some relief when it was eventually paved over in the 1890s, allowing the **Naschmarkt** (Mon–Sat 10am–6pm; Ⓦwww.wienernaschmarkt.eu) to move from the square to its present site over the old course of the river, between the Linke and Rechte Wienzeile. The market – its name translates literally as "nibble market" – is now the city's premier source of fruit and vegetables, and is one of the few places where you get a real sense of the city's multicultural make-up: Turkish, Arab, Slav and Chinese stall-holders vie for customers all the way to the Kettenbrückengasse U-Bahn. It's a great place to eat, either on the hoof or in one of the trendy cafés that have begun to colonise the place, and on Saturdays the market extends even further west as the weekly flea market joins in. The Linke and Rechte Wienzeile, on either side of the market, now function as a six-lane motorway. There are, however, a couple of sights along the Linke Wienzeile that make a stroll through the market doubly rewarding.

### Theater-an-der-Wien

The **Theater-an-der-Wien** opened in 1801 under the directorship of Emanuel Schikaneder at Linke Wienzeile 6. Schikaneder wrote the libretto for Mozart's *Die Zauberflöte* (Magic Flute), and is depicted above the main portico as the feathered bird-catcher Papageno, a role he played in the première. Schikaneder was also instrumental in supporting Beethoven, putting the theatre at his disposal, and even allowing him to live here on and off. Beethoven's opera *Fidelio* premiered here on November 20, 1805, exactly a week after the French had marched into Vienna. Under such extreme conditions – French soldiers made up much of the audience – it's hardly surprising that the opera flopped, running for just three performances. The theatre is also intimately connected with many other Austrian classics: Franz Grillparzer's *Ahnfrau*, almost all of Johann Nestroy's farces, Johann Strauss's *Die Fledermaus* and Franz Lehár's *Die lustige Witwe* (The Merry Widow) were all first performed here. After World War II, while the Staatsoper was being repaired, the theatre once more staged operas, but it now concentrates on popular musicals.

### Otto Wagner

Two of Otto Wagner's most appealing Secession buildings from 1899, the adjacent apartment blocks of **Linke Wienzeile 38** and **40**, stand a good 500m further west of the Theater-an-der-Wien, on the same side of Linke Wienzeile. Wagner's ultimate aim was to transform the Wienzeile – which leads eventually to Schön-brunn – into a new Ringstrasse, though stylistically both buildings signal a break with the Ringstrasse style. Eschewing any pretensions to resemble a palace, the separation between the commercial ground floor and the residential apartments above is deliberately emphasized. The right-hand building (no.#38) is richly embossed with gold palm fronds and medallions – the latter designed by Kolo Moser – and even features an elaborate top-floor loggia with Art Nouveau swags, urns and a couple of figures. The left-hand building (no. 40) is more unusual, its pollution-resistant cladding of majolica tiles giving rise to the nickname, **Majolika-haus**. To contemporary eyes, the facade looks highly decorative, but what mattered to the Viennese was that – as with the Looshaus – there was virtually no sculptural decoration, and no mouldings or pediments above the windows. Instead, Wagner weaves an elaborate floral motif – a giant, spreading rose tree or a vine of sunflowers – on the tiles themselves.

## Schwarzenbergplatz

Bombarded by the din of cars and trams whizzing across its cobbles, it's difficult to believe that the large, rectangular traffic intersection of **Schwarzenbergplatz** was once a fashionable address. The aristocracy, though they owned up to a third of the property on the Ring, usually turned their noses up at actually living here – but with Schwarzenbergplatz they made an exception. The square became the nobility's own personal enclave, centred on an equestrian statue of one of their own, Prince Karl von Schwarzenberg, a member of one of the most powerful Austrian families, commander-in-chief (and victor over Napoleon) at the Battle of Leipzig in 1813.

At the southern end of the square, dramatically floodlit at night and spurting water high into the air, the **Hochstrahlbrunnen** (High Jet Fountain) was erected in 1873 to celebrate the city's nascent modern water-supply system. Once the focal point of the square, it is now thoroughly upstaged by the bombastic **Russen Heldendenkmal** (Russian Heroes' Monument), which rises up behind the jet of water. A giant curving colonnade acts as the backdrop to the central column, crowned by the Unknown (Soviet) Soldier in heroic stance, flag aloft, sporting a gilded shield and helmet; the red granite plinth bears the names of the fallen and a quote from Stalin (after whom the square was briefly renamed in 1945). For the Viennese, though, it's more a grim reminder of the brutality of the liberators and the privations suffered by those in the city's postwar Russian zones. No doubt aware of their unpopularity, the Soviets made sure that a clause ensuring the proper upkeep of the monument was written into the 1955 Austrian State Treaty.

Before the erection of the Soviet war memorial, the backdrop to the fountain was the **Palais Schwarzenberg**, Lucas von Hildebrandt's grandiose Baroque palace, begun in 1697 and now hidden behind foliage. It was finished in 1728 by the Schwarzenbergs who employed Hildebrandt's arch rival, Fischer von Erlach; a riding school and orangerie were added in 1751. A bomb lopped off the central dome in World War II, and destroyed most of the frescoes by Daniel Gran, but the palace is otherwise well preserved. The Schwarzenbergs still own the place, though they've turned the best rooms into a hotel and restaurant, and rented out one of the outbuildings to the Swiss Embassy. Sadly, the palace and its extensive gardens are closed except to hotel and restaurant guests, or embassy staff.

More accessible, though rather more specialist, is the **Arnold Schönberg Center** (Mon–Fri 10am–5pm; €3; ⓦ www.schoenberg.at), situated in the Palais Fanto, east of the Soviet war memorial, on the corner of Zaunergasse and Daffin-gerstrasse. The centre holds vast archives, and puts on talks, concerts and temporary exhibitions about the composer, held on the second floor of the

Shortly before the Konzerthaus was built, Klimt and his followers, who had left the Secession in 1905, staged their own exhibition, **Kunstschau Wien 1908**, on the empty site. Josef Hoffmann designed the pavilion and formal garden as a sort of stripped-down summerhouse, Oskar Kokoschka designed the poster, the Wiener Werkstätte took part, and the centrepiece was a retrospective of Klimt's work hung in a room designed by Kolo Moser. The show was an outstanding success, and even before the exhibition closed, the Austrian state had purchased Klimt's *The Kiss* (now in the Belvedere).

The next year, with Klimt's blessing, Egon Schiele exhibited his work for the first time at the **Kunstschau Wien 1909**. Klimt expected the exhibition to cause a scandal, but it was actually Kokoschka's brutal, sexually aggressive play, *Mörder, Hoffnung der Frauen* (Murderer, Hope of Women), premiered in the Kunstschau's garden theatre, which proved the most controversial. Some imperial army soldiers from Bosnia in the audience took exception to the play and started a riot. Archduke Franz Ferdinand, reading the newspaper reports the next day, memorably opined, "Every bone in that young man's body should be broken." Though Kokoschka avoided that particular fate, his art school stipend was withdrawn at the instigation of the Ministry of Culture.

building (the entrance is on Zaunergasse). Considered the father of atonal music, Schönberg was the leading figure in what has become known as the Second Viennese School. He was an accomplished artist, too, and several of his drawings are usually on display as part of the exhibitions – most people find his artwork a lot easier on the eye than his atonal works are on the ear. There's also a reconstruction of Schönberg's study in Los Angeles (to which he fled in the 1930s), containing original furniture and objects, many of which he himself designed from recycled materials. Whatever you do, don't forget to ask about Schönberg's greatest invention: chess for four players.

After the Musikverein (see p.104), Vienna's most illustrious concert venue is the **Konzerthaus**, east of Schwarzenbergplatz on Lothringerstrasse, home to the Wiener Symphoniker, three concert halls, the Akademietheater and a studio theatre. Built in late Secessionist style in 1913 by the great Austrian theatre-building firm Fellner & Helmer, it boasts a lovely, illuminated wrought-iron-and-glass canopy, surmounted by octagons and a half-moon gable.

## Stadtpark

Straddling the canalized River Wien much as the *glacis* once did, the **Stadtpark** is the largest of the Ringstrasse parks. Opened in 1862 as the city council's first public park, it's best known for Edmund Hellmer's eye-catching, over-the-top **Strauss Monument** from 1925, with its statue of the "Waltz King", Johann Strauss Junior, violin in hand. Gilded from head to toe and dramatically floodlit at night, the composer stands framed by a stone arch of naked, swirling naiads. Tour groups turn up at regular intervals to admire the monument, while the benches close by are a favourite spot for Vienna's elderly population. Vienna's younger generation also like to hang out here, too, in the summer, smoking and drinking on the grass; the authorities occasionally move the scene on, but without any great enthusiasm.

Several other artistic types are honoured with statues in this park, but none deserves much attention. You're better off heading for the much-diminished River Wien itself, where the **Wienflussportal** – a series of rather wonderful Jugendstil pavilions and quaysides – was constructed in 1905 by Friedrich Ohmann, nicely complementing Otto Wagner's adjacent Stadtbahn station, which survives as the Stadtpark U-Bahn. The other architectural landmark is the **Kursalon**, built in neo-Renaissance style at the same time as the park, daubed in soft *Kaisergelb* (imperial yellow) and still a prime venue for waltzing. Another possible focus for your wanderings is the state mint or **Münze**, built in the 1830s on the eastern edge of the Stadtpark. Somewhat surprisingly, the Münze puts on excellent temporary exhibitions (Mon–Fri 10am–4pm, Wed until 6pm), often with only a tenuous numismatic bent.

## MAK

North of the Stadtpark, the **Österreichisches Museum für angewandte Kunst** (Austrian Museum of Applied Art) – better known simply as the **MAK** (Tues 10am–midnight, Wed–Sun 10am–6pm; €9.90, free on Sat; Ⓦwww.mak.at) – ranks among Vienna's most enjoyable museums. The highlights of its superlative, highly eclectic selection of *objets d'art*, stretching from the Romanesque period to the twentieth century, are **Gustav Klimt**'s *Stoclet Frieze* and the unrivalled collection of **Wiener Werkstätte** products. But what really sets it apart is its interior design; in the 1990s, the MAK gave some of Austria's leading designers free rein to create a unique series of rooms.

The MAK was founded as the Museum für Kunst und Industrie in the 1860s by Rudolf von Eitelberger, who was inspired by a visit to what is now London's Victoria and Albert Museum. Designed by **Heinrich Ferstel** in a richly decorative neo-Renaissance style in 1872, the building was later extended to house the Kunstgewerbeschule (Arts and Crafts School), where Kokoschka and Klimt both trained. At the end of the nineteenth century the school became a stronghold of the Secession movement, handing out faculty positions to Josef Hoffmann and Kolo Moser, and promoting the work of the Wiener Werkstätte.

At the **ticket office**, you'll be given a museum plan in German and English, and offered an audiovisual guide (also €2), which is worth considering. There's no labelling, but each room features a slightly pretentious, bilingual introduction by the designer, and a leaflet in English explaining each exhibit. Most temporary exhibitions are held in the Ausstellungshalle, whose main entrance is on Weiskirchnerstrasse; the café is excellent (see p.210).

### Romanesque to Rococo

To follow the collection chronologically, start with the **Romanik, Gotik, Renaissance** room, on the ground floor, off the beautiful, glass-roofed courtyard, with its wacky sofas and double-decker loggia. The minimalist display cabinets in this room are beautifully offset by deep cobalt-blue walls. The curators have restricted the number of items on show, so you can pay detailed attention to each exhibit, though inevitably you also end up with a slightly staccato history of the applied arts. Aside from a few pieces of beautifully inlaid sixteenth-century furniture and some very early thirteenth-century canonical garments, most of the exhibits are items of Italian sixteenth-century majolica, decorated with richly coloured mythological scenes and grotesque faces.

The main focus of the next-door room – **Barock, Rokoko, Klassizismus** – is a room within a room. Acquired by the museum in 1912, the mid-eighteenth-century Porcelain Room was removed piece by piece from the Palais Dubsky in Brno and reassembled here. It derives its name from the ceramics used to decorate everything right down to the wall panelling, candelabra, chandeliers and table-tops. Outside the Porcelain Room exhibits include two huge late eighteenth-century maple and walnut marquetry panels, an unusually large section of Chinese wallpaper from the same period, portraying an idealized landscape, and a pair of powder-pink, gilded double doors salvaged from the Palais Paar in the Innere Stadt in 1938.

## Renaissance to Art Deco and the Orient

As you cross the courtyard to the next set of rooms, the designers begin to impose themselves more emphatically. **Renaissance, Barock, Rokoko** consists of two long, central glass cabinets displaying Bohemian, Silesian and Venetian glass, with examples of Italian, French and Flemish lacework set against a black background all along the walls. The **Empire, Biedermeier** room is much quirkier. A parade of early nineteenth-century Viennese chairs, arranged as if for a game of musical chairs, occupies the central space, while, up above, the cornice is broken by fast-moving, polemical, multilingual LED text on the social history of the era. To take it all in, sit down on the aluminium version of one of the Biedermeier sofas on display.

The museum's *pièce de résistance*, though, in terms of design, comes in the **Histor-ismus, Jugendstil** room. Two parallel shadow screens, running the length of the room, create a corridor down which you can stroll while admiring the changing geometry of chair design over the last hundred years in silhouette. For a 3D look at the chairs, simply go round the back of the screens. The exhibits include modernist designs by the likes of Josef Hoffmann, Otto Wagner and Adolf Loos, and, of course, the bentwood Thonet chair that became an inexpensive design classic, selling millions around the world.

The final ground-floor room, **Orient**, contains Europe's finest collections of oriental carpets, all laid out on the walls and floors, creating a mosque-like atmos-phere. Mostly from the sixteenth and seventeenth centuries, the carpets were avidly collected by the Habsburgs, and include a wonderfully decorative silk hunting carpet and the world's only surviving silk Mamluk carpet.

## The twentieth century and beyond

Three rooms on the first floor are given over to the permanent collection. One is devoted to the **Wiener Werkstätte** (see box, p.112), whose archives were donated to the museum in 1955. The range and scope of the WW is staggering, and just about every field in which they were active is represented here, from jewellery and metalwork, primarily by Peche and Hoffmann, to the WW's prolific fashion offshoot. One of the finest works is Kolo Moser's wood-inlaid writing desk, which includes a retractable armchair that can be slotted into place to make the whole thing appear like a chest of drawers.

The **Jugendstil, Art Deco** room is dominated by Gustav Klimt's working designs for his *Stoclet Frieze*, a series of mosaics commissioned in 1904 for the dining room of the Palais Stoclet in Brussels. Predominantly gold, with Byzantine and Egyptian overtones, the frieze marks the climax of Klimt's highly ornamental phase (the finished product was inlaid with semiprecious stones). The tree of life is the central motif, the birds of prey in its branches symbolizing death, and the figures below representing paradise. Close by the Klimt hangs a frieze by Margaret Macdonald, executed for Fritz Wärndorfer, and clearly inspired by Klimt's own *Beethoven Frieze*. Also on show is outstanding furniture by the likes of Otto Wagner and Kolo Moser, Charles Rennie Mackintosh, and an amazing selection of Bohemian glass – from the Lötz factory's iridescent, plant-like Art Nouveau vases to monochrome, geometric bowls from Haida (Nový Bor) – displayed in a glass cabinet suspended from the ceiling. A staircase leads up to **Gegenwart-skunst**, an entire room of contemporary art.

Finally, there's a **20/21 Jahrhundert Architektur** room, filled with models of realized and unrealized architectural works ranging from Frank O. Gehry's Santa Monica residence from 1978 to Daniel Libeskind's recently completed Jüdisches Museum in Berlin.

## Studiensammlung

If you've got the time and energy, head off down to the museum's **Studiensammlung** (Study Collection), hidden away in the basement. The rooms here are as crowded with exhibits as those in the permanent collection are sparse. The central room is used for temporary exhibitions drawn from the museum's vast Asian ceramics collection. The two rooms devoted to **Sitzmöbel** (Furniture) hold truly democratic changing displays: a Baroque settee happily shares space with a bean bag, a De Stijl chair, classic Wiener Werkstätte works and the director's daybed from the Postsparkasse by Otto Wagner.

The two **Keramik, Glas** rooms boast a collection ranging from Meissen porcelain figures to Jugendstil and Wiener Werkstätte produce. The glass, which kicks off with medieval stained-glass windows, ends with another incredible

---

## Wiener Werkstätte

After the Secession, probably the most important Austrian art movement was the **Wiener Werkstätte** (Vienna Workshop), founded in 1903 by the architect Josef Hoffmann, the designer Kolo Moser and the rich Jewish textile merchant, Fritz Wärndorfer. Hoffmann and Moser, both founder-members of the Secession, were initially inspired by William Morris and the English Arts and Crafts Movement. As with Morris & Co, the idea was to grant designers and craftsmen equal status – all Wiener Werkstätte produce bears the WW monogram, and the name of both the artist and craftsman. The other parallel with Morris & Co was the sheer range and breadth of the WW, whose work encompassed furniture, glassware, metalwork, porcelain, fashion, children's toys, postcards and even wrapping paper.

Artistically, the WW drew on a wide range of talents, including the likes of Oskar Kokoschka, Egon Schiele and Gustav Klimt. However, the strongest influences on Hoffmann and Moser were the Glaswegians **Charles Rennie Mackintosh** and his wife, **Margaret Macdonald**, who exhibited at the Secession in 1900 – their rectilinear, geometrical style became the hallmark of the WW in their first decade. In 1907, the WW made a big splash in Vienna with the opening of the legendary *Cabaret Fledermaus* on Kärntnerstrasse, which they had designed, from the toilets to the cutlery. However, despite winning numerous international prizes, and opening shops as far afield as New York and Zürich, the WW was not a financial success. Unlike Morris & Co or Bauhaus, their works were not meant for mass production, and they remained attached to the old-fashioned idea of the single, unrepeatable object, designed for rich patrons, the majority of whom recoiled from such avant-garde designs. Though from 1915 onwards, Dagobert Peche's softer, more decoratively playful style, dubbed *spitzbarok* (spiky Baroque), significantly widened the appeal of the WW, the company eventually folded in 1932.

The most complete WW work – the 1905 Palais Stoclet designed by Hoffmann (in collaboration with Klimt) – is actually in Brussels, but the room devoted to the WW in the MAK is the next best thing. There are also exhibits in the Wiener Glasmuseum. Another good place to head for is the Backhausen interior-design shop, just off the Ringstrasse at Schwarzenbergstrasse 10, which not only still produces WW pieces, but also has a charming **Wiener Werkstätte Museum** (Mon–Fri 10am–6pm, Sat 10am–5pm; free; Ⓦ www.backhausen.com) in the basement. Beautifully laid out, it explains the history of the shop's connection with the WW, and exhibits a mixture of original textiles, reproductions, design sketches and samples.

# The Secession

In 1897, a number of artists broke away from the Künstlerhaus, Austria's leading independent artists' association, and set up their own organization, which they named the Secession. The second half of the nineteenth century had seen the ossification of the arts in Vienna, exemplified in architecture by the heavy-handed historicism of the Ringstrasse, and epitomized in painting by the flattery of Hans Makart (1840–84). Broadly speaking, the new group aimed to regenerate the arts in Vienna, and to promote "art for art's sake", in particular the latest style, Art Nouveau, known in German as Jugendstil (literally "Youth-style").

illustration from *Ver Sacrum* ▲

*Beethoven Frieze* ▼

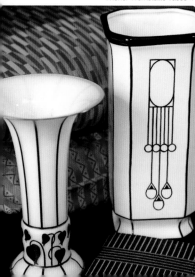

Wiener Werkstätte vases ▼

# Klimt and his followers

The artist **Gustav Klimt** (1862–1918), who became the first president of the Secession in 1897, remained its driving force for the next eight years. Klimt had begun his career as a promising young master of the old ideology. In the movement's striking, purpose-built headquarters, however, in full view of the Künstlerhaus, he now helped to stage a series of exhibitions of new work. Initially, the reception among the Viennese critics and public was good; the emperor himself visited, and several Secessionists went on to receive faculty appointments at the Arts and Crafts School. However, the movement ran into trouble when Klimt exhibited *Medicine* here, part of his controversial mural intended for the University. The ensuing public scandal (see p.90), and the mixed reception given to the group's fourteenth exhibition in 1902, for which Klimt painted the *Beethoven Frieze*, eventually prompted Klimt, along with a select group of followers, to leave the Secession and retreat from public life for several years.

Between 1898 and 1903, the Secession group also published *Ver Sacrum*, a successful arts journal employing lavish Jugendstil typography and layout. Instrumental in its production and design were two of the Secession's co-founders, **Josef Hoffmann** (1870–1955) and **Kolo Moser** (1868–1918). Hoffmann and Moser went on to pursue their interest in applied art, forming the craft-based Wiener Werkstätte in 1902 (see p.112), and eventually leaving the Secession along with Klimt in 1905. All three later worked together to organize the **Kunstschau** exhibitions of 1908 and 1909 (see p.109), which rejected the decorative art of the Secession in favour of Expressionism.

# Kunsthistorisches Museum

... a city somewhat overloaded with museums, Vienna's **Kunsthistorisches ...useum** (Art History Museum) stands head and shoulders above the rest. ...anks to the wealth and artistic pretensions of successive Habsburg rulers, it ...ntains not only the fourth largest collection of paintings in the world, but ...gyptian, Greek and Roman antiquities, plus sundry more recent *objets d'art*. ...merous are the exhibits that several of the museum's departments are now ...d in the Neue Burg wing of the Hofburg (see p.82).

... bulk of the art collection is comprised of sixteenth- and seventeenth-...ry masters. Most people come to see the collection of **Bruegels** – the largest ... world – but the museum is also loaded with **Venetian** works by the likes of ...retto, **Veronese** and **Titian**, and a goodly selection of **Velázquez** portraits. ...dition, there are plenty of paintings by **Rembrandt**, **Cranach** and **Dürer**, ...whole rooms devoted to **Van Dyck** and **Rubens**. Lastly, don't miss the ...alled collection of Mannerist works from the court of Rudolf II, especially ...rrealist court painter, **Giuseppe Arcimboldo**.

... of the glories of the Kunsthistorisches Museum is, of course, the **building** ... especially the main foyer and staircase, which are sumptuously decorated, ...the monochrome marble floor to the richly stuccoed dome and well. Don't ...ok Canova's *Theseus and the Minotaur*, which greets you on the main staircase, ...te the lunettes, spandrel and intercolumnar murals on the first-floor balcony,

## ...iting the museum

**Kunsthistorisches Museum** (Ⓦ www.khm.at) is open Tuesday to Sunday 10am ...pm; the picture gallery is also open on Thursdays until 9pm. The **admission fee** ...12 includes entry to the museum's temporary exhibitions; the museum is free ...ublic holidays. Even if you spend the whole day here, you'll be pushed to see ...rything, so it's best to concentrate on just one or two areas. If you're peckish, ...d for the *Gerstner* **café** in the stylish upper foyer, which offers snacky meals and ...es for under €10. You are also allowed to nip out for a picnic (or a cigarette break), ...ng as you inform the museum staff. The painting titles are all in German; in our ...ount they're given the English names by which they're usually known. **Guided** ...s of the museum in English set off daily at 3pm and cost €3. The nearest **U-Bahn** ...useumsquartier.

## Wagner and Loos

As Hermann Bahr wrote, "without Wagner, there would be no Secession, no Klimt group, no applied art". Though only peripheral in the Secessionist organization, the architect **Otto Wagner** (1841–1918) was a seminal figure in the Viennese art world throughout the period. Wagner not only completed more buildings than any other Secession architect, he also designed the entire Stadtbahn system between 1894 and 1901, including all the stations and bridges, many of which still adorn the U4 and U6 metro lines. Though he remains the highest-profile exponent of the Secession style, his works in fact range from nineteenth-century historicism to twentieth-century modernism. Having started out as a Ringstrasse architect, he had become an establishment figure by the time he joined the Secession in 1899. During the next decade he executed some of his finest work, initially opting for ornate curvilinear motifs derived from nature, but later moving towards more rectilinear, abstract forms. Wagner's shift towards minimalism and his enthusiastic adoption of new materials such as concrete and aluminium – best seen in his **Postsparkasse** (see p.113) – make him a key figure in the emergence of modernism.

It's also worth mentioning **Adolf Loos** (1870–1933), who published two articles in *Ver Sacrum*, one of which was a stinging attack on Ringstrasse architecture. Loos's relationship with the Secession was brief, however, and in 1908 he published a thinly veiled criticism of the movement in an article entitled *Ornament is Crime*. As an architect, Loos went on to design some of Europe's first truly modernist buildings, most notably the Looshaus (see p.55) and his villas in Hietzing (see p.176).

▲ Postsparkasse

▼ Karlsplatz station

Majolikahaus ▲

Portois & Fix ▼

Secession ▼

## A Jugendstil hitlist

### Otto Wagner

▶▶ **Döblergasse 4**, Spittelberg. Wagner's apartment and studio in town is now a museum.

▶▶ **Hofpavillon Hietzing**, Hietzing p.175. Wagner's most ornate U-Bahn station, built outside Schönbrunn for the imperial family.

▶▶ **Kirche am Steinhof**, Baumgarte Höhe p.180. The world's most beautiful psychiatric hospital church.

▶▶ **Majolikahaus**, Naschmarkt, Ringstrasse p.108. Ceramic-clad apartment block sporting a lively floral motif, overlooking the Naschmarkt.

▶▶ **Nussdorfer Wehr- und Schleusen-anlage**, Nussdorf. Never have municipal weirs and locks looked so good.

▶▶ **Postsparkasse**, Stubenring, Ringstrasse p.113. The architect's iconic modernist building.

▶▶ **Rennweg**, Landstrasse, Vorstädte p.130. A trio of early Wagner houses.

▶▶ **Schützenhaus**, Donaukanal, Leopoldstadt p.156. A dinky little lock-keeper's house on the banks of the Danube Canal.

▶▶ **Pavillon Karlsplatz**, Resselpark, Ringstrasse p.104. Two preserved ornate U-Bahn stations.

▶▶ **Wagner Villas I & II**, Hütteldorf p.180. Two country villas built at either end of his career.

### Others

▶▶ **Artaria Haus**, Kohlmarkt, Innere Stadt p.55. Max Fabiani's marble-faced precursor to the Postsparkasse.

▶▶ **Portois & Fix**, Landstrasse, Vorstädte p.130. Fabiani's ceramic-clad exterior looks like digital art.

▶▶ **Secession**, Karlsplatz, Ringstrasse p.103. The movement's landmark headquarters, popularly known as the "Gilded Cabbage".

▶▶ **Zacherlhaus**, Hoher Markt, Innere Stadt p.64. Josip Plečnik's remarkably eclectic inner-city apartment block.

---

display of Jugendstil and Art Nouveau glassware similar to th collection, with works from Gallé, Tiffany and Lobmeyr as w pieces. In the **Metall** room, a watering can from Wolverha among gold goblets, silver chalices, Art Nouveau candelabra teapots. In **Textil**, you can view everything from napkins and vestments and festive dresses from all around the Mediterra miss the partial reconstruction of the utopian **Frankfurter Kü** designed in 1926 by Margarete Schütte-Lihotsky, and r aluminium pull-out drawers and a fold-down ironing board.

## Postsparkasse and around

The final segment of the Ringstrasse, **Stubenring**, was the erected mostly in the decade before World War I. The two bigg built here were the former Kriegsministerium (War Ministry) ar of the Postsparkasse or **PSK** (Postal Savings Bank). The latter attempt to counteract the perceived threat of Jewish capital, ir the Rothschilds. With this duo in place, the Ringstrasse had, ir full circle: having begun with a barracks and a church – the V 1850s, it was to end with another reassertion of the army and (

Despite the reactionary politics behind the **Postsparkasse** (M Thurs until 5.30pm), the design with which Otto Wagner wc for its construction was strikingly modern. The building is by devoid of ornament – this is, after all, a prime Ringstrasse site. a pergola hung with laurel wreaths on the roof, flanked by two The rest of the building, though, looks something like a giant s its otherwise smooth facade studded with aluminium rivets, use grey marble slabs in place. Aluminium – a new and expensive used for the delicate glazed canopy over the entrance, and, mos heating cowls, which rise up into the main banking hall like gi It's worth exploring beyond counter 13 to the **museum** (€5), w see, among other things, Wagner's now defunct stripey Kleine Banking Hall) and a model of the building.

As you leave, check out Emperor Franz-Josef's ceramic bus staircase. Moves by the Christian Socials to have the bust of t founder, government bureaucrat **Georg Coch** (1842–90), place foiled, allegedly by high-placed Jewish opposition. The anti-Se Lueger (see p.92) stepped into the breach and got the square nam – with Wagner's consent – placed Coch's bust on a plinth in the

Archduke Franz Ferdinand remained unimpressed by Wagner's made sure the competition for the **Kriegsministerium**, situa Postsparkasse, was won by Ludwig Baumann's conservative ne Completed in 1912, it's a thoroughly intimidating building, smacki bombastic militarism, personified by the equestrian figure ( Radetzky, scourge of the 1848 revolution in northern Italy, which the main entrance. Grim busts of the empire's soldiers keep watch f above the ground-floor windows, while armed cherubs and a vast guarded by a giant double-headed eagle with wings outstretched, the pediment. The building now houses various governmental dep

Stubenring ends at the Danube Canal, beside which stand **Urania** (Ⓦ www.urania-sternwarte.at), built in the shape of an in 1910. Conceived as an adult education centre, it remains a mu tution, housing a cinema, puppet theatre, planetarium, observato **café** (see p.210).

which illustrate the history of art from ancient Egypt to Florence. Hans Makart only managed to complete the lunettes before his death from syphilis in 1884; the remaining murals were completed, in Makart's classical style, by the youthful trio of Franz Matsch, Ernst Klimt and his more famous brother Gustav; diagrams point out which mural was painted by which artist.

## The Gemäldegalerie

Around eight hundred paintings – a mere tenth of the museum's total catalogue – are on display at any one time in the **Gemäldegalerie** (Picture Gallery) on the first floor. Unlike most big galleries, however, the Kunsthistorisches makes no attempt to cover a broad span of art history – the collection has changed little since the Habsburgs bequeathed it. Consequently, British and French artists, and the early Italian Renaissance, are all under-represented, and the collection stops at the late eighteenth century.

The paintings are arranged in parallel rooms around two courtyards: the Italians, plus a few French and Spanish, lie to one side, and the Germans, Dutch and Flemish to the other. The larger rooms – prefixed by the word Saal – that face onto the courtyards sport Roman numerals (I–XV), while the smaller outer rooms use the standard form (1–24), though the latter are often unmarked. It would be difficult to concoct a more confusing numerical system, but at least both wings are laid out (vaguely) chronologically. The account below starts with the Bruegels.

However you plan your itinerary, be sure to avail yourself of one of the great assets of the Gemäldegalerie, the comfy sofas in the larger rooms.

### Bruegel and his contemporaries

The great thing about the museum's works by **Pieter Bruegel the Elder** (c.1525–69), in Saal X, is the breadth and range of the collection, from innovative interpretations of religious stories to allegorical peasant scenes. Though well connected in court circles in Antwerp and, later, Brussels, Bruegel excelled in these country scenes, earning himself the soubriquet **"Peasant Bruegel"** – the story goes that he used to disguise himself in order to move freely among the peasantry. A classic

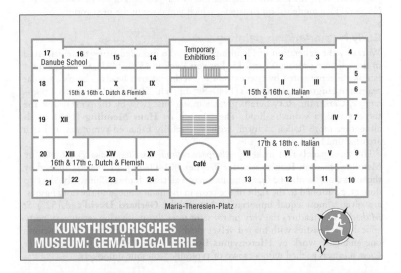

example of the genre is his incredibly detailed *Children's Games*, in which more than 230 children play 83 different games. Perhaps the most beguiling of all Bruegel's works within the peasant genre is the **cycle of seasons**, commissioned by a rich Flemish banker. Three (out of six) hang in this room: *The Gloomy Day*, *The Return of the Herd* and, the most famous of all, *Hunters in the Snow*, in which Bruegel perfectly captures a wintry monochrome landscape.

Several of Bruegel's peasant works have a **moral message**, too, as in the *Peasant Dance*, where the locals revel irreverently under an image of the Madonna. Similarly, the *Peasant Wedding* comes over less as a religious occasion than as another excuse for gluttony. Others, such as *The Peasant and the Bird-Thief*, are more difficult to interpret, though it's thought to illustrate the inscrutable Flemish proverb: "He who knows where the nest is, has the knowledge; he who robs it, has the nest."

In *The Procession to Calvary*, we are confronted with a typically vigorous Bruegelian crowd, who seem unmoved by the tragedy quietly and inconspicuously unfolding in their midst. Gruesome characters, revealing the influence of Bosch, inhabit *The Fight between Carnival and Lent*, a complex painting in which the orgy of Shrove Tuesday is contrasted with the piety of Ash Wednesday. *The Tower of Babel* (inspired, it's thought, by Rome's Colosseum) illustrates the vanity of King Nimrod – the **detail** on both the tower and the city below it is staggering.

Bruegel lived through a particularly turbulent period when the Netherlands was under Spanish Habsburg rule, and many have tried to read allusions to contemporary **political events** into his paintings (Austrian troops accompany Christ in *The Procession to Calvary*, for example). However, the most oft-quoted example, *The Massacre of the Innocents*, was, in fact, painted prior to the appointment of the Duke of Alba, and therefore cannot refer to the duke's Council of Blood, during which twelve thousand were executed.

Note that before you get to the Bruegels, you must pass through Saal IX, which contains works by **Pieter Aertsen** (c.1508–75), a contemporary of Bruegel's who also worked in the peasant genre. *Vanity – Still Life* is typical of his style: the detailed still life of the feast being prepared by Martha upstages her sister Mary at the feet of Jesus, portrayed in the background. **Frans Floris** (1516–70), a painter more famous in his day than Bruegel ever was, contributes a gruesome *Last Judgement*, while the five surviving months of the year by Lucas van Valckenborch (1535–97) are modelled on Bruegel's, which you'll see in the next room.

## Early Netherlandish painting

Works by the generation of Flemish painters who preceded Bruegel are displayed in the adjoining rooms 14 and 15. **Jan van Eyck** (c.1390–1441), by far the most famous, is represented by two extremely precise portrait heads. There's a similar realism in **Hugo van der Goes**'s (1440–82) diptych, *The Fall of Man and the Lamentation of Christ*; the story here is given a misogynist twist by the portrayal of the serpent with a woman's head. The triptych by **Hans Memling** (1440–94) is altogether more Italian in form, with its carefully balanced symmetry and rich architectural framing.

The three panels that make up *Altarpiece with the Crucifixion and Two Donors* by Memling's teacher, **Rogier van der Weyden** (c.1400–64), are cleverly unified by the undulating landscape that continues across all three frames. Unusually, the two donors, positioned to the right of the cross in the main scene, and the holy figures, are given almost equal importance. Meanwhile, **Gerhard David**'s (d.1523) *St Michael's Altar* features the very pretty saint serenely smothering seven very nasty apocalyptic beasties with his red velvet cloak. Also in this room is the museum's one and only work by **Hieronymus Bosch** (c.1450–1516), *Christ Carrying the Cross*, a canvas packed with a crowd of typically grotesque onlookers.

## Dürer, Cranach and Holbein

If you continue with the smaller rooms, you come to the excellent German collection. Room 16 shelters a colourful *Adoration of the Trinity* altarpiece by **Albrecht Dürer** (1471–1528). Amid his gilded throng are the donor, Matthäus Landauer (lower row, to the left), his son-in-law (lower row, to the right) and, with his feet firmly on the ground, Dürer himself (bottom right). The frame (a modern copy) bears closer inspection, too, with those not heading for heaven being chained up and devoured by the devil. Dürer also appears, somewhat incongruously dressed in black, in the centre of his *Martyrdom of the Ten Thousand*; amid scenes of mass murder on Mount Ararat, he strolls, deep in conversation, with his recently deceased friend, the humanist Conrad Celtes.

Room 17 contains more Dürer, including his portrait of Emperor Maximilian I, from the year the latter died; the emperor holds a pomegranate, symbol of wealth and power. *The Crucifixion*, an early work by **Lucas Cranach the Elder** (1472–1553), depicts a gory Christ, spattered with, and vomiting up, blood, against a rugged Danubian landscape. Later, after Cranach became court painter to the Elector of Saxony, his style became more circumspect. In *Judith with the Head of Holofernes*, the Biblical heroine is depicted as an elegant Saxon lady, while his *Stag Hunt of Elector Frederick the Wise*, in which numerous stags are driven into the water so the royals can pick them off with crossbows, is almost playful, with little sense of the impending butchery. His son, Lucas Cranach the Younger (1515–86), contributes an equally jolly scene of slaughter in *Stag Hunt of the Elector John Frederick*, which hangs close by.

The large collection of works in room 18 by **Hans Holbein the Younger** (1497–1543) date from his period as court painter to King Henry VIII. One of his first royal commissions was a portrait of *Jane Seymour*, lady-in-waiting to Henry VIII's second wife, Anne Boleyn, who, after the latter's execution, became his third wife. (She died giving birth to Henry's one and only son, the future Edward VI.) The portrait of Emperor Karl V with his Ulm Mastiff in Saal IX, by Austrian artist **Jakob Seisenegger** (1505–67), helped popularize the full-length portrait among the European nobility, and was undoubtedly the model for Titian's more famous portrait of the emperor, which hangs in the Prado in Madrid.

## Brueghel, Arcimboldo and van Dyck

Room 19 contains several works by the son of "Peasant Bruegel", **Jan Brueghel the Elder** (1568–1625), whose detailed still lifes of flowers were highly prized, his luminous paintwork earning him the nickname "Velvet Brueghel". Among his best known, non-flowery paintings is his reverential *Adoration of the Kings*, a beautifully detailed work that's a firm favourite on Christmas cards.

Also in room 19 are several works from the court of Rudolf II (1576–1612), the deeply melancholic emperor who shut himself up in Prague Castle surrounded by astrologers, alchemists and artists – it's Rudolf we have to thank for the museum's Bruegels and Dürers. Probably Rudolf's most famous court artist was **Giuseppe Arcimboldo** (1527–93), whose "composite heads" – surrealist, often disturbing, profile portraits created out of inanimate objects – so tickled the emperor that he commissioned portraits of every member of his entourage, down to the cook. All the four in room 7 are allegorical, and include *Water*, in which the head is made of sea creatures, and *Fire*, where it's a hotchpotch of burning faggots, an oil lamp and various firearms.

**Anthony Van Dyck** (1599–1641) predominates in the adjacent room (XII). Some pieces, like *Samson and Delilah*, date from the time when Van Dyck was working closely with Rubens, hence the characteristic, "ruffled" brushstrokes.

Others – mostly portraits – date from after his appointment as court painter to King Charles I of England.

## Rubens

Thanks to the Habsburgs' long-term control of the southern Netherlands, the Kunsthistorisches boasts one of the largest collections of paintings by **Peter Paul Rubens** (1577–1640) in existence, spread over three rooms (room 20, Saal XIII & XIV). As is clear from his self-confident self-portrait at the age of 62, Rubens was a highly successful artist, who received so many commissions that he was able to set up a studio and employ a group of collaborators (among them Van Dyck and Jordaens). Rubens would supply the preliminary sketches – witness the sketches for giant high-altar paintings commissioned by the Jesuits in Saal XIV, and the end result, in the same room.

Perhaps the best-known of all the Rubens works is *The Fur*, in Saal XIII, a frank, erotic testament to the artist's second wife, Hélène Fourment, who was 37 years his junior. Rubens was clearly taken with his 16-year-old wife, who appears as an angel and as a saint (or possibly deity) in two other late works: the *Ildefonso Altar* and, looking directly at the viewer, in the *Meeting near Nördlingen*. The loose brushwork and painterly style in these two bear comparison with Titian's late work in room I, and Rubens pays tribute to the Italian in *The Worship of Venus*, a veritable chubby cherub-fest set in a classical landscape.

### Rembrandt, Vermeer and the Brits

Rubens' Baroque excess is a million miles from the sparse, simple portraits by **Rembrandt van Rijn** (1606–69), several of which hang in room 21. There's a sympathetic early portrait of his mother (now thought to be a copy), the year before she died, depicted in all the fragility and dignity of old age, and a dream-like later study of his son, Titus, reading. Three self-portraits date from the 1650s, when, as the art critics love to point out, Rembrandt was beginning to experience financial difficulties. Whether you choose to read worry into Rembrandt's face or not, these are three superb studies of the human face.

Next door, in room 22, is the museum's one and only painting by **Jan Vermeer**, *The Art of Painting*, considered by many to be among his finest and thought to have been one of the artist's favourites – he never parted with it or sold it even when he was in debt. The bright light from the onlooker's left; the yellow, blue and grey; the simple poses, are all classic Vermeer trademarks, though the symbolic meaning, and even the title, of the work have provoked fierce debate. Close by, in room 24, are the museum's only **British paintings**: a gentle, honey-hued *Suffolk Landscape* by Thomas Gainsborough, a portrait of painstaking realism by Joseph Wright, an unfinished portrait of a young woman by Joshua Reynolds, and a Henry Raeburn portrait.

### Titian and the Venetians

Over in the west wing, the museum boasts a superb selection of Venetian paintings, especially works by **Titian** (c.1488–1576), which span all sixty years of his artistic life. Very early works like *The Gypsy Madonna* in Saal I reveal Titian's debt to Giovanni Bellini, in whose studio he spent his apprenticeship. The colours are richer, the contours softer, but the essentially static composition is reminiscent of Bellini's own *Young Woman with a Mirror* (see below). The largest canvas here is Titian's complex *Ecce Homo*, in which, amid all the action and colour, Christ and Pontius Pilate are relegated to the top left-hand corner.

In *Girl in a Fur* and the portrait of the Elector of Saxony, Titian shows himself equally capable of sparing use of colour, allowing the sitters' individual features maximum effect. By contrast, Titian's very last portrait, of the art dealer Jacopo Strada, whom the painter disliked, is full of incidental detail, colour and movement. Don't miss the portrait of Isabella d'Este, depicted wearing a "borzo", a turban-like headgear that she was instrumental in popularizing – she was 62 when the portrait was painted but insisted on being depicted forty years younger. Towards the end of his life, Titian achieved a freedom of technique in his own personal works, in which "he used his fingers more than his brush", according to fellow painter Palma il Giovane. His masterpiece of this period is the *Nymph and Shepherd*, painted without a commission, using an autumnal palette and very loose brushwork.

A fragment of an altarpiece by Antonello da Messina, who is credited with introducing oil painting to northern Italy, hangs in room 2, along with *Young Woman with a Mirror* and *Presentation of Christ in the Temple*, both by **Giovanni Bellini** (1460–1516), and a sculptural *St Sebastian* by Bellini's brother-in-law, **Andrea Mantegna** (c.1430–1506). *The Three Philosophers* is almost as mysterious as its (probable) painter, **Giorgione**. All we know about him is that he was tall, handsome and died young (possibly of the plague); as for the painting, no one's sure if it depicts the Magi, the three stages of man's life or some other subject. The sensuous portrait, *Laura* – fur and naked breasts are a recurring theme in the gallery – is one of Giorgione's few works to be certified and dated.

Colourful, carefully constructed, monumental Mannerist canvases by **Paolo Veronese** (1528–88) fill the walls of Saal II – his early *Anointing of David* is a classic example, with the subject matter subordinated to the overall effect. Saal III holds several impressive portraits by **Tintoretto** (1518–94), and a voluptuous *Susanna and the Elders*, full of contrasts of light and shade, old age and youthfulness, clothed and naked. It's also worth looking at the horizontal panels, depicting scenes from the Old and New Testaments and intended for use on furniture, not least for their refreshing immediacy and improvised brushstrokes.

## Raphael, Bronzino and Caravaggio

In room 3, **Antonio Correggio** (c.1489–1534) puts his bid in for the gallery's most erotic painting with *Jupiter and Io*, in which the latter is brought to the verge of ecstasy by Jupiter in the form of a lecherous cloud. In room 4, the masterly *Madonna in the Meadow* is a study in Renaissance harmony and proportion, painted by **Raphael** (1483–1520) at the tender age of 22. Further on, room 8 holds a typically icy *Holy Family* by **Agnolo Bronzino** (1503–72).

**Caravaggio** (1571–1610), several of whose works hang in Saal V, was nothing if not controversial. His chief artistic sin, in the eyes of the establishment, was his refusal to idealize his Biblical characters, frequently using street urchins as models, as in *David with the Head of Goliath*; he also painted his self-portrait as the severed head of Goliath. He may have managed to outrage more than a few of his religious patrons, but his works had a profound effect on artists like Rubens and Brueghel, each of whom at one time or another owned the *Madonna of the Rosary*.

## Velázquez, Bellotto and Canaletto

If the Italians start to get you down, head for the Spanish in rooms 9 and 10. Here you can see Alonso Sánchez Coëllo's portrait of **Don Carlos**, Philip II's mentally and physically handicapped son, who was incarcerated by his father some four years later, and died shortly afterwards. Another Coëllo portrait depicts Elisabeth of Valois, Philip II's third wife, whom he married despite the fact that she was already betrothed to Don Carlos – events familiar to those who know the plot of Verdi's opera *Don Carlos*.

The smattering of works by **Diego Velázquez** (1599–1660) in room 10, most of them gifts from the Spanish Habsburgs to the Austrian side of the family, include a portrait of Queen Maria-Anna of Spain, whose hairdo is twice the size of her face. Charles II of Spain looks utterly grotesque in the portrait by Juan Carreño de Miranda – it's scary to think that he probably looked even worse in real life. The most famous works are those of the Infanta Margarita Teresa, who was betrothed to her uncle, the future Emperor Leopold I, from the age of three, married him at the age of 15, and died at the age of 21.

Lastly, you might want to take a look at the large eighteenth-century views of Vienna in room VII, commissioned by the court from **Bernardo Bellotto**, to see how little the view from the Belvedere has changed over the centuries. The Viennese insisted on calling Bellotto "Canaletto", though he was in fact the latter's nephew and pupil. For real **Canalettos**, you must go next door, to room 13, where his much smaller, picture-postcard views of Venice hang alongside works by his compatriot, Francesco Guardi.

### Vermeyen and the Coin Cabinet

On the little-visited second floor, a series of sixteenth-century cartoons and tapestries by **Jan Cornelisz Vermeyen** are displayed. Vermeyen accompanied Emperor Karl V in 1535 during his crusade to recapture Tunis from the Ottoman Turks, at the head of a vast army of thirty thousand troops and over four hundred ships, and his detailed depictions of the maritime scenes, cityscapes, cavalry charges and hand-to-hand combat boast a remarkable topographical veracity and a skilful use of perspective.

The **Münzkabinett** (Coin Cabinet) also occupies several second-floor rooms, and includes a display of piggy banks from Roman times to the 1990s. Naturally enough, there are also coins, some dating as far back as 650 BC, others from more recent times: the Habsburg Empire, the Austro-fascist state, the Nazi period and even a few token euros. Also here, you'll find **Archduke Ferdinand II of Tyrol**'s remarkable collection of more than one thousand postcard-sized portraits of popes, dukes, generals, poets and philosophers.

# The ground-floor galleries

Laid out chronologically, the **ground floor** kicks off with the Egyptian and Near Eastern Collection (I–VIII), passes through Greek and Roman Antiquities (IX–XVIII) and heads off into the Kunstkammer (XIX–XXXVII).

### Egyptian and Near Eastern Collection

Immediately to the right as you enter the museum, the purpose-built galleries of the **Egyptian and Near Eastern Collection** sport appropriately hieroglyphic decorations. Pink granite papyrus-stalk columns from around 1410 BC are even incorporated into the construction of Saal I, which is devoted to the **Egyptian death cult**. The entrance to the room is guarded by two statues of the fearsome lion-headed goddess, Sekhmet – the museum owns four out of the six hundred that once formed a colossal monument to the deity erected at Thebes by Amenophis III.

In the room itself, there's one actual mummy, wrapped in papyrus leaves, and numerous wooden inner **coffins**, smothered with polychrome symbols and hieroglyphs. Below these are the canopic jars containing the entrails removed during mummification, with lids carved in the shape of animal deities. Saal III holds cabinets full of *shabti* figurines, in wood, stone and pottery, which were placed in the tomb to perform any task the gods might require (there had to be at least 365 in each tomb, plus 36 overseers). Notice, too, the cabinet of heart scarabs, placed

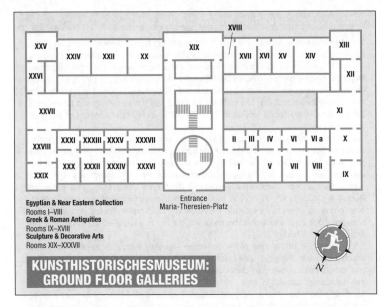

Egyptian & Near Eastern Collection
Rooms I–VIII
Greek & Roman Antiquities
Rooms IX–XVIII
Sculpture & Decorative Arts
Rooms XIX–XXXVII

Entrance
Maria-Theresien-Platz

**KUNSTHISTORISCHESMUSEUM:
GROUND FLOOR GALLERIES**

upon the chests of mummies, bearing a spell that implored the deceased's heart not to bear witness against him or her during the Judgement of Osiris. Finally, don't miss the mummified bestiary – everything from crocodiles to dormice – in Saal IV.

While the Kunsthistorisches owns some superb **Egyptian sculpture**, beginning in Saal VII, the most popular item is the winsome **blue pottery hippo**, whose body is tattooed with papyrus leaves, lotus flowers and a bird, pictorial elements from its natural swamp habitat. Saal VII contains another prized possession, the *Ersatz Kopf* or **Reserve Head** from around 2450 BC, a smooth, stylized, deliberately mutilated head carved in limestone, which exudes an extraordinary serenity. Excavated a century ago by Austrian archeologists at Giza, it is thought to be a surrogate head for the immortal *ka*.

## Greek and Roman Antiquities

Many of the museum's finest **Greek and Roman Antiquities** are displayed in the large, arcaded Saal XI, which is lined with richly carved sarcophagi, and has, at the centre, the magnificent fourth-century AD **Theseus Mosaic**, discovered in 1815 in a Roman villa near Salzburg. Theseus and the Minotaur are depicted in the middle of a complex geometric labyrinth, out of which the hero escapes with the help of the red thread given to him by Ariadne, who is pictured abandoned to the right.

Anyone in search of **Greek vases** need look no further than Saal XIV, which contains an excellent selection, from early Geometric vases from the eighth century BC to the sophisticated black-and-red-figure vases of the Classical period. Among the many onyx cameos in the adjoining Saal XVI is one of the finest in the world, the first-century AD **Gemma Augustea**, which is surprisingly large at 19cm in height. The upper scene depicts the emperor Augustus in the guise of Jupiter, seated on a bench alongside Roma, with the emperor's star sign, Capricorn, floating between them; the lower scene shows the Romans'

## Kunstkammer (Sculpture and Decorative Arts)

The **Kunstkammer**, which occupies half the ground floor galleries, closed in 2003, following the theft of its most famous exhibit, Benvenuto Cellini's **Saliera**. The *Saliera* – a slightly ludicrous sixteenth-century salt cellar upon which the gold figures of Neptune, holding a phallic trident, and Earth, squeezing her own nipple, appear to be engaged in some sort of erotic see-saw – was rediscovered, buried in a forest near the town of Zwettl in 2006. The galleries, however, will have been closed for nearly a decade when they finally reopen in 2013. Below is a very brief account of some of the highlights.

It's a patchy collection, with some real gems, and a lot of objects of great crafts-manship, but dubious artistic taste. *Kunstkammern* (Chambers of Marvels) became *de rigueur* among German-speaking rulers during the Renaissance and most of the exhibits were purchased or specially commissioned for such collections. The most avid collectors were **Archduke Ferdinand II of Tyrol** (died 1595) and **Emperor Rudolf II** (1576–1612). Rudolf, in particular, took collecting very seriously indeed, even going so far as to incarcerate the Augsburg clockmaker, Georg Roll, when the celestial globe he made for him broke down, but the one supplied to his brother, the Archduke Ernst, had not.

To get an idea of the tone of the collection – slightly vulgar, exquisitely executed kitsch – consider the gold vase holding tulips made from agate, jasper, chalcedony and rock crystal, or the gold chain, inset with rubies and made up of 49 portraits of the Habsburgs carved in shell. Most of the exhibits have no particular function; however, some, like the rock-crystal dragon-lions were clearly something of a party piece: liquid poured into their tails would gush into a shell through nozzles in the beast's breasts.

All in all, the collection is a compelling hotchpotch, ranging from a striking six-winged sixteenth-century altarpiece, comprised of 156 panels, to a dubious trio of pearwood cherubs playing with one another's private parts, and a richly carved backgammon set featuring erotic scenes on each of the counters. Elsewhere, you'll find some remarkable miniature mining scenes carved out of tiny rocks, and some exquisitely beautiful scientific instruments, including one of Georg Roll's aforementioned celestial globes.

victory over the Dalmatians under Tiberius. Look out, too, for the oldest Latin Edict of Senate in existence, dating from 186 BC, and rather hopefully forbidding Bacchic orgies.

Saal XVII contains **goldwork**, much of which – like Visigoth King Alaric II's sapphire ring seal – strictly speaking postdates the collapse of the Roman Empire. The chain of honour with 52 pendants is an excellent example of early Germanic gold, its centrepiece a bead of smoky topaz, mounted with two tiny pouncing panthers. The most impressive haul is the treasure from Nagyszentmiklós (Sînicolaul Mare) in Romania, 23 pure gold vessels, weighing a total of 20kg, with runic inscriptions that continue to fox the experts.

Before you leave this section, admire one of the most famous classical statues here, the **Youth of Magdalensberg**. It is, in fact, a sixteenth-century bronze copy of the Roman original, something that was only discovered in 1983 when research was being conducted into the methods used in the casting.

# 5

# The Vorstädte

O nce the Turks were beaten back from the city gates in 1683, Vienna could, at last, spread itself safely beyond the confines of the medieval town walls. A horseshoe of districts, known as the **Vorstädte** (Inner Suburbs), quickly grew up and engulfed the villages around the old town, beyond the *glacis* (the open ground outside the city walls). In 1704, the great military leader, Prince Eugène of Savoy, ordered the construction of a second, outer line of fortifications or *Linienwall*, to protect the new suburbs. Later, the *Linienwall* became the municipal boundary, where, in a Habsburg custom going back to the Middle Ages, everyone entering the city was searched, and made to pay a tax on goods purchased outside Vienna.

As the city spread still further out into the *Vororte* or rural parishes, the *Linienwall* was demolished in 1890. It became what's known today as the **Gürtel** – literally "belt" – a thunderous ring road that has the added indignity of doubling as the city's red-light district. The seven districts of the Vorstädte – the third to the ninth – are neatly confined between the Ringstrasse and the Gürtel. They remain residential for the most part, though each has its own commercial thoroughfare, the largest of which is the city's main shopping drag, **Mariahilferstrasse**, which divides the sixth and seventh districts. Sights in the Vorstädte are widely dispersed, so it pays to be selective – a *Netzkarte* and a grasp of the transport system are useful (see p.23). The following account starts with the third district and finishes with the ninth. The second district, Leopoldstadt, east of the Danube Canal, is covered in Chapter Six.

The one sight in the Vorstädte that no visitor should miss is the **Belvedere**, in the third district, with its formal gardens and twin-set of Baroque palaces housing some superb works of art, including the city's finest collection of paintings by Gustav Klimt. Two other sights that heave with visitors in summer are the **Hundertwasserhaus**, a wacky piece of council housing in the third district, and the **Freud–Museum**, in the psychoanalyst's former apartment in the ninth. The other reason to explore the Vorstädte is to wander round the shops, restaurants and bars in districts like Neubau (seventh) and Josefstadt (eighth).

## The districts of the Vorstädte

| | |
|---|---|
| Third – Landstrasse | Seventh – Neubau |
| Fourth – Wieden | Eighth – Josefstadt |
| Fifth – Margareten | Ninth – Alsergrund |
| Sixth – Mariahilf | |

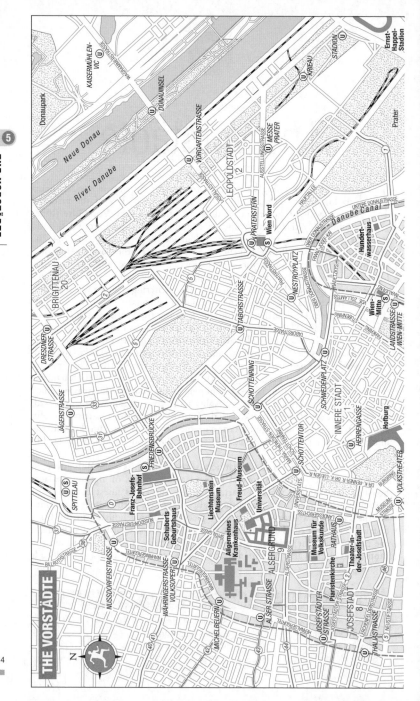

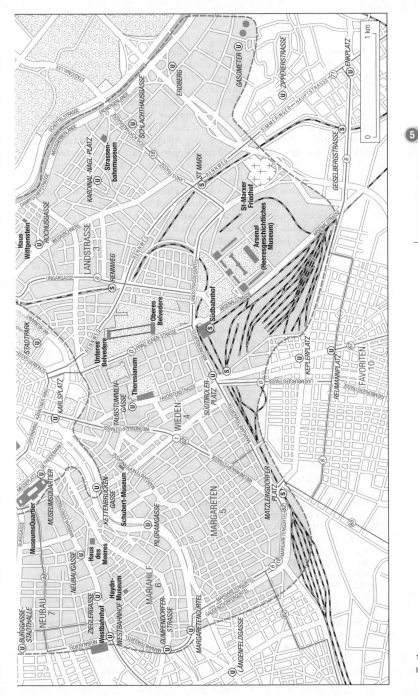

1 km

# Landstrasse

**Landstrasse** – Vienna's third district – lies to the east and southeast of the Innere Stadt, framed by the Danube Canal (Donaukanal) to the east, and to the west by Prinz-Eugen-Strasse and Arsenalstrasse. By far the largest of the Vorstädte, it remains a predominantly working-class area, with a high immigrant population, mostly from Eastern Europe and the Balkans. The one exception is the diplomatic quarter around the **Belvedere**, where the summer palaces of Prince Eugène of Savoy house a feast of fine art from medieval times to the early twentieth century. Just south of the Gürtel lies the city's former **Arsenal**, home to the **Heeresgeschichtliches Museum**, built to glorify the Imperial Army and worth admiring for its quasi-Moorish architecture, even if you're not keen on military paraphernalia.

Other sights are more widely dispersed. The **Hundertwasserhaus**, an idiosyncratic housing development in the nub of land to the north of the district, is now one of Vienna's top tourist attractions, something which cannot be said for the nearby modernist **Haus Wittgenstein**, designed by the famous philosopher. An incredible number of diehard fans make it out to the **St Marxer Friedhof**, where Mozart is thought to be buried – no one is quite sure where his bones actually lie. Finally, for tram-lovers, the **Strassenbahnmuseum** beckons in the far southeast of the district.

## Hundertwasserhaus and KunstHausWien

In 1983, following his philosophy that "the straight line is godless", Friedensreich Hundertwasser, and his colleague Josef Krawina, transformed a dour apartment block on the corner of Löwengasse and Kegelgasse into **Hundertwasserhaus** (Ⓦ www.hundertwasserhaus.com; tram #1 to Hetzgasse), a higgledy-piggledy, kitsch, childlike jumble of brightly coloured textures that caught the popular imagination, while enraging the architectural establishment. It certainly runs the

### Friedensreich Hundertwasser (1928–2000)

Born in Vienna, under the name Friedrich Stowasser, **Friedensreich Hundertwasser** was brought up singlehandedly by his Jewish mother, who wisely had him baptized and enrolled him into the Hitler Youth shortly after the Anschluss, thus saving both their lives. Having spent just three months training as an artist at the Akademie der bildenden Künste, Hundertwasser left formal education in 1948 and shortly afterwards adopted his *nom de plume*. He established himself as an artist in the 1950s, using distinctive coiling forms to produce "kaleidoscopic landscapes", reminiscent of Gustav Klimt, with a dash of Paul Klee. In the late 1960s, at the height of the hippy era, he achieved even greater notoriety for his speeches given in the nude, one of which was his architecture boycott manifesto *Los von Loos* (Down with Loos), in which he attacked the modernist establishment.

In many ways, Hundertwasser anticipated the current, widely accepted critique of modernism – that its emphasis on machine-like, undecorated flat surfaces was dehumanizing and alienating – stressing green issues and arguing for architectural variety. However, as an unrepentant hippy, experienced self-publicist and shrewd businessman, he also made no small number of enemies along the way, not least among contemporary Viennese architects, who felt his forays into their art form – his "painted boxes" – were crass, irreverent and populist. As one critic put it, his wavy lines and individually designed windows are akin to "a nineteenth-century quack flogging his bottles of coloured horsepiss as a miracle cure for all diseases".

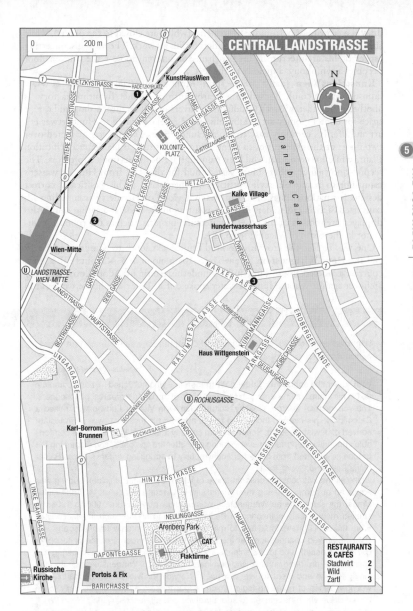

gamut of styles, consisting of a frenzy of oriel windows, loggias, shiny ceramic pillars, glass embellishments, a gilded onion dome, roof gardens and even a slice of the pre-1983 building.

Residents were none too happy when hordes of pilgrims began ringing on their doorbells, asking to be shown round, so Hundertwasser obliged with an even tackier shopping arcade opposite, called **Kalke Village** (daily 9am–6pm; free), providing a café (with a stream running along the bar) and information centre to draw the crowds away from the apartments (which are closed to the public), while simultaneously increasing the sales outlets for his artwork. The most disconcerting aspect of his architecture is his penchant for uneven floors ("the uneven floor becomes a symphony, a melody to the feet").

**KunstHausWien** (daily 10am–7pm; Mon €4.50, Tues–Sun €9; ⓦ www .kunsthauswien.com), housed in a nearby former Thonet furniture factory, is another of Hundertwasser's Gaudíesque conversions; it features a shop and café, a space for contemporary art exhibitions and a gallery devoted to Hundertwasser's art and life. It's certainly easy to mock Hundertwasser's *bons mots*, scattered over two floors of the gallery, not to mention inventions such as his Water Purification Plant, while his colourful, childlike paintings are not everyone's cup of tea. The second-floor gallery offers more varied food for thought, from Hundertwasser's campaign to retain old-style Austrian number plates to his politically correct designs for national flags. You can watch a video of Hundertwasser sailing his converted Sicilian salt trader, *Regentag*, painting in the nude and eating soup. Also displayed are models of his other architectural projects, such as the rubbish incinerator in the north of Vienna; see p.183.

One way to lose the crowds is to head four blocks south to Kundmanngasse 19 and the **Haus Wittgenstein** (Mon–Thurs 10am–noon & 3–4.30pm; €3), a grey, concrete-rendered house built in the modernist spirit of Adolf Loos, the very architect against whom Hundertwasser spoke out in 1968. The house was built in

## Ludwig Wittgenstein (1889–1951)

*Whatever can be said can be said clearly, and that of which one cannot speak, one must remain silent about.*

*Tractatus Logico-Philosophicus*

With such pithy aphorisms, **Ludwig Wittgenstein** – who published just one complete text in his entire lifetime – made his name as one of the world's greatest philosophers. The youngest of a large, wealthy, cultured family in Vienna, Ludwig was raised a Catholic like his mother, though his father, a leading industrialist, was a Protestant convert of Jewish descent. Sceptical from an early age, Ludwig rejected his comfortable upbringing, reportedly never wearing a tie after the age of 23, and dispersing the fortune he inherited from his father anonymously to struggling writers such as Rainer Maria Rilke and Georg Trakl.

Like all the Wittgenstein children (three of whom committed suicide), Ludwig was educated at home, entering the Gymnasium in **Linz** at the age of 14 (Adolf Hitler, almost the same age as Wittgenstein, was a fellow pupil). From 1906 to 1908, he studied mechanical engineering in Berlin, completing his research in Manchester. From there, his interests shifted to mathematics and eventually to philosophy – in 1911 he arrived unannounced at the Cambridge college rooms of the philosopher **Bertrand Russell**, who took a shine to the eccentric young Austrian, considering him "passionate, profound, intense and domineering". In 1913, Wittgenstein inherited the family fortune and went to live in a hut in Norway for two years, meditating and writing a series of notes on logic, which he put forward as his degree, only to be turned down when he refused to add a preface and references. During World War I, in between winning several medals for bravery, and being taken prisoner on the Italian front, he completed his *Tractatus Logico-Philosophicus*, seventy pages of musings on a wide range of subjects, including logic, ethics, religion, science, mathematics, mysticism and, of course, linguistics.

After the war, Wittgenstein handed the rest of his fortune over to his brothers and sisters. He trained as a teacher, writing a spelling dictionary for schools, and working the late 1920s by Margarethe Stonborough-Wittgenstein, a leading light among the Viennese intelligentsia, a personal friend of Freud and the sister of the philosopher Ludwig Wittgenstein. She employed the architect Paul Engelmann, a pupil of Loos, but her brother couldn't resist getting involved. As rigorous in his architecture as in his philosophical thinking, Wittgenstein advocated an austere functionalism, eschewing bourgeois trappings such as lampshades, carpets and curtains. His sister no doubt saw the funny side of making her 1905 wedding portrait, by Secession artist Gustav Klimt, the focal point of the house's implacably minimalist interior. The building now belongs to the Bulgarian embassy – hence the bronze statues of the Slav saints, Cyril and Methodius, in the garden – who use it for exhibitions of Bulgarian art.

To the west, on the other side of Landstrasser Hauptstrasse, two blocks up Rochusgasse, the little-known and rather unusual **Karl-Borromäus-Brunnen** was erected in 1909 by the sculptor Josef Engelhart, one of the founders of the Secession, and the Slovene architect Josip Plečnik. Set within its own little sunken square, whose entrances are flanked by flowerpots sporting rams' and eagles' heads, the fountain is centred on a plain triangular obelisk, shaped like a three-leaved clover, and covered with salamanders, bog-eyed frogs and assorted reptiles. Rings of cherubs holding hands dance beneath the leaves, while above, three groups of diminutive, free-standing figures tell the story of the saint, to whom the Karlskirche is also dedicated (see p.104).

in several villages south of Vienna. Prone to pulling a pupil's hair if he or she failed to understand algebra, he wasn't greatly liked by the locals, and eventually returned to Vienna to design a house for his sister, Margarethe (see p.128). In 1927, Wittgenstein came into contact with members of the **Vienna Circle**, a group of philosophers, scientists and mathematicians, including Karl Popper, Kurt Gödel, Rudolf Carnap and Moritz Schlick, who rejected traditional philosophy and espoused, instead, logical positivism. The Circle had chosen *Tractatus* as their working text, but their interpretation of it as an anti-metaphysical tract infuriated Wittgenstein, who preferred to dwell on its ethical and mystical aspects.

He was persuaded to return to Cambridge in 1929, putting forward *Tractatus* as his PhD, and consoling his examiners – among them Russell – with the remark, "Don't worry, I know you'll never understand it." He became a legend in his own lifetime: scruffily dressed, discussing philosophy with his chambermaid, devouring American pulp fiction, delivering lectures without notes, gesticulating violently and cursing himself at his own stupidity or maintaining long silences. Such was his ambivalence towards the smug, unnatural world of academia, and his conviction that philosophy precludes improvement, that he frequently tried to dissuade his students from continuing with the subject. He succeeded in persuading his lover, a promising young mathematician called **Francis Skinner**, to give up his studies and become a factory mechanic.

In 1939, Wittgenstein acquired **British citizenship** and returned to Vienna (by now part of Nazi Germany) to secure the declassification of his family as Jewish. Wittgenstein considered it intolerable to be teaching philosophy in time of war, so he took a job as a porter at London's Guy's Hospital and as a lab assistant in Newcastle's Royal Victoria Infirmary researching wound shock. In 1946, he fell in love with another undergraduate, a medic forty years his junior called Ben Richards, with whom he stayed until his death from prostate cancer in 1951. He is buried in Cambridge.

Another arresting architectural sight is the **Portois & Fix** building, one block west of the fountain, at Ungargasse 59–61. Designed by Max Fabiani in 1900, this Jugendstil building copies Otto Wagner's innovative use of tiling for the facade of his Majolikahaus (see p.108). Instead of Wagner's more conventional floral pattern, however, Fabiani creates a strikingly modern, abstract, dappled effect with his tiles in various shades of lime green and brown, topped by a decorative wrought-iron balustrade.

## Along Rennweg

"East of Rennweg, the Orient begins" is one of Prince Metternich's much-quoted aphorisms, though he clearly meant a bit further along the road than his own house at no. 27 (now the Italian embassy), where he lived until forced to flee the city in 1848. **Rennweg** runs for several kilometres through Landstrasse towards Hungary, but the section close to the Belvedere has always had a certain cachet. Nowadays, the streets immediately north are more desirable, dotted with embassies, among them the German, British and Russian legations. The last two are provided with their own churches, a red-brick Anglican one and an onion-domed Orthodox one, both on Jaurèsgasse.

When **Otto Wagner** built himself a "town house" at Rennweg 3 in 1891, it was clearly still des res. Now known as the Palais Hoyos and occupied by the Serbian embassy, this early Wagner work is very much in the Ringstrasse style, with its elaborate wrought-iron balconies, but you can discern hints of his later work in touches such as the projecting cornice and the very fine reliefwork in the upper floor. Wagner also designed the houses on either side, including no. 5, where Gustav Mahler lived from 1898 to 1907 (see p.98).

Close by, on Rennweg, stands the **Gardekirche**, completed by Nicolo Pacassi in 1763, but refaced in a rather dour, Neoclassical style just six years later. The Rococo interior, however, was left alone, and still retains its richly gilded stuccowork, ribbed dome, bull's-eye windows and lantern. Built as the chapel of the imperial hospital, it was handed over to the Polish Guards in 1782, holds services in Polish and is popularly known as the Polnische Kirche.

## Belvedere

Forget the Hofburg or even Schönbrunn – the **Belvedere**, to the south of Rennweg, is the finest palace complex in the whole of Vienna, at least from the outside. Two magnificent Baroque mansions, designed in the early eighteenth century by Lukas von Hildebrandt, face each other across a sloping formal garden, commanding a superb view over central Vienna. The man for whom all this was built was **Prince Eugène of Savoy**, Austria's greatest military leader (see p.133), whose campaigns against the Turks enabled the city, at last, to expand beyond the walls of the old town. Today, the loftier of the two palaces, the Oberes Belvedere, houses a popular art gallery, with an unrivalled collection of paintings by Gustav Klimt plus a few choice works by contemporaries such as Egon Schiele and Oskar Kokoschka.

Prince Eugène himself was a great patron of the arts, but he left no direct heirs. After his death in 1736, a distant cousin, Anna Victoria, inherited the estate and sold off his possessions. The menagerie fell into disrepair, but Emperor Karl VI bought the prince's personal library, which now resides in the Prunksaal of the Nationalbibliothek (see p.79). Finally, in 1752, the Belvedere itself was snapped up by Empress Maria Theresia, who used it to house the Habsburgs' art collection, and opened the palace gardens to the public in 1779.

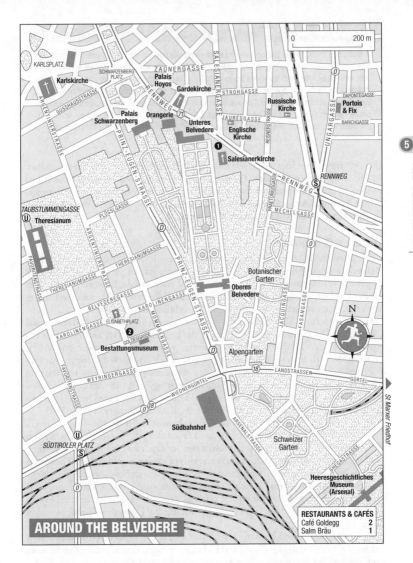

.. 

The imperial art collection moved into the purpose-built Kunsthistorisches Museum in the 1890s, while the Oberes Belvedere was taken over by **Archduke Franz Ferdinand** until his assassination in Sarajevo in 1914. He stayed here infrequently, preferring to reside at his Bohemian estate, since his wife was snubbed by the Habsburgs. Thanks to the patronage of Archduchess Valerie, Emperor Franz-Josef's daughter, the ailing composer **Anton Bruckner** was granted the ground-floor flat in the gatehouse of the Oberes Belvedere in July 1895 and spent the remaining sixteen months of his life here.

After World War I, both palaces were used as state art galleries (as they are today), though under the Austro-fascists (1934–38), Chancellor **Kurt Schuschnigg** also

## Visiting the Belvedere

A **ticket** to the Oberes Belvedere or Unteres Belvedere costs €9.50; entrance to both costs €13.50. Both galleries are open daily from 10am to 6pm (Ⓦ www.belvedere .at), with the Unteres Belvedere open until 9pm on Wednesdays. Entry to the gardens is free. You'll find a pleasant café on the ground floor in the east wing of Oberes Belvedere, and a pub called *Salm Bräu* round the corner from the Unteres Belvedere, on Rennweg (see p.130). The easiest way to reach the Oberes Belvedere is to hop on tram #D; to reach the Unteres Belvedere, take tram #71 from the Ringstrasse.

chose to reside here, before he was interned by the Nazis following the Anschluss. In 1955, the **Austrian State Treaty**, or Staatsvertrag, was signed by the Allied Powers in the Marmorsaal of the Oberes Belvedere. Fifteen years later, the superpower **Stategic Arms Limitation Talks** (SALT) were opened in the same room by the then Foreign Minister, Kurt Waldheim.

### Unteres Belvedere

Completed in 1716 at the very bottom of the formal gardens, the **Unteres Belvedere** (Lower Belvedere) is a relatively simple garden palace, built for Prince Eugène's personal use, rather than for affairs of state. Inside, however, it preserves more of its lavish original decor than the Oberes Belvedere, and is now used, along with the adjacent Orangerie, for temporary exhibitions.

The architectural highlight of the interior, the richly decorated **Marmorsaal** (Marble Hall), extends over two floors at the building's central axis. The hall is a hymn to Prince Eugène's military prowess, white stucco trophies and reliefs contrasting with the rich red marbling. Extra depth is achieved through trompel'oeil niches and balconies, and illusory moulding, leading up to Martino Altomonte's fresco featuring Prince Eugène enjoying his apotheosis in the guise of Apollo. At ground level, admire the original lead statues from the Donnerbrunnen on Neuer Markt (see p.48), sculpted by Georg Raphael Donner (1693–1741).

At the far end of the wing, the **Groteskensaal** – now the shop – has a "grotesque" decor of birds and beasts, and fanciful floral murals. The inspiration for this style of painting, very fashionable in its day, came from ancient Roman wall decoration, discovered during excavations of underground rooms. The rooms became known as "grottos" and the style of decor was dubbed "grotesque". Next comes the **Marmorgalerie**, a richly stuccoed white-and-red reception room built by Prince Eugène to house his trio of classical statues from Herculaneum. Now in Dresden, these inspired the Neoclassical sculptures by Domenico Parodi in niches along the walls.

By far the most mind-blowing room, though, is the adjacent **Goldkabinett**, a cabinet of mirrors, dating from Maria Theresia's reign, dotted with oriental vases and adorned with yet more "grotesques" painted onto a vast expanse of gaudy, 23-carat-gold panelling. *The Apotheosis of Prince Eugène*, displayed here (or in the adjacent room), is an explosion of marble by the Dresden court sculptor Balthasar Permoser, in which a tangle of figures struggles to stay on the plinth. The prince is depicted in full armour, trampling on the enemy, while attempting modestly to muffle the horn of Fame.

### The gardens

The Belvedere's formal **gardens** (daily: April–Oct 6am to dusk; Nov–March 6.30am to dusk; free) are laid out on a wide slope, punctuated with box hedges,

## Prince Eugène of Savoy (1663–1736)

The Austrians have never enjoyed the greatest of military reputations, so it comes as little surprise that their most revered military figure is a Frenchman, **Prince Eugène of Savoy**. His first taste of warfare came at the age of 20, when he offered his services to Emperor Leopold I, partly to avenge his brother, Louis Julius, who had recently died fighting the Turks. Eugène immediately fought in the front line against the 1683 Turkish siege of Vienna, earning himself a pair of golden spurs for his bravery. Subsequently, Leopold gave him command of a regiment; by 30, he was a field marshal. After his victory over the Turks at Zenta in 1697 helped win back Hungary for the Habsburgs, he was made president of the Imperial War Council. His capture of Belgrade in 1718 was the single most important act in making Western Europe safe from the Ottomans. In between times, he even fought against his fellow countryman, Louis XIV, in the Spanish Wars of Succession (1701–14), assisting the Duke of Marlborough in the victories at Blenheim, Oudenarde and Malplaquet. Meanwhile, back in Vienna, he became a great patron of the arts, building fabulous Baroque palaces, and amassing a huge library, art collection and menagerie.

Very little is known about the prince's childhood or personal life. Born in **Paris** into a leading aristocratic family, Eugène was brought up in extraordinary circumstances. His mother, the Countess of Soissons, was not only a mistress of Louis XIV, but also a wild party animal, with a penchant for intrigue and black magic. She was eventually exiled from France in 1680, on suspicion of having poisoned her husband, and of plotting to kill the king himself. Whether the infant Eugène participated in the trans-vestite orgies in his childhood home will never be known. He remained unmarried all his life, and there is no mention of his ever having taken a mistress. Whether this was due to his own sexual preference, his troubled relationship with his mother, or his notoriously unprepossessing appearance, remains a mystery. Certainly, the Duchess of Orléans' description of him as a boy is far from flattering: "It is true that his eyes are not ugly, but his nose ruins his face; he has two large teeth which are visible all the time. He is always dirty and has lanky hair which he never curls… and an upper lip so narrow that he cannot close his mouth." As a result of the child's physical deficiencies, Louis XIV decided he should be brought up for the church rather than follow a military career, and denied him admission into the French army in 1683. Louis lived to rue his decision when the prince went on to repeatedly humiliate him on the battlefield.

fountains, waterfalls and statuary, and centred on a grand vista culminating in the magnificent Oberes Belvedere itself. The central axis, flanked by statues of the Eight Muses, leads up to the **Lower Cascade**, a giant shell held up by tritons and sea nymphs. To either side are sunken bosquets, or hedge gardens, two circular and two square, with statues of Pluto and Proserpina from the Underworld. The balustrades that line the steps either side of the cascade are peppered with putti representing the seasons, and, beyond, the first of the sphinxes for which the Belvedere is famous. Fearsome beasts spurt water over the crest of the **Upper Cascade**, from where the water flows over a set of steps. The upper section of the garden was meant to represent Olympus, but its Greek gods were replaced in the nineteenth century by yet more sphinxes.

The main entrance of the Oberes Belvedere looks south onto the busy Landstrasser Gürtel, its wonderful wrought-iron gateway flanked by standing lions clasping the Savoy coat of arms. The prince himself, a keen gardener, brought rare and exotic plants and trees from all over the world to his garden. He also established a **menagerie**, with a lion, a wolf, a porcupine, several ostriches, a cassowary

133

and a pet eagle that he fed by hand every day. East of the Oberes Belvedere, its ground plan of radial paths can still be seen.

East of the main entrance on Landstrasser Gürtel, Europe's oldest **Alpengarten** (April–July daily 10am–6pm; €3.20), was founded in 1803. It's a small, walled garden, packed with hardy alpine heathers, shrubs and flowers that stick close to the rockery to escape the chilling winds. North of the Alpengarten lies the university's **Botanischer Garten** (Easter–Oct daily 9am to 1hr before dusk; free), founded in 1754, and as large again as the Belvedere's formal gardens. The layout is more like an English park, with a woodier section popular with red squirrels, sloping down to another pseudo-alpine shrubbery near the Mechelgasse entrance.

## Oberes Belvedere

Completed in 1724, the **Oberes Belvedere** (Upper Belvedere) is twice as grand as the Unteres Belvedere. Its unusual roofline, like a succession of green tents, seems to echo the camps erected by the Turks during the siege of Vienna; others have interpreted the domed octagonal pavilions as quasi-mosques. The whole building was purpose-built for the prince's lavish masked balls, receptions and firework displays. Guests would pull up in their coaches underneath the central *sala terrena*, thickly adorned with white stucco, its four columns decorated with military trophies and held up by writhing Atlantes.

Originally an open arcade, the *sala terrena* was glassed in during the nineteenth century and is now the main entrance to the museum. If you're here for the Klimts and Schieles, head straight upstairs to the **Marmorsaal**, a lighter and loftier concoction than the one in the Unteres Belvedere; it was here that the Austrian State Treaty of 1955 was signed, guaranteeing the withdrawal of foreign troops in return for Austria's neutrality.

### Wien around 1900: Gustav Klimt

Beyond the smattering of Impressionist and Secession works that lie to the right of the Marmorsaal, two rooms display the gallery's major works by **Gustav Klimt** (1862–1918). The most famous is *The Kiss*, displayed behind a protective glass shield, and depicting Klimt himself embracing his long-term mistress, Emilie Flöge. Klimt's use of gilding, derived partly from his engraver father, proved extremely popular; the painting was bought for the Austrian state during the Kunstschau of 1908 (see p.109), a rare seal of official approval for an artist whose work was mostly frowned upon by the establishment.

Klimt's ethereal 1898 *Portrait of Sonja Knips* marked his breakthrough as an independent artist, and was the first of several **portrait commissions** of the wives of the city's wealthy Jewish businessmen. In a later example, the 1906 *Portrait of Fritza Riedler*, Klimt's love of ornamentation comes to the fore, with the sitter engulfed in Egyptian eyes and sporting a Velázquez headdress. *Judith I*, an early gold work from 1901, depicts the Jewish murderess in sexual ecstasy having beheaded Holofernes. Every summer Klimt spent his vacations at the Flöge family house on the Attersee in the Salzkammergut. As a way of relaxing, he painted **landscapes** alfresco straight onto a square canvas, without preliminary sketches. Like Monet, he used to row out into the middle of the lake and set up his easel on board, finishing the works off in his Vienna studio. Rich, almost flat, one-dimensional tapestries of colour – some almost pointillist – they're easy on the eye, and sold extremely well in the salons.

The gallery has recently been forced to relinquish five Klimts, including two portraits of Adele Bloch-Bauer, which came into its hands via the Nazis. After a seven-year **legal battle**, the 90-year-old niece of Bloch-Bauer succeeded in winning back the paintings in 2006, and promptly sold the lot at auction for more than $327 million – they are now in the Neue Galerie in New York.

From one of the rooms dedicated to the artist's work, you can look down into the richly gilded, octagonal **Schlosskapelle**, looking pretty much today as it would have in Eugène's day.

## Egon Schiele and Oskar Kokoschka

Klimt actively supported younger artists like **Egon Schiele** (1890–1918), even, in the case of Schiele, passing on his young models after he'd finished with them. Such was the case with the 17-year-old Wally Neuzil, with whom Schiele enjoyed a four-year affair. In *Death and the Maiden* – a disturbingly dispassionate farewell portrait to Wally, painted in 1915, the year they split up – Wally clings to Schiele, in deathly, detached decay. The gallery also owns one of Schiele's most famous erotic oil paintings, *The Embrace*, a double nude portrait of the artist and his model.

Schiele went on to marry **Edith Harms**, who came from a respectable middle-class family, that same year. *The Artist's Wife* was bought directly from the artist by the gallery, though only after the director had got Schiele to repaint Edith's tartan skirt, which he felt was too "proletarian". Edith's pregnancy in spring 1918 was the inspiration for *The Family*, Schiele's last great painting, which remained unfinished at the time of his death from the influenza epidemic that had claimed Edith's life just three days earlier (and Klimt's eight months before that). Schiele is the father figure, the child is Schiele's nephew, Toni, but Edith had reservations about posing nude, and is clearly not the model for the mother. Though melancholic, the painting is positively upbeat compared with the harrowing *Mother with Two Children* from 1915, with its skeletal mother and two mannequin-like children.

Displayed alongside Schiele's works are a couple of paintings by **Richard Gerstl**, including his manic *Laughing Self-Portrait* from 1908. This is a deeply disturbing image given that its subject was, in fact, in a deep depression at the time – his lover, Mathilde, whose portrait also hangs here, had gone back to her husband, the composer Arnold Schönberg. Gerstl committed suicide the very same year at the age of just 28.

The gallery's works by **Oskar Kokoschka** (1886–1980) mostly date from his first ten creative years, when he lived in Vienna. Kokoschka's portraits contrast sharply with those of Schiele. "A person is not a *still* life," Kokoschka insisted, and he encouraged his sitters to move about and talk, so as to make his portrayals more animated. Among the portraits here is one of fellow artist Carl Moll, who was stepfather to Alma Mahler (widow of the composer) with whom Kokoschka had a brief, passionate affair. Other works by Kokoschka include his primeval *Tiger-Lion*, painted in London Zoo, and *Still Life with Lamb and Hyacinth* from 1910, painted in the kitchen of the art collector Dr Oskar Reichel, who had commissioned him to paint a portrait of his son.

## Wien 1880–1900

The rooms in the west wing, on the other side of the Marmorsaal, are given over to **late nineteenth-century art**. In the first, it's hard not to be somewhat taken aback by Max Klinger's gargantuan *Judgement of Paris*, surrounded by an incredible 3D frame, within which a bored Paris is confronted by a boldly naked goddess, while the two others get ready to strip in the wings. Giovanni Segantini's *Evil Mothers* is a misogynist piece of anti-abortion propaganda, donated by the Secession to the gallery shortly after its foundation in 1903.

Less well known, and less well thought of now, is the Austrian artist **Hans Makart** (1840–84), to whom the westernmost room is devoted. A high-society favourite who was in great demand during his lifetime, Makart had the posthumous misfortune of being one of Hitler's favourite artists. One wall is almost entirely taken up with his gigantic, triumphant flesh-fest of *Bacchus and Ariadne*; on the opposite wall in long vertical panels are four of the *Five Senses*, featuring typically sensuous Makart nudes.

Makart's fame so eclipsed several of his contemporaries, among them **Anton Romako** (1832–89), that the latter's death was rumoured to be a suicide. Compared with Makart's studied flattery, Romako's uncomfortably perceptive psychological portraits were less popular – consider how far removed from official portraiture his portrait of the Empress Elisabeth is, with its gloomy palette and its emphasis on Sisi's defensive body language. Look out, too, for Romako's most famous work, *Tegetthoff at the Naval Battle of Lissa*, which again reveals his unconventional approach; there's no hint of heroics, but simply manic fear and foreboding in the expressions of the crew.

### Biedermeier, Neoclassical and Romantic art

If you thought the previous 1880–1900 section was patchy, the top-floor galleries are positive deserts. One or two works do stand out: Scheffer von Leonhardshoff's *The Dead Saint Cecilia*, a remarkable Raphaelite religious pastiche that was a personal favourite of Franz I; the superlative Romantic *Seashore in Mist* by **Caspar David Friedrich** (1774–1840); and Gérard's rigidly Neoclassical portrait of the fabulously rich Fries family, who are deliberately posing like some sort of latter-day Holy Family.

### Baroque and Medieval art

Back down on the ground floor, the **Baroque art** collection in the east wing features studies for larger works by all the great Austrian fresco painters, among them Paul Troger, Franz Maulbertsch and Johann Maichael Rottmayr. There are also one or two real masterpieces such as **Angelika Kaufmann**'s relaxed *Portrait of Lord John Simpson*, executed during her lengthy sojourn in England. Look out, too, for the room of bizarre, hyperrealist "character heads", carved by the eccentric sculptor **Franz Xaver Messerschmidt** (1732–83), which are usually displayed here.

Over in the west wing, the **medieval art** collection includes several paintings by the fifteenth-century Tyrolean artist **Michael Pacher**, whose works mark the transition between the more static Gothic period and the love of perspective that heralds the Renaissance. The same is true of the seven large-scale works by **Rueland Frueauf**, who, like Pacher, spent most of his career in Salzburg. Look out, too, for two panels from the altarpiece in Vienna's Schottenstift (see p.58). The most remarkable work here, however, is the vast crucifixion altarpiece, probably carved in Vienna in the 1440s, from a church in Znaim (Znojmo) in South Moravia. The main crucifixion scene features an incredible crush of polychrome figures and animals in high relief fighting, mourning and gesticulating.

# Wien Hauptbahnhof and Wieden

Having lost all its wonderful nineteenth-century railway stations in World War II, Vienna has recently destroyed the postwar **Südbahnhof**, on the other side of the Landstrasser Gürtel from the Belvedere, to make way for **Wien Hauptbahnhof**, the city's new main station (due to be completed in 2015).

West of Prinz-Eugen-Strasse, **Wieden** – Vienna's fourth district – is worth a mention for the **Bestattungsmuseum** (Undertakers' Museum), run by the state funeral company, at Goldeggasse 19. It's open by appointment (Mon–Fri

## Adolf Eichmann

The innocuous-looking Kammer für Arbeiter und Angestellte (Chamber of Workers and Employees), Prinz-Eugen-Strasse 20–22, on the west side of the Belvedere, was the site of the Palais Rothschild. Appropriated by the Nazis, it became home to the euphemistically named "Central Office for Jewish Emigration", where **Adolf Eichmann** oversaw forced expulsion of thousands of Jews from Austria and relieved them of their possessions. At his trial, Eichmann remembered his days there as "the happiest and most successful of my life". Round the corner, on Theresianumgasse 16–18, another former Rothschild palace served as the headquarters of the Nazi SD, the security service of the SS. Both palaces were destroyed in World War II.

noon–3pm; €4.50; ☎501 95) for guided tours (in German), so this is really only for those who share the morbid Viennese fascination with death. Many Viennese still aspire to the custom of magnificent funerals, known as having a "beautiful corpse" or *schöne Leiche*; only eighteen percent opt for cremation. Inside the museum, you can admire the elaborate costumes of undertakers over the years, their banners, equipage and so on, and learn about the more bizarre rituals associated with Viennese funerals. Dead Habsburgs, for instance, used to have their faces smashed in, to make them appear more humble in the eyes of God, and it was common practice to install a bell inside the coffin, for the deceased to ring in case they came back to life. There are some wonderful examples of funereal merchandising: matches, photo albums, toy cars, and, best of all, undertakers' cigarettes, with the motto *Rauchen sichert Arbeitsplätze* ("Smoking guarantees work"). The *pièce de résistance*, though, is the reusable coffin instigated by Emperor Josef II.

# Arsenal and the Heeresgeschichtliches Museum

A short distance south of the Belvedere, down Arsenalstrasse, lies the city's former **Arsenal**, a huge complex of barracks and munitions factories, built on these strategic heights in the wake of the 1848 revolution. An integral part of the Arsenal was the **Heeresgeschichtliches Museum** (daily 9am–5pm; €5.10, free first Sun of month; ⓦwww.hgm.or.at), the city's first purpose-built museum, housed in a marvellous red-brick neo-Byzantine edifice by Theophil Hansen. Designed to glorify the Imperial Army, it's adorned with light-brick crosses and machicolated crenellations.

The ticket office and cloakroom are in the vaulted foyer or **Feldherrnhalle** (Hall of the Generals), crowded with life-sized marble statues of pre-1848 Austrian military leaders. Pick up the excellent free audioguide (in English) and head upstairs to the **Ruhmshalle** (Hall of Fame), a huge domed, arcaded hall of polished marble, decorated with worthy frescoes depicting Austrian military victories over the centuries.

### From the Thirty Years' War to the Austro-Prussian War

The museum kicks off with the **Thirty Years' War** (1618–48), to the left as you reach the top of the stairs, and tells the story of the rise of the musketeer over the pikeman – there's an informative video showing how hellish it was to try and fire a musket. Beyond hang twelve huge battle paintings by the Dutch artist Pieter Snayers portraying the decisive encounters of the war.

The rich pickings to be had during the **Turkish Wars** proved a useful incentive to the imperial troops. Among the most impressive of the fine trophies displayed here is the Great Seal of Mustafa Pasha, which the Grand Vizier wore round his neck as a symbol of his absolute authority, and which fell into the hands of **Prince Eugène of Savoy** at the 1697 Battle of Zenta. Other bits and bobs relating to Prince Eugène include his minuscule vest, his marshal's baton, and the pall and cortège decorations from his state funeral. The end room contains the Grand Vizier's vast tent, which Prince Eugène later used on hunting trips. The Grand Vizier was killed at the 1716 Battle of Peterwardein, when Prince Eugène defeated an Ottoman army more than twice the size of his. Also displayed is the "Mortar of Belgrade", a shot from which hit the Turkish powder magazine during the siege of 1717, killing three thousand Ottoman soldiers in one go and considerably aiding Prince Eugène's victory.

To continue chronologically, head for the east wing. Most items here relate to the **Napoleonic Wars**: Field-Marshal Radetzky's hat, map bag and sword, Prince Karl von Schwarzenberg's hat, sword and medals, and Napoleon's Russian greatcoat, thought to have been worn during his exile on Elba.

## The road to World War I

The ground-floor west wing displays the glorious **uniforms of the Imperial Army** and their opponents. At the start of the twentieth century, the Habsburgs had the best-dressed army in Europe – while the other superpowers were donning dull khaki for camouflage, their pristine white and cream won the prize for the most elegant uniform at the 1900 Paris Exhibition. The uniforms were at their most resplendent during the ball season, and certainly had the right effect on many female guests, as Anthony Trollope's mother, visiting in 1836, swooned:

I really know nothing at once so gorgeous and picturesque as the uniform of the Hungarian noble bodyguard, with their splendid silver accoutrements, their spotted furs, uncut, hanging at their backs, and their mustard-yellow Morocco boots. The rich and beautiful skins which they all carry, apparently in the very shape in which they came off the animal, give the most striking air of primitive and almost barbarous magnificence.

By far the most famous exhibits in this wing relate to the **Archduke Franz Ferdinand**, in particular the splendid Gräf & Stift convertible in which the archduke and his wife, Sophie, were shot dead on June 28, 1914, by the Bosnian Serb terrorist Gavrilo Princip. The car still has a bullet hole in it, but even more macabre is the archduke's reverentially preserved bloodstained light-blue tunic and unblemished, slightly comical hat with green feathers (the ceremonial uniform of an Austrian cavalry general), and the chaise-longue on which he expired.

Devoted to **World War I**, the final room of the wing includes video footage of the Habsburgs' various (mostly disastrous) campaigns. The room itself is dominated by a massive 38cm Howitzer, designed by Ferdinand Porsche, which had a range of 15km. Overlooking the gun is Albin Egger-Lienz's chilling *To the Unknown Soldier*, whose repetitive image of advancing infantry perfectly captures the mechanical slaughter of modern warfare.

## Republic and Dictatorship

Beyond the café in the east wing of the ground floor, the excellent **Republic and Dictatorship** section takes you through the heady, violent interwar years that ended with the Anschluss in 1938. Period posters depict both sides of the spectrum, and there's plenty of fascinating interwar video footage. You can view the couch on which Dollfuss died during the abortive Nazi coup of 1934 (see p.258), and a bust of his successor Kurt Schuschnigg, by Anna Mahler, the composer's daughter, who was a committed Austro-fascist. Nazi memorabilia includes the bust of Hitler that once stood in the museum's Ruhmshalle.

## Naval Power

The last room in the east wing is concerned with Austria's **Naval Power**, not something normally associated with a land-locked country, though, of course, under the Habsburgs, the empire had access to the Adriatic. Amid the model ships, figureheads and nauticalia there's a model of the U-27 submarine commanded by Austria's most famous naval captain, Georg Ritter von Trapp of *Sound of Music* fame. Among the more surprising material is the video of the Austrian navy's involvement in the Boxer Rebellion, and the section on the Austrian Arctic expedition (1872–74), which discovered and named Franz Josef Land, an archipelago in the Barents Sea.

If you're keen on tanks, don't miss the **Panzergarten**, with its international parade of tanks from Soviet T34s to British Centurions.

# St Marxer Friedhof

In the 1780s, Emperor Josef II closed the inner-city cemeteries, and decreed that all burials, for health reasons, should take place outside the city walls. The first of these out-of-town graveyards was the **St Marxer Friedhof** (daily: April & Oct 7am–5pm; May & Sept 7am–6pm; June–Aug 7am–7pm; Nov–March 7am–dusk; tram #18 or #71 to St Marx stop), founded in 1784 near the Landstrasser Gürtel, closed down in 1874, and also known as the Biedermeier cemetery. It was here, on a rainy night in December 1791, that **Wolfgang Amadeus Mozart** was given a pauper's burial in an unmarked mass grave, with no one present but the gravediggers.

To contemporary minds Mozart's final journey seems particularly cruel for one widely considered the greatest composer ever; the reality is less tragic. Following Josef II's reforms, **mass burials** were the rule; only the very wealthy could afford a family vault, and the tending of individual graves was virtually unknown. Funeral services took place in churches (Mozart's was in the Stephansdom), and mourners did not customarily accompany the cortège to cemeteries. In fact, bodies could only be taken to the cemetery after nightfall, and left in the mortuary overnight for burial the next day.

By the mid-nineteenth century, when the Viennese had adopted lavish tastes for funerals and monuments, it became a scandal that no one knew where Mozart was buried. As graves were usually emptied every eight years and the bones removed to make way for more corpses, the most Mozart's wife Constanze could discover was that he had probably been buried three or four rows down from the cemetery's central monumental cross. In 1859, the **Mozart-Grab** was raised in this area, featuring a mourning angel and a pillar, broken in half to symbolize his untimely death. Nowadays, the St Marxer Friedhof gives little indication of the bleak and forbidding place it must have been in Mozart's day, having been tidied up in the early part of the twentieth century and planted with a rather lovely selection of trees.

# Strassenbahnmuseum (Tram Museum)

Occupying three brick-built sheds in the eastern corner of Landstrasse, the **Strassenbahnmuseum** (May–Sept Sat & Sun 10am–5pm; €6; ⓦwww.tram.at), on Ludwig-Koessler-Platz, houses examples of just about every type of tram that has trundled across the city, with a few buses thrown in for good measure. The vast majority sport the familiar municipal red livery, with the exception of the wartime exhibits, the horse-drawn trams from the 1870s, and the wonderful steam tram (still working). Children will be disappointed not to be able to climb on any of the exhibits, although the model tram railway in the ticket office might mollify them.

# ⑤ Mariahilf, Neubau and Josefstadt

**Mariahilf and Neubau** – Vienna's sixth and seventh districts – lie on either side of **Mariahilferstrasse**, the city's busy, mainstream shopping street, which stretches for more than 2km from the Ringstrasse to the Westbahnhof. A few minor tourist sights are scattered across both districts, but the only area that merits a stroll is the narrow network of eighteenth- and early nineteenth-century streets in Neubau known as **Spittelberg**. You might also find yourself wandering up Burggasse or Neustiftgasse, further north, in search of some of the area's numerous restaurants, cafés and pubs. The eighth district, **Josefstadt**, to the north, is a slightly more homogenous residential area, created in the eighteenth century. It, too, has its sprinkling of sights; it's also popular with students, owing to its proximity to the university.

## On and off Mariahilferstrasse

The district of Mariahilf takes its name from the **Mariahilferkirche**, the big Baroque church set back from the street between nos. 55 and 57 and providing a welcome escape from the rampant consumerism outside. The miraculous *Mariahilf* (Mary's help) picture in the main altar is actually a seventeenth-century copy of the original Passau Madonna by Lucas Cranach. One of the most striking furnishings is the *Schutzengelgruppe*, opposite the pulpit, in which a gilded angel and child are set against an iridescent blue-and-gold-curtained baldachin. Glance up to admire the ceiling frescoes by pupils of Paul Troger, and the Rococo organ, with a gilded filigree clock suspended between its pipes.

### Esterházypark and Haus des Meeres

One block south of Mariahilferstrasse, the diminutive **Esterházypark** is dominated by a Flakturm, or anti-aircraft tower, daubed with the gnomic "smashed into pieces (in the still of the night)". The hand- and footholds of an artificial climbing wall now pepper the exterior, while a sloping green-glass aviary juts out on one side. The interior houses the **Haus des Meeres** (daily 9am–6pm, Thurs until 9pm; €12.50; ⓦwww.haus-des-meeres.at), a collection of reptiles, amphibians and fish – the crocs and snakes could do with larger tanks, but the tropical fish are spectacular. So too is the tropical aviary in whose dense foliage and flora you can spot tortoises, turtles, monkeys and vibrantly colourful birds.

The Flakturm's air-raid shelter contains the Torture Museum or **Foltermuseum** (daily: April, Sept & Oct 11am–5pm May & June 10am–6pm; July & Aug 10am–8pm; €6; ⓦwww.folter.at). With various tableaux illustrating tortures through the ages, the museum treads a fine line between using torture as entertainment and putting across a serious message. The final Amnesty International video

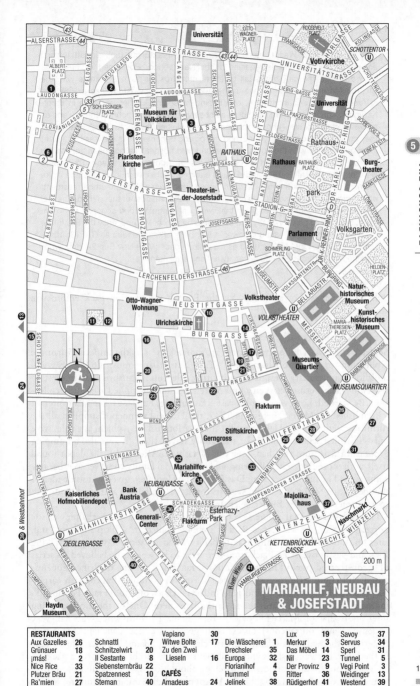

MARIAHILF, NEUBAU
& JOSEFSTADT

0 _____ 200 m

| RESTAURANTS | | | | Vapiano | 30 | Die Wäscherei | 1 | Lux | 19 | Savoy | 37 |
|---|---|---|---|---|---|---|---|---|---|---|---|
| Aux Gazelles | 26 | Schnattl | 7 | Witwe Bolte | 17 | Drechsler | 35 | Merkur | 3 | Servus | 34 |
| Grünauer | 18 | Schnitzelwirt | 20 | Zu den Zwei | | Europa | 32 | Das Möbel | 14 | Sperl | 31 |
| ¡más! | 2 | Il Sestante | 8 | Lieseln | 16 | Florianihof | 4 | Nil | 23 | Tunnel | 5 |
| Nice Rice | 33 | Siebensternbräu | 22 | | | Hummel | 6 | Der Provinz | 9 | Vegi Point | 3 |
| Plutzer Bräu | 21 | Spatzennest | 10 | CAFÉS | | Jelinek | 38 | Ritter | 36 | Weidinger | 13 |
| Ra'mien | 27 | Steman | 40 | Amadeus | 24 | Kafka | 29 | Rüdigerhof | 41 | Westend | 39 |
| Schilling | 15 | Una Abraham | 11 | Bar Italia | 28 | | | St Josef | 25 | Wirr | 12 |

## Flaktürme

Built during World War II, Vienna's six unsightly **Flaktürme** (anti-aircraft towers) are among the few visible legacies of the Nazi period. Positioned in three sets of two across the city, these tall concrete monstrosities form a triangle with the Stephansdom at the centre: two in the Augarten in Leopoldstadt (see p.158), two in Arenbergpark in Landstrasse, one behind MuseumsQuartier, and one in Ester-házypark. The towers were used both as observation posts to light up the sky and as anti-aircraft gun posts – hence their name FLAK (Flieger Abwehr Kanone). In addition, they could house up to thirty thousand troops and become completely self-sufficient in an emergency, with their own underground field hospital, munitions factory, water and power supply, and even air filters in case of a poison-gas attack. The towers were built to last; after the war the Nazis planned to clad them in marble and make them into victory monuments. Many Viennese view them with acute embarrassment; others argue that they serve as a useful and indelible reminder of that period. The real reason for their survival, though, is that, with walls of reinforced concrete up to 5m thick, they would be very costly and difficult to demolish. More recently the Flaktürme have been put to good use: one tower in Arenbergpark, rebranded as CAT (Contemporary Art Tower) by MAK, is used as exhibition space (May–Nov Sun 2–6pm), while the one in Esterházypark houses an aviary and aquarium.

pulls no punches, however. Ask for the English information pack before you wander round.

### Hofmobiliendepot

Set back from Mariahilferstrasse itself, at Andreasgasse 7, is the Imperial Furniture Collection or **Hofmobiliendepot** (Tues–Sun 10am–6pm; €6.90; ⓦ www .hofmobiliendepot.at). Despite its uninviting title, this is a surprisingly interesting museum – like a cross between a junk warehouse and an applied arts study collection. Be warned, however, that it's vast – fascinating, but best taken at a canter.

Established by Maria Theresia in 1747, the Hofmobiliendepot supplied all the furniture needed by the Habsburgs for their various palaces, which, as a rule, were only furnished when members of the family stayed there. It was also a dumping ground for furniture that had gone out of fashion. After 1918, the depot found itself with more than 650,000 items, and no imperial family to serve, so it became a museum. The first huge room, **Das Erbe** (The Heritage), gives you some idea of the sheer scale of the collection, with its forests of candelabra and coat stands, not to mention the bevy of Biedermeier spittoons.

The **Habsburgersaal** panders to imperial nostalgia with Winterhalter's classic portrait of Sisi, Crown Prince Rudolf's ebony highchair, scallop-shell cot, and, later on, funeral crown, while Maximilian of Mexico's serpent-wrapped walking stick and vastly oversized black sombrero have to be seen to be believed. A series of reconstructed **period interiors** follows, ranging from one of Prince Eugène's wonderful chinoiserie rooms to Rudolf's Turkish boudoir, draped with carpets snapped up on his oriental Grand Tour in 1881 – check out, too, Franz Ferdinand's monster walk-through wardrobe from the Belvedere. One of the most arresting interiors is that of Maria Ludovica d'Este, Franz I's third wife, who had very expensive (and outrageous) tastes. You get to see her penchant for South American–themed murals, featuring genocidal acts by Spanish invaders; downstairs in the foyer, her vogueish Egyptian cabinet from the Hofburg is worth a peek.

Displays on the upper floors are patchier, though the special exhibitions can be fun. The second-floor highlight is the **Hygienemöbel** (Sanitary Furniture), which displays imperial commodes, bedpans and spittoons through the ages. On the third floor, there are some Jugendstil pieces by the likes of Josef Hoffmann, original furniture from Adolf Loos's *Café Museum* (see p.209) and Mies van der Rohe's Tugendhat Haus, plus an entire reconstruction of Ernst Plischke's 1928 modernist design for potter Lucie Rie's bedroom in London. Before you head back down the stairs, however, make sure you take a look inside the **Wappensaal**, a library from a swanky villa in Mödling, its ceiling smothered in imperial coats-of-arms, originally designed in the 1880s to glorify the Habsburgs, but later modified to give it a more Pan-German character.

### Haydn-Memorial

The composer **Josef Haydn** (1732–1809) spent much of his life in the service of the Esterházy family at their seats in Eisenstadt and Esterháza (now in Hungary). With the death of his chief patron, Prince Nikolaus Esterházy, in 1790, however, he was free to settle permanently in Vienna. In 1793, he bought a house two blocks south of Mariahilferstrasse, in which he lived until his death in 1809; it's now the **Haydn-Memorial** (Tues–Sun 10am–1pm & 2–6pm; €4; ⓦ www.wienmuseum .at), at Haydngasse 19. Here he wrote, among other works, his great oratorio *Die Schöpfung* (The Creation), and spent his last few months sitting at home, silently handing visitors a specially printed calling card, which began with a quote from one of his own texts, "Gone is all my strength..." At the time of his death, Vienna was occupied by Napoleonic troops, but such was his renown, that – so the story goes – Napoleon himself ordered a guard of honour to be stationed outside his house, and a French Hussars officer came and sang an aria from *Die Schöpfung* at his deathbed. Sadly, none of the original fittings survive from Haydn's day, and you'll learn little about the composer's life from this formulaic museum. The house also contains an equally unenlightening memorial room dedicated to the composer **Johannes Brahms** (1833–97), who lived near Karlsplatz.

## Spittelberg and Neubau

Few areas in the Vorstädte have retained their original eighteenth- or early nineteenth-century appearance like the half-dozen parallel, narrow cobbled streets between Siebensterngasse and Burggasse known as **Spittelberg** (ⓦ www .spittelberg.at). Traditionally a working-class and artisan quarter, it doubled as the red-light district, conveniently backing onto two sets of barracks full of sex-starved soldiers. The area was saved from demolition in the 1970s, its Baroque and Biedermeier houses restored – and inevitably gentrified – and many streets pedestrianized. While it's a pleasant place to wander any day, the small summer Saturday **craft market** around Spittelberggasse makes the stroll even more enjoyable. This functions daily during Easter and in Advent, when the streets heave with folk drinking *Glühwein* and *Punsch*. Spittelberg also boasts a dense concentration of bars, cafés and restaurants, not so much throbbing as gently swaying until the early hours.

One church worth seeking out in Neubau is the **Altlerchenfelder Kirche**, up Lerchenfelderstrasse. Begun in 1848, its neo-Romanesque exterior is a slightly sickly salmon colour, but its vast interior is spectacular, thanks to Eduard van der Nüll, architect of Vienna's opera house. The walls and the saucer-domed ceiling are absolutely smothered in mid-nineteenth-century Romantic frescoes – where most churches have stained-glass windows, this one has murals and mosaics, ranging from the small saintly roundels in the nave to the richly gilded vision of the *Seven Sanctuaries* in the apse.

## Josefstadt

**Josefstadt** – Vienna's eighth district – was laid out in the early eighteenth century and named after Emperor Josef I (1705–11). Almost immediately, the Piarists were given a large slice of the land for their monastery, the Maria-Treu Kloster, which now forms an impressive Baroque ensemble, centred on a cobbled square with its own Marian column, off Piaristengasse. Overlooking the square are the splendid convex Baroque facade, tall pediment and twin towers of the monastery church, the Hildebrandt-designed **Piaristenkirche**. The light interior is a glorious slice of High Baroque, full of playful oval shapes and faded frescoes by the youthful Franz Anton Maultbertsch, though it's difficult to see outside of services. After the young Anton Bruckner was examined on the church's still extant nineteenth-century organ, one of the judges exclaimed: "He should have been testing us!"

Close by the monastery, across Piaristengasse, facing Josefstädter Strasse, the **Theater-in-der-Josefstadt** (ⓦwww.josefstadt.org) was founded in 1788 as a variety theatre. Remodelled in Neoclassical style by Josef Kornhäusel, it reopened in 1822 with a premiere of Beethoven's *Consecration of the House* overture, conducted by the composer himself. Between the wars, the theatre director was Max Reinhardt, the great theatrical innovator who helped found the Salzburg Festival, staged incredible large-scale productions, and eventually fled to Hollywood. Today, the theatre has returned to its light-entertainment roots, staging comedies, melodramas and farce.

Three blocks north, in Hildebrandt's Baroque Palais Schönborn on Laudongasse, the folk art collection of the **Österreichisches Museum für Volkskunde** (Tues–Sun 10am–5pm,; €5; ⓦwww.volkskundemuseum.at) seems out of place in such an urban setting. Founded in 1894, the museum has been sensitively modernized, with enough variety to keep you entertained for an hour or so. Exhibits range from grass raincoats and magnificent Tyrolean wardrobes to an incredible limewood shrine to Emperor Karl I.

# Alsergrund

**Alsergrund** – Vienna's large, roughly triangular ninth district – is dominated by its medical institutions and associations. A vast swathe is taken up with the **Allgemeines Krankenhaus** or AKH (General Hospital), both old and new, originally established by Josef II in 1784. The following year, Josef founded the **Josephinum**, an academy for training military surgeons, next door. Since then, various university science faculties have relocated here, and the area remains popular with doctors and medical students, as it has been since **Freud**'s day – his museum is now Alsergrund's chief tourist attraction. Alsergrund also boasts one of the few aristocratic summer palaces to survive into the modern era, now the **Liechtenstein Museum**, home to the prince's private art collection.

## Allgemeines Krankenhaus

The **Allgemeines Krankenhaus** (General Hospital) was one of the most modern medical institutions in the world in 1784 when it replaced the Grossarmenhaus (Great Poor House). From its foundation, its overriding philosophy was therapeutic nihilism. At its best, this meant letting nature take its course, rather than relying on the quack remedies popular at the time. At its worst, it meant neglecting

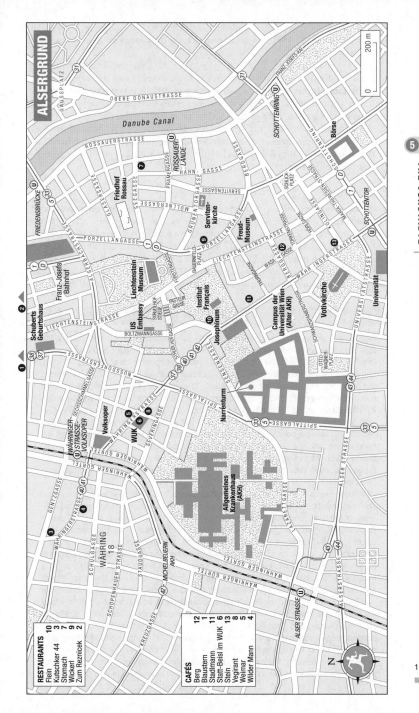

# ALSERGRUND

THE VORSTÄDTE

**RESTAURANTS**

| | |
|---|---|
| Flein | 10 |
| Kutschker 44 | 3 |
| Stomach | 7 |
| Wickerl | 9 |
| Zum Reznicek | 2 |

**CAFÉS**

| | |
|---|---|
| Berg | 12 |
| Blaustern | 11 |
| Stadtmann | 1 |
| Statt-Beisl im WUK | 6 |
| Stein | 13 |
| Vegirant | 8 |
| Weimar | 5 |
| Wilder Mann | 4 |

5

145

patients while they were alive, and then concentrating on autopsy as a means of prognosis instead. By 1850, it was claimed that the only medicine used at the AKH was cherry brandy.

East of Spitalgasse and known as the Altes Allgemeines Krankenhaus, the original buildings have been handed over to the university and converted into the **Universitätscampus Wien**. The courtyards and various bars within the complex spill over with students, especially in summer when the whole place becomes one enormous beer garden. The prime motive for exploring the old hospital court-yards, however, is to visit the former lunatic asylum of the Narrenturm (see below). West of Spitalgasse, the modern **Neues Allgemeines Krankenhaus** is one of the largest hospitals in Europe; its lengthy construction was plagued by corruption at the highest level.

## Narrenturm

Looking something like a converted gasometer, the circular, unprepossessing **Narrenturm** (Wed 3–6pm, Thurs 8–11am & Sat 10am–1pm; €2; Ⓦwww .narrenturm.at) or "Fools' Tower" is situated in a scruffy, neglected courtyard (no. 13) of the Altes Allgemeines Krankenhaus. Built in 1784 as a lunatic asylum with five floors, each housing 28 cells that feed off a circular corridor, it was nicknamed the "Guglhupf", after the ring-shaped cake. Despite its forbidding, prison-like design and slit windows, conditions were exceptionally humane. It fell into disuse

### Sigmund Freud (1856–1939)

Few people are so intimately associated with one place as **Freud** is with Vienna. He was born to a Jewish wool merchant in Freiberg, Moravia in 1856, and died in 1939 in exile in London, but in the intervening 83 years, he spent most of his life in Vienna. The family moved here when Freud was just four years old, and in 1873 he entered the university determined to be a scientist. He took three years longer than usual to complete his degree, and then decided to train as a medic at the **Allgemeines Krankenhaus**. In 1887 Freud began practising as a neuropathologist, experimenting with cocaine, electrotherapy and hypnosis, before coming up with the "pressure technique", using a couch for the first time and asking questions while pressing his hand on the patient's forehead. He later switched to the method of "free association", during which the patient says whatever comes into their mind. "The aim is modest," Freud said when describing his new science: "to turn neurotic misery into common unhappiness."

In 1896, Freud coined the term **"psychoanalysis"**, and four years later published *The Interpretation of Dreams*. The book argued that "all dreams represent the fulfill-ment of wishes", and that these wishes are often (but not always) sexual. Freud's impact on modern thought has been profound, and several of his discoveries – the death wish, the Oedipus complex, transference, the Freudian slip, penis envy, the oral, anal and phallic stages of childhood, and so on – have become common parlance. This popularization has often come at the expense of Freud's original meaning – "Freudian symbols", for example, used exclusively by Freud for dream interpretation, are now widely used simply as a day-to-day form of sexual innuendo.

In 1902, Freud founded the **Psychoanalytical Society**, which met every Wednesday evening in his apartment, his wife serving *Guglhupf* and coffee, while academic papers were read and discussed. Freud ruled his disciples with an iron hand, ejecting anyone who disagreed with him, most famously Carl Jung, in 1913. Jung later accused Freud of having slept with his sister-in-law, Minna, who lived with the family in Berggasse. In reality, Freud was a disappointingly conventional Viennese paterfa-milias. "What a terrible man! I am sure he has never been unfaithful to his wife. It is in 1866, and now houses the **Pathologisch-anatomisches Bundesmuseum** (Federal Museum of Pathological Anatomy).

The museum is popular with medical students, and it certainly helps to have a strong stomach. The ground-floor cells contain a mock-up of Dr Robert Koch's 1882 discovery of the bacillus that causes tuberculosis, an apothecary from 1820, a section on artificial limbs, a mortuary slab, wax models of TB sufferers and the odd piece of anatomy preserved in formaldehyde. If you're already feeling queasy, don't, whatever you do, venture upstairs where the cells and corridors are filled with yet more examples of abnormalities and deformities from autopsies conducted around a hundred years ago.

## Josephinum

Northeast of the **Universitätscampus Wien**, the **Josephinum** (Mon–Fri 9am–3pm, first Sat of the month 10am–2pm; €2) is housed in an austere silver-grey palace, set back from Währingerstrasse behind a set of imposing wrought-iron railings. Having observed the primitive techniques used by army surgeons at first hand during his military campaigns, Emperor Josef II set up an Institute for Military Surgery. The institute was closed in 1872, and now houses the Pharmacological Institute for Medicine and History of Medicine Institute instead – plus a museum run by the latter, known as the Museum für Geschichte der Medizin or Medizinhistorisches Museum.

quite abnormal and scandalous," reported one fan, the French poet Countess Anna de Noailles, after meeting him. He was happily married all his life to **Martha Bernays**, a good Jewish *Hausfrau*, who gave birth to and brought up six healthy children. He saw patients without appointment daily from three to four in the afternoon, using the profits to buy the (occasionally erotic) antiquities that filled his study; afterwards he would write until as late as three in the morning. Every afternoon, he walked the entire circuit of the Ringstrasse at a brisk pace; every Saturday evening he played the card game Tarock, and every Sunday in summer, Freud would don his Lederhosen, and go mushroom-picking with the family in the Wienerwald.

In 1923, he was diagnosed with **cancer of the jaw** (he was an inveterate cigar-smoker) and given five years to live. A year later, aged 68, he was granted the Freedom of Vienna, two years earlier than was the custom. As he joked to a friend, they clearly thought he was going to die. In the end, he lived another 16 years in considerable pain, taking only aspirin, undergoing 33 operations, and having his mouth scraped daily to accommodate an ill-fitting prosthesis.

Shortly after the **Anschluss** in March 1938, the SS raided Freud's flat. Martha, ever the accommodating host, asked them to put their rifles in the umbrella stand and to be seated. The Freuds' passports were subsequently confiscated and their money taken from the family safe. Freud dryly commented that *he'd* never been paid so much for a single visit. Before being allowed to leave the country, he was forced to sign a document to the effect that he had been treated with respect and allowed "to live and work in full freedom" after the Anschluss. This he did, but he asked to be allowed to add the following sentence: "I can heartily recommend the Gestapo to anyone." Through the efforts of his friends Freud was able to **escape to Britain** on June 3, 1938. Four of his sisters were not allowed to join him and died in the Holocaust. Just over a year after having arrived in London, when the pain became too much, Freud's doctor fulfilled their eleven-year-old pact, and gave him a lethal dose of morphine.

Aside from the leech cups, amputation saws, dental instruments and the odd pickled stomach, the chief attraction is the museum's remarkable collection of anatomical **wax models**, commissioned by Josef II from a group of Florentine sculptors in 1780. The models are serene, life-sized human figures, for the most part, presented as if partially dissected, revealing the body's nerves, muscles and veins in full gory technicolour. Equally beautiful are the original display cases, fashioned from rosewood and fitted with huge, bobbly, hand-blown panes of Venetian glass. There's also a model of the Allgemeines Krankenhaus and the Narrenturm as they would have appeared in 1784, just for good measure.

## Sigmund-Freud-Museum

Sigmund Freud moved to the second floor of Berggasse 19 in 1891 and stayed here until June 3, 1938, when, unwillingly, he and his family fled to London. Now the **Sigmund-Freud-Museum** (daily: July–Sept 9am–6pm; Oct–June 9am–5pm; €7; Ⓦ www.freud-museum.at), his apartment is a place of pilgrimage, though he took almost all his possessions – bar his library, which he sold – into exile (where they can be seen in London's Freud Museum). His hat, coat and walking stick are still here, and there's home-movie footage from the 1930s, but only the waiting room retains any original decor, with the odd oriental rug, a cabinet of antiquities, and some burgundy-upholstered furniture sent back from London by his daughter Anna after the war. Otherwise, there are a couple of rooms of photographs, a few rooms of Freud-inspired art, a library and a shop. English translations of the museum's captions are available, as are guided tours at 10am & 4pm (for an extra €1).

## Servitenkirche and Friedhof Rossau

If you're heading from Freud's apartment to the Liechtenstein Museum, it's worth taking a slight detour to visit the **Servitenkirche**, an early Baroque gem up Servitengasse, designed in the mid-seventeenth century by Carlo Carnevale, and the only Vorstädte church to survive the 1683 Turkish siege. Its oval-shaped nave – a first for Vienna – was a powerful influence on the layout of the Peterskirche and Karlskirche. You can only peek through the exquisite wrought-iron railings, but that's enough to get a feel for the cherub-infested, stucco-encrusted interior, which features an exuberant gilded pulpit by Balthasar Moll. Of the two side-chapels, the one to the north of the entrance holds a stucco relief of St John of Nepomuk taking confession from the Bohemian queen, and its very own grotto of the Virgin Mary.

Gravestones at Vienna's oldest surviving Jewish cemetery, **Friedhof Rossau**, a couple of blocks north at Seegasse 9–11, date back to 1540. Disused for two centuries, it remains hidden from the street behind a supremely ugly, 1970s old-people's home, on the site of the former Jewish Hospital and Old People's Home. It's possible to visit the cemetery at any reasonable time by simply walking through the foyer to the back of the building, where the graves that survived Nazi desecration shelter under tall, mature trees. The most famous person buried here was Samuel Oppenheimer (1630–1703), the first of the Court Jews to be allowed to settle in Vienna after the 1670 expulsion. He supplied the Habsburg army for its war with France, and organized the logistics of the defence of Vienna in 1683. When he died, however, the Habsburgs refused to honour their debts to his heirs, causing the family to go bankrupt, which in turn caused a major European financial crisis.

# Liechtenstein Museum

At the end of the seventeenth century, when the enormously wealthy Liechtenstein family commissioned Domenico Martinelli to build a summer palace, Alsergrund was still a rural idyll. Now hemmed in by nineteenth-century apartment blocks, the Baroque Palais Liechtenstein comes as a surprise, hidden away down the backstreet of Fürstengasse. Built on a giant scale, it houses the **Liechtenstein Museum** (Fri–Tues 10am–5pm; €10; ⓦwww.liechtensteinmuseum.at), which provides a suitably grandiose setting for the family's private art collection, best known for its series of paintings by Rubens. The collection was actually displayed here until World War II, then, with the Red Army approaching, smuggled back to Liechtenstein. The Austrian government argued that the collection had been illegally exported but eventually came to an agreement that has allowed the paintings to return.

The **ticket office** is in the imposing *sala terrena*, flanked by two grandiose marble staircases and decorated with frescoes by Johann Michael Rottmayr and Andrea Pozzo. Originally open to the elements, the *sala terrena* now shelters the family's eighteenth-century gilded coach with its panels of celestial cherubs. The east wing of the ground floor is used for temporary exhibitions; the west wing is occupied by the family's gargantuan library with its green-brown marbling decoration and Rottmayr's trompe-l'oeil frescoes. Heading up the east staircase, which retains its Rottmayr fresco, you come to the **Herkulessaal**, the largest secular Baroque hall in Vienna (and there's a fair bit of competition). Lined with red marble half-pillars topped by gilded composite capitals and interspersed with paintings and gilded reliefs, the hall's crowning glory is the Pozzo's ceiling fresco, which depicts the life of Hercules from the strangling of the snake in his cot to his final suicide. Regular classical concerts take place in the hall on Sunday afternoons.

The paintings of **Pieter Paul Rubens** (1577–1640) dominate the first-floor galleries. The largest room, Saal VII, is taken up almost entirely with the Decius Mus Cycle, depicting the life of the Roman consul, who sacrificed his own life in order to secure victory for his army over the Latins. The colours are fabulously strong, and the centrepiece of the cycle, *The Death of Decius Mus*, is a masterpiece of action-packed drama. Saal VIII holds a lovely portrait by Rubens of his 5-year-old daughter, painted with a refreshing informality and intimacy, next to a more formal one of his two sons. *Mars and Rhea Silva*, in Saal IX, provides a striking contrast between the god's red cloak and the priestess's golden one. It's not all rippling flesh, however, as there are plenty of sober portraits to bring you down to earth, one by Frans Hals and a whole series by **Van Dyck**, including a superb portrait of the 19-year-old Maria de Tassis. Lastly, don't miss the surrealist head, *Terra*, by Rudolf II's court painter, Giuseppe Arcimboldo.

If you're in need of refreshment, you can pay a visit to the museum's *Rubens* café on the east side of the forecourt, or take a picnic into the landscaped **gardens** round the back of the palace.

# From the Strudlhofstiege to Schuberts Geburthaus

If you've just been to the Liechtenstein Museum, you might as well take a stroll up the **Strudlhofstiege**, an imaginative set of Jugendstil steps designed in 1910 by Theodor Jäger, which link Pasteurgasse with Strudlhofgasse above it. They may not have the fame nor the setting of Rome's Spanish Steps, but they are a beguiling vignette of fin-de-siècle Vienna, and provided the inspiration for a long novel of the same name written in 1951 by Heimito von Doderer, dear to the hearts of many Viennese.

## Franz Schubert (1797–1828)

Of all the composers associated with Vienna, **Franz Schubert** fulfils more Romantic criteria than most. He died of syphilis at the age of just 31 (younger even than Mozart), he really was penniless (unlike Mozart, who was just careless with his money), and never lived to hear any of his symphonies performed (the first one wasn't published until fifty years after his death). The picture would be complete had he died while writing his eighth (unfinished) symphony – in fact, he abandoned it before he died, and went on, instead, to complete a ninth symphony.

Born the eleventh child (and fourth son) of an impoverished teacher, Schubert played viola in a string quartet with his older brothers. Aged 9 or 10, he won a scholarship to boarding school, earning a place as a chorister at the **Hofburgkapelle**, and studying with the court organist at the local church on Marktgasse, where he had been baptized, and with Antonio Salieri, Mozart's court rival. He went on to become the church organist, and composed his first Mass aged 17. After working as an assistant teacher at his father's school, he became a freelance musician, thanks to financial help from his friends, and spent two summers as music tutor for the **Esterházy family**.

His intensely lyrical chamber music, fragile songs and melodic piano works were popular among the Viennese bourgeoisie, and he performed at numerous informal social gatherings, known as "Schubertiaden". His personal life was dissolute; a heavy drinker, who frequented "revolutionary" circles, he remained unmarried all his life, possibly gay, and died of syphilis. Towards the end of his short life, he fulfilled his ambition to meet up with Beethoven, though there are no reliable details of the encounter. A torchbearer at the composer's funeral, he was buried, according to his wishes, three graves away from him in Währinger Friedhof the following year (he now lies near Beethoven in the **Zentralfriedhof**; see p.190).

## Schuberts Geburtshaus

Further north still, at Nussdorferstrasse 54, **Schuberts Geburtshaus** (Tues–Sun 10am–1pm & 2–6pm; €2; ⓦ www.wienmuseum.at), is the unassuming, two-storey house where the composer was born in 1797. Inside, the charming courtyard has been lovingly restored, its wooden balconies festooned with boxes of geraniums. As so often with Vienna's musical memorials, however, no attempt has been made to reconstruct Schubert's family home, which consisted of just one room and a kitchen (the latter survives). In any case, Schubert wouldn't recognise the place; the family moved down the road, to Säulengasse 3, when he was four. Nevertheless, you can admire the composer's broken spectacles and his half-brother's piano, and listen to excerpts of his music. Several rooms are given over to idyllic Biedermeier landscapes by **Adalbert Stifter**, the writer and artist from the Böhmerwald who slit his throat in 1868 rather than suffer cancer of the liver.

Schubert's brother's house – 4, Kettenbrückengasse 6 (Wed & Thurs 10am–1pm & 2–6pm; €2), near the Naschmarkt – the **Sterbewohnung** in which the composer died in 1828, has been made into a similarly unenthralling museum for the truly dedicated.

# Leopoldstadt and the east

L eopoldstadt – the city's second district – is separated from the centre of Vienna by the Danube Canal. Along with the twentieth district of Brigittenau, it forms a misshapen island bordered to the east by the main arm of the Danube. For the most part, it's a drab residential suburb, only redeemed by the **Prater**, the vast city park, with its funfair, its famous Ferris wheel and its woods. However, Leopoldstadt also boasts a long history as the city's foremost Jewish quarter, faint traces of which still survive. More recently, the arrival of immigrants from Turkey, the Balkans and Africa has made this one of the city's more ethnically diverse central districts.

East of Leopoldstadt and the Danube's main channel is an area quite unlike anywhere else in Vienna. First off, there's the Donauinsel where the Viennese go to cool off in summer, then there's the **Vienna International Centre** or UNO-City, seat of various UN organisations, and finally there's the placid waters of the **Alte Donau**, where you bathe and sail away a lazy summer's day.

## Prater

Of all the places in Leopoldstadt, it's the **Prater** – from the Spanish *prado* (plain) – which draws the biggest crowds. This large, flat tract of land, taking up almost half the island, includes vast areas of mixed woodland, sports stadiums, racecourses, a miniature railway, allotments, a trade-fair centre, a planetarium, an amusement park and, most famously of all, Vienna's giant Ferris wheel. Aside from the Wienerwald, the Prater is by far the most popular weekend destination for any Viennese searching for a breath of fresh air.

Traditionally a royal hunting preserve, the Prater was opened to the public in 1766 by Josef II. Throughout the nineteenth century, it continued to be *the* place to be seen. On Sundays, the long, central chestnut-lined Hauptallee was the scene of the **Praterfahrt**, when "the newest shape in carriages, the last 'sweet thing in bonnets', the most correct cut of coat *à la Anglaise*, is to be seen, walking, riding, or driving up and down." On public holidays, nearly half the population of the city would turn up for the *Praterfahrt*. As one historian put it: "Everyone in Vienna joined in... if they could call a carriage their own or anything else on wheels with

## Jewish Leopoldstadt

It was probably Leopoldstadt's physical separateness that persuaded Emperor Ferdinand II to establish a **walled Jewish ghetto** here in 1625. The Habsburgs happily exploited the financial acumen and clout of its wealthiest burghers to fund the Thirty Years' War, but as the Counter-Reformation gathered pace, there were increasingly vociferous calls from devout Catholics – including the city council and the emperor's Spanish wife – to banish the community entirely. In 1670, Emperor Leopold I bowed to the zealots' pressure and expelled Jews on charges of spying for the Turks and blasphemy against the Virgin Mary; the area was named after him in celebration.

Leopoldstadt enjoyed a second period of Jewish settlement following the 1848 revolution, when official restrictions on Jews within the empire were abolished. Thousands left the *shtetls* of Bohemia, Moravia, Hungary and Galicia and migrated to the capital. Most arrived by train at the Nordbahnhof (Wien-Nord) and settled, initially at least, in the surrounding district of Leopoldstadt, which became known as **Mazzeinsel**, after the unleavened bread or *Matzoh* eaten at Passover. The Strauss family, Sigmund Freud, Gustav Mahler, Arthur Schnitzler, Billy Wilder, Viktor Frankl and Theodor Herzl all lived here at some point, before moving to the city's richer suburbs.

This time around, Leopoldstadt was only an unofficial Jewish quarter – at their peak, between the wars, Jews comprised around forty percent of the population, a high proportion of whom were orthodox **Hasidic Jews**, with their distinctive eighteenth-century dress. With the richer Jewish families moving out, and poorer families constantly arriving to fill their place, the district remained trapped in a cycle of poverty. By the start of the twentieth century the area was notorious as a hotbed of prostitution, much to the satisfaction of the city's anti-Semites.

After the Anschluss, the Nazis destroyed all the area's synagogues, and then turned Leopoldstadt into the official ghetto, forcibly resettling the city's remaining Jews. **Deportations** to the camps began in earnest in 1941 and by the end of 1942 the Jewish population was reduced to eight thousand, most of whom were married to gentiles. Just five hundred Jews returned to Vienna after the war, although numbers have since increased to around seven thousand, many of whom have chosen to settle once more in Leopoldstadt. The pockets of kosher shops on Hollandstrasse and Tempelgasse, and the Jewish school on Castellezgasse, are evidence of the area's modest Jewish renaissance. Four newly erected columns, a plaque, a mosaic and the surviving north wing of what was once Vienna's largest synagogue, the neo-Byzantine **Leopoldstädter Tempel**, on Tempelgasse, give an idea of the building's former glory. Throughout the district, plaques and **Steine der Errinnerung** (commemorative stones) record the former locations of Jewish synagogues, cafés, schools and theatres, plus the assembly points, at Kleine Sperlgasse 2a and Malzgasse 7, used by the Nazis to round up the city's Jews for deportation.

a nag to pull it. If not, they walked. Vienna had no more glamorous sight to offer, nor any which united all classes in this way."

In 1873, the Prater was the venue for the empire's *Weltausstellung* or **World Trade Fair**. Some fifty thousand exhibitors from forty countries set up displays in the exhibition's rotunda, topped by a huge cupola 108m in diameter. Unfortunately, just eight days after the emperor opened the fair on May 1, the Vienna stock exchange collapsed, and what had been touted as a celebration of the empire's thriving liberal economy became a charade. In July, to further dampen the mood, a cholera epidemic broke out in the city, claiming three thousand victims. By November, seven million admissions were recorded – thirteen million fewer than expected – and the fair was forced to close.

In 1890, the First of May *Praterfahrt* was appropriated by the Socialist leader Viktor Adler, who organized the first **May Day Parade** of workers down the Hauptallee, though he himself was in prison on the actual day. There was panic among the ruling classes: "Soldiers are standing by, the doors of the houses are being closed, in people's apartments food supplies are prepared as though for an impending siege, the shops are deserted, women and children dare not go out into the street," reported the *Neue Freie Presse*. Even so, thousands took part, marching

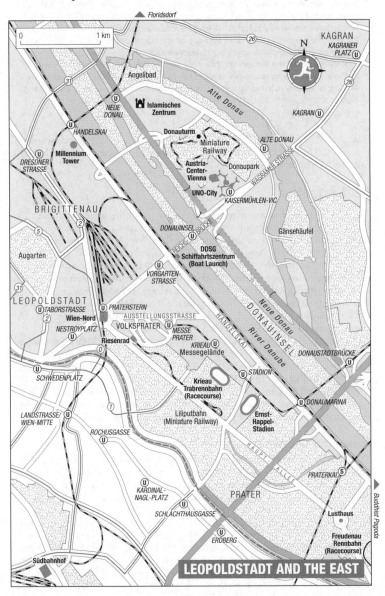

The Prater is vast; its backbone, the chestnut-lined **Hauptallee**, runs dead straight for 5km, from the Ferris wheel in the northwest to the woody section around the Lusthaus to the southeast.

Several **U-Bahn** stations lie along the Prater's northern edge. The park is also an easy stroll from Wien-Nord station (U-Bahn Praterstern), the terminus for **trams** #5 and #O. Alternatively, tram #1 terminates right by the Hauptallee, a third of the way down from the Ferris wheel. Halfway down, bus #84A (every 10min) crosses the Hauptallee en route to and from U-Bahn Schlachthausgasse. Finally, bus #77A (every 30min) from the same U-Bahn will take you all the way to or from the Lusthaus, even travelling some of the way down the Hauptallee itself.

**Getting around the Prater**, you can walk, jog, rollerblade, cycle, take a *Fiaker*, or rent one of the **pedal carriages**, which seat two adults (plus two kids if you wish). Another possibility is to buy a one-way ticket on the miniature railway or **Liliputbahn** (see opposite), which will get you almost halfway down the Hauptallee.

four abreast, carrying red flags and singing, and the demonstration passed off peacefully. The May Day Parade quickly became a permanent fixture in the city's calendar of celebrations.

# Volksprater

The easiest point of access from the city centre – and the busiest section of the Prater – is the northwest end, where you'll find the park's funfair, known as the **Volksprater** (mid-March to Oct daily 10am–1am; free; ⓦwww.prater.at). While tourists come to the Volksprater for the Ferris wheel or Riesenrad, the Viennese are here for the **funfair**, which ranges from high-tech white-knuckle affairs to old-fashioned fairground rides like ghost trains, dodgems and strength contests that judge participants from *Weichling* (weakling), through *Fräulein* (girly) to *Weltmeister* (world champion). In addition, there's a tawdry "Sex-Museum" and a "Jack the Ripper" dark ride. For the kids, there are bouncy castles, horse rides and even a rather sad sleigh carousel pulled by real ponies.

The atmosphere is relaxed during the day, though it can get a little more charged at night. If you get lost, you can orientate yourself by one of the two open areas, Rondeau and Calafattiplatz, the latter named after the man who set up the first carousel in the Prater in 1840. The easiest point of reference of all is, of course, the Riesenrad. Sadly, there are no longer more than fifty restaurants and pubs to choose from as there were a century ago, but if you want a bite to eat or a drink, head for the *Schweizerhaus* (see p.221), whose roast pig is legendary.

### Riesenrad (Ferris Wheel)

Taking a ride on the **Riesenrad** (daily: March, April & Oct 10am–9.45pm; May–Sept 9am–11.45pm; Nov–Feb 10am–7.45pm; €8.50; ⓦwww.wienerriesenrad .com) is one of those things you simply have to do if you go to Vienna – it's the place in front of which Orson Welles does his famous "cuckoo clock" speech in *The Third Man*. Built in 1898 for Emperor Franz-Josef I's golden jubilee, the Riesenrad was designed by the British military engineer Walter Basset, who constructed similar Ferris wheels in Blackpool and Paris (both long since demolished). Its cute little red gondolas were destroyed during World War II, and only half were replaced after 1945 in deference to the wheel's old age. Acrophobes can reassure themselves with the fact that the gondolas, which hold up to twelve people standing, are entirely enclosed, though they do tend to wobble around a bit. The wheel reaches a height of 65m and doesn't so much spin as stagger slowly round over the course of twenty minutes, as each gondola fills with passengers.

## Prater Museum and Planetarium

If the Volksprater amusements don't grab you, head instead for the nearby **Prater Museum** (Fri–Sun 10am–1pm & 2–6pm; €2, first Sun of month free; ⓦ www .wienmuseum.at), which records the golden age of the *Wurstelprater* funfair, destroyed in 1945. Old photographs of the likes of Semona, the fiery Amazonian snake-charmer, and Liliputstadt, an entire miniature city inhabited by dwarves, give something of the nineteenth-century flavour. Also displayed are characters from Hanswurst, various antique slot-machines (some of which you can play on) and a model of the 1873 *Weltausstellung*. The museum is housed in one room of the **Planetarium** (shows Tues–Sun; €8; ⓦ www.planetarium-wien.at), founded by the German optician Carl Zeiss in 1927, and puts on a varied programme, with commentary nearly always in German. For the latest listings, pick up a leaflet or visit the website.

## Kugelmugel

A short way along the Hauptallee from the Planetarium, the **Kugelmugel** (ⓦ www.republik-kugelmugel.com) is a spherical terracotta-coloured house belonging to the artist Edwin Lipburger. Following arguments over planning permission, Lipburger declared his house a self-governing republic or micro-nation, refused to pay taxes and began printing his own stamps. It was for this latter act that he received a prison sentence, though he was pardoned by the Austrian president. The republic's territory is marked out by a barbed-wire fence and its unofficial address is Antifaschismus-Platz.

# Beyond the Volksprater

The quirkiest method of escape from the Volksprater is by the miniature railway, built in 1928 and known as the **Liliputbahn** (mid-March to mid-Oct Mon–Fri 10am–1pm every 30min; 1–6.30pm every 15min, Sat & Sun 10am–6.30pm every 15min; ⓦ www.liliputbahn.com), which runs from near the Riesenrad over to the main stadium, a return trip of around 4km (€4). The engines are mostly diesel, but some steam trains run in the summer. There are three stations: Prater, by the Riesenrad, the mid-point station Rotunde, named after the now-defunct exhibition hall of the 1873 *Weltausstellung*, and Stadion. En route, you pass the Hockey-Stadion and Bowling-Halle to the south, the ugly, expansive Messegelände (trade-fair grounds) and the **Krieau** Trabrennbahn (trotting-racecourse), to the north. **Trotting races** are held on Sundays from September to June (ⓦ www.krieau.at; tickets from €5).

## Ernst-Happel-Stadion

Beyond Krieau lies the **Ernst-Happel-Stadion** (aka the Wiener or Prater Stadion), Austria's largest stadium, with a capacity of over fifty thousand. It opened in 1931 with the second Workers' Olympiad, during which eighty thousand athletes took part and four thousand musicians, actors and gymnasts re-enacted the struggle of Labour over Capital from the Middle Ages to the present day. As a grand finale, the giant gilt idol representing capitalism was toppled, while youths dressed in white marched forward carrying red flags and singing the *Internationale*. The show was one of the cultural highpoints of interwar "Red Vienna" (see p.185). During World War II, the stadium was used by the Nazis as a collection point for Jews awaiting deportation to the camps. In 1992, it was re-named after the Austrian football coach

Ernst Happel (1925–1992), who won the European Cup twice (once with Feyenoord and once with Hamburg).

## Beyond the Stadion

The autobahn and the railway line cut across the southeastern half of the Prater, but the woods beyond the Stadion are still the most peaceful sections of the park, perfect for a picnic. If you've no provisions, walk to the far end of the Hauptallee where you'll find the **Lusthaus** restaurant (see p.221), a pretty octagonal building, remodelled from a hunting lodge into a pleasure palace in 1783. Originally surrounded by water, it served as the centrepiece for a mass picnic for twenty thousand soldiers during the Congress of Vienna. It preserves its original frescoed interior, and remains a popular spot for lunch, as is the more rustic *Altes Jägerhaus*, opposite (see p.220).

Southeast of the *Lusthaus*, **Freudenau** is a lovingly restored, late nineteenth-century racecourse. The racing season traditionally opens on Easter Sunday, with races every other weekend until November. The Derby, a race organized by the Austrian Jockey Club since 1868, is held on a Sunday in June; it used to be attended by the emperor himself, with various aristocrats often among the riders, and the wealthy young Viennese crowd dressed to the nines.

# Central Leopoldstadt

The rest of Leopoldstadt boasts only minor sights such as the **Johann-Strauss-Museum**, the sculptures in the **Gustinus-Ambrosi-Museum** in the Augarten, and the Meissen porcelain in the Augarten **Porzellanmanufaktur**.

## The Danube Canal

Separating Leopoldstadt from the old town, the **Danube Canal** (Donaukanal) is the narrowest of the River Danube's four arms. As the channel nearest to the city, this was the first section of the Danube to be regulated, around 1600. The canal was an easy target for Allied bombs during World War II, and the only building of note is Otto Wagner's dinky **Schützenhaus** (literally "defence tower"), below Obere Donaustrasse. Clad in white marble (and smothered in graffiti) it features a playful wave pattern of cobalt-blue tiles, and is best viewed from the opposite embankment below Franz-Josefs-Kai.

## Praterstrasse

Once a majestic boulevard, traversed by trams and peppered with Yiddish theatres, **Praterstrasse** is now just a busy wide street leading to the Prater. Fans of the "Waltz King", however, should head for the **Johann-Strauss-Wohnung** (Tues–Sun 10am–1pm & 2–6pm; €2; Ⓦwww.wienmuseum.at) on the first floor of no. 54, where the composer lived from 1863 until the death of his first wife, the singer Jetty Treffz, in 1878. Some attempt has been made to recreate a period interior; one room, decorated with ceiling panels of cherubs, contains his grand piano, house organ and standing desk at which he used to compose. There's also a fascinating collection of ephemera from the balls of the day, with various gimmicky dance cards – one laid out in the form of a staircase – and quirky ball pendants, kept as mementoes of the evening.

## The Strauss family

Of all the many tunes associated with Vienna, perhaps the best known are the waltzes composed by the Strausses. Born in Vienna to a Jewish innkeeper in Leopoldstadt, **Johann Strauss the Elder** or I (1804–49) kept quiet about his origins, though it was the Nazis themselves who felt the need to falsify the parish register of Vienna's Stephansdom in order to make the Strauss family appear as true Aryans (a similar leniency was shown towards Hitler's much-loved composer Franz Léhar, whose wife was Jewish). Strauss began his career serenading diners in Viennese restaurants, along with Josef Lanner, who became his chief musical rival. However, it was in Zum Sperl in Leopoldstadt that Strauss the Elder made his name as a band leader, conducting a mixture of dances, orchestral phantasies and more serious music. His gypsy-like features, and wild, vigorous conducting style soon became very popular in Vienna. Later, he and his orchestra toured Europe, and he was eventually appointed *Hofballmusikdirektor*. Strauss created a public scandal in 1842, when he left the family home and moved in with a young seamstress, who bore him several illegitimate children.

His eldest son, **Johann Strauss the Younger** or II (1825–99), followed in his father's footsteps, writing his first waltz at the age of six, though much against the latter's wishes (he wanted him to be a banker). It was, in fact, Johann's long-suffering mother, Anna, who directed her sons into musical careers. Father and son soon became rivals, both musically and politically. In 1848, while the Elder was busy conducting his famous *Radetzky March*, the signature tune of the *ancien régime*, the Younger was composing tunes such as the *Revolution March* and the *Song of the Barricades*. Strauss the Younger was appointed *Hofballmusikdirektor* in 1863, and rapidly surpassed even his father's enormous fame. Among the world's first international celebrities, he was feted on both sides of the Atlantic. On one memorable occasion in Boston, he conducted *The Blue Danube* with twenty thousand singers, an orchestra of over one thousand, and twenty assistant conductors, to an audience of more than 100,000. Johann's operetta, *Die Fledermaus*, written to take Viennese minds off the economic crash of 1873, was another huge success – by the end of the decade, it was playing in some 170 theatres.

Despite his success, Johann, a difficult character like his father, was something of an outsider. He was constantly irked by his lack of acclaim among serious musical critics, and his several attempts at straight opera flopped. Again like his father, he too caused a scandal: his first wife was seven years older than him, and he divorced his second wife, Lili, to marry his mistress, Adele. As the Vatican would not annul his marriage, he was forced to convert to Lutheranism and become a citizen of Saxony, though he continued to live in Vienna until his death in 1899.

At the far end of Praterstrasse, nearest the Prater, stands the splendid **Tegetthoff Monument,** a tall rostral column, complete with frolicking sea-horses and topped by a statue of Wilhelm von Tegetthoff himself, celebrating his 1866 naval victory over the Italians at the Battle of Lissa.

# Kriminalmuseum

Leopoldstadt's most popular museum is the **Wiener Kriminalmuseum** (Tues–Sun 10am–5pm; €5; Ⓦ www.kriminalmuseum.at), a prurient overview of Vienna's most gruesome crimes, at Grosse Sperlgasse 24. In between the voyeuristic photos of autopsies interesting sections cover the city's social and political history, though with labelling in German only, these are lost on most foreign visitors. To cap it all, there's a fairly gratuitous section on flagellation, while the biggest criminals of the lot – the Nazis – get only the very briefest of mentions. A more edifying museum on a similar subject is the Foltermuseum (Torture Museum), described on p.140.

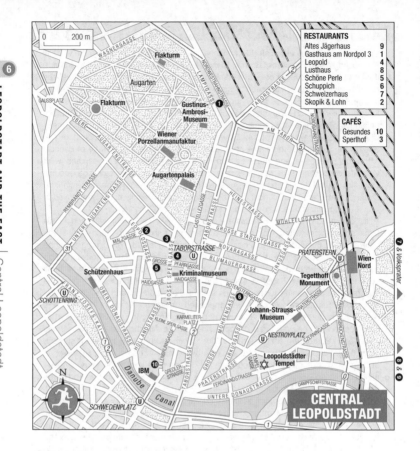

RESTAURANTS
| Altes Jägerhaus | 9 |
| Gasthaus am Nordpol 3 | 1 |
| Leopold | 4 |
| Lusthaus | 8 |
| Schöne Perle | 5 |
| Schuppich | 6 |
| Schweizerhaus | 7 |
| Skopik & Lohn | 2 |

CAFÉS
| Gesundes | 10 |
| Sperlhof | 3 |

## Augarten

The **Augarten** (open dawn to dusk), in the north of Leopoldstadt, is one of Vienna's oldest parks, laid out in formal French style in 1650, and opened to the public in 1775 by Josef II. Sadly, it's come down in the world since its fashionable halcyon days when Mozart gave morning concerts here, and, a century later, Strauss the Younger championed Wagner's overtures. That said, the park does pull in the crowds in the summer, thanks to its open-air cinema, Kino unter Sternen (see p.232). A slightly melancholic air is lent by the forbidding presence of not one, but two World War II Flaktürme (see p.140). These sinister concrete hulks put the dampeners on the park's formal section; to escape them, head off into the woody network of chestnut-lined paths to the north, home to some very tame red squirrels and elusive woodpeckers.

Hidden in this dense section of the park, by the eastern boundary, is the intriguing, but little-visited **Augarten Contemporary** (Thurs–Sun 11am–7pm; €5). The gallery stages contemporary art shows and also displays a permanent collection of the prolific Austrian sculptor **Gustinus Ambrosi** (1893–1975), whose larger works are clearly influenced by Auguste Rodin. However, Ambrosi is at his best with his bronze portrait heads, of which there are plenty here, his subjects drawn mainly from the artistic and political circles of the interwar period. Note the emaciated Otto Wagner the year before his death, a suitably overblown Nietzsche, and a youthful Mussolini (with hair).

On the ruins of the Alte Favorita, Leopold I's summer palace, burnt to the ground by the Turks in 1683, Josef II erected a long, low-lying garden pavilion. From 1782, the pavilion's restaurant was the venue of the fashionable *Morgenkonzerte* conducted by the likes of Mozart and Beethoven; the building now serves as the headquarters of the **Wiener Porzellanmanufaktur** (Mon–Fri 9.30am–5pm; free; Ⓦ www.augarten.at), founded in 1718, eight years after Meissen. The factory's famous "flower and figure" porcelain is displayed in the Silberkammer in the Hofburg (see p.70), though temporary exhibitions are also staged in the showroom foyer. The adjacent shop sells the factory's current offerings, from gaudy Rococo to modernist designs by the likes of Josef Hoffmann. Hour-long **guided tours** of the entire production process take place Monday to Friday at 10am (€6).

The **Augartenpalais**, east of the Porzellanmanufaktur, was designed by Johann Bernhard Fischer von Erlach at the end of the seventeenth century, and bought as a hunting lodge by Emperor Josef II in 1780. Unfortunately, you can't get a good look at the building, as it's now the boarding school of the Wiener Sängerknaben (Vienna Boys' Choir; see p.76). The choir's kindergarten and primary school are housed in the **Kaiser-Josef-Stöckl**, a pavilion hidden behind the palace, designed by Isidor Canevale in 1781 for Josef II, who preferred the Augarten above all his other residences.

# Donauinsel and Kaisermühlen

During the second half of the nineteenth century, the main course of the River Danube was straightened to allow larger vessels to dock. A parallel channel, the slow-flowing Neue Donau, was cut in the 1970s, thus creating a long, thin, artificial island, officially known as the **Donauinsel**, but dubbed variously Spaghetti Island or Copa Cagrana (after the end station on the nearby U-Bahn line). The Danube's original course, known as the Alte Donau, east of the Neue Donau, was simultaneously dammed to create perhaps the most attractive stretch of water. The semicircular nub of land encompassed by the Neue and Alte Donau is known as **Kaisermühlen**, home to Vienna's UNO-City and the accompanying Donaupark. Neither deserves to top your itinerary, but each provides an interesting insight into modern Viennese life.

## Donauinsel

To be perfectly honest, the **Donauinsel** – measuring 20km by just 200m – is pretty bleak, a situation not helped by the views over to the unsightly east bank. Nevertheless, when the summer heat starts to kick in, the Viennese flock to the beaches here in droves, and the island's numerous bars, discos and food stalls, centred around Donauinsel U-Bahn station, start to get busy. Joggers, skateboarders and cyclists also use the island, which every June becomes the focus for the open-air *Donauinselfest*, a rock festival with fireworks organized by the Social Democrat Party (SPÖ). To the north, a huge watersports complex has a 200m-long water slide, boat rental, windsurfing and the like. To the south, there are fixed barbecue spots, and a nudist beach (FKK). Wherever you decide to go, don mosquito repellent in summer.

# Vienna International Centre (UNO-City)

East of the Danube, six Y-shaped, glass-fronted high-rise offices soar to a height of 110m, and radiate from a central block like a three-legged man on the run. Built in the 1970s, the **Vienna International Centre** (ⓦ www.unis.unvienna.org) – known as VIC to its inmates, and UNO-City to the mapmakers – has been the United Nations' number-three base (UNOV), after New York and Geneva. The idea was first mooted by Austrian Chancellor Bruno Kreisky, and its construction nearly bankrupted the country. The UN functionaries, until then housed in the Hofburg, were none too happy either. Today, the VIC is home to numerous bureaucracies, including the International Atomic Energy Agency, the Office for Outer Space Affairs, the Office on Drugs and Crime, and the ever-busy High Commission for Refugees (UNHCR).

Of the five thousand folk employed here, only a third are Austrians, but the place is an important source of income for the city, and has ensured Vienna a bit part on the international stage. The adjacent conference-centre monstrosity – imaginatively named Austria Center Vienna – has proved less of a money-spinner. Whatever the financial benefits, UNO-City is not a beautiful place to visit. Within earshot of a roaring autobahn, cordoned off with wire fencing, and bristling with armed police and CCTV cameras, the whole place is alienating and, essentially, ugly. **Guided tours** (Mon–Fri 11am & 2pm; €6), which start from the visitor centre at Gate 1 (take ID), will explain Vienna's role within the UN and allow you to admire the contemporary Austrian art with which the interior is generously sprinkled.

# Donaupark and the Alte Donau

It's with a certain amount of relief that you descend from the VIC to the adjacent **Donaupark**, laid out on an old rubbish dump in 1964 as part of the Vienna International Garden Show. The best section is around the artificial lake, Irissee, and in the rose garden and walled Chinese garden beyond, both accessible on the miniature railway, the 3.4km **Donauparkbahn**, which wends its way around the park (mid-March to mid-Oct Mon–Fri 10am–6pm every 10–25min, Sat & Sun 10am–6pm every 10–15min; round trip €4; ⓦ www.liliputbahn.com). Anyone with kids should consider treating them to a trip to **Minopolis** (Fri–Sun 1–7pm; adults €6, children €15; ⓦ www.minopolis.at), on the other side of the VIC and Wagramerstrasse from the park, where children can pretend to be fire fighters, pharmacists, refuse collectors or a baker, and get paid in "Eurolinos".

Overlooking the Donaupark, the futuristic **Donauturm** (daily 10am–midnight; €6.90; ⓦ www.donauturm.at) reaches a height of 252m. To enjoy the view, either simply take the lift to the viewing platform (at 155m), or eat in one of the tower's two revolving restaurants (at 160m and 170m). Clearly visible to the west, by Handelskai on the Danube, Vienna's **Millennium Tower** is a shiny double-glazed cylinder that's 171m tall, plus antennae.

The Donaupark stretches from UNO-City to the **Alte Donau**, the old course of the Danube, which is undoubtedly the most attractive and peaceful section of the river. Several bathing areas lie south of Wagramerstrasse and on the **Gänsehäufel**, the large island in the middle of the Untere Alte Donau, which has its own beach area. Opposite the Gänsehäufel, you'll find numerous places to enjoy an alfresco drink along the eastern bank – again, mosquito repellent is a good idea. Probably the most accessible (and popular) public bathing area is the **Angelibad**, in the north near Neue Donau U-Bahn, with a popular *Schnitzel* place close by. Along the eastern bank there are also a number of sailing schools, which rent out boats and windsurfers and offer lessons too.

# Schönbrunn, the Wienerwald and the Zentralfriedhof

Vienna's outer suburbs or *Vororte*, which lie beyond the *Gürtel*, are predominantly residential. Chief among the few top-drawer sights they contain is **Schönbrunn**, the Habsburgs' former summer residence, west of the city centre, and one of Vienna's most popular tourist destinations after the Hofburg. The palace boasts some of the finest Rococo interiors in central Europe, while the surrounding **Schlosspark** is home to the **Tiergarten**, Vienna's delightful zoo, and various other attractions. To the west of the neighbouring villa district of **Hietzing**, the wooded parkland of the **Lainzer Tiergarten** is a former royal hunting-ground that's now a haven for wildlife.

The rest of the suburbs hold a scattering of interesting museums and sights that call for a targeted approach, relying on the tram system to get you around. To the north, several wine-producing villages have been subsumed into the city; their **Heurigen** (wine taverns) are a natural magnet for the Viennese in the summer, as well as for busloads of tourists (see p.222). Vienna is also very lucky to have the **Wienerwald** (Vienna Woods) on its doorstep, just beyond the *Heurigen*, and a trip up to one of its forested hills is rewarded with glorious views over the entire city.

Finally, in the southeast, there's the **Zentralfriedhof**, Vienna's truly awesome Central Cemetery, with a population almost twice that of the city itself, and featuring musical graves of the likes of Beethoven, Schubert, Brahms, Schönberg and the Strauss family.

## Schönbrunn

Compared with the hotchpotch that is the Hofburg, the Habsburgs' summer residence of **Schönbrunn** (@www.schoenbrunn.at) is everything an imperial palace should be: grandiose, symmetrical and thoroughly intimidating. Built over the course of the eighteenth century, it contains nearly 1500 rooms, and, in its day,

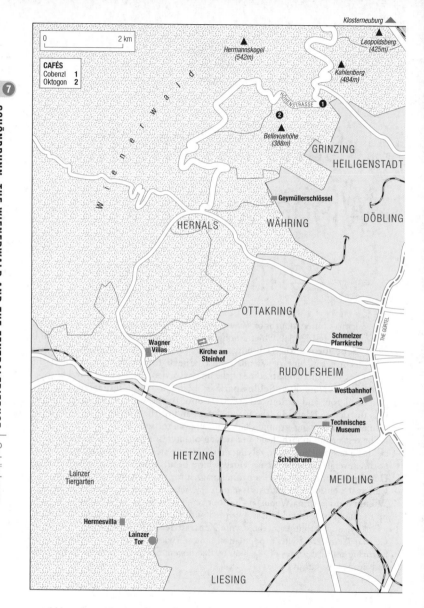

CAFÉS
Cobenzl 1
Oktogon 2

0        2 km

would have housed more than a thousand servants. However, while the sheer scale of the place is undeniably impressive, the building itself is something of an acquired taste, its plain facade painted a rather sickly mustard yellow.

The riches are inside, with its superb array of Baroque and Rococo **Prunkräume** (State Rooms), from the time of Empress Maria Theresia, the first Habsburg to make Schönbrunn the official imperial summer residence. There's also a fine collection of imperial carriages in the outbuilding of the **Wagenburg**, as well as

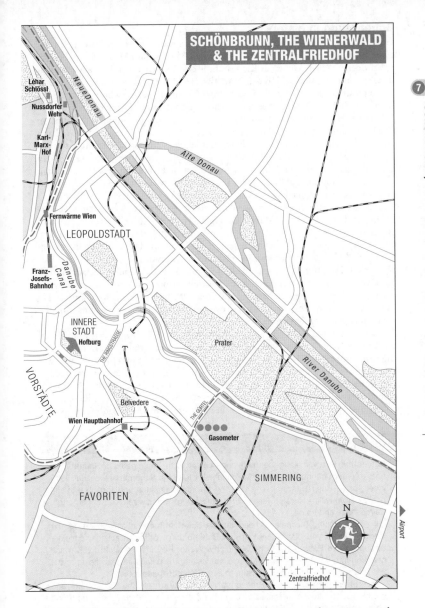

Léhar Schlössl

Nussdorfer Wehr

Karl-Marx-Hof

Neue Donau

Alte Donau

Fernwärme Wien

LEOPOLDSTADT

Franz-Josefs-Bahnhof

Danube Canal

INNERE STADT

Hofburg

THE RINGSTRASSE

Prater

River Danube

VORSTÄDTE

Belvedere

Wien Hauptbahnhof

THE GÜRTEL

Gasometer

SIMMERING

FAVORITEN

N

Airport

Zentralfriedhof

temporary exhibitions in the **Orangerie** and puppet performances in the **Marionettentheater**.

In the **Schlosspark**, you'll find the **Tiergarten** (Zoo), far more uplifting than most inner-city zoos, and close by, the tropical **Palmenhaus** and the desert-like **Wüstenhaus**. Last, but not least, there's the magnificent Schlosspark itself, and its **Irrgarten** (maze) and follies, to explore.

## Schönbrunn in history

Compared with the Hofburg, Schönbrunn has a short Habsburg history. It only came into imperial ownership in 1569, when **Maximilian II** (1564–76) bought the property – then known as Katterburg – close to what is now the Meidlinger Tor, as a hunting retreat. His son **Matthias** (1612–19) had the place rebuilt after marauding Hungarians laid it to waste in 1605, and it was he who discovered the natural spring, from which the name Schönbrunn (Beautiful Spring) derives.

After the Habsburgs themselves destroyed the place in anticipation of the Turks in 1683, **Leopold I** (1657–1705) commissioned a new summer palace from Johann Bernhard Fischer von Erlach. The latter's initial plans envisaged a structure to rival Versailles, perched atop the hill and approached by a series of grandiose terraces. In the end, a more modest building was agreed upon, and work began in 1696. Enough was built to allow Leopold's son **Josef I** (1705–11) to occupy the central section, but construction was stymied by the War of the Spanish Succession (1701–14).

Josef I's successor, Karl VI, was only interested in pheasant-shooting at Schönbrunn, and it was left to **Maria Theresia** (1740–80) to create the palace and gardens that we see today. Employing her court architect, Nicolo Pacassi, she added an extra floor to the main palace, to accommodate her ever-increasing family, and had the interior transformed into a sumptuous Rococo residence. Her son, **Josef II** (1780–90), rearranged the gardens in Classical style, adding the largest of the garden's monuments, the Gloriette triumphal arch, and growing his own tea, coffee and sugar, which he took great pleasure in serving to his guests. He did not, however, share his mother's love of Schönbrunn, and had much of the palace boarded up to save money.

**Napoleon** stayed at Schönbrunn in 1805 and 1809 – his eagles can still be seen on the main gates – and his son, the Duke of Reichstadt, lived out most of his brief life here, too (see p.171). However, not until the reign of **Franz-Josef I** – who was born here in 1830 and died here in 1916 – did Schönbrunn once more occupy centre stage in court life. In November 1918, the last of the Habsburgs, **Karl I**, signed away all hopes of preserving the monarchy, in the palace's Blue Chinese Salon, and thereafter the entire place became state property. Badly damaged in

---

### Visiting Schönbrunn

Rather than struggle along the multi-lane freeway to the main gates or Haupttor, it's best to enter Schönbrunn via the Meidlinger Tor (U-Bahn Schönbrunn), or the Hietzinger Tor (U-Bahn Hietzing). The Hietzing approach enables you to pop into the nearby Hofpavillon Hietzing (see p.175), and brings you nearer to the Tiergarten, Palmenhaus and so on.

If you're visiting the palace, head for the **ticket office** first as queues can be lengthy. And if you plan to visit any of Schönbrunn's other attractions, consider buying a **Gold Pass** (April–Oct; €39), or the Winter Pass (Nov–March; €25), which gets you into them all. Equally, if you're not visiting the palace, but are going to the zoo, mazes and glasshouses, be sure to buy a **Kombi-Karte** (€18).

For **refreshments**, there's a reasonably-priced *Beisl* near the Wagenburg, and a coffee shop beyond the ticket office in the palace itself. Whatever you do, don't be hoodwinked into going to the overpriced café-restaurant on the east side of the main courtyard. Tea and cakes are also on offer in the wonderful surroundings of the Gloriette, overlooking the Schlosspark, and there are usually a few food stalls in the main palace courtyard. The Tiergarten holds still more eating options, from *Würst* stands to restaurants – you can even fix your own picnic from the shop in the zoo's Tirolerhaus. Nevertheless, by far the cheapest and most convenient option in fine weather is to bring your own picnic and find somewhere to relax in the park.

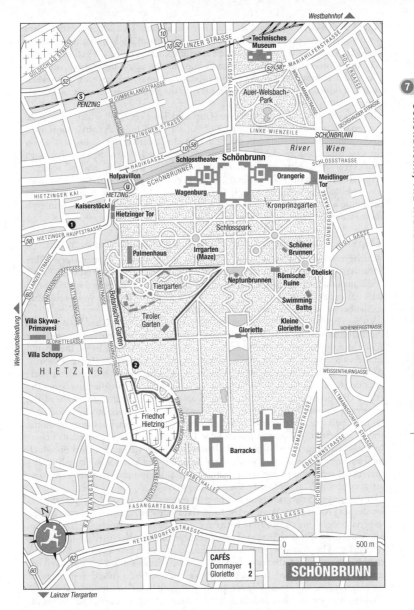

Map labels: Westbahnhof; Technisches Museum; LINZER STRASSE; GOLDSCHLAGSTRASSE; MARIAHILFER STRASSE; HOFERGASSE; PENZING; CUMBERLANDSTRASSE; Auer-Welsbach-Park; WINCKELMANNSTRASSE; SECHSHAUSER STRASSE; PENZINGER STRASSE; LINKE WIENZEILE; SCHÖNBRUNN; HADIKGASSE; Schlosstheater; Schönbrunn; River Wien; SCHLOSSSTRASSE; Hofpavillon; SCHÖNBRUNNER; Orangerie; Meidlinger Tor; HIETZINGER KAI; HIETZING; Wagenburg; Kronprinzgarten; GRÜNBERGSTRASSE; TIROLI GASSE; Kaiserstöckl; Hietzinger Tor; Schlosspark; Schöner Brunnen; LAINZER STRASSE; Palmenhaus; Irrgarten (Maze); Römische Ruine; Obelisk; HIETZINGER HAUPTSTRASSE; WATTMANNGASSE; Botanischer Garten; Tiergarten; Neptunbrunnen; Swimming Baths; WATTMANNSDORFFGASSE; MAXINGGASSE; Villa Skywa-Primavesi; Tiroler Garten; Gloriette; Kleine Gloriette; HOHENBERGSTRASSE; GLORIETTEGASSE; Villa Schopp; HIETZING; WEISSENTHURNGASSE; SECKENDORFF-GUDENTWEG; Friedhof Hietzing; GASSMANNSTRASSE; ALTMANNSDORFER STRASSE; Barracks; EDELSINNSTRASSE; ELISABETHALLEE; SCHÖNBRUNNER ALLEE; SCHLÖGLGASSE; FASANGARTENGASSE; HETZENDORFERSTRASSE; Werkbundsiedlung; STRANZENBERGGASSE; N; 0 500 m; Lainzer Tiergarten

CAFÉS
Dommayer 1
Gloriette 2

SCHÖNBRUNN

World War II, Schönbrunn served first as the Soviet, and then the British, army headquarters before being handed back to the state in 1947.

## The palace

Compared to the sterility of the Hofburg's state apartments, Schönbrunn's **Prunk-räume** (daily: April–June, Sept & Oct 8.30am–5pm; July & Aug 8.30am–6pm;

Nov–March 8.30am–4.30pm) are a positive visual feast. That said, not every room is worthy of close attention, so don't feel bad about walking briskly through some of them. Visits to the Prunkräume are carefully choreographed. First, make your way to the ticket office on the ground floor of the east wing, where you'll be allocated a visiting time; if the palace is busy, you may well have to wait several hours, in which case you should head off into the gardens, or visit one of Schönbrunn's other sights.

There's a choice of two tickets: the "**Imperial Tour**" (€9.50), which takes in 22 state rooms, and the "**Grand Tour**" (€12.90), which includes all forty rooms open to the public. Even if you're no great fan of period interiors, it's pointless to go on the first, since it skips the palace's most magnificent Rococo delights. For both tours, you get a hand-held audioguide in English, lasting 35 and 50 minutes respectively; with the "Grand Tour", you also get the option of paying €1.50 extra for an hour-long tour with a guide (total price €14.40). The disadvantage of following a tour guide is that they give you the same, short space of time in each room, whether it's worth pausing in or not.

## Emperor Franz-Josef I and Empress Elisabeth's apartments

Whichever tour you're on, you enter the palace via the **Blauerstiege** (Blue Staircase) on the ground floor of the west wing. If you're on the "Imperial Tour", you'll miss the nine **private apartments of Franz-Josef** – no great loss, as anyone who has experienced his dreary quarters in the Hofburg will tell you – entering at Elisabeth's Salon, just after the couple's bedroom.

Visitors on the "Grand Tour", meanwhile, pass through the **Guard Room** into the **Billiard Room**. In Franz-Josef's day, supplicants wishing for an audience with the emperor were made to wait here. While kicking their heels, they could admire the paintings, but sadly weren't invited actually to play billiards. Audiences with the emperor were given in the **Walnut Room** (Nussholzzimmer) next door, named after the walnut chairs and gilded Rococo panelling; even the gilded chandelier is carved from wood. A nasty brown hue lines the walls of the emperor's gloomy **Study**, where Franz-Josef spent much of the day stood over his desk, pedantically reading and signing thousands of official documents; on the wall is a portrait of Empress Elisabeth at 16, when she was betrothed to Franz-Josef. Next comes the widower's **Bedroom**, with the simple iron bed on which the emperor died on November 21, 1916, aged 86; beside it stands Franz Matsch's reverential rendition of the scene. To one side is his imperial majesty's lavatory, installed in 1899 "according to the English system".

Passing through two tiny rooms – the empress used one as her study, the other as her dressing room – you come to the **Imperial Bedroom**, decorated in time for the imperial couple's nuptials in 1854 with matching blue Lyon silk upholstery, and twin rosewood beds. Elisabeth managed to avoid consummating the marriage for the first two nights. The story goes that at family breakfast on the first morning, Elisabeth's crabby mother-in-law, the formidable Archduchess Sophie, asked her how well her son had performed in bed, at which the young bride broke down and wept. Though the empress dutifully produced a son and heir (Rudolf, who later committed suicide; ), within five years she had fled the marital bed entirely, apart from a brief reconciliation in 1867, so it's unlikely Elisabeth spent many nights here.

Not surprisingly, Empress Elisabeth's personal apartments smack even less of her personality than those in the Hofburg. The decor, in fact, dates from the time of **Empress Maria Theresia**, a century or so earlier, and the walls of three rooms – the Marie-Antoinette Room, the Nursery and the Yellow Salon – are lined with portraits of the empress's sixteen offspring. Her father, Karl VI, failed to produce a male heir, leaving Maria Theresia with an uphill struggle to convince the rest of

Europe she was "man" enough for the job. She herself was determined to produce a good cropful of heirs – after the birth of her fourth child, she was heard to comment "I wish I were already in the sixth month of a new pregnancy." Nine of her children survived to adulthood.

While two of her sons went on to become emperors, Josef II and Leopold II, the most famous of the lot was her youngest daughter, **Marie-Antoinette**, who

## Empress Maria Theresia (1740–80)

In 1740, Emperor Karl VI died suddenly, leaving no male heir. That the emperor's daughter, **Maria Theresia**, was able to ascend the throne was thanks to the Pragmatic Sanction of 1713, passed by her father, granting her the right of inheritance. But as she herself put it, "I found myself without money, without credit, without an army, without experience and knowledge, even without counsel, because all my ministers were wholly occupied in trying to discover which way the cat was going to jump." Despite this inauspicious beginning, she survived against the odds – no thanks to her husband, Franz Stephan of Lorraine, who was good at fencing, hunting, shooting and womanizing, but not much else.

Throughout Europe she was known as the "Virgin Empress", though with sixteen children to her name, she clearly wasn't in the literal sense. She was, however, out of step with the promiscuity of the period. Jesuit-educated and deeply pious, she insisted, much to her husband's discomfort, that they share a marital bed (this was by no means the usual custom). It was partly her husband's extramarital activities that prompted her to set up the **Chastity Commission** in 1747. Its commissioners were empowered to search houses, and to arrest any man found entertaining an opera singer, dancer or any other woman of loose morals; offending ladies were locked up in a convent or banished from the realm. Though in the end the commission fizzled out after just six months, it caused a certain amount of havoc – several acting troupes fell foul of the commission, as did Casanova himself, and the celebrated soprano Santini, who was escorted to the Venetian border.

Like her son, Josef II (see p.77), Maria Theresia was a keen reformer, establishing one of the best education systems in Europe at the time, with compulsory education for both sexes. However, she was no liberal, holding notoriously rabid **anti-Semitic** views. Though Vienna had barely five hundred Jews, the empress considered them to be an abomination, expelling them all from the city in 1777, stating: "I know no worse public plague than this people, with their swindling, usury, and money-making, bringing people to beggary, practising all evil transactions which an honest man abhors; they are therefore to be kept away from here and avoided as far as possible." Normally, she would only communicate with them from behind a screen, though she happily used their money to help build Schönbrunn, and made an exception of the baptized Jew, Josef von Sonnenfels, who was one of her chief advisers.

Though Maria Theresia acquired a fun-loving reputation early in her reign, playing cards and dancing until all hours, her demeanour changed after the unexpected death of her husband on August 18, 1765. Thereafter she went into **perpetual mourning**, cutting her hair short, and wearing no jewellery or make-up. For the next fifteen years, she heard Mass every day in the Kaisergruft at the foot of the sepulchre containing her dead husband, spending every 18th of the month and the whole of August in silent prayer. On Franz Stephan's death, she immediately appointed her son, Josef, **co-regent**, and pretty much left him to take over the day-to-day running of the state. In her old age, she grew so large she found it hard to walk and rarely left Schönbrunn at all. She had difficulty breathing, and would keep the windows at the palace constantly open, though the wind and rain which came in gave her terrible rheumatism, and prevented her from writing the sackful of letters she liked to wing off to her children.

married Louis XVI and followed him to the guillotine in 1793. Under her portrait in the Nursery, to the right of the door to Empress Zita's private bathroom, is the only piece of furniture sent back to Vienna by the French after her execution. Off the Empire-style Yellow Salon lies the intimate **Breakfast Room (Frühstücks-kabinett)**, a frothy Rococo concoction decorated with gilded cartouches containing floral silk embroidered by Maria Theresia and her daughters.

## The state apartments

The first of the more elaborate state apartments is the **Mirrors Room** (Spiegel-saal), where, in 1762, the precocious seven-year-old Mozart performed a duet with his older sister Nannerl, in the presence of Maria Theresia and family, and famously "sprang on the lap of the empress, put his arms round her neck and vigorously kissed her", according to his father. From here you enter the **Large Rosa Room**, named for the idealized landscapes executed by the Polish court painter Josef Rosa in the 1760s, set into gilded frames on the walls.

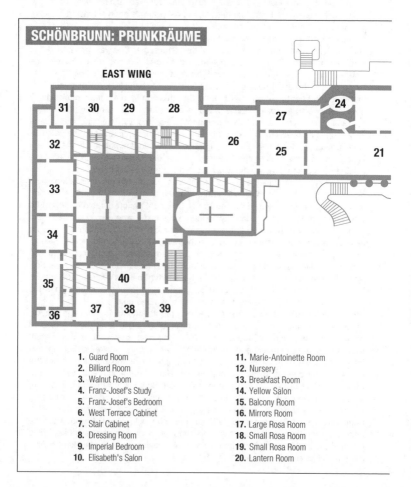

**SCHÖNBRUNN: PRUNKRÄUME**

EAST WING

| | |
|---|---|
| **1.** Guard Room | **11.** Marie-Antoinette Room |
| **2.** Billiard Room | **12.** Nursery |
| **3.** Walnut Room | **13.** Breakfast Room |
| **4.** Franz-Josef's Study | **14.** Yellow Salon |
| **5.** Franz-Josef's Bedroom | **15.** Balcony Room |
| **6.** West Terrace Cabinet | **16.** Mirrors Room |
| **7.** Stair Cabinet | **17.** Large Rosa Room |
| **8.** Dressing Room | **18.** Small Rosa Room |
| **9.** Imperial Bedroom | **19.** Small Rosa Room |
| **10.** Elisabeth's Salon | **20.** Lantern Room |

The **Great Gallery** is, without doubt, the most splendid of all the rooms so far, a vast long hall, heavy with gilded stucco embellishments, lined with fluted pilasters sporting acanthus capitals, and originally lit by over four thousand candles. Of the ceiling frescoes by Guglielmo Guglielmi glorifying the Habsburgs, the last – depicting Austria's military prowess – was, ironically enough, destroyed by World War II bomb damage, and is therefore a copy. The hall was used for banquets during the 1815 Congress of Vienna, and it was here, in 1961, that J.F. Kennedy and Nikita Krushchev held their historic détente meeting.

Venture into the **Small Gallery**, which lies through the three arches to the south of the Great Gallery, to peek at the two Chinoiserie rooms – one round, one oval – to either side. The parquet flooring is sublime, but it's the oriental lacquer panels set into the wainscoting, and the blue-and-white Chinese porcelain, that give the rooms their names. Of the two, the **Round Chinese Cabinet** is the most renowned, as this was where Maria Theresia held her secret meetings with, among others, her chief adviser, Prince Kaunitz, whose apartments were linked to the room by a spiral

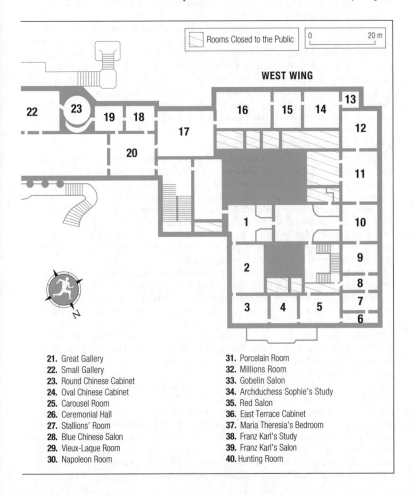

Rooms Closed to the Public

0     20 m

**WEST WING**

21. Great Gallery
22. Small Gallery
23. Round Chinese Cabinet
24. Oval Chinese Cabinet
25. Carousel Room
26. Ceremonial Hall
27. Stallions' Room
28. Blue Chinese Salon
29. Vieux-Laque Room
30. Napoleon Room

31. Porcelain Room
32. Millions Room
33. Gobelin Salon
34. Archduchess Sophie's Study
35. Red Salon
36. East Terrace Cabinet
37. Maria Theresia's Bedroom
38. Franz Karl's Study
39. Franz Karl's Salon
40. Hunting Room

staircase hidden behind one of the doors in the panelling. Another quirky feature of the room was the table designed to rise up through the floor, laden with food and drink, allowing the empress to dine without the need of servants, who might otherwise eavesdrop on matters of state. Kaunitz himself was particularly fond of food, and his table manners were legendary; on one memorable occasion, he "treated the company with the cleaning of his gums, a nauseous operation which lasted a prodigious long time and was accompanied with all manner of noises".

At the far end of the Great Gallery, you must pass through the **Carousel Room**, which gets its name from the painting of the special ladies' tournament held in the Winter Reitschule in 1743 (the sleighs used can be viewed in the Wagenburg). The final room for those on the "Imperial Tour" is the **Ceremonial Hall**, displaying five large paintings by pupils of the court painter, Martin van Meytens. Most depict the elaborate festivities that accompanied the wedding of Maria Theresia's eldest son, Josef II, to Isabella of Parma, in 1760. The magnifying glass, over one section of the painting of the wedding's opera performance, helps you pick out Mozart and his father from the crowd, though the family didn't, in fact, arrive in Vienna until two years after the event.

It was in the beautiful surroundings of the **Blue Chinese Salon**, on November 11, 1918, that the last Habsburg emperor, Karl I, signed the document renouncing "all participation in the affairs of state". (He refused formally to abdicate or to renounce his claim to the throne, and made two unsuccessful attempts to regain the Hungarian half of his title in 1921, before dying in exile on Madeira the following year.) As the name suggests, the room is another Chinoiserie affair – all the rage in the eighteenth century – lined with yellow wallpaper, hand-painted on rice paper, and inset with serene scenes of Chinese life on a deep-blue background.

### The audience rooms

The lightness of the Blue Chinese Room is in complete contrast to the oppressively opulent **Vieux-Laque Room**, with its black-and-gold lacquer panels, exquisite parquetry and walnut wainscoting. During his two sojourns at Schönbrunn, Napoleon is thought to have slept in the neighbouring walnut-panelled **Napoleon Room**, lined with Brussels tapestries depicting the Austrian army in Italy. It was also here that Maria Theresia is thought to have given birth to her brood, and where Napoleon's son by Archduchess Marie-Louise died in 1832, aged just 21. He had been kept a virtual prisoner in Schönbrunn, the stuffed skylark on the table among his few companions (see opposite).

Despite its name, only three items in the remarkable **Porcelain Room**, designed by Isabella of Parma, are actually genuine Meissen porcelain: the chandeliers, the clock and the wall bracket. The rest of the decor is carved from wood and painted to appear like porcelain. The delicate ink drawings set into the walls are signed works by Empress Maria Theresia's daughters, copied from French originals.

The most precious of all the rooms in Schönbrunn is the **Millions Room**, so called because it's estimated that Maria Theresia paid more than a million silver florins to have it decorated. Unfortunately the most priceless items here – the miniature seventeenth-century Persian watercolours of life in the Moghul court – are somewhat overwhelmed by the surrounding, richly gilded cartouches set into the Caribbean rosewood panelling. Just off the Millions Room, the handy little breakfast room, known as the **Miniatures Room (Miniaturenkabinett)**, contains more works by the talented archduchesses. Next door the **Gobelin Salon** holds yet more Brussels tapestries, not only decorating the walls but also upholstering the six chairs, which depict the twelve months. Tapestries were a status symbol, partly because they were so labour-intensive, and therefore very expensive; the central tapestry in this room took eight people twelve years to complete.

When Napoleon's only son, **Napoleon Franz Joseph Karl** (1811–32) was born to his second wife, nineteen-year old Archduchess Marie-Louise (aka Maria Ludovica), daughter of Emperor Franz I, he was destined to inherit a vast empire. Just four years later, in a futile gesture shortly after Waterloo, Napoleon abdicated and proclaimed his infant son Emperor Napoleon II of France in his place, saying: "I would rather my son were strangled than see him brought up as an Austrian prince in Vienna." It was, however, too late for Napoleon to have any say in the destiny of **L'Aiglon** or the "Little Eagle", as his son was known. Marie-Louise had already returned to Vienna with Franz during Napoleon's exile to Elba, and, after his death in 1821, went on to marry a dashing cavalry officer called Count Neipperg, with whom she had three more children.

Franz, or "der kleine Napoleon", as the Viennese dubbed him, was left, orphaned, in Schönbrunn and given precisely the Habsburg aristocratic upbringing his father had dreaded. Abandoned by his parents, who lived in Parma, the little boy enjoyed a privileged but lonely childhood: his language of instruction was switched to German, all reminders of his past life, including toys, were removed. As Napoleon's son, he had been declared King of Rome, but under the Habsburgs, who had no use for him at all, he was given the title **Duke of Reichstadt**, a duchy that didn't in fact exist.

Franz's health deteriorated badly from 1830 onwards, and by the winter of the following year he was seriously ill with **tuberculosis**. He was prevented from moving to a drier climate, or even to the Habsburg spa of Bad Ischl. He died at the age of 21 in the same room his father had slept in during his stay at Schönbrunn. Rumour had it that he had been poisoned by Prince Metternich, who saw him as a political embarrassment; others alleged that he had overindulged in sex; tuberculosis seems the most likely cause.

Passing quickly through the Archduchess Sophie's Study, the Red Salon and the East Terrace Cabinet, with its trompe-l'oeil fresco of cherubs "in an azure firmament", as the brochure puts it, you reach **Maria Theresia's Bedroom** (Reiches Zimmer). The empress never actually slept in the red velvet- and gold-embroidered four-poster bed, which was brought here from the Hofburg. Instead, the room was used exclusively for levées – a kind of official breakfast-in-bed – during her frequent pregnancies. This was also the modest little room in which Franz-Josef was born in 1830.

The last few rooms of the "Grand Tour" are those used by **Archduke Franz Karl** (Franz-Josef's epileptic father) and his wife, Archduchess Sophie, decked out in the usual red-damask and white panelling, and stuffed full of Habsburg portraits, including several by Martin van Meytens. The only items of note are the miniatures, in Franz Karl's Study by the window, by Maria Christina – Maria Theresia's favourite daughter, who was also the lover of Josef II's wife, Isabella of Parma. After Isabella's death from smallpox, Maria Christina went on to marry Albrecht of Saxony-Tetschen, with whom she helped found the Albertina (see p.81).

## Kindermuseum and Berglzimmer

On weekends and in school holidays, the palace organizes a **Kindermuseum** (Sat, Sun & school hols 10am–5pm; adults €6.50, children €4.90) for kids aged between 4 and 12. The children get to dress up, learn to dance the quadrille and find out about court life under the Habsburgs for everyone from the servants to the emperor and empress. The museum, on the ground floor, also allows kids access to the **Berglzimmer**: four relatively informal, though highly decorated, eighteenth-century rooms, all of which look out onto the Schlosspark. The colourful floor-to-ceiling frescoes, abounding in exotic flora, fauna and trompe-l'oeil trelliswork, are the work of the Bohemian painter Johann Wenzel Bergl. Make sure your kids check out the astonishing gilded Baroque stove in the shape of a tree trunk, with birds and animals frolicking on it.

## The outbuildings

With two exceptions (the Orangerie and the Wagenburg), most of the yellow outbuildings that radiate from the main palace at Schönbrunn are closed to the public. A few, like the small Baroque **Schlosskapelle** in the ground floor east wing close to the ticket office, have limited opening hours (Sun 8–11am; ⓦwww .schlosskapelle.at). The ornate **Schlosstheater**, built in 1747 by Pacassi on the west side of the main courtyard, is open only occasionally for summer opera performances (ⓦwww.musik-theater-schoenbrunn.at) or for the Marionettentheater (ⓦwww.marionettentheater.at); pick up a leaflet in the main ticket office.

The vast **Orangerie**, east of the palace, is used for temporary exhibitions, usually on an appropriately imperial theme, for which there is an additional charge. Nearby is the Privy Garden or **Kronprinzengarten** (daily: April–June, Sept & Oct 8.30am–5pm; July & Aug 8.30am–6pm; Nov–March 8.30am–4.30pm; €2), a formal garden laid out in 1870 for the ill-fated Crown Prince Rudolf.

### Wagenburg

By far the most rewarding of the Schönbrunn outbuildings is the **Wagenburg** (daily: April–Oct 9am–6pm; Nov–March 10am–4pm; €6; ⓦwww.khm.at), housed in the former winter riding school west of the palace. The initial section is crowded with nineteenth-century carriages, which are of limited interest to the non-specialist. Head instead for the far end of the hall, where, below the gallery, there's an odd assortment of carriages and sleighs used to transport the imperial offspring. The most poignant is the phaeton designed for Napoleon's son, Franz (see p.171), with mudguards in the shape of eagles' wings, and bees, the Bonaparte family symbol, on the sides.

The highlights of the collection, though, lie beyond the gallery, where you'll find the Habsburgs' Baroque and Rococo carriages. The most outrageous is the enormously long **coronation carriage of Franz Stephan**, Maria Theresia's husband, dripping with gold plating, and fitted with windows of Venetian glass. The painted panels were added for Josef II's coronation as Holy Roman Emperor in 1764. The whole thing weighs an incredible 4000kg, and yet it was transported on several occasions for coronations in Budapest, Frankfurt and Milan. Check out the wonderful horses' harnesses, too, embroidered in red velvet and gold, and the horses' ostrich feather plumes.

The equally ornate carriage opposite, painted entirely in black, was used during periods of official imperial mourning. The relatively modest **red-leather litter**, which stands close by, studded with more than eleven thosand gold-plated nails and buckles, is also worth a look. From 1705 onwards, it was used solely for transporting the Archduke of Austria's hat from Klosterneuburg to Vienna and back for oath fealty ceremonies.

The richly carved, gold-plated carousel or **racing sleigh of Maria Theresia** is the sole survivor of a whole set built in the shape of giant scallops for the special ladies' tournament held in the Winter Reitschule in 1743; note the sleigh bells on the horses' mane decoration. Sleighs were frequently used during *Fasching* for rides in the parks and on the *glacis* outside the city walls. The wheels, on hand in case there was no snow, would be removed and the sleighs pulled by horses, steered by drivers who sat in the back seats and controlled the reins over the heads of the seated ladies.

The gallery is also the place to head if you've a yen to see Empress Elisabeth's horsewhip, with a photo of her husband set into the ivory handle, or the hoof of the horse used by Emperor Franz-Josef I during his coronation as King of Hungary in 1867.

# Schlosspark

Even if you're not going to visit the interior of Schönbrunn, it's worth coming here to enjoy the glorious **Schlosspark** (daily: April–Oct 6am–dusk; Nov–March 6.30am–dusk; free), behind the palace. Like the Belvedere, the park is laid out across a sloping site ideal for the vistas and terraces beloved of Baroque landscape gardeners. Yet despite the formal French style of the gardens, there are also plenty of winding paths in the woods on the slopes to give a hint of wildness, the result of modifications made by Josef II. The latter was also responsible for the park's numerous architectural follies and features, and it was Josef who opened the Schlosspark to the public back in 1779.

## The lower park

The lower section of the Schlosspark is laid out in the formal French style, with closely cropped trees and yew hedges forming an intricate network of gravel paths. Approaching from the palace, however, the first thing that strikes you is the central axis of the **parterre**, decorated with carefully regimented flower beds, leading to the Neptunbrunnen and, beyond, to the triumphal colonnaded arch of the Gloriette. Along the edges are just some of the park's tally of stone statues, more of which lie concealed in its lower section.

Erected in 1781 at the foot of the hill rising up to the Gloriette, the theatrical **Neptunbrunnen** (Neptune Fountain) is by no means upstaged by its grand setting. The eponymous sea god presides over a vast array of wild sea creatures and writhing Tritons and naiads attempting to break in their sea-horses. Kneeling below Neptune, Thetis pleads with the sea god for calm seas to speed her son Achilles to Troy.

Several architectural follies are hidden among the foliage east of the Neptunbrunnen. Particularly fine are the **Römische Ruine** (Roman Ruins), designed to tickle the imperial fancy and serve as a stage set for open-air concerts and theatre. The idea was that these were the remains of some Corinthian palace – they were, in fact, taken from the Schloss Neugebäude (see p.194) – whose fallen stones now provide a watery retreat for a couple of river gods. Close by is the outlet of the original **Schönerbrunnen**, a small grotto pavilion in which the nymph, Egeria, dispenses mineral water from a stone pitcher into a giant-scallop basin.

Further east still stands an **Obelisk**, smothered in hieroglyphs glorifying the Habsburgs, topped by an eagle and an orb, and supported at the base by four, originally gilded, long-suffering turtles. Below the obelisk is a giant cascade of grottos, and a pond inhabited by yet more river gods. Up the hill, past Schönbrunn's municipal swimming baths, stands the **Kleine Gloriette**, where the imperial family used to breakfast. The real reason to explore this heavily wooded part of the park, however, is to feed the red squirrels, tits and nuthatches, which are all tame enough to eat out of your hand. Look out, too, and listen, for the park's numerous **woodpeckers**.

## The Gloriette

If you do nothing else in the Schlosspark, you should climb the zigzag paths from the parterre to admire the triumphal **Gloriette**, and, of course, the view. Designed in Neoclassical style to celebrate the 1757 victory of the Habsburgs over the Prussians at the Battle of Kolín, the Gloriette is the park's focal point, where Fischer von Erlach originally intended to build Schönbrunn itself. One eighteenth-century visitor found the whole thing a bit *de trop*, describing it as a "long portico kind of building, as ugly as possible". It's certainly an overblown affair, its central arch flanked by open colonnades of almost equal stature, and surmounted by trophies and an enormous eagle, wings outstretched; yet more colossal trophies, guarded by lions, stand at either end of the colonnades.

The central trio of arches have been glazed and now house a **café**, from which – if you can get a window table – you can enjoy the view down to the palace. Alternatively, you can climb to the **observation terrace** atop the colonnades (daily: April–June & Sept 9am–6pm; July & Aug 9am–7pm; Oct 9am–5pm; €2).

## Tiergarten (Zoo)

A substantial segment of the palace gardens is taken up by the **Tiergarten** (daily: Feb 9am–5pm; March & Oct 9am–5.30pm; April–Sept 9am–6.30pm; Nov–Jan 9am–4.30pm; adults €14, children €6; Ⓦwww.zoovienna.at), which, founded as an imperial menagerie by Franz Stephan back in 1752, is the world's oldest **zoo**. Here, the imperial couple would breakfast among the animals, in the octagonal pavilion designed for them by Jean-Nicholas Jadot, and decorated with frescoes by Guglielmi depicting Ovid's *Metamorphoses*. Now a very pleasant café-restaurant, the pavilion has miraculously survived to this day, along with several of the original Baroque animal houses, making this one of the most aesthetically pleasing zoos any captive animal could hope for.

The Tiergarten has three **entrances**: the main entrance closest to Hietzing; the Neptunbrunnen entrance; and the Tirolergarten entrance up in the woods to the south. Once inside, you'll find all the usual attractions – elephants, tigers, lions, giraffes, zebras, penguins, camels, monkeys – plus a few less common inhabitants such as beavers, wolves, polar bears, pandas and giant tortoises. Money has been lavished on the zoo, to great effect: the state-of-the-art aquarium has a wonderful walk-through tank, marmosets run freely in the funky monkey-house, and the rainforest glasshouse features tropical birds aplenty, plus fruit bats and terrapins. Those with small kids should head for the *Streichelzoo* (literally "stroking zoo"), where they can get a bit closer to the more benign animals.

The nicest feature of the zoo, by far, is the **Tirolergarten**, on whose woody slopes perches a large timber-framed farmhouse from the Tyrol. The original Tirolergarten was the dreamchild of Archduke Johann, younger brother of Franz II. Fond of the Alps, he commissioned two Tyrolean houses and an alpine garden, in which the imperial family could dispense with the formalities of court life and "get back to nature". Sheep, cows and horses occupy the lower floors of the farm, while upstairs there's an exhibition on the building's history. If you're peckish, check out the traditional Tyrolese soup, bread, cheese and cold meats in the farmhouse kitchen/shop.

## Irrgarten and Labyrinth

Schönbrunn also boasts two mazes, known as the **Irrgarten and Labyrinth** (daily: April–June & Sept 9am–6pm; July & Aug 9am–7pm; Oct 9am–5pm; adults €2.90, children €1.70), situated adjacent to one another near the Neptunbrunnen. The **Irrgarten** – literally "Mad Garden" – is a conventional, head-height yew-hedge maze, based on the original that existed here from 1698 to 1892. While it's easy to get lost for some considerable time in the Irrgarten, the **Labyrinth** is only laid out with small knee-high yew and beech hedges. What the Labyrinth does have, however, are fun stepping-stones, a glockenspiel grid, some zany mirrors and a mathematical teaser.

### Palmenhaus, Wüstenhaus and the Botanischer Garten

While its claim to be the world's largest greenhouse, when it opened in 1882, may well be suspect, Schönbrunn's **Palmenhaus** (daily: May–Sept 9.30am–6pm; Oct–April 9.30am–5pm; €4) is certainly one of the most handsome, with its gracefully undulating wrought-iron frame. Inside, three climate-controlled rooms each have a glorious canopy of palm trees and lots of rhododendrons, lilies, hydrangeas and begonias to add a splash of colour below.

Next door, in the old Sonnenuhrhaus (Sundial House), completed in 1904, is the **Wüstenhaus** (daily: May–Sept 9am–6pm; Oct–April 9am–5pm; €4), a dry hothouse filled with cacti and inhabited by desert mammals, geckos, lizards and "peaceful doves". Schönbrunn also has a small **Botanischer Garten** of its own, established by Franz Stephan west of the Tiergarten, tucked away between the zoo and Maxingstrasse, and a beautiful place in which to escape the crowds.

# Hietzing

With the imperial family in residence at Schönbrunn for much of the summer, the neighbouring quarter of **Hietzing** – now Vienna's thirteenth district – soon became a very fashionable suburb. Still a favourite with Vienna's wealthier denizens, it now boasts some of the city's finest garden villas, ranging from the Biedermeier summer residences of the minor nobility to the Jugendstil and modernist villas of the capital's more successful artists and businessmen. If you've a passing interest in architecture, check out several villas within easy walking distance of Schönbrunn. The incumbents of the local cemetery also reflect the area's cachet, and include the likes of Gustav Klimt and Otto Wagner. In the far west, the **Lainzer Tiergarten**, the former imperial hunting ground, is today a vast, woody retreat for the hoi polloi.

## Hietzinger Hauptstrasse

On the whole, Hietzing is just a sleepy little suburb now, with little to evoke the social whirl that was a feature of the place in the nineteenth century. The *Café*

### Hofpavillon Hietzing

If you're coming to Schönbrunn or Hietzing on a Sunday, pop into the **Hofpavillon Hietzing** (Sun 10.30am–12.30pm; €2; @www.wienmuseum.at), a one-off, Jugendstil pavilion built on the initiative of Otto Wagner in 1899 for the exclusive use of the imperial family and guests whenever they took the Stadtbahn (as the U-Bahn was then known). On the palace side of the gleaming white pavilion, Wagner provided a graceful wrought-iron canopy topped with miniature gilded crowns, underneath which the imperial carriage could shelter. In the octagonal waiting-room, "in order to shorten the seconds spent waiting by the monarch with the sight of a work of art", there hangs a painting by Carl Moll, giving an eagle's-eye view of Vienna's Stadtbahn system. Wagner also tried to ingratiate himself with the emperor by decorating the interior with patterns formed out of Empress Elisabeth's favourite plant, the split-leaved philodendron. Despite Wagner's best efforts, however, the pavilion was used just twice by the emperor, who had a pathological distrust of all things modern.

*Dommayer*, on the corner of **Hietzinger Hauptstrasse**, is one of the few social institutions of the period to have survived (see p.213). Johann Strauss the Younger gave his first public concert here in 1844, playing six of his own waltzes and one of his father's. Round the corner from the café, the enormous *Parkhotel Schönbrunn*, built in 1907 for the emperor's personal guests, is another Hietzing landmark that's still going strong; the Kaiserstöckl, opposite, once the foreign minister's summer residence, is now a post office.

## Friedhof Hietzing

The one and only entrance to the **Friedhof Hietzing** cemetery (daily: March, April, Sept & Oct 8am–5pm; May–Aug 8am–6pm; Nov–Feb 9am–4pm) is on Maxingstrasse. Once inside, despite the smallness of the graveyard, it's actually quite difficult to locate individual tombs. Still, with perseverance, you can find Otto Wagner's rather pompous tomb from the early 1890s, designed by the architect himself, with some gloriously exuberant ironwork, but disappointingly devoid of the Jugendstil motifs that became his trademarks. Plans for a sarcophagus designed by Josef Hoffmann over Gustav Klimt's grave were never carried out; a simple slab with gold lettering is all that marks the artist's resting place. Other notables buried here include the artist Kolo Moser; the Austro-fascist leader Engelbert Dollfuss, murdered by the Nazis in 1934; Franz Grillparzer, Austria's greatest nineteenth-century playwright; Katharina Schratt, Emperor Franz-Josef's mistress; and Alban Berg, the composer, who died in 1935 after an insect sting led to septicaemia.

## Hietzing's villas

A short stroll down **Gloriettegasse** immediately west of the Schlosspark gives a fair indication of the variety of architecture in Hietzing's villa-encrusted backstreets. Only fans of the international modern movement need continue further west to the **Werkbundsiedlung**; the rest can take tram #60 back to Hietzing U-Bahn, or continue west to the Lainzer Tiergarten.

### Gloriettegasse

Your first port of call should be the modest Biedermeier villa at Gloriettegasse 9, with its delicate window pediments of necking swans, where Franz-Josef's mistress, the Burgtheater actress **Katharina Schratt**, used to live. It was procured for Ms Schratt by the emperor himself, so that he could pop in for breakfast at around 7am, to enjoy a bit of intimacy before continuing with his paperwork. "Do not get up too early tomorrow morning, I beg of you," he would write to her, "Allow me to come and sit on your bed. You know that nothing gives me greater pleasure." Afterwards they would go for a stroll in Schönbrunn, where onlookers would applaud the happy couple, who regularly fed the remains of their imperial breakfast to the bears in the Tiergarten.

Turning right down Wattmanngasse to no. 29 brings you to a terraced apartment block embellished by Ernst Lichtblau in 1914 with bands of majolica between the windows, depicting various quasi-medieval figures holding fruits and flowers. Back on Gloriettegasse, at no. 21, stands the **Villa Schopp**, a wonderful 1902 Jugendstil house designed by Friedrich Ohmann, set back from the street behind curvaceous railings, and flanked by hefty gateposts topped by big, black-capped lamps.

Opposite, at Gloriettegasse 14–16, is one of the most unusual Hietzing pads, the **Villa Skywa-Primavesi**. Built in 1913–15 by Josef Hoffmann for the wealthy Wiener Werkstätte patrons, this huge house is designed in Neoclassical vein, with fluted pillars and huge triangular pediments. Nude miniatures perch on shelves at the tops of the pillars, while two larger figures recline in the pediments. Unfortunately, from the street, there's no way to see the bizarre, modern Teetempelchen (Little Tea Temple) Hoffmann built in the garden, complete with pergola and pond.

## Adolf Loos and the Werkbundsiedlung

"Loos swept clear the path before us. It was a Homeric cleansing: precise, philosophical, logical. He has influenced the architectural destiny of us all," Le Corbusier effused in the 1930s. The building authorities were less enthusiastic in 1912 when Adolf Loos sought planning permission for his first Hietzing villa, **Haus Scheu**, at Larochegasse 3, on the other side of Lainzerstrasse from Gloriettegasse. As with the infamous Looshaus in the old town (see p.55), the architect's almost religious aversion to exterior ornament provoked a hostile reaction, as did the building's asymmetry, caused by the series of west-facing terraces that give the house its "stepped" look. Loos completed four other houses in Hietzing alone – Villa Strasser, Kupelwiesergasse 28; Villa Rufer, Schliessmanngasse 11; Haus Steiner, St-Veit-Gasse 10; and the "Wagonhaus", Haus Horner, at Nothartgasse 7, with its barrel-shaped roof – though they're widely dispersed across the district. The main frustration, however, when visiting Loos's houses is that it was in his use of the open plan, and of in-built furniture, that Loos truly excelled – neither of which can be appreciated from his ornament-free exteriors.

Anyone in search of Bauhaus-style inspiration would do better to head for the **Werkbundsiedlung**, a model housing-estate of seventy houses, on Veitingergasse, a short walk up Jagdschlossgasse from the terminus of tram #62. It was laid out between 1930 and 1932 by the Socialist city council for an exhibition of the Wiener Werkbund, an association for the advancement of industrial design, inspired by a similar housing-estate exhibition held at Stuttgart in 1927. Josef Frank invited an international posse of modernists, including Adolf Loos and Josef Hoffmann, to take part. The emphasis was not on technical innovation, but on creating cheap, single-family houses using minimal space, Frank's "planned randomness" offering a more human alternative to the big housing projects of Red Vienna (see p.185). The most surprising thing about the whole project is how small the houses are, with miniature, winding roads to match. Within Werkbundsiedlung, at Woinovichgasse 32 (designed by Frank himself), there's a small documentation centre with information on the estate.

# Lainzer Tiergarten

In the far west of Hietzing lies the former imperial hunting reserve of **Lainzer Tiergarten** (daily: April–Oct 8am–6.30pm or later; Oct–March 9am–5pm or

## Egon Schiele in Hietzing

In 1912, the painter **Egon Schiele** rented a studio at Hietzinger Hauptstrasse 101, and, in between canvases, began flirting with the two respectable middle-class girls, Adele and Edith Harms, who lived opposite at no. 114. Edith and Schiele were ultimately married in 1915, and were expecting their first child when they were both killed in 1918 by the influenza pandemic that claimed more fatalities in Austria than World War I itself. Edith died first at their new studio flat at Wattmanngasse 6. Schiele succumbed three days later at his mother-in-law's house and is buried in the nearby **Friedhof Ober-St-Veit**, beneath a tombstone sculpted by the Hungarian Benjamin Ferenczy, commissioned by Schiele's friends on the tenth anniversary of his death.

later; free), enclosed within a 25km-long wall by Emperor Josef II. It's now the wildest of Vienna's public parks, with virtually no traffic, and no formal gardens at all – head here if you want to leave the urban sprawl far behind. It may not boast the views of the Wienerwald, but you're more likely to spot wildlife, including wild boar, mouflon, woodpecker, and, most easily, red squirrels and deer; in addition, the famous Lipizzaner horses of the Spanische Reitschule spend their summer holidays in the park.

The main entrance is the **Lainzer Tor**, at the end of Hermesstrasse (tram #60 or #62 and then bus #60B), where a **visitor centre** can help you get your bearings. The park's chief sight, the **Hermesvilla** (see below), is ten minutes' walk from here. Those with more energy might aim for the **Hubertuswarte**, an 18m-high lookout tower at the top of Kaltbrundlberg (508m), beyond the Hermesvilla in the centre of the park. **Refreshments** are available in the Hermesvilla restaurant, and also from the *Rohrhaus* and the *Hirschgstemm*, both of which are signposted (with approximate walking times) from the Hermesvilla. Note that the St-Veiter Tor (tram #62 to terminus and then walk or hourly bus #55B), to the north of Lainzer Tor, is only open from mid-February to early November, and that in November and December, only the section of the park around the Hermesvilla is open to the public.

## Wien Museum Hermesvilla

In 1882, in an effort to ingratiate himself with his estranged wife, Emperor Franz-Josef decided to build Elisabeth an informal new residence, which she named **Hermesvilla** (Easter–Oct Tues–Sun 10am–6pm; €5; Ⓦwww.wienmuseum.at) after her favourite Greek deity, the god of travel. Karl Hasenauer designed the building, while Gustav Klimt and Hans Makart helped decorate the interior; there was even a purpose-built exercise room in which the empress could indulge in her daily gymnastics. In the end, though, the villa failed to entice Elisabeth back to Vienna, and she stayed here only very occasionally. The interior is now used for exhibitions put on by the Wien Museum, and there's not much on the Hermesvilla's imperial days, nor anything specific on Empress Elisabeth herself (for more on whom, see p.71).

Less of a villa and more of a mini-chateau, the Hermesvilla is a rather overwrought mixture of Renaissance and Baroque, surrounded by outbuildings linked by a wonderful parade of wrought-iron colonnades. Inside, the decor has that heavy, slightly sterile, strangely unweathered look common to Historicist architecture. Downstairs, the **Dining Hall** serves up rich helpings of marble and stucco, but the best stuff is preserved upstairs. Elisabeth's **Gym** is suitably decorated in Pompeiian style, with muscle men and lusty satyrs engaging in feats of strength. The **Empress's Bedroom** is smothered floor-to-ceiling in one of Makart's sumptuous trompe-l'oeil frescoes depicting Elisabeth's favourite Shakespearean text, *A Midsummer Night's Dream*, with Titania and Oberon in a chariot pulled by leopards. The four-poster bed, with its oppressive double-headed eagle over the headboard, seems designed to guarantee a disturbed night's sleep. The central chamber or **Kirchensaal** is similarly overwrought, with gilded wood-panelling and a shallow oval dome.

# Further afield

The sights in this section are widely dispersed across the great swathe of the city's western suburbs from Hietzing to the Wienerwald. While the **Technisches Museum** is within easy walking distance of Schönbrunn, the others require careful route-planning on the Viennese transport system. Of these, the most rewarding is the **Kirche am Steinhof**, Otto Wagner's Jugendstil masterpiece, high up on Baumgartner Höhe; two more **Wagner villas** can be admired in the leafy surroundings of neighbouring Hütteldorf. In the otherwise dour suburb of Ottakring lies the **Schmelzer Pfarrkirche**, an early modernist work by the spiritual godfather of postmodernism, Josep Plečnik. Further north still, in Pötzleinsdorf, the city's premier collection of Biedermeier furniture is housed in the peaceful **Geymüllerschlössel**.

## Technisches Museum

Across Auer-Welsbach-Park from the main gates of Schönbrunn, the **Technisches Museum** (Mon–Fri 9am–6pm, Sat & Sun 10am–6pm; €8.50; ⓦ www.tmw.at), was conceived in the last decade of Habsburg rule, and opened in 1918. The museum has recently undergone a massive transformation to become a truly innovative, hands-on place, with just about enough information to enable English speakers to enjoy the exhibits. With five floors to explore, you should leave yourself at least half a day to do the museum justice, safe in the knowledge that the ground floor café serves decent food. Note that a few of the exhibits have timed showings, for which you must pay extra and book in advance.

The museum's main entrance is down in the basement, where you'll also find the **Nature and Knowledge (Natur und Erkenntnis)** section. Here, you can learn about basic scientific concepts from gravity to electromagnetism, while being entertained at the same time – don't miss the fog chamber at the far end. Also on this level is the interactive **Phenomena and Experiments (Phänomene und Experimente)** gallery, where, among other things, you can play at animation and doodle with a giant spirograph. Upstairs on the ground floor is the hangar-like main hall, with an early aeroplane and a satellite suspended above it. The oldest train displayed here is *Ajax*, built in Warrington in 1841 for Austria's first steam railway; the most luxurious, Empress Elisabeth's *Hofsalonwagen* (imperial sleeping car) from 1873. The nearby **Heavy Industry (Schwerindustrie)** section is dominated by the giant Linz-Donawitz basic oxygen furnace, developed at the giant steelworks in Linz, an interactive model of which stands close by. The **Energy (Energie)** gallery, on the other side of the main hall, is a lot more fun, however, especially the giant, wind-up energy contraption by the entrance.

With the help of a Van de Graaff generator and a Tesla transformer, you can experience some hair-raising forms of energy in the first-floor **High Voltage Room (Hochspannungsraum),** one of the museum's highlights, for which you have to book on arrival (€2). At the far end of the Energy gallery, you can don a hard hat to visit the mock-up **Mine (Bergwerk)**, though, again, you need to book onto a tour in advance (€2). The special exhibitions on the second floor up are always worth investigating, while those with small kids should head for **das mini**, where 3-to-6-year-olds can romp around and have fun.

The **Transport (Verkehr)** collection on the top floor is deservedly popular, boasting vintage vehicles by Porsche, Benz, and Graf & Stift, and a whole load of old bicycles, motorbikes, model ships, trams and trains. Look out, too, for the rare sight of an Austrian lighthouse from the Dalmatian coast. Also on this level are the **Musical Instruments (Musikinstrumente)** – a good place for a breather, as you can sit down at one of the listening stations. Meanwhile, the **medien.welten** section concentrates on digital technology and its application in printing, photography and music. For something more immediately appealing, though, head for the **Everyday Life (Alltag)** section, which has a wonderful display of domestic appliances through the decades, a 1908 urinal you can wander into, and a bizarre collection of historic prosthetic limbs.

## Kirche am Steinhof

Anyone with a passing interest in Jugendstil architecture should head out to the **Kirche am Steinhof** (Sat 3–5pm; Mon–Fri by appointment ☎910 60-11 204; free), completed in 1907 by Otto Wagner as a chapel for the city's main psychiatric hospital. The church occupies a fantastic site on the commanding heights of the Baumgartner Höhe, overlooking the hospital's grid-plan terraces below. Like the Karlskirche (see p.104), it's topped by a giant copper dome and lantern (both originally gilded) and features two belfries capped with copper statues of seated saints; only the Karlskirche's columns are missing.

Inside, the church is organized on a north–south axis to allow more light to stream through Kolo Moser's glorious mosaic windows. Health and safety informed much of the design: continuously running holy water in the fonts, no sharp edges to the pews, a raked floor to facilitate cleaning, and special doors flanking the altar to allow hospital staff rapid access to the patients in emergencies. The main altar features an eye-catching, cage-like, gilt baldachin, against a backdrop mosaic featuring Christ at the top of a Hollywood-style staircase crowded with sundry saints. Sadly, the church is little used nowadays; it's too cold for services during the winter, and even in summer there are few takers among the patients.

To reach the church, take bus #47A (every 15min) from U-Bahn Unter-St-Veit, after which it's a good ten-minute hike uphill to the church itself. There's a **guided tour** – more of a dull monologue (in German only) really – but from 4pm you're free to wander around. Alternatively, you can sign up for a guided tour (in English) of the church and some of the other hospital buildings (April–Sept Fri 3.30pm; €10).

Close by, below the church in Pavillon V, a permanent exhibition commemorates those who suffered here during the war due to the hospital's shocking involvement in the **Nazi euthanasia** campaign (Wed–Fri 10am–5pm, Sat 2–6pm; free; ⓦwww.gedenkstaettesteinhof.at). The museum tells the story of the thousands of patients who were put on transports to be gassed at Schloss Hartheim in Upper Austria, and the hundreds of (already ill) children who were experimented on at the hospital itself.

## Two Wagner villas

If you're fired with enthusiasm for Otto Wagner's works, head for the woody suburb of **Hütteldorf**, where two contrasting villas, built at either end of his career, stand side by side on Hüttelbergstrasse; take tram #49 to its terminus, then walk along the Halterbach stream (10min) or the U-Bahn to Hütteldorf and then three stops on bus #148 or #152.

**Villa Wagner I**, at no. 26, is an early work from 1888, designed as a luxurious Palladian villa for Wagner's own use. It's a grandiose, typically Ringstrasse building, with a central Ionic portico flanked by two Doric pergolas. Badly damaged in World War II, the building was saved from demolition in the 1960s thanks to being squatted by the artists Friedensreich Hundertwasser and Ernst Fuchs. Fuchs, a purveyor of "fantasy-realism" from the *Judge Dredd* school of painting, bought the property in 1972, and, since going into tax exile in Monaco, has turned it into the self-aggrandizing **Ernst-Fuchs Privatstiftung** (March–Oct daily except Sat 10am–6pm; Nov–Feb Mon–Fri 10am–5.30pm; €11; ⓦwww.ernstfuchs-zentrum.com). Wagner devotees come out of it worse than Fuchs fans.

The latter can lap up his lurid nudes and admire the rock'n'roll decor; all that survives of Wagner's work are the ceilings, and the north pergola, which retains its vegetal, Jugendstil windows added in 1900. The psychedelic touches on the exterior, such as the multicoloured cornice, are by Fuchs, though the wrought ironwork is original. Fuchs is, naturally, responsible for the huge fertility goddess with decorated mammaries that fronts the building, and has also added his very own Gaudí-, not to say gaudy, style Nymphaeum fountain-house in the garden.

Providing a perfect contrast to its neighbour is the cube-shaped **Villa Wagner II** (closed to the public), at no. 28, into which Wagner moved in 1913. It was to be his last work, and, with its austere, ornament-free facade, and its use of reinforced concrete and aluminium, conforms to his later conversion to rationalism and modernism. The exterior decoration is limited to a distinctive band of indigo-blue glass tiles alternating with aluminium bolts. Above the building's two entrances are the only other gratuitous decoration: the glass mosaic over the front door depicting Athene sporting her Gorgon's-head shield, and the series of colourful, mythological mosaics, which also feature under the side portico.

## Schmelzer Pfarrkirche

Don't be put off by the brutal, concrete classicism of its exterior: the **Schmelzer Pfarrkirche**, designed by the Slovene architect Josep Plečnik on Herbststrasse in 1913, is one of Vienna's hidden suburban gems. The city's first-ever concrete church, it caused huge controversy, provoking Archduke Franz Ferdinand to pronounce it a ridiculous mixture "of a temple to Venus, a Russian bath, and a stable or hayloft". Despite such confusion, the main body of the church is surprisingly light and modern, while Otto Holub's Jugendstil high altar is simply outstanding. A dove flanked by two angels, all in aluminium low-relief, are framed against a semicircular golden sunburst, in turn set off against a "luxuriant gold and purple wall mosaic featuring the seven levitating attributes of the Holy Spirit, from *Frömigheit* (Piety) to *Gotesfurcht* (Fear of God)".

The church's *pièce de résistance*, however, is the concrete **crypt**, which you enter from stairs either side of the main altar; in order to see anything, you need to feed the light-meter. Several Jugendstil masterpieces brighten this gloomy underworld, with its low ceiling and trio of grottoes. Murals on either side of the altar feature Klimt-like celestial creatures: *Rachel Weeping for Her Dead Children* and *The Creation of Water*. Even more magical is the marble font, capped by a golden lid frothing with fish, out of which a heavenly figure rises up brandishing a cross.

## Geymüllerschlössel

In the 1800s, the wealthy banker Johann Heinrich von Geymüller had a luxury summer house, the **Geymüllerschlössel** (May–Nov Sun 11am–6pm; €7.90 includes admission to the MAK, see p.110), built in the sleepy village (now city suburb) of Pötzleinsdorf. The Geymüllers were an archetypal wealthy Biedermeier family, though the house itself is, in fact, an exotic mixture of Gothic and Moorish elements. It has the appeal of a garden folly, and the colour – white walls and green shutters – of an Italianate villa.

Rich in Biedermeier associations – Schubert and Grillparzer were frequent visitors – and decor, the house displays a magnificent collection of **early nineteenth-century furniture** and clocks. The most startling room is the **Salon mit Panoramatapete**, a drawing room equipped with period furniture made from ebony and gold and upholstered in deep blue, and dominated by the panoramic murals of idealized Oriental landscapes.

To reach the house, take tram #41 to its terminus, and either bring a picnic to have in the extensive gardens, or pop across the road into the local *Heuriger*. Those with children might consider combining a trip out here with a visit to the nearby **Pötzleinsdorfer Schlosspark**, by the tram terminus, which has a big playground, red-squirrel-infested woods, and a small farm with hens, goats, sheep and guinea fowl.

# Döbling and the Wienerwald

Once a little village to the north of Vienna, **Döbling** is now the city's vast nineteenth district which stretches right up into the **Wienerwald** or Vienna Woods. Though built-up in parts, the district is still peppered with vineyards and the remnants of several old villages, making it a unique mixture of city and countryside. Tourists and locals alike flock here in summer to drink the local wine in the numerous *Heurigen*, or to get some fresh air during a walk in the hills. Nearer town, there are a couple of places of pilgrimage devoted to Beethoven, and a housing estate, which remains a symbol of both the success and failure of interwar "Red Vienna".

## Oberdöbling

Döbling used to be two separate villages: Unterdöbling and **Oberdöbling**. Lying just outside the *Linienwall* (now the *Gürtel*), these were popular summer retreats for the wealthier denizens of Vienna. The district's chief sight is the **Eroicahaus**, but if you're here at the weekend, it's worth visiting nearby **Villa Wertheimstein**, a rambling, fin-de-siècle house that once attracted the city's literati to its door.

### Beethoven Eroicahaus

In the summer of 1803, Beethoven took lodgings in a single-storey vintner's house – today's **Eroicahaus** (by appointment ℡505 87 47; €2; ⓦwww.wien museum.at), at Döblinger Hauptstrasse 92. Surrounded by gardens and vineyards, with a view across to Heiligenstadt, he grappled with the "heroic" (*eroica* in Italian) concepts that would crystallize in his third symphony. The inspiration for the piece was Napoleon, whom Beethoven saw as the embodiment of the French Revolution. He dedicated the work to Napoleon, but on receiving news that the former First Consul had crowned himself Emperor, Beethoven flew into a rage, tore up the dedication, and renamed the symphony *Eroica*. The rooms in which Beethoven lodged have been preserved, though the building's upper storey is a later addition. The museum contains none of the composer's personal effects, and is really only for those with a specialist interest. Passing Beethoven fans would be better off visiting the composer's other memorial house in Heiligenstadt (see p.186).

### Villa Wertheimstein

Up the street from the Eroicahaus, at the end of a driveway, a much more enjoyable house-museum, the **Villa Wertheimstein** (March–Oct Sat 10am–5pm, Sun 10am–3pm; free), doubles as the local museum or Döblinger Bezirksmuseum. Built in the 1830s by silk manufacturer and patron of the arts Rudolf Arthaber, it was bought in 1870 by the Jewish financier Leopold Wertheimstein, manager of the Vienna branch of the Rothschild bank. Leopold spent most of his time in the

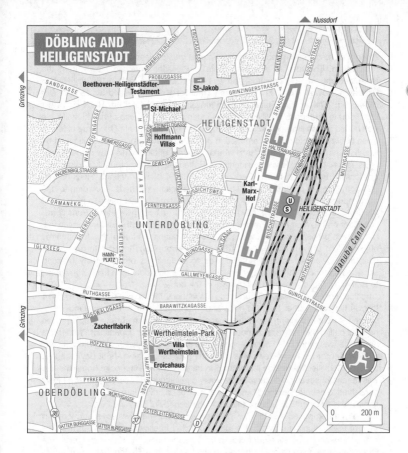

family's town house, while his young wife, Josephine, stayed at the Döbling villa, presiding over one of Vienna's most celebrated salons, along with her only daughter, Franziska. The pianist Artur Rubinstein played here on more than one occasion, while more frequent visitors included the artist Hans Makart, the philosopher Franz Brentano, the poets Eduard Bauernfeld and Ferdinand Saar, and the writer Hugo Hoffmannsthal. When Franziska died in 1907, villa and contents were bequeathed to the city. The rooms given over to the local museum contain few surprises, but the three final rooms retain their hotchpotch decor from the salon's heyday, and include commemorative rooms for the two poets.

## Heiligenstadt

**Heiligenstadt** is typical of Vienna's outlying suburbs, a combination of barracks-like housing and remnants of the old wine-making village. It became a fashionable spa retreat for the Viennese from 1784 onwards, thanks to the discovery of a curative mineral spring. Nowadays, the easiest way to get here is on the U-Bahn, from which you get a great view of Friedensreich Hundertwasser's funky **Fernwärme Wien** (guided tours by appointment ☏313 26) in neighbouring Spittelau, his colourfully decorated paper-incineration plant from the late 1980s,

## Theodor Herzl (1860–1904)

Along with fascism, psychoanalysis and atonal music, Vienna is also the birthplace of **Zionism**. The idea of a Jewish state in Palestine emerged slowly from the mid-nineteenth century onwards, and was only coined as a term in 1893 by Nathan Birnbaum. However, only in 1896, when **Theodor Herzl** published his seminal *Der Judenstaat* (The Jewish State), did the movement really take off. Herzl spent his childhood in Budapest, but lived in the Austrian capital for much of his adult life. He was buried in Döbling's Jewish cemetery until the establishment of the state of Israel, when he was disinterred and reburied in Jerusalem. Yet despite his beatification by Israel, it's not at all clear what Herzl would have thought about his new place of rest.

His family, though Jewish residents of Budapest, were thoroughly assimilated, politically liberal and culturally German. While studying law in Vienna, Herzl himself was something of a dandy, "dark, slim, always elegantly clothed", according to one contemporary. His true ambition was to be a playwright, or at a push, "a member of the Prussian nobility". Having failed on both counts, he became, instead, Paris correspondent of the *Neue Freie Presse*. Herzl had experienced **anti-Semitism** in Vienna, but nothing prepared him for the bigotry aroused during the trial of the Jewish army officer, Alfred Dreyfus, in 1893–94. During this period, Herzl toyed with the idea of challenging Vienna's leading anti-Semites to a duel; his other, equally madcap scheme was to lead the Jews of Vienna into the Stephansdom for a mass conversion to Roman Catholicism, with the approval of the pope.

Ironically enough, it was a performance of Wagner's *Tannhäuser* – in which the hero follows his heart rather than his head and returns to his spiritual homeland – that spurred Herzl into thinking about the creation of a new **Jewish state**, a utopian vision he later outlined in his most famous political pamphlet, *Der Judenstaat*. Yet Herzl's new state was more of a liberal utopia than a specifically Jewish one. The principal inducement for his fellow Jews was to be the new state's seven-hour day (one less than the Socialist International promised to deliver); to drive the point home the flag was to feature seven gold stars. Yet he was no revolutionary, decrying "That a highly conservative people, like the Jews, have always been driven into the ranks of revolutionaries, is the most lamentable feature in the tragedy of our race."

Initially, he proposed that the European powers grant the Jews sovereignty over a slice of their colonial territories. He tried, but failed to elicit the support of the likes of the Rothschilds; he even approached the Tsar, the pope, the Kaiser and finally the Ottoman sultan, from whom he hoped to secure Palestine. Failing that, Herzl, unlike most of his followers, was prepared to accept a portion of Argentina or take up the British offer of Uganda. Despite his rejection by most wealthy, assimilated Jews, and by the Orthodox Jewry, Herzl's movement flourished, especially in the ghettos of Eastern Europe. In 1897, Herzl convened and chaired the first **World Zionist Congress** in Basel, where he was elected president and hailed "King of the Jews". By the time of his death in 1904, the Zionist bank in London boasted 135,000 shareholders, the largest number financing any enterprise in the world.

which provides electricity for the surrounding district. Architecturally, it is, as one critic caustically dubbed it, merely "a painted shed", though it's certainly a lot more visually entertaining than most industrial plants, looking something like a psychedelic mosque.

### Karl-Marx-Hof

If one housing complex has come to symbolize the interwar municipal socialism of "Red Vienna", it is the **Karl-Marx-Hof**, the kilometre-long, peach-and-salmon-coloured "people's palace", whose distinctive giant archways greet you as you exit from Heiligenstadt U-Bahn. Though right-wing critics charged that these housing complexes were built as fortresses by the socialists to protect their workers in case of civil war, their fragility was proved on February 12, 1934, when the World War I artillery of the Austro-fascist government reduced much of the Karl-Marx-Hof to rubble in a few hours. It took another four days for the government forces to flush the last defenders out, however. This is only the most famous of the battles of the civil war, which was fought just as keenly and bloodily in numerous other working-class housing estates in Vienna and other Austrian cities. Shortly after the battle, the future King Edward VIII visited Vienna and endeared himself to the Viennese socialists by asking to be taken to see the Karl-Marx-Hof – it would be difficult to think of a more unlikely political sympathizer.

## Hohe Warte

During the first decade of the twentieth century, the architect Josef Hoffmann built five houses in the fashionable **Hohe Warte**, the high ground above the village church of Heiligenstadt, at the terminus of tram #37. A pupil of Otto Wagner, Hoffmann was one of the founders of the Secession and of the Wiener Werkstätte (see p.112), but his architectural style, with its pared-down classicism and minimal decoration, is very much his own.

### Red Vienna

Its bloody history and colourful, monumental exterior have made Karl-Marx-Hof a potent symbol of **Red Vienna** (Rotes Wien), the city's Austro-Marxist experiment in municipal socialism (1919–33). While other European socialist parties attempted piecemeal reforms, the Social Democratic Workers' Party (SDAP) developed a comprehensive **proletarian counterculture** that was intended to serve as an alternative to both bourgeois culture and the Bolshevik experiment in Russia. Cheap tickets to the theatre and opera were provided for the workers, and workers' symphony concerts were held under the baton of one of Schönberg's pupils, Anton Webern. Perhaps the most powerful display of Red Vienna took place during the **International Worker Olympics** in 1931, when 100,000 people marched through the city to take part in a mass festival held in the Prater Stadion (see p.155), watched by countless more thousands.

Though one cannot but be impressed by the ambition and scope of the SDAP's social and cultural programme, a large section of the working class remained untouched by either initiative. Throughout, the SDAP remained controlled and led by an oligarchy of party elite, which held a patronizing and deeply paternalistic view of the rank and file, who, by and large, fulfilled a passive role in the whole process. While the real achievements and failures of Red Vienna have become lost in the myths of time, its legacy remains highly visible in the huge **housing complexes** that punctuate Vienna's outer suburbs. These workers' enclaves – purpose-built with communal laundries, bathhouses, kindergartens, libraries, meeting rooms, cooperative shops and health clinics – were designed to help create the "neue Menschen" of the Socialist future. They may have failed in that lofty aim, but they continue to provide cheap and well-maintained housing for a populace who had, until then, been crowded into unsanitary tenements within the *Vorstädte*.

**Karl-Marx-Hof** is the most famous, but by no means the largest, of Red Vienna's housing complexes. Though all are imposing, none are architecturally innovative, eschewing the modernist, avant-garde aesthetic of the interwar era for a more traditional, monumental architecture. If you're interested, there are guided tours organized by the city council, or you can visit them off your own bat. After Karl-Marx-Hof, the most impressive architecturally are Reumann-Hof, 5, Margaretengürtel (tram #6 or #18), and Raben-Hof, 3, Rabengasse (Kardinal-Nagl-Platz U-Bahn).

The best-preserved house, the ivy-strewn **Villa Spitzer**, Steinfeldgasse 4, is an idiosyncratic mixture of the classical and the medieval, completed in 1902. The **Villa Ast** (now the Saudi Arabian embassy), at no. 2, completed nearly a decade later at the height of Hoffmann's classical period, provides an interesting contrast. Earliest of the lot, the semi-detached double **Villa Moser-Moll I**, built for his fellow Secession artists, Kolo Moser and Carl Moll, at no. 6 and no. 8, features decorative half-timbering similar to that of the Villa Spitzer. Carl Moll was, of course, the stepfather of Alma Mahler-Werfel (née Schindler), and it was to no. 8 that the composer Gustav Mahler went a-courting in the winter of 1901–02 (see box, p.98).

## Beethoven-Wohnung-Heiligenstadt

In 1802, on the advice of his doctor, who hoped the country air would improve his hearing, Beethoven moved out to the **Beethoven-Wohnung-Heiligenstadt** (Tues–Sun 10am–1pm & 2–6pm; €2; ⓦwww.wienmuseum.at), Probusgasse 6. Here he wrote his **"Heiligenstadt Testament"** – a facsimile of which is at the

### Ludwig van Beethoven (1770–1827)

Born in 1770 in Bonn, **Ludwig van Beethoven** came to Vienna in 1787, but remained for just a few months owing to his mother's illness. Her death, and his father's later death from alcoholism in 1792, freed Beethoven to return to the Austrian capital, where he lived until his own demise in 1827. Like Mozart, he was taught by his father and played piano in public at a very early age (though his father used to pretend he was younger than he actually was). Again like Mozart, Beethoven was a **virtuoso pianist**, yet their techniques couldn't have been more different: Mozart gliding over the keys with smooth fluency, Beethoven smashing the keys with such force that he regularly broke the strings. Unlike both Haydn and Mozart, Beethoven was never a slave to the aristocracy, but an independent artist, whose patrons clubbed together to pay him an annuity just to keep him in Vienna, and prevent him having to take up the post of *Kapellmeister* at Westphalia which was offered him in 1809.

Though recognized as a genius by Viennese high society, he was also regarded as something of a freak: unprepossessing, scruffily dressed, reeking of body odour and swearing like a trooper. Despite such shortcomings, he was clearly attractive to women, and was, in his own words, "generally involved in one entanglement or the other". The objects of his affections were almost invariably young, beautiful, educated, aristocratic, and occasionally even married – in other words, unobtainable. One theory put forward as to why Beethoven never married is that he had syphilis, which would explain why he frequently changed doctors, and talked in his letters of "a malady which I cannot change and which brings me gradually nearer to death" – some suggest it may even have been the cause of his **deafness**.

In 1815, Beethoven's brother, Karl, died and Beethoven made the fateful decision to adopt his nephew, also named Karl, no doubt hoping that he would be the son the composer never had. After a long custody battle with his sister-in-law, Beethoven succeeded in removing the boy from his mother in 1820, only to send him to boarding school. Beethoven proved totally unsuitable as a father, and Karl's misery reached such a pitch that in 1826, the 15-year-old tried unsuccessfully to shoot himself. He was immediately removed from Beethoven's care, at which point the composer fell into despair, eventually dying on March 26, 1827, during a thunderstorm. His **funeral**, in contrast to Mozart's, attracted a crowd of twenty thousand to the Dreifaltigkeitskirche on Alserstrasse, with Austria's chief poet, Franz Grillparzer, composing the funeral oration, and Schubert as one of the torchbearers. Beethoven was buried in Währinger Friedhof, but now rests in the Zentralfriedhof (see p.190).

museum – addressed but never sent to his brothers. In it he apologizes for appearing "unfriendly, peevish, or even misanthropic", talks honestly about his **deafness**: "a sense which in me should be more perfectly developed than in other people", and the pain and embarrassment it brought him: "I was on the point of putting an end to my life – the only thing that held me back was my art." It reads like a will, though it was more of a confession, the cathartic soliloquy of someone who had reached rock bottom.

After the onset of his deafness, Beethoven kept a **Conversation Book** and a pencil with him at all times. He would offer the book and pencil to whomever he was trying to communicate with, though he himself rarely wrote in it, simply bellowing his replies to his companions. By the time of his death in 1827 there were four hundred "conversations", 136 of which have survived (and are kept in Berlin's Royal Library). Despite his personal distress, while resident at Probusgasse Beethoven completed his joyful second symphony, "brought home right from the meadows of Heiligenstadt, so full is it of summer air and summer flowers" – a keen antidote to the theory of trying to fit the works to a composer's mood and life.

Beethoven changed addresses more times even than Mozart (see p.50), and spent a further four summers at various locations in Heiligenstadt. Despite the lack of original furnishings, the house in Probusgasse is the most rewarding of the city's three memorial museums to the composer. On the far side of a shady, cobbled courtyard, the museum occupies the rooms thought to have been rented by Beethoven, and contains a lock of the composer's hair, his death mask, and the original doorhandle and lock from the Schwarzspanierhaus (now demolished), in which he died in 1827.

## Grinzing

The last village you come to as you ascend the slopes towards the Wienerwald is **Grinzing**, by far the most famous of the wine-making districts, whose *Heurigen* are mobbed by tour groups throughout the summer. To find a more authentic *Heuriger*, you're better off in any of the less well-known neighbouring districts (see p.222), but fans of Gustav Mahler (see p.98) might consider taking tram #38 to **Grinzinger Friedhof** (daily: May–Aug 7am–7pm; March, April, Sept & Oct 7am–6pm; Nov–Feb 8am–5pm). The composer was buried here in 1911, having converted to Catholicism earlier in his career to make himself more acceptable to the anti-Semitic Viennese establishment that ran the opera house. His modernist tombstone, designed by Josef Hoffmann, was commissioned by his widow, Alma Mahler-Werfel, who lies close by. Other notable corpses include the one-armed pianist Paul Wittgenstein (brother of philosopher Ludwig), and the writer Heimito von Doderer.

## Wienerwald

The forested hills of the **Wienerwald** (Vienna Woods) reach from the north-western city limits to the foothills of the eastern Alps to the southwest. The peaks you can see northwest of Vienna make an uplifting spectacle – few other European capitals can boast such an impressive green belt on their doorstep. In the eighteenth century, wealthier folk used to move out into the villages on the vine-clad slopes of the Wienerwald for the duration of the summer. With the arrival of public transport, even those without such means could just hop on a tram to the end of the line, and enjoy a day in the countryside. To this day, the Wienerwald remains a popular weekend jaunt, and throughout the summer, the wine gardens of the local *Heurigen* are filled not only with tour groups, but also the Viennese themselves, who come here to sample the new wine.

## Approaching the Wienerwald

There are several approaches to the Wienerwald. **Tram #38** terminates in the centre of Grinzing. If you walk up Cobenzlgasse, turn right up Krapfenwaldgasse and then go straight on at the crossroads, up Mukenthalerweg, you'll find yourself on the right path to Kahlenberg. To avoid the worst of the crowds and the traffic, though, it's better to start walking from the terminus of **tram #D**, following Beethovengang past the Beethoven memorial, then going up Kahlenbergerstrasse. Either way, it's a good 3km uphill to Kahlenberg itself. The shortest, stiffest climb is from **Kahlenbergerdorf S-Bahn** station up Nasenweg, a kilometre-long path of tight switchbacks that takes you to the top of Leopoldsberg.

The lower reaches of the Wienerwald are no longer the rural idyll they once were, partly owing to the winding corniche, known as the Höhenstrasse, built in the 1930s to allow access to Kahlenberg and Leopoldsberg. **Bus #38A** from Heiligenstadt U-Bahn will take you all the way to Kahlenberg, Cobenzl and (less frequently) Leopoldsberg. Although it is nice to bring your own picnic, there are several restaurants and cafés to fall back on.

## Kahlenberg, Leopoldsberg and around

One of the most popular places from which to admire the view over Vienna is **Kahlenberg** (484m), the higher of the two hills that rise to the north of the city, close by the Danube. There's a café, with a magnificent terrace and a viewing platform, but the whole place is literally mobbed on summer weekends. According to tradition, this was where the papal legate, Marco d'Aviano, and the Polish king, Jan Sobieski, celebrated Mass in 1683, before Sobieski led the Polish army down the mountain to relieve the city from the Turks. The Baroque **Josefskirche**, in which the event supposedly took place, is now run by the Poles, and the church's Sobieski chapel is a Polish national shrine. The most striking thing about the plain interior is the hundreds of rosaries, pendants, and lucky Madonna and Child talismans, which hang on the walls from floor to ceiling.

Tradition notwithstanding, it has been proved fairly conclusively that the aforementioned Mass actually took place on the neighbouring peak of **Leopoldsberg** (425m), just over 1km by road east of Kahlenberg. To confuse matters further, the two hills swapped names after the Leopoldskirche was built on what is now Leopoldsberg in 1693. This is certainly a more beguiling spot in which to relax and enjoy the view – the courtyard and café are shaded by pine trees, and there's a more dramatic view from the restored ramparts, originally built by the Babenbergs in 1135. The main lookout-point doubles as a memorial for those Austrian POWs who finally returned from the Soviet Union in the 1950s. The church itself is also better looking than the one on Kahlenberg, and has a historical display of prints and documents relating to the Turkish siege.

If you'd like a longer walk in the woods, it probably makes more sense to get off bus #38A in the big car park at **Am Cobenzl**. Cobenzl itself offers assorted eating and drinking options, from the posh *Schlossrestaurant Cobenzl* to the more modest *Café Cobenzl*, both of which enjoy extensive views over Vienna. If you have children with you, be sure to check out the wild boar penned up round the back of the *Schlossrestaurant*. A nicer spot for something to drink or eat is the *Oktogon*, a modern octagonal café, off the road, five minutes' walk west at Am Himmel. Behind the café, a musical tree-circle is worth a quick look.

From Cobenzl, it's around 3km via Bei der Kreuzeiche and Jägerkreuz to the lookout tower on **Hermannskogel** (542m). Alternatively, you can enjoy the view while walking downhill from Am Himmel or Am Cobenzl via the **Bellevuehöhe**

(388m), where a plaque commemorates Freud's discovery of the secret of dreams. At the bottom of the hill, you can catch bus #39A to Oberdöbling.

# Klosterneuburg

Just north of the city limits, hidden from the capital by the Wienerwald, the chief attraction in the village of **Klosterneuburg** is its imposing Augustinian **monastery** – the oldest and richest in Austria, its Baroque domes and neo-Gothic spires soar above the right bank of the Danube. Klosterneuburg also has a spanking-new private **modern art museum**, hidden in its peripheral streets and filled with postwar Austrian art.

## The monastery

The **Stift Klosterneuburg** (daily 9am–5pm; ⓦ www.stift-klosterneuburg.at) was founded in the twelfth century by the Babenberg Duke Leopold III, who, so the story goes, vowed to build an abbey on the spot where he found his wife's veil, carried off by the wind from a nearby castle. Leopold himself was canonized in 1485, and later became the patron saint of Austria, making Klosterneuburg a popular place of pilgrimage. Having withstood the Turkish siege of 1683, the monastery enjoyed a second golden age under the Emperor Karl VI (1711–40), who planned a vast imperial palace here, along the lines of the Escorial in Spain. Although the project was never fully realized, the one wing that was completed gives some idea of Karl's grandiose plans.

To reach the monastery, take **S-Bahn** line S40 from Franz-Josefs Bahnhof (every 30min) to Klosterneuburg-Kierling. The monastery is clearly visible from the station; head up Hundskehle, then take the steps to your left. Of the various tours on offer, the main two are the guided **Sakrale Tour** (hourly 10am–4pm; €9), which lets you see the Stiftskirche, the cloisters and the Verduner Altar, and the **Imperiale Tour** (May to mid-Nov only; €9), which allows visitors to explore the state rooms of the Residenztrakt.

The Sakrale Tour starts with the **Stiftskirche**, which still hints at its origins as a Romanesque basilica, despite over-zealous nineteenth-century restoration. Neo-Gothic finials and other details obscure the west front, but the south door, with its blind arcading, is much as it would have been in the Babenbergs' day. Inside, it's a riot of early Baroque stuccowork and frescoes. The most impressive craftsmanship is in the chancel: the richly gilded choirstalls, exuberant high altar, and, above all, Johann Michael Rottmayr's *Assumption*, without doubt the pick of the frescoes.

North of the church are the **medieval cloisters**, built in the late thirteenth century. The central courtyard is encroached upon in the southwest corner by the little L-shaped Freisingerkapelle, containing the episcopal tomb of its namesake, who died in 1410. More intriguing is the polygonal wellhouse, which juts out into the courtyard from the eastern cloister, and boasts some fine tracery over the portal; the highlight is the magnificent, giant bronze candelabra, crafted in Verona in the twelfth century.

The monastery's most outstanding treasure is the **Verduner Altar**, in the Leopoldskapelle, east of the cloisters. This stunning winged altar, completed in 1181 by Nikolaus of Verdun, is comprised of over fifty gilded enamel plaques, depicting Biblical scenes from both testaments. Sadly, you can't get close enough to appreciate the detail, but the overall effect is dazzling. The top half of St Leopold is buried in the Wiener Werkstätte casket underneath the altar; his legs are beneath the nearby wrought-iron grille.

In the **Residenztrakt**, east of the medieval buildings, you can get some idea of the Spanish-bred Emperor Karl VI's ambitious plans for a vast imperial edifice, in deliberate imitation of El Escorial in Spain, which the Habsburgs had recently lost to the Bourbons. The building was to sprout numerous domes, due to be capped by crowns, each representing one of the Habsburg lands. In the end, the money ran out and the roof sports just two domes, one capped with the imperial crown, the other with the archducal hat of Lower Austria. The showpiece of the Baroque wing is the **Marmorsaal** (Marble Hall), with its giant oval dome, supported by coupled composite columns, and decorated with frescoes by Daniel Gran glorifying the Habsburg dynasty.

## Essl Museum

Klosterneuburg is also home to Austria's largest private art collection, the **Essl Museum** (Tues–Sun 10am–6pm, Wed until 9pm; free; ⓦwww.sammlung-essl .at), displayed in a concrete modernist gallery designed by Heinz Tesar, down by the Danube. Featuring just about every renowned postwar Austrian artist, the collection has been accumulated over the last fifty years by Karlheinz and Agnes Essl, inheritors of the bauMax chain of DIY stores, which has its corporate headquarters in Klosterneuburg. To reach the Sammlung Essl, take **S-Bahn** line S40 from Franz-Josefs Bahnhof to Klosterneuburg-Weidling, then walk under the railway tracks and turn left, following the signs to the gallery. To walk to the gallery from the monastery, head down Leopoldstrasse and cross over the railway tracks.

The big white rooms on the first floor display a sort of overview of the collection, which is characterized by large abstract canvases, but ranges from Surrealist works by Maria Lassnig and "kaleidoscopic landscapes" by Friedrich Hundertwasser to works by the leading lights of Aktionismus, Vienna's very own extremely violent version of 1960s performance art. In addition to the Austrian pieces, there are works by international contemporary artists such as Britain's Sean Scully and the American Nam June Paik. At least half the gallery space is given over to temporary exhibitions drawn from the collection. On the second floor, you'll find the Grosser Saal, with its distinctive floating, curved ceiling, and a café and bookshop.

# Zentralfriedhof

In a city where some people still keep a separate savings account in order to ensure an appropriately lavish funeral, it comes as little surprise that the **Zentralfriedhof** (daily: March & Oct 7am–6pm; April & Sept 7am–7pm; May–Aug 7am–8pm; Nov–Feb 8am–5pm) is one of the biggest cemeteries in Europe. Larger than the Innere Stadt, and with a much greater population – 2.5 million – than the whole city, it's so vast it even has its own bus service to help mourners get about. It was opened in 1874, at the height of Viennese funereal fetishism, when having *eine schöne Leich* (a beautiful corpse) was something to aspire to. Today, it's still very much a working graveyard, and is particularly busy on Sundays and on religious holidays, most notably All Saints' Day (November 1), when thousands of Viennese

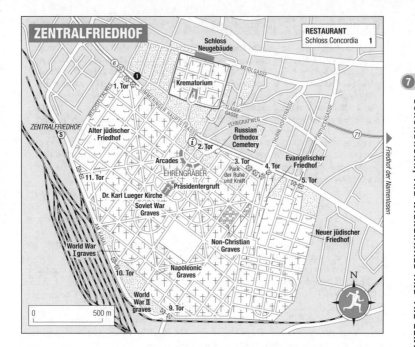

*Friedhof der Namenlosen*

make the trip out here and virtually every grave is left with a candle burning in remembrance.

## The Ehrengräber

Passing through the monumental Jugendstil **main gates** (2. Tor), designed by Max Hegele in 1905, you come to a semicircular sweep of red-brick arcades, which, though a little uncared for, contain some very elaborate tombs. The most extraordinary is in the first alcove on the left: a mock-up mine entrance guarded by lantern-wielding dwarves, commemorating the Austrian mining magnate August Zang.

As you approach the central church, you pass through the main area of the so-called **Ehrengräber** (Tombs of Honour). Gruppe 32A, to the left, facing the main avenue, holds the cemetery's most famous musicians. Centre stage is a memorial to Mozart, topped by a woman trying to stop a load of books from falling off. (He is, in fact, buried in St Marxer Friedhof; see p.139.) Behind him, at a respectful distance, lie the graves of **Ludwig van Beethoven**, emblazoned with a busy gilded bee, and **Franz Schubert**, whose bust is about to receive the posthumous honour that eluded him during his lifetime in the shape of a garland. Beethoven and Schubert were disinterred from Währinger Friedhof in 1889, and reburied here – fellow composer Anton Bruckner managed to get his hands on both composers' corpses during the operation, before being physically restrained by those present. Another composer reburied nearby is Maria Theresia's favourite, Christoph Willibald Gluck, who died in 1779 after refusing his doctor's orders that he drink no alcohol after dinner. Other composers to look out for include **Johannes Brahms**, Josef Lanner, Hugo Wolf, who died of syphilis in 1903, and

**7**

The quickest way to **reach the Zentralfriedhof** is on tram #6 or #71 from Simmering U-Bahn. The cemetery has three separate tram stops on Simmeringer Hauptstrasse: the 1. Tor, the first stop, deposits you outside the old Jewish section; the second stop, the **2. Tor**, serves the main entrance; the third stop (and the terminus for tram #6) is the 3. Tor, close to the entrance to the Protestant section, and within easy walking distance of the new Jewish section. In addition, there's an S-Bahn station, Zentralfriedhof, at the western edge of the cemetery, a short walk from the 11. Tor and 12. Tor; the station is on the S7 line to the airport, which calls at Wien-Nord, Wien-Mitte and Rennweg. The Rundkurs bus does a circuit of the graveyard every thirty minutes and there's an **information centre** (Mon–Fri 8am–2pm) in the building to the right of the 2. Tor, where you can buy a guide with a plan (in English) of the cemetery.

the entire **Strauss** clan; Johann Jr's tomb, in particular, features a fine collection of musical cherubs.

The Ehrengräber on the opposite side of the main avenue, in Gruppe 14A, are the more eye-catching tombs of fin-de-siècle Vienna's wealthier denizens. Few of the names mean much to non-Austrians, with the possible exception of Ringstrasse architect **Theophil Hansen** and artists Emil Jakob Schindler, father of Alma Mahler-Werfel, and **Hans Makart**, another victim of syphilis. Continuing towards the church, you come to a sort of sunken roundabout surrounded by shrubs; this is the illustrious **Präsidentergruft**, containing the remains of the presidents of the Second Republic, from **Dr Karl Renner**, the first postwar president to the former Nazi officer, **Kurt Waldheim**.

To the right of the presidents, in Gruppe 14C, lie several other notable politicians, including the former chancellors Julius Raab and Leopold Figl; the architect **Josef Hoffmann** is also buried here. To the left of the presidents, in Gruppe 32C, you'll find more intriguing incumbents like the sculptor **Fritz Wotruba**, who lies under a self-designed tombstone. He also provided the highly appropriate cuboid tombstone for the atonal composer **Arnold Schönberg**, who died in Los Angeles in 1951. Adjacent to Schönberg, and more universally mourned by the Viennese, is **Bruno Kreisky**, the populist Austrian chancellor (1970–83). Nearby lie the graves of the writer **Franz Werfel**; the composer **Alexander Zemlinsky**, Schönberg's mentor, who died in exile in the USA in 1942; and the architect **Adolf Loos**, whose tomb is a typically ornament-free block of stone. Loos designed a similarly minimalist tombstone for his friend, the poet **Peter Altenberg**, who is buried in Gruppe O, by the wall to the left of the main gates. Those on the search for Austria's most famous pop star, Hans Hölzel – better known as **"Falco"**, the man responsible for the hit *Rock Me Amadeus* – will find him buried in Gruppe 40.

### Dr-Karl-Lueger-Kirche and beyond

The focal point of the cemetery is the gargantuan Friedhofskirche or **Dr-Karl-Lueger-Kirche** (daily: March–Oct 8am–5pm; Nov–Feb 8am–4pm; free), completed by Max Hegele, a pupil of Otto Wagner, in 1910. Initially at least, this domed church resembles Wagner's Jugendstil Kirche am Steinhof (see p.180), but on closer inspection, it's clear that Hegele has taken a more austere Neoclassical approach. There are guided tours of the church on the first Sunday of the month after Mass (9.45am). Its chief vault is that of the anti-Semitic city mayor, Karl Lueger (see p.92) below the high altar.

Few tourists venture further than the Ehrengräber and the Friedhofskirche, but there are plenty of other points of interest, if you've got the legs for it. Directly behind the church a large **Soviet war cemetery** contains the graves of those who fell during the 1945 liberation of Vienna, centred on a statue of two Red Army soldiers, flags downcast, with patriotic quotes from Stalin around the plinth. Continuing down the central avenue, you come to Anton Hanak's despairing memorial to those who fell in **World War I**; behind it, in Gruppe 91, is a semicircular green field, its soft turf studded with small graves. To the southeast, in Gruppe 88, are the graves of Napoleonic troops who died during the 1809 French occupation of Vienna, the majority inscribed with the words "Français non identifié". More than seven thousand Austrians who died fighting in the Nazi Wehrmacht in **World War II** are commemorated by a field of black crosses to the southwest in Gruppe 97.

Those who died fighting for the freedom of their country from 1934 to 1945 have their own memorial – a big, heroic bronze man accompanied by two mourning women – at the giant intersection to the southeast of the Lueger-Kirche. Nearby are the uniform graves of those who died in the riot outside the Justizpalast on July 15, 1927 (see p.94), and a memorial to war victims from the Czechoslovak section of the Austrian Communist Party. To the east, in Gruppe 28, the victims of the civil war of February 1934 (see p.257), those who died under the Austro-fascists, and martyrs of the Spanish Civil War, have their own memorial. Further east still, the **Social Democrats** have their own Ehrengräber featuring their early leaders, among them Otto Bauer, Viktor Adler, and the latter's brother, Friedrich Adler, who assassinated the prime minister Count Karl von Stürgkh in 1916 (see p.48). Opposite, the casualties of the 1848 revolution are commemorated by a simple obelisk.

Several non-Catholic denominations share the Zentralfriedhof: there's an **Evangelischer Friedhof** (Protestant Cemetery), accessible from 4. Tor, a growing Islamic section in Gruppe 26 and 36, and a small Russian Orthodox section around the onion-domed church in Gruppe 21, to the left of the main gates. In Gruppe 23, you'll also find the **Park der Ruhe und Kraft** (Park of Peace and Strength), a laudable attempt to address the spiritual needs of those who don't subscribe to an organized religion, with five symbolic areas to wander through, ranging from a stone circle to a labyrinth.

By far the largest non-Catholic sections, however, are the two Jewish cemeteries. The **Alter jüdischer Friedhof** (Old Jewish Cemetery), founded in 1863 and accessible from 1. Tor, was desecrated by the Nazis on *Kristallnacht*, though some sixty thousand graves are still standing. Among those buried here are the Viennese branch of the Rothschild family and the playwright Arthur Schnitzler. The **Neuer jüdischer Friedhof** (New Jewish Cemetery), accessible from 5. Tor, on the other side of the Zentralfriedhof, was inaugurated in 1917, and, despite being damaged during *Kristallnacht*, still functions today. The sheer size of these two graveyards is a testament to the prewar magnitude of Vienna's Jewish community – testament also to the several generations systematically wiped out in the Holocaust.

# The Krematorium and the Friedhof der Namenlosen

For the terminally obsessed, the city's **Krematorium** (hours as for Zentral-friedhof) is but a short stroll from the main gates (2. Tor) of the Zentralfriedhof; take the underpass to the other side of Simmeringer Hauptstrasse and walk in a northwesterly direction. While the Roman Catholic Church had a deep-seated opposition to cremation, the practice was championed by the anticlerical Social Democrats between the wars as a secular alternative. The Viennese have never been entirely convinced by this ecologically sound form of burial and less than twenty percent opt for it even today.

Nevertheless, the central complex of buildings is worth checking out, a startling work designed in the early 1920s by Clemens Holzmeister. The central courtyard, with its arcade of Gothic lancet arches, is the most impressive section, along with the zigzag roofline of the crematorium itself, all smothered in smooth, grey, rendered concrete. The crenellated perimeter walls of the crematorium date back to the **Schloss Neugebäude**, built as a magnificent Mannerist palace by the emperor Maximilian II. What remains of the palace can be seen at the far end of the Garden of Rest, behind the crematorium building.

Last, and probably least, is the **Friedhof der Namenlosen** (Cemetery of the Nameless Ones), east of the Zentralfriedhof at Alberner Hafen, containing the graves of the poor souls fished out of the Danube each year. Some of the corpses are later identified (and therefore no longer "nameless"), but the majority are not, and the overriding feeling is one of melancholy. To get here, you have to study the timetable of bus #76A very carefully; it leaves from the terminus of tram #71, but only occasionally makes it as far as the cemetery – at other times, you'll have to alight at Sendnergasse and walk east down Mannswörtherstrasse.

# Listings

# Listings

# 8

# Accommodation

A s you might expect, Vienna has some of the most opulent, historic **hotels** in Europe, with mesospheric prices to match. However, reasonably priced, central accommodation can be found, especially in the numerous **pensions**. These are not necessarily inferior in quality or price to hotels – in fact some are a whole lot better. The distinction is purely technical: pensions occupy one or more floors, but not the whole, of a building, whereas to be a hotel, the entire block must be occupied.

Vienna also has plenty of **hostels**, although these tend to be booked up months in advance, so try to ring ahead or email and make a reservation before you leave. Inveterate **campers** have a wide choice of peripheral sites.

**High season** for accommodation in Vienna is from April to October, plus the two weeks over Christmas and New Year (when there is sometimes a surcharge). It can also be difficult to find a room on spec during the week running up to Lent, when *Fasching* reaches its climax (see p.231). That said, some hotels drop their rates in July and August, when the opera houses and theatres are on vacation. (The room price should, by law, be displayed in your room.)

You can book accommodation for free **online** at ⓦ www.wien.info; payment is made directly to the hotel on checking out. If you arrive without a booking, any of the **tourist offices** mentioned on p.35 can make a reservation for you, for which they charge a small fee.

## Hotels and pensions

**Hotels and pensions** in Vienna tend to adhere to the standards of efficiency, modernity and cleanliness you'd expect in Austria. It's perfectly possible to stay right in the **Innere Stadt** without totally breaking the bank, although the cheapest places tend to be in the districts beyond the Ringstrasse. This is no bad thing, as areas like **Margareten**, **Mariahilf**, **Neubau** and **Josefstadt** have a wider choice of reasonably priced restaurants and trendy bars than the central tourist zone.

It's always worth having a look at a room before you commit yourself, as **natural light** is in short supply in some buildings in Vienna. Many old blocks of flats retain their beautiful antique **lifts**, some of which are so ancient they carry passengers up and not down, and can only be operated by placing a coin in the slot.

**Breakfast** is included in the price at most hotels and pensions, though what it actually amounts to can differ enormously. "Continental breakfast" means coffee and a couple of rolls; "full continental breakfast" means you should get a bit of choice, perhaps cold meats and cheeses, and if you're really lucky a hot egg-based snack; and "buffet" means you can gorge yourself on as much cereal, muesli, eggs, bread, rolls, cheese and meat as you can eat.

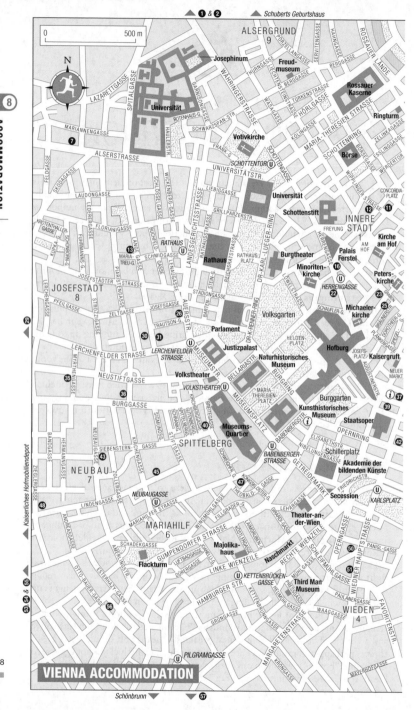

**VIENNA ACCOMMODATION**

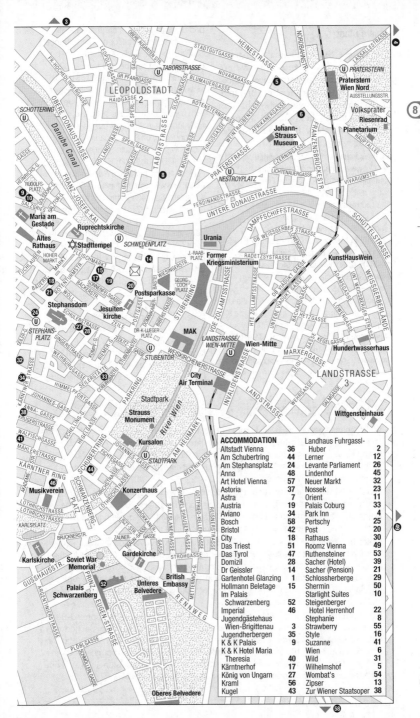

**ACCOMMODATION**

| | | | |
|---|---|---|---|
| Altstadt Vienna | 36 | Landhaus Fuhrgassl- | |
| Am Schubertring | 44 | Huber | 2 |
| Am Stephansplatz | 24 | Lerner | 12 |
| Anna | 48 | Levante Parliament | 26 |
| Art Hotel Vienna | 57 | Lindenhof | 45 |
| Astoria | 37 | Neuer Markt | 32 |
| Astra | 7 | Nossek | 23 |
| Austria | 19 | Orient | 11 |
| Aviano | 34 | Palais Coburg | 33 |
| Bosch | 58 | Park Inn | 4 |
| Bristol | 42 | Pertschy | 25 |
| City | 18 | Post | 20 |
| Das Triest | 51 | Rathaus | 30 |
| Das Tyrol | 47 | Roomz Vienna | 49 |
| Domizil | 28 | Ruthensteiner | 53 |
| Dr Geissler | 14 | Sacher (Hotel) | 39 |
| Gartenhotel Glanzing | 1 | Sacher (Pension) | 21 |
| Hollmann Beletage | 15 | Schlossherberge | 29 |
| Im Palais | | Shermin | 50 |
| Schwarzenberg | 52 | Starlight Suites | 10 |
| Imperial | 46 | Steigenberger | |
| Jugendgästehaus | | Hotel Herrenhof | 22 |
| Wien-Brigittenau | 3 | Stephanie | 8 |
| Jugendherbergen | 35 | Strawberry | 55 |
| K & K Palais | 9 | Style | 16 |
| K & K Hotel Maria | | Suzanne | 41 |
| Theresia | 40 | Wien | 6 |
| Kärntnerhof | 17 | Wild | 31 |
| König von Ungarn | 27 | Wilhelmshof | 5 |
| Kraml | 56 | Wombat's | 54 |
| Kugel | 43 | Zipser | 13 |
| | | Zur Wiener Staatsoper | 38 |

## Innere Stadt

The **Innere Stadt**, Vienna's old town and commercial centre, is where everyone wants to stay. Prices reflect this and there is a surfeit of upper-range hotels (most of which we haven't bothered listing below), and a corresponding dearth of inexpensive places (most of which we *have* listed).

**Hotel am Schubertring** 1, Schubertring 11 ☎717 02-0, ⓦ www.schubertring.at; U-Bahn Stadtpark. Solid choice on the Ring, and one of the few options not run by a hotel chain. The rooms (all on the fifth floor) are spacious and a/c; some have views over the Ringstrasse. Free wi-fi in the lobby and ethernet in the rooms. Doubles from €135.

**Hotel am Stephansplatz** 1, Stephansplatz 9 ☎534 05-0, ⓦ www.hotelamstephansplatz.at; U-Bahn Stephansplatz. Newly refurbished rooms are modern, comfortable and spacious, and it's just about as central as you can get without actually being inside the Stephansdom. Doubles from €180.

**Hotel Astoria** 1, Kärntnerstrasse 32–34 ☎515 77-0, ⓦ www.austria-trend.at; U-Bahn Karlsplatz. Grandiose, century-old flagship of the *Austria Trend* hotel chain, and preferred pad of visiting opera stars thanks to its proximity to the Staatsoper. The entrance is on Fürichgasse. Rack rates are high, but online doubles can be had from €130.

**Hotel Austria** 1, Fleischmarkt 20 ☎515 23, ⓦ www.hotelaustria-wien.at; U-Bahn Schwedenplatz. Plush, traditional family-run hotel, with a wonderful circular staircase, pleasantly located in the quiet cul-de-sac of Wolfengasse, off Fleischmarkt. Cheaper rooms without en-suite facilities – all have free wi-fi. Doubles from €100.

**Pension Aviano** 1, Marco d'Avianogasse 1 ☎512 83 30, ⓦ www.secrethomes.at; U-Bahn Karlsplatz. Squeezed onto the top floor of a building just off Kärntnerstrasse, *Aviano*'s en-suite rooms have low ceilings, but are nevertheless spacious, with old-fashioned floral décor. Free wi-fi. Doubles from €125.

**Pension City** 1, Bauernmarkt 10 ☎533 95 21, ⓦ www.citypension.at; U-Bahn Stephansplatz. On the second floor of a wonderful late nineteenth-century building (birthplace of Franz Grillparzer) and run by a friendly female proprietor. Tastefully decorated rooms, all en-suite. Buffet breakfast until 11am. Doubles from €85.

**Hotel Domizil** 1, Schulerstrasse 14 ☎513 31 99, ⓦ www.hoteldomizil.at; U-Bahn Stephansplatz. Clean, bright pension with simple, smartly

## Vienna's Big Three

While Vienna specializes in big **luxury hotels**, three Ringstrasse piles stand head and shoulders above the others for their heavy, late nineteenth-century decor and their historical associations. During the Allied occupation following the end of World War II, the Americans took over the *Bristol*, the Russians occupied the *Imperial*, and the British holed up in the *Sacher*.

**Hotel Bristol** 1, Kärntner Ring 1 ☎515 16-0, ⓦ www.bristolvienna.com; U-Bahn Karlsplatz. The least remarkable of the three from the outside, but a feast of marble inside, with barley-sugar columns in the *Korso* restaurant, and opulent repro decor in all the rooms. Doubles can be had online from as little as €200.

**Hotel Imperial** 1, Kärntner Ring 16 ☎501 10-0, ⓦ www.hotelimperialvienna.com; U-Bahn Karlsplatz. Incredibly lavish converted palace, built for the Duke of Württemberg, and later the "favourite hostelry of crowned heads, their heirs-apparent, and ambassadors", according to one observer in 1877. Hitler stayed here on his return to the city in 1938, and it's still the first choice for visiting heads of government. Doubles can be had online for around €300.

**Hotel Sacher** 1, Philharmonikerstrasse 4 ☎514 56-0, ⓦ www.sacher.com; U-Bahn Karlsplatz. The most famous of the lot, not only because of its legendary Sachertorte, but also because this was where the aristocratic playboys used to hang out in the imperial days; see p.100 for a fuller account of its history. The new rooms eschew the traditional heavy, wood-panelled, red velvet approach of the rest of the hotel, and opt for a more pared-down opulence. Double rooms from around €350.

furnished en-suite rooms, just seconds from Stephansplatz. Doubles from €135.

**Pension Dr Geissler 1, Postgasse 14** ☎533 28 03, 🖰 www.hotelpension.at; U-Bahn Schwedenplatz. On the eighth floor, this is an anonymous, modern place; the rooms are clean, however, and those with shared facilities are among the cheapest in the Innere Stadt. Doubles from €40.

🏃 **Hollmann Beletage 1, Kollnerhofgasse 6** ☎961 19 60, 🖰 www.hollmann-beletage .at; U-Bahn Karlsplatz/Stephansplatz. Small boutique hotel whose bright and cheery rooms are replete with contemporary furnishings. Service is pretty low-key, and there's no reception at night; breakfasts are excellent. Doubles from €140.

**K & K Palais Hotel 1, Rudolfsplatz 11** ☎533 13 53, 🖰 www.kkhotels.com; U-Bahn Schwedenplatz. Built in 1890 and once the town house of Franz-Josef's mistress Katharina Schratt, the *K & K* retains an appropriately imperial ambience in the lobby. Breakfasts are king-sized and the a/c rooms kept in tip-top condition. Doubles from €210.

**Hotel Kärntnerhof 1, Grashofgasse 4** ☎512 19 23, 🖰 www.karntnerhof.com; U-Bahn Schwedenplatz/Stephansplatz. Located in a cul-de-sac off Köllnerhofgasse, with some very pleasant, characterful rooms, and others that are a little dingy. Make sure you see yours before checking in. Free wi-fi. Doubles from €120.

**Hotel König von Ungarn 1, Schulerstrasse 10** ☎515 84-0, 🖰 www.kvu.at; U-Bahn Stephansplatz. Tastefully modernized hotel with a remarkable wooden-panelled, covered courtyard bar/lounge. Rooms are fair-sized, pleasantly decorated and a/c. Service is top notch and the location dead central. Doubles from €220.

**Pension Lerner 1, Wipplingerstrasse 23** ☎533 52 19, 🖰 www.pensionlerner.com; U-Bahn Stephansplatz. Small, super-central, seven-room pension with friendly staff, free wi–fi and super breakfasts. Cheaper rooms have shared facilities; they also offer a few apartments to let in Schulerstrasse. Doubles from €70.

**Pension Neuer Markt 1, Seilergasse 9** ☎512 23 16, 🖰 www.hotelpension.at; U-Bahn Stephansplatz. Very popular, central pension on the second floor of a lovely old patrician building. Only a few of the rooms have views over Neuermarkt, but all are clean, comfortable and modern, and those without

en-suite toilet are a relative bargain. Doubles from €60; en-suite from €95.

**Pension Nossek 1, Graben 17** ☎533 70 41, 🖰 www.pension-nossek.at; U-Bahn Stephansplatz. Large, old-fashioned, family-run pension on three floors of an old building on the pedestrianized Graben. En-suite doubles of varying sizes, and some real bargain singles with shared facilities. It's popular, so book in advance. Doubles from €115.

**Hotel Orient 1, Tiefer Graben 30** ☎533 73 07, 🖰 www.hotelorient.at; U-Bahn Herrengasse. Vienna's equivalent of a Tokyo "love hotel", with rooms rented by the hour and per night. Couples come for the mind-boggling exotic decor, and the wide range of themed rooms; it's all terribly discreet. Doubles from around €100.

**Palais Coburg 1, Coburgbastei 4** ☎518 18-0, 🖰 www.coburg.at; U-Bahn Stubentor. One of Vienna's seriously sumptuous palace hotels, a Neoclassical affair built for Duke Ferdinand of Saxe-Coburg & Gotha (Queen Victoria's uncle) in the 1840s. There's a stunning lobby and rooftop pool, while the suites themselves have all mod cons and a fully equipped kitchen. Prices start at around €670.

🏃 **Pension Pertschy 1, Habsburgergasse 5** ☎534 49-0, 🖰 www.pertschy.com; U-Bahn Stephansplatz. Flagship of the *Pertschy* pension chain, with rooms off a series of plant-strewn balconies looking onto a lovely old courtyard. The characterful rooms have high ceilings, tasteful furnishings, TV and free wi-fi. Doubles from €150.

🏃 **Pension Sacher 1, Rotenturmstrasse 1** ☎533 32 38, 🖰 www.pension-sacher.at; U-Bahn Stephansplatz. Family-run pension in an incredible location on the seventh floor on the corner of Stephansplatz itself. There are nine apartments, with lovely parquet flooring and pleasant furnishings. All have TV, free wi-fi, shower, toilet, fridge and cooking facilities, and most have views out on to the Stephansdom. No breakfast. Doubles from €100.

**Starlight Suites 1, Salzgries 12** ☎535 92 22-0, 🖰 www.starlighthotels.com; U-Bahn Schwedenplatz. Totally modernized apartments for around €180 and upwards, in a quiet but central backstreet, not far from Schwedenplatz. Buffet breakfast is provided (though not always included in price) as there are only limited kitchen facilities. Two other branches exist at Renngasse 13 and Am

Heumarkt 15, both a stone's throw from the Ring. Apartments from €195.

**Steigenberger Hotel Herrenhof 1, Herrengasse 10** ☏ 534 04-0, Ⓦ www.steigenberger.com; **U-Bahn Herrengasse.** The rooms at this five-star hotel are modern and unfussy; all come with air-con, free wi-fi and free minibar; the hotel also has a gym, sauna, steam room and spa treatments available. Check the website for special offers – breakfast not always included. Doubles from €160.

**Style Hotel 1, Herrengasse 12** ☏ 227 80-0, Ⓦ www.stylehotel.at; **U-Bahn Herrengasse.** Now part of the Radisson chain, this boutique hotel has a contemporary aesthetic, and rooms with every possible gadget. Breakfast not always included in the rates. Doubles online from €140.

**Pension Suzanne 1, Walfischgasse 4** ☏ 513 25 07, Ⓦ www.pension-suzanne.at; **U-Bahn Karlsplatz.** Family-run pension just off Kärntnerstrasse, furnished in tasteful period style; rooms are spacious, and many have baths, balconies and even small kitchens (though breakfast is included). Doubles from €105.

**Hotel zur Wiener Staatsoper 1, Krugerstrasse 11** ☏ 513 12 74, Ⓦ www.zurwienerstaatsoper.at; **U-Bahn Karlsplatz.** Despite the flamboyant late nineteenth-century facade and foyer, this is a family-run hotel with small, simply furnished, clean rooms. The location, just off Kärntnerstrasse, is pretty good for the price. Closed for three weeks in Nov. Doubles from around €120.

## Landstrasse, Wieden and Margareten

The only area of **Landstrasse** (third district) where it's worth basing yourself is in the vicinity of the Belvedere. **Wieden** (fourth district) and **Margareten** (fifth district) are quieter, residential areas, to the south of Karlsplatz and convenient for the Naschmarkt.

**Art Hotel Vienna 5, Brandmayergasse 7–9** ☏ 554 51 08, Ⓦ www.thearthotelvienna.at; **tram #6 or #18 from U-Bahn Margaretengürtel.** Margareten hotel with a penchant for wacky modern art and designer furnishings. All rooms are en-suite; free wi-fi only in the lobby. Doubles from €80.

**Pension Bosch 3, Keilgasse 13** ☏ 798 61 79, Ⓦ www.hotelpensionbosch.com; **S-Bahn Rennweg or tram #0, #18 or #71.** Friendly pension in a quiet residential backstreet behind the Belvedere, an easy tram-ride into town. The thirteen rooms have lots of character; the cheapest share facilities. Closed Jan & Feb. Doubles from €50.

**Hotel im Palais Schwarzenberg 3, Schwarzenbergplatz 9** ☏ 798 45 15, Ⓦ www.palais-schwarzenberg.com; **tram #D.** Hidden behind the Soviet War Memorial, this Baroque palace, with its own extensive gardens, was designed by Hildebrandt and Fischer von Erlach, with period furnishings courtesy of, among others, Rubens, Meissen and Gobelins. Doubles from €350.

**Hotel-Pension Shermin 4, Rilkeplatz 7** ☏ 586 61 83, Ⓦ www.hotel-pension-shermin.at; **U-Bahn Karlsplatz.** The lobby's a bit lugubrious, but the rooms are clean and spacious and the staff very friendly. Good location, just off Karlsplatz, and they have apartments nearby, too. Doubles from €90.

**Das Triest 4, Wiedner Hauptstrasse 12** ☏ 589 18-0, Ⓦ www.dastriest.at; **U-Bahn Karlsplatz.** Designer hotel hidden away in a nondescript building a short stroll from Karlsplatz. The super-smooth, minimalist interior comes courtesy of Terence Conran and the Italians, and is quirky in an understated way. Service is excellent and the rooms are immaculate; those on the top floor have great views across the city skyline. Doubles from €245.

## Mariahilf, Neubau and Josefstadt

As home to some of Vienna's liveliest bars and choicest restaurants, the sixth, seventh and eighth districts make ideal bases. **Neubau** includes the lively Spittelberg area, while **Josefstadt** is more studenty.

**Altstadt Vienna 7, Kirchengasse 41** ☏ 522 66 66, Ⓦ www.altstadt.at; **U-Bahn Volkstheater.** A cut above most other pensions, with laid-back, well-informed staff, a relaxing lounge and full-on buffet breakfast. Tastefully decorated en-suite rooms with high ceilings and a great location, near Spittelberg, and within easy walking distance of the U-Bahn and Ring. Doubles from €140.

**Pension Anna 7, Zieglergasse 18** ☏ 523 01 60, Ⓦ www.pension-anna.at; **U-Bahn Zieglergasse.** First-floor, twenty-room pension run by a friendly couple. The startling light-blue decor doesn't extend into the fourteen bedrooms, all of which have en-suite shower and toilet and free wi-fi. Closed Christmas. Doubles from €90.

**Pension Astra 8, Alserstrasse 32** ☎402 43 54, ⓦ www.hotelpensionastra.com; U-Bahn Alserstrasse. Mid-sized pension on the mezzanine of an old patrician building. Friendly staff and a range of modernized rooms, from simple doubles without toilet to roomy apartments. Doubles from €60.

🏃 **Pension Kraml 6, Brauergasse 5** ☎587 85 88, ⓦ www.pensionkraml.at; U-Bahn Zieglergasse/Neubaugasse. Probably the friendliest and most reliable of the cheap pensions in the quiet streets off Mariahilferstrasse. Large, smart, clean, modern rooms, some with en-suite facilities. Doubles from €56.

**Hotel Kugel 7, Siebensterngasse 43** ☎523 33 55, ⓦ www.hotelkugel.at; U-Bahn Neubaugasse. Long-established, family-run hotel within spitting distance of Spittelberg's numerous restaurants and bars. Bright, clean, en-suite rooms (some with modern four-posters), plus a few bargain singles with shared facilities. Closed Jan. Doubles from €85.

**K & K Hotel Maria Theresia 7, Kirchberggasse 6** ☎521 23 70, ⓦ www.kkhotels.com; U-Bahn Volkstheater. Hotel within easy walking distance of the Innere Stadt, with a modern contemporary feel to the furnishings. Impeccable service and a/c rooms that are kept in tip-top condition; there's free wi-fi and the vast buffet breakfasts are available until 11am. Doubles from €180.

**Levante Parliament 8, Auerspergstrasse 9** ☎228 28-0, ⓦ www.thelevante.com; U-Bahn Volkstheater. Chic designer hotel, a stone's throw from the Ring, with resolutely modernist decor throughout and all mod cons of course. They also have apartments for €120 a night deeper in Josefstadt. Doubles from around €300.

**Pension Lindenhof 7, Lindengasse 4** ☎523 04 98, ⓦ www.pensionlindenhof.at; U-Bahn Neubaugasse. On the first floor of a lugubrious turn-of-the-century building at the Spittelberg end of this long street. Lovely, up-only lift, a plant-strewn communal area, and endearingly old-fashioned rooms (some of which are en-suite), with high ceilings and creaky parquet flooring. Doubles from around €50.

🏃 **Hotel Rathaus 8, Lange Gasse 13** ☎400 11 22, ⓦ www.hotel-rathaus-wien.at; U-Bahn Rathaus. Discreet boutique hotel with bright, contemporary, wine-themed rooms

in an old patrician building a few blocks west of the Rathaus. Breakfasts are superb, and you can opt (later) for some wine-tasting too. Doubles from €200; suites from €400.

**Das Tyrol 6, Mariahilferstrasse 15** ☎587 54 15, ⓦ www.das-tyrol.at; U-Bahn Museumsquartier. Boutique hotel off Vienna's main shopping street, with a beautiful antique lift. The rooms are quite small, but the décor is fresh, modern and deliberately arty; everything is spotlessly clean and smart and the staff are very helpful. Doubles online from €180. ❽

**Pension Wild 8, Lange Gasse 10** ☎406 51 74, ⓦ www.pension-wild.com; U-Bahn Volkstheater. Friendly, laid-back pension, a short walk from the Ring in a student district behind the university. Especially popular with backpackers and gay travellers; booking essential. Doubles from around €50.

**Hotel Zipser 8, Lange Gasse 49** ☎404 54-0, ⓦ www.zipser.at; U-Bahn Rathaus. Well-equipped modern pension, offering a buffet breakfast – a reliable choice, just a short walk from the Ring behind the Rathaus. Doubles from €95.

## Leopoldstadt

Cut off from the Innere Stadt by the Danube Canal, **Leopoldstadt**, Vienna's second district and former Jewish quarter, is quiet and seldom visited by tourists. Yet the area lies just a couple of tram stops from the central district and the greenery of the Prater.

**Hotel Wien 2, Praterstrasse 72** ☎211 30-0, ⓦ www.classic-hotelwien.at; U-Bahn Nestroyplatz/Praterstern. If you want to stay in the second district, then the birthplace of Max Steiner, composer of film music for *Gone With the Wind* and *Casablanca*, is a good choice. It's now a large, pleasantly modernized hotel with shower, toilet, TV and free wi-fi in all rooms. Doubles from €120.

**Park Inn 2, Wagramerstrasse 16–18** ☎260 40-0, ⓦ www.parkinnvienna.at; U-Bahn Kaisermühlen-VIC. Plain, modern hotel that's perfect if you're heading for the UNO City or Vienna International Center, but also close to the U-Bahn if you need to go into town. Free parking, too. Doubles online from around €150.

**Hotel Stephanie 2, Taborstrasse 12** ☎211 50-0, ⓦ www.schick-hotels.com; U-Bahn Schwedenplatz. A touch of well-worn splendour to the public areas, and some modern comforts in the rooms. Excellent breakfast, good restaurant, charming staff and a short stroll to the Innere Stadt. Doubles from €145.

**Hotel Wilhelmshof 2, Kleine Stadtgutgasse 4** ☎214 55 21, ⊛www.wilhelmshof.at; U-Bahn **Praterstern.** Old patrician building a short stroll from Wien Nord and the Prater, with simple, plain, modern furnishings and air conditioning, and free wi-fi in all the rooms. Doubles from around €105.

## The suburbs

**Gartenhotel Glanzing 19, Glanzinggasse 23** ☎470 42 72-0, ⊛www.gartenhotel-glanzing. at; tram #41. Classic interwar modernist villa in the northern suburbs. Some of the en-suite rooms and apartments have amazing views over Vienna, and there's a lovely shady garden. Sauna, solarium and mini-gym on site. Under-14s free. Doubles from €110.

**Landhaus Fuhrgassl-Huber 19, Rathstrasse 24** ☎440 30 33, ⊛www.fuhrgassl-huber.at; bus #35A from U-Bahn Nussdorferstrasse. A genuine *gemütlich* country hotel/wine producer right out in the vineyards at the foot of the Wienerwald. Sauna available. It takes a while to get into town by public transport. Doubles from €115.

**Roomz Vienna 11, Paragonstrasse 1** ☎743 17 77, ⊛www.roomz-vienna.com; U-Bahn **Gasometer.** Designer functionalist budget hotel out by the awesome Gasometer development. Clean and efficient, it has everything from air conditioning and wi-fi to a 24hr bar, and is just minutes from the U-Bahn. Doubles from €60.

# Hostels, student rooms and camping

Vienna's official **Hostelling International** *Jugendherbergen* or *Jugendgästehäuser* (youth hostels) are efficient, clean and, occasionally, even friendly. However, all, with just one exception, are a long way from the centre. Beds are in segregated dorms or bunk-bed doubles and many have en-suite facilities. You can join Hostelling International on the spot at any hostel listed below (if you're already a member of your national hostelling association, you're automatically in the HI). Last, but by no means least, you should make an **advance reservation by email or phone** as soon as you know when you might be arriving, as places often get booked up in advance; at the very least, call before turning up on spec.

The biggest practical drawback to the official hostels is that they throw you out of your room each day at the ungodly hour of 9am in order to clean, and won't let you back in until 3 or 4pm. Most hostels have 24hr receptions or they'll give you a night key on request. The lure of the **independent hostel**, then, is that while the prices are much the same as the HI hostels, the atmosphere is a bit less institutional, and there's either no lockout or a more generous one allowing a longer lie-in. However, the places are sometimes, though not always, a bit more run-down and ramshackle.

Finally, Vienna's **campsites** are all quite far out from the centre, on the perimeter of the city, and so for committed campers only. They charge around €7 per person, with tent pitches from around €5.

## Hostels

**Jugendgästehaus Wien-Brigittenau 20, Friedrich-Engels-Platz 24** ☎332 82 94-0, ⊛www.oejhv.or.at; U-Bahn **Handelskai.** Huge, clean, modern HI hostel in a dour working-class suburb; 3–6 bed dorms from around €17, plus en-suite bunk-bed twins from €35. Breakfast included. There's also an adjacent "youth palace" with 90 en-suite twins from €45.

**Jugendherbergen Wien-Myrthengasse 7, Myrthengasse 7** ☎523 63 16, ⊛www.oejhv .or.at; bus #48A or 10min walk from U-Bahn **Volkstheater.** The most central of all the HI hostels has 200-plus dorm beds divided between two addresses around the corner from each other. Breakfast included. Book well in advance. Dorms (2–6 beds) from around €17.

**Hostel Ruthensteiner** 15, Robert-Hamerling -Gasse 24 ☎893 42 02, ⓦwww.hostel ruthensteiner.com; U-Bahn Westbahnhof. Excellent, quiet hostel with a nice courtyard to hang out in, within easy walking distance of the Westbahnhof. Good kitchen and laundry. Free wi-fi. Discounts for HI members. Dorms (4–8 beds) from €14; doubles from €40.

**Hostel Schlossherberge** 16, Savoyen- strasse 2 ☎481 03 00, ⓦwww.hostel.at; bus #146B or #46B from U-Bahn Ottakring. Also known as the *Palace Hostel*, and beautifully located next to a Neoclassical mansion in the Wienerwald, this place is great as a quiet, bucolic base, and has excellent transport links. Breakfast included. Free wi-fi. Dorms from around €22; twins from around €70.

**Strawberry Summer Hostel** 6, Mittelgasse 18 ☎599 79 66-0, ⓦstrawberryhostels.com; U-Bahn Westbahnhof or Gumpendorfer Strasse. Former hotel, now student hall and summer- only hostel a short distance from the Westbahnhof. The en-suite rooms are clean and spacious, and have fridges. There's a kitchen and free wi-fi in the lobby, but no bar. Dorms (3–4 beds) from €21; doubles from €56. July–Sept only.

**Wombat's** ☎897 23 36, ⓦwww .wombats.at. *Wombat's* run a small chain of modern hostels, which are friendly, laid-back places with clean en-suite dorms and bunk-bed doubles, and a party atmos- phere. Computers in the communal areas are not free, but wi-fi is free if you have your own device. Their first branch, known as "The Base", at 15, Grangasse 6, is within easy walking distance of Westbahnhof. 24hr reception. Breakfast extra; no kitchen. There's another great branch – "The Lounge" – around the corner at 15, Maria- hilferstrasse 137; it has a kitchen and laundry. A third even funkier branch – "The Naschmarkt" – opens in 2011 at 4, Rechte Wienzeile 35. Dorms from €20; doubles from €58.

## Campsites

**Camping Klosterneuburg Donaupark** An der Au ☎02243/258 77, ⓦwww.campingklosterneuburg .at; S-Bahn Klosterneuburg-Kierling. Squeezed between the town centre and the Danube, just outside the city limits, this busy site has very fast transport connections to Vienna. Open mid-March to Oct.

**Camping Neue Donau** 22, Am Kleehäufl ☎202 40 10, ⓦwww.wiencamping.at; S-Bahn Lobau or bus #91A from U-Bahn Kaisermühlen-VIC. Not a first choice, as it's squeezed between the Autobahn and the railway lines on the east bank of the Danube. Shop, laundry, bike hire and free wi-fi. Open mid-April to mid-Sept.

**Camping Rodaun** 23, An der Au 2 ☎888 41 54; tram #60 from U-Bahn Hietzing to its terminus, then 5min walk. Nice rural location by a stream on the southwestern outskirts of Vienna, near the Wienerwald. Open mid-May to Oct.

**Wien West** 14, Hüttelbergstrasse 80 ☎914 23 14, ⓦwww.wiencamping.at; bus #152 from U-Bahn Hütteldorf or 15min walk from tram #49 terminus. Very popular site in the plush, far western suburbs of Vienna, close to the Wienerwald; bungalows (April–Oct) from around €70. Free wi-fi. Closed Feb.

# Cafés

*You have troubles of one sort or another – to the COFFEEHOUSE!*
*She can't come to you for some reason no matter how plausible –*
   *to the COFFEEHOUSE!*
*You have holes in your shoes – the COFFEEHOUSE!*
*You have a salary of 400 crowns and spend 500 – THE COFFEEHOUSE!*
*You are frugal and permit yourself nothing – THE COFFEEHOUSE!*
*You find no woman who suits you – THE COFFEEHOUSE!*
*You are SPIRITUALLY on the threshold of suicide – THE COFFEEHOUSE!*
*You hate and disdain people and yet cannot do without them –*
   *THE COFFEEHOUSE!*
*Nobody extends you any more credit anywhere – THE COFFEEHOUSE!*

*The Coffeehouse* Peter Altenberg (1859–1919)

More than a century on, the traditional Viennese **Kaffeehaus** remains a haven of old-fashioned values. For the price of a small coffee, you can still sit for as long as you like without being asked to move on or buy another drink. Understandably, then, the price of this first drink is fairly steep, and will set you back around €2.50–3.50.

*Kaffeehäuser* always have at least a selection of **cakes**. Many will also offer a midday meal, and some will set aside a number of tables for customers who wish to eat. The food is generally traditional Austrian fare, inexpensive and tasty. As well as the traditional *Kaffeehaus*, there is also the **Kaffee-Konditorei**, where the coffee is a mere sideshow to the establishment's cakes and pastries. Modern variants on the *Kaffeehaus* theme continue to evolve, particularly in the Vorstädte or inner suburbs. Such places generally eschew the formality and heavy menu of the older *Kaffeehäuser* and consequently attract a younger crowd. For more on Vienna's café culture, coffee and cakes, see the colour section.

Lastly, some cafés have what is known as a *Schanigarten* – named after the assistant waiter or *Schani*, whose job it is to set out the tables and chairs – don't get too excited, however, as this is rarely much of a **garden**, simply a few tables alfresco.

All cafés detailed in this chapter are marked on the relevant **map** in the Guide – you'll find a page reference taking you there at each review. For a German food and drinks **glossary**, see p.278.

## Innere Stadt (1st district)

The following places are marked on the map on pp.40–41.

**Aera** 1, Gonzagagasse 11 ⓦ www.aera.at; U-Bahn Schwedenplatz. Relaxing, upstairs café serving tasty food to a mixed crowd – some smart, some trendy. Live bands perform in the dimly lit cellar downstairs. Daily 10am–1am.

**Aida** 1, Singerstrasse 1; 1, Bognergasse 3 ⓦ www.aida.at; 1, Rotenturmstrasse 24; U-Bahn

## Cheap eats

The most obvious snack in Vienna is, of course, a *Wurst* or **hot dog** – *Hasse* in the local dialect – from one of the ubiquitous *Würstelstandln* around town. Numerous varieties are available: the *Bratwurst* (fried sausage) or *Burenwurst* (boiled sausage) are the most common, but you could also try a *Debreziner*, a spicy Hungarian sausage, a *Currywurst*, which speaks for itself, or a *Tirolerwurst*, a smoked variety. To accompany your sausage, you usually get a roll and some *Senf* (mustard), which can be either *scharf* (hot) or *süss* (sweet).

For something a bit healthier, a number of **takeaway stands** sell grilled **Maiskolben** (corn on the cob), roasted **Maroni** (chestnuts), **Bratkartoffeln** (roast potatoes) and **Kartoffelpuffer** (potato puffs), depending on the season. Anker, the largest **bakery** chain in the country, with branches right across Vienna, produces excellent bread, rolls and pastries, and serves coffee too.

The best place to grab a quick bite and eat cheaply at the same time, however, is the **Naschmarkt** (see p.236), Vienna's premier fruit and vegetable market (Mon–Sat), where you can feast on seafood, kebabs, falafel, **burek**, noodles and much more besides, or, if you prefer, assemble a king-sized picnic.

As well as the student **Mensen** (see p.210), there are plenty of other **self-service** places, such as the fish and seafoody **Nordsee**, 1, Kärntnerstrasse 25 (U-Bahn Stephansplatz); the Middle Eastern **Levante**, 1, Wollzeile 19 (U-Bahn Stephansplatz); and the **Schnitzelhaus**, 7, Zieglergasse 35 (tram #49). Again, each has numerous other branches. At all these places you'll get fast and efficient service and filling snacks for less than €10, but they are not places to idle away several hours.

---

Stephansplatz. The largest Viennese *Konditorei* chain, serving a staggering selection of calorific cakes and coffee in dodgy 1960s and 1970s decor. Branches all over Vienna. Hours vary, but usually Mon–Fri 7am–8pm, Sun 9am–8pm.

**Alt Wien** 1, Bäckerstrasse 9; U-Bahn Stephansplatz. Bohemian *Kaffeehaus* with *Beisl* decor, posters on nicotine-stained walls, and a dark, smoky atmosphere even on the sunniest day. Daily 10am–2am.

**Café Bräunerhof** 1, Stallburggasse 2; U-Bahn Herrengasse. Thomas Bernhard's favourite has a real *Kaffeehaus* atmosphere: nicotine-coloured walls, slightly snooty tuxedoed waiters and simple food. Live music Sat 3–6pm. Mon–Fri 8am–9pm, Sat 8am–7pm, Sun 10am–7pm.

**Café Central** 1, Herrengasse 14 ⓦ www.ferstel.at; U-Bahn Herrengasse. The most famous of all Viennese cafés, resurrected in the 1980s and still the most architecturally interesting (see p.56). Trotsky was once a regular. Piano music daily 5–10pm. Free wi-fi. Mon–Sat 7.30am–10pm, Sun 10am–10pm.

**Delia's Caffè** 1, Tuchlauben 8 ⓦ www.caffedelias.com; U-Bahn Stephansplatz. The decadent décor overwhelms this small central café, and attracts a dressed-up crowd. Mon–Sat 8am–midnight, Sun 11am–11pm.

**Demel** 1, Kohlmarkt 14 ⓦ www.demel.at; U-Bahn Herrengasse. The king of the *Kaffee-Konditorei* – and one of the priciest. The cake display is a work of art, as is the interior. Daily 9am–7pm.

**Café Diglas** 1, Wollzeile 10 ⓦ www.diglas.at; U-Bahn Stephansplatz. Smoky old *Kaffeehaus* – once Franz Lehár's favourite haunt – with burgundy upholstery and piles of cakes and papers to choose from. Piano music Tues, Wed, Fri & Sat 8–11pm. Daily 8am–11pm.

🏃 **Café Engländer** 1, Postgasse 2 ⓦ www.cafe-englaender.com; U-Bahn Stubentor. Great *Kaffeehaus* with a very long pedigree, currently sporting a smart modernist look and serving good food. Free wi-fi. Mon–Sat 8am–1am, Sun 10am–1am.

**Eissalon am Schwedenplatz** 1, Franz-Josefs-Kai 17 ⓦ www.gelato.at; U-Bahn Schwedenplatz. The locals' favourite Italian ice-cream parlour, right by the U-Bahn on Schwedenplatz – grab a cone before you jump on the tram home. Daily 10am–11pm.

🏃 **Café Frauenhuber** 1, Himmelpfortgasse 6; U-Bahn Stephansplatz. The oldest *Kaffeehaus* in Vienna – Beethoven was a regular (as patron and pianist) – with vaulted ceiling, deep burgundy upholstery and an excellent menu. Mon–Sat 8am–midnight, Sun 10am–10pm.

**Café Griensteidl 1, Michaelerplatz 2; U-Bahn Herrengasse.** After nearly a hundred-year caesura, the literary *Griensteidl* was resurrected (at least in name) in 1990 – it's perfectly OK, but not what it was in 1897 (see p.56) and still needs the patina of age. Daily 8am–11.30pm.

**Café Hawelka 1, Dorotheergasse 6; ⓦwww .hawelka.at; U-Bahn Stephansplatz.** Small, smoky bohemian café, run for sixty years by the same couple; Leopold was born in 1911, but still works on. You may have to fight for a table. Mon & Wed–Sat 8am–2am, Sun 10am–2am.

**Kleines Café 1, Franziskanerplatz 3; U-Bahn Stephansplatz.** Cosy little café on a quiet square, an early crossover between traditional *Kaffeehaus* and modern bar, designed by the Viennese architect Hermann Czech in the 1970s. Mon–Sat 10am–2am, Sun 1pm–2am.

**Café Korb 1, Brandstätte 9 ⓦwww.cafekorb.at; U-Bahn Stephansplatz.** Traditional, endearingly worn 1950s formica-style *Kaffeehaus* tucked away in the backstreets of the Innere Stadt; rather surprisingly you can play skittles in the basement. Mon–Sat 8am–midnight, Sun 11am–11pm.

**Café Krugerhof 1, Krugerstrasse 8; U-Bahn Karlsplatz.** No-nonsense classic *Kaffeehaus* just off Kärntnerstrasse, with well-worn, flock beige upholstery, coat stands, newspapers, billiards, food and comfy booths. Mon–Fri 7am–5pm, Sat 7am–4pm.

**Café Markusplatz 1, Tuchlauben 16 ⓦwww .markusplatz.at; U-Bahn Stephansplatz.** Slip into one of the retro 1950s booths at the resurrected Café Tuchlauben and enjoy great coffee, patisserie, food and free wi-fi. Mon–Fri 7.30am–9pm, Sat 8.30am–7pm, Sun 9.30am–7pm.

**Pat's Brainfood 1, Plankengasse 4 ⓦwww .pats-brainfood.com; U-Bahn Stephansplatz.** Funky, modern lunchtime spot serving up high-energy, gluten-free but not necessarily veggie soups, stews and salads, with a few high stools for those eating in. Mon–Fri 11am–3pm.

**Soho 1, Burggarten; U-Bahn Karlsplatz.** A cut above your average student canteen, this is the Nationalbibliothek's groovy café near the Palmenhaus, with a daily lunchtime menu for under €6; pay for the food at the bar and hand your counter in at the kitchen. Mon–Fri 9am–4pm, Sat 11am–4pm.

**Café Tirolerhof 1, Tegetthoffstrasse/Fürichgasse; U-Bahn Karlsplatz.** A real, peaceful, old-fashioned *Kaffeehaus*, with classic decor and ambience, conveniently situated just behind the opera house. Mon–Fri 7am–9pm, Sat 7am–2am, Sun 9am–midnight.

**Trześniewski 1, Dorotheergasse 1 ⓦwww.trzesniewski.at; U-Bahn Stephansplatz.** Minimalist sandwich bar that's a veritable Viennese institution, serving tiny mouthwatering slices of rye *Brötchen*(€1 each) topped with fishy, eggy and meaty spreads – wash it all down with a *Pfiff*. Stand-up tables and a few seats. Branches elsewhere in Vienna. Mon–Fri 8.30am–7.30pm, Sat 9am–5pm.

**Wrenkh Natürlich 1, Rauhensteingasse 12; U-Bahn Stephansplatz.** A small weekday-only snack bar around the back of the Steffl department store on Kärntnerstrasse; soup or salad and a main course for around €8. Mon–Fri 11am–7pm, Sat 10am–4pm.

**Zanoni & Zanoni 1, Lugeck 7 ⓦwww.zanoni .co.at; U-Bahn Stephansplatz.** Primarily an ice-cream parlour or *gelateria* – though also a *pasticceria* – and one of the few that's open all year round. Daily 7am–midnight.

**Zum schwarzen Kameel 1, Bognergasse 5 ⓦwww.kameel.at; U-Bahn Herrengasse.** A terribly smart, convivial deli that's not exactly cheap, but is a venerable Viennese institution, with stand-up tables and an excellent but expensive restaurant attached. Mon–Sat 9am–midnight.

## Vegetarians

**Vegetarianism** has not caught on in a big way in Vienna – and there are remarkably few vegetarian restaurants – but most places have at least one veggie dish available. The key phrases are *Ich bin vegeterianisch(e)* ("I'm vegetarian") and *Ist das ohne Fleisch?* (literally "Is that without meat?"). There are usually a few traditional vegetarian dishes on most *Beisl* and *Kaffeehaus* menus: *Gebackener Emmenthaler* (or some other kind of cheese), which is breaded and deep-fried; *Knödel mit Ei* (dumplings with scrambled egg); *Spinatnockerl* (spinach pasta).

# Coffee and cakes

**Paris may have more of them, but Vienna is the spiritual home of the café or *Kaffeehaus*. Legend has it that coffee was first introduced to Vienna by a certain Georg Franz Kolschitzky, an Austrian spy who regularly penetrated the Turkish camp during the siege of 1683. When the siege was finally lifted, Kolschitzky was asked what he wanted in return for his services. He requested to be given the "camel fodder" – in actual fact sacks of coffee beans – left behind by the hastily departed Turks, and went on to open the first coffeehouse in Vienna the same year.**

Café Schwarzenburg ▲

Café Central ▼

# A Viennese institution

By the late nineteenth century, the *Kaffeehaus* had become Vienna's most important social institution. It was described by writer Stefan Zweig as "a sort of democratic club to which admission costs the small price of a cup of coffee. Upon payment of this mite, every guest can sit for hours on end, discuss, write, play cards, receive his mail, and above all, can go through an unlimited number of newspapers and magazines". For its *Stammgäste* or regulars, the *Kaffeehaus* served as an informal office where they could work, relax and receive clients in warmth and comfort.

At certain cafés, the head waiter or *Herr Ober* could direct each customer to a certain table or *Stammtisch* depending on what subject he (or less frequently she) wished to debate.

Even today, there is still something unique about the institution that makes a visit worthwhile. While the rest of the world queues up for fast food, the Viennese *Kaffeehaus* implores you to slow down; as the sign in one café puts it, "Sorry, we do not cater for people in a hurry". In his own time, a tuxedoed waiter will ask for your order and, for the price of a small coffee, allow you to sit for as long as you like without asking you to move on or buy another drink.

At this point, you should admire your surroundings: the high ceiling, the marble table-tops, the velvety upholstery, the bentwood coat stands, perhaps a billiard table or two. Select yourself a newspaper and – thanks to the absence of piped music and the general censure on mobile phones – appreciate the timeless tranquillity of the *Kaffeehaus*.

**Österreicher im MAK** 1, Stubenring 5 ⓦwww
.oesterreicherimmak.at; U-Bahn Stubentor. This
museum café, with its wonderfully high
nineteenth-century coffered ceiling, was by
Eichinger oder Knechtl, and, like the MAK
itself (see p.110), is a trendy little spot; it also
serves really delicious food. Daily 10am–2am.

🏃 **Café Palmenhaus** 1, Burggarten ⓦwww
.palmenhaus.at; U-Bahn Karlsplatz. Stylish
modern café set amid the palms of the
greenhouse in the Burggarten. Breakfasts are
great and the daily menu specializes in grilled
fish and meats. A wonderful treat after
visiting the Hofburg. DJs Fri from 8.30pm.
March–Oct daily 10am–2am; Nov–Dec
Mon–Thurs 11.30am–midnight, Fri & Sat
10am–2am, Sun 10am–midnight; Jan & Feb
closed Mon & Tues.

🏃 **Café Prückel** 1, Stubenring 24 ⓦwww
.prueckel.at; U-Bahn Stubentor. The
*Prückel* has lost two-thirds of its original
interior, but the retro 1950s refurbishment
has given it a new lease of life, and draws
in a great mix of young things, elderly
shoppers and dog-owners from the
nearby Stadtpark. Piano music Mon, Wed
& Fri 7–10pm. Free wi-fi. Daily
8.30am–10pm.

**Café Sacher** 1, Philharmonikerstrasse 4;
ⓦwww.sacher.com; U-Bahn Karlsplatz. For all
its fame (see p.100), the *Sacher* is a bit
of a let-down. The decor is imperial red
and gold, but the *Sachertorte* overrated –

practically the only folk who come here
nowadays are tourists. Daily 8am–midnight.

**Café Savoy** 6, Linke Wienzeile 36; U-Bahn
Kettenbrückengasse. A gay café for most of
the week, with wonderfully louche, camp
fin-de-siècle decor, and packed with
bohemian bargain-hunters during the
Saturday flea market. Mon–Fri 5pm–2am,
Sat 9am–2am.

**Café Schottenring** 1, Schottenring/ Börsegasse;
ⓦwww.café-schottenring.at; U-Bahn Schottentor/
Schottenring. L-shaped 1879 *Kaffeehaus*,
with a high stuccoed ceiling, this is an
old-fashioned place, an oasis of calm on the
Ringstrasse. Live piano daily 3–7pm. Mon–Fri
6.30am–11pm, Sat & Sun 8am–9pm.

**Café Schwarzenberg** 1, Kärntner Ring 17
ⓦwww.cafe-schwarzenberg.at; U-Bahn
Karlsplatz. Opulent café with rich marble,
ceramic and wood-panelled decor, plus
huge mirrors and a great cake cabinet. The
super-snooty waiters can make it a bit of an
ordeal. Live piano music Wed & Fri
7.30–11pm, Sat & Sun 5–8pm. Mon–Fri &
Sun 7am–midnight, Sat 9am–midnight.

**tewa** 4, 672 Naschmarkt 1 ⓦwww.tewa672
.com; U-Bahn Kettenbrückengasse. Popular
oriental café in the Naschmarkt serving a
whole range of breakfasts for around €8
until 2pm, salads and wraps for the rest of
the day. Daily 8am–midnight.

**Urania** 1, Uraniastrasse 1 ⓦwww.barurania
.com; U-Bahn Schwedenplatz. Grafted onto

---

## Mensen and student cafés

If you're on a tight budget, then it's worth considering using one of the city's
numerous university cafés or **Mensen** (ⓦwww.mensen.at) – Mensa is the singular –
which are open to the general public (you get an extra discount with student ID). It
might not be cordon bleu, but the food is generally perfectly decent, traditional
Viennese fare, and you usually get a couple of courses for around €6.

**Al-Wien** 9, Türkenstrasse 3; U-Bahn Schottentor. Vienna's most multiethnic Mensa,
situated on the ground floor of the Afro-Asiatisches Institut. The *Café Afro* in the
same building also serves food (and drink) and is open longer hours. Mensa: Mon–Fri
11.30am–3.30pm; Café: Mon–Fri 8.30am–10pm, Sat & Sun 10am–10pm.

**TU Wien** 4, Wiedner Hauptstrasse 8–10; U-Bahn Karlsplatz. The wonderfully-named
*Café Schrödinger* and the Mensa are in the building behind the main Technische
Universität block on Karlsplatz. Mon–Thurs 11am–3pm, Fri 11am–2.30pm.

**UNI Wien NIG** 1, Universitätsstrasse 7; U-Bahn Schottentor. This is the main university Mensa; take the dumbwaiter lift to floor 6 and then walk up another flight of stairs
– you get a nice view over to the Votivkirche. Mon–Thurs 8am–5pm, Fri 8am–4pm.

**WU Wien** 9, Augasse 2–6; U-Bahn Spittelau. The Mensa Markt at the Wirtschaftsu-
niversität always has some veggie options, and the café is good for breakfast. Mensa
Markt: Mon–Fri 11am–2.30pm. Café: Mon–Thurs 8am–7pm, Fri 8am–6pm.

---

# Coffee

On average, the Austrians drink almost
twice as much **coffee** as beer (more than
a pint a day per head of the population).
When ordering, few Viennese ever
actually ask for a straight *Kaffee*, as the
varieties are legion. However, whatever
you order, it will come on a little silver
tray, accompanied by a glass of water.

▲ *Kaffeehaus* waiter

▼ An Austrian cappuccino

▸▸ **Brauner** Black coffee with a small
amount of milk.

▸▸ **Cappuccino** The Austrian version
of a cappuccino comes with whipped
cream (*Schlagobers*).

▸▸ **Einspänner** Small black coffee,
served in a tall glass and topped with
whipped cream.

▸▸ **Eiskaffee** Iced coffee with ice cream
and whipped cream.

▸▸ **Fiaker** A coffee with a shot of rum
and whipped cream.

▸▸ **Kaffee Crème** Coffee served with a
little jug of milk.

▸▸ **Konsul** Black coffee with a spot of
cream.

▸▸ **Kurz** Viennese version of an espresso.

▸▸ **Mazagran** Coffee served with an ice
cube and laced with rum, to be drunk in
one gulp.

▸▸ **Mélange** (pronounced like the
French). Equal measures of frothed milk
and coffee – more of a cappuccino than
an Austrian *Cappuccino*.

▸▸ **Milch Kaffee** Large hot, frothy, milky
coffee.

▸▸ **Pharisäer** Coffee in a glass topped
with whipped cream, served with a
small glass of rum on the side.

▸▸ **Schwarzer** or **Mokka** Small or large
black coffee.

▸▸ **Türkische** Coffee grains and sugar
boiled up together in individual copper
pots to create a strong, sweet brew.

▸▸ **Verlängerter Brauner** or **Schwarzer**
Slightly weaker than normal coffee.

# Cakes

Many *Kaffeehäuser* in Vienna will have *Torten* piled high in a display cabinet, in which case you can simply point to the one that takes your fancy.

The best cafés still bake their own cakes on site, and all can be served with a helping of *Schlagobers* (whipped cream).

The box below details some of the more common choices.

Apfelstrudel ▲

The definitive Sachertorte ▼

Demel ▼

▶▶ **Apfelstrudel** Apple and raisins wrapped in pastry and sprinkled with icing sugar.
▶▶ **Biskuitroulade** The basic roulade is a jam roll, but it comes in various other creamier versions.
▶▶ **Dobostorte** A rich Hungarian cake made up of alternate layers of biscuit sponge and chocolate cream.
▶▶ **Esterházytorte** Several layers of cream and sponge coated in white icing with a feather design on top.
▶▶ **Guglhupf** Sigmund Freud's favourite, at its most basic a simple sponge cake baked in a fluted ring mould and cut into slices.
▶▶ **Linzertorte** Essentially a jam tart made with almond pastry.
▶▶ **Mohnstrudel** A bread-like pudding rather like an *Apfelstrudel*, but with a poppy seed-and-raisin filling.
▶▶ **Powidltascherl** This is basically a Danish pastry, filled with plum jam.
▶▶ **Punschkrapfen** More of a *petit four* than a proper slice of cake, this is a mouthful of cake filled with jam, rum and chocolate and encased in icing.
▶▶ **Sachertorte** The most famous of the Viennese cakes, and in some ways the least interesting: a chocolate sponge cake coated in chocolate, most often with a layer of apricot jam beneath the chocolate coating.
▶▶ **Topfenstrudel** Like an *Apfelstrudel*, but with a sweet curd cheese filling.
▶▶ **Zwetschgenkuchen** A spongy tart dotted with halved plums.

## Ringstrasse

The list here includes cafés inside the MuseumsQuartier and around the Naschmarkt, which begins at Karlsplatz. Unless otherwise specified, the following places are marked on the map on pp.88–89.

**Am Heumarkt 3**, Am Heumarkt 15; U-Bahn **Stadtpark**. Venerable weekday *Kaffeehaus* with giant stone pillars, red booths, parquet floor and billiard tables. Mon–Fri 9am–11pm.

**Café Amacord 4**, Rechte Wienzeile 15; U-Bahn **Karlsplatz**. Fashionable smoky *Kaffeehaus* by the Naschmarkt, with cool (occasionally live) music, lots of newspapers and inexpensive food on the menu. Mon–Wed & Sun 10am–1am, Thurs–Sat 10am–2am.

**Café Bendl 1**, Landesgerichtsstrasse 6; ⓦcafe -bendl.at; U-Bahn **Rathaus**. Nicotine-stained favourite with the local student population for its cheap Austrian comfort food and late hours. Mon–Thurs 8am–2am, Fri 8am–4am, Sat 6pm–4am, Sun 6pm–2am.

**Do & Co Albertina 1**, Albertinaplatz 1 ⓦwww .doco.com; U-Bahn **Karlsplatz**. Beautifully posh café with striking onyx interior and a raised terrace overlooking the Burggarten. Daily 9am–midnight.

**Deli 5**, Naschmarkt Stand 421–436; ☎585 08 23, ⓦwww.naschmarkt-deli.at; U-Bahn **Karlsplatz**; see map, p.102. Very busy, trendy Turkish café in the Naschmarkt, whose famous breakfasts are super-popular. DJs keep things funky in the evening. Mon–Sat 8am–midnight.

**Café Drechsler 6**, Linke Wienzeile 22 ⓦwww .cafedrechsler.at; U-Bahn **Kettenbrückengasse**; see map, p.102. Terence Conran has given what was an endearingly scruffy *Kaffeehaus* by the Naschmarkt a modernist makeover, and it's as popular as ever, especially with clubbers attracted by the late/early opening hours. Mon 8am–2am, Tues–Sat 3am–2am, Sun 3am–midnight.

**Café Eiles 8**, Josefstädterstrasse 2; U-Bahn **Rathaus**. Very traditional *Kaffeehaus* set back from the Ringstrasse, behind the Rathaus. The decor dates from the 1930s, when the café was the meeting point for the Nazis who assassinated the Austro-fascist leader, Englebert Dollfuss. Mon–Fri 7am–10pm, Sat & Sun 8am–10pm.

**Halle 7**, Museumsplatz 1; U-Bahn **Museums quartier**. The biggest and vibiest of the MuseumsQuartier cafés, the multilev... throbs to funky music under a slice o... Fischer von Erlach's old ceiling, and ... produces pricey Italian-fusion food. Fr... wi-fi. Daily 10am–2am.

**Café Imperial 1**, Kärntner Ring 16; U-Bahn **Karlsplatz**. Seriously intimidating, palatia... in the hotel of choice for visiting statesm... and business folk. Live piano Sat & Sun... 3.30–7.30pm. Daily 7am–midnight.

**Kantine 7**, Museumsplatz 1; U-Bahn **Museum quartier**. Simple, relaxed café near the MuseumsQuartier bookshop, with emerald green furniture, and a simple snacky men... of breakfasts, pitta sandwiches and salads... Mon–Sat 10am–2am, Sun 9am–midnight

**Café Landtmann 1**, Dr-Karl-Lueger-Ring 4 ⓦwww.landtmann.at; U-Bahn **Herrengasse/ Schottentor**. One of the poshest of the *Kaffeehäuser* – and a favourite with Freud – with impeccably attired waiters, and a high quota of politicians and Burgtheater actors. Live music Mon, Tues & Sun 8–11pm. Free wi-fi. Daily 7.30am–midnight.

**Café Leopold 7**, Museumsplatz 1 ⓦwww.café -leopold.at; U-Bahn **Museumsquartier**. Stylish modernist Leopold Museum café, with a summer terrace overlooking the courtyard. Sink into the beige-and-black leatherette armchairs inside and tuck into the tasty dishes all under €10. DJs after 10pm. Free wi-fi. Mon–Wed & Sun 10am–2am, Thurs– Sat until 4am.

**Milo 7**, Museumsplatz 1; U-Bahn **Museumsquartier**. The best of the MuseumsQuartier cafés, *Milo* boasts a wonderful, vaulted floral ceramic ceiling, an imaginative menu and a friendly vibe. Free wi-fi. Mon–Fri 9am–midnight, Sat 10am– midnight, Sun 10am–6pm.

**Café Ministerium 1**, Georg-Coch-Platz 4 ⓦww .cafeministerium.at; U-Bahn **Stubentor**. Not quite a classic *Kaffeehaus* – the streaked yellow paintwork puts paid to that – but th... lunchtime cooking is excellent and it's popular with local civil servants. Free wi-f... Daily 7am–11pm.

**Café Museum 1**, Friedrichstrasse 6 ⓦwww .cafe-museum.at; U-Bahn **Karlsplatz**. L-sha... café that was once a favourite haunt of... Klimt, Kokoschka and Schiele, among others. Refurbishment has returned the... place to the original 1899 Adolf Loos c... scheme, but a lick of paint is really the... thing an old *Kaffeehaus* needs. Mon–S... 8am–midnight, Sun 10am–midnight.

the canalside of the Urania building is this smart, modern café-bar, with a fabulous terrace overlooking the Donaukanal. Daily 9am–midnight.

## Landstrasse and Wieden (3rd & 4th districts)

**Café Anzengruber 4, Schleifmühlgasse 19; U-Bahn Karlsplatz; see map, p.102.** Classic L-shaped *Kaffeehaus* with lino floor and formica tables, last refurbished sometime after World War II, and with some shockingly bad art on the walls. The soupy *pasta fagioli* is famous, filling and just €3.50. Mon–Sat 4pm–2am.

**Café Goldegg 4, Argentinerstrasse 49; U-Bahn Südtiroler Platz; see map, p.127.** Archetypal no-nonsense *Kaffeehaus* a short stroll from the Belvedere in the backstreets of Wieden. Mon–Fri 8am–9pm, Sat 8am–8pm, Sun 9am–8pm.

**The Point of Sale 4, Schleifmühlgasse 12 ⓦwww.thepointofsale.at; U-Bahn Karlsplatz.** Cool neighbourhood corner café, with a casual modern, slightly ad hoc feel. Breakfast and brunch, washed down with juices, are especially popular. Mon–Thurs & Sun 10am–1am, Fri & Sat 10am–2am.

**Café Zartl 3, Rasumofskygasse 7; tram #N or U-Bahn Rochusgasse; see map, p.127.** Local corner *Kaffeehaus* – here since 1883 and frequented over the years by everyone from Robert Musil to Hundertwasser himself – with cream and green decor, billiards, booths and lots of ice-cream sundaes. Daily 7am–midnight.

## Margareten and Mariahilf (5th & 6th districts)

**Bar Italia 6, Mariahilferstrasse 19–21 ⓦwww.baritalia.net; U-Bahn Museumsquartier; see map, p.141.** Very posey, sleek, modern bar set in subterranean vaults not far from the MuseumsQuartier; great coffee, pastries and breakfasts and a cheap midday Italian menu. Mon–Fri 8.30am–2am, Sat 9am–2am, Sun 9am–2am.

**Cuadro 5, Margaretenstrasse 77; U-Bahn Pilgramgasse; see map, p.102.** Modern café in the lovely Biedermeier courtyard of the Schlossquadrat; defined by its vast backlit glass wall, and well loved for its organic breakfasts and square burgers. Free wi-fi. Mon–Sat 8am–midnight, Sun 9am–11pm.

**Café Jelinek 6, Otto-Bauer-Gasse 5; U-Bahn Webgasse; see map, p.141.** Lovely, battered old *Kaffeehaus* tucked away in the backstreets south of Mariahilferstrasse, this is a rare survivor, still serving an exclusively local clientele. Daily 9am–9pm.

**Café Kafka 6, Capistrangasse 8; U-Bahn Museumsquartier; see map, p.141.** Old, smokey *Kaffeehaus* near the MuseumsQuartier that's home (once a month) to Labyrinth (ⓦwww.labyrinthpoetry.com), Vienna's English poetry group, and serves up veggie and vegan dishes. Mon–Sat 8am–midnight, Sun 2–11pm.

**Café Ritter 6, Mariahilferstrasse 73; U-Bahn Neubaugasse; see map, p.141.** Vast, venerable, high-ceilinged V-shaped café popular with veteran card-players and shoppers. Live piano Thurs–Sat 8–10pm. Daily 7.30am–11.30pm.

**Café Rüdigerhof 5, Hamburger Strasse 20; U-Bahn Kettenbrückengasse; see map, p.141.** Wonderful Jugendstil building on the outside, mishmash of 1950s kitsch on the inside. The food is cheap and filling, but the riverside terrace is marred by the nearby busy road. Daily 9am–2am.

**St Josef 7, Mondscheingasse 10; tram #49; see map, p.141.** Functional, friendly self-service canteen (with shop at back) serving tasty veggie dishes for under €10. No smoking. Mon–Fri 8am–5pm, Sat 8am–4pm.

**Servus 6, Mariahilferstrasse 57–59 ⓦwww.servus-café.at; U-Bahn Neubaugasse; see map, p.141.** Smart, traditional *Kaffeehaus*, with red and white decor, that gets busy with shoppers at lunchtime. Live music Tues, Thurs & Sat 8–11pm. Mon–Sat 10am–midnight.

**Sperl 6, Gumpendorfer Strasse 11 ⓦcafesperl.at; U-Bahn Karlsplatz/Babenbergerstrasse; see map, p.102.** One of the classics of the *Kaffeehaus* scene, just off Mariahilferstrasse: L-shaped, with billiard tables and a hint of elegant, bohemian shabbiness. Free wi-fi. Mon–Sat 7am–11pm, Sun 11am–8pm (July & Aug closed Sun).

## Neubau (7th district)

Unless otherwise specified, the following places are marked on the map on p.141.

**Café Amadeus 15, Märzstrasse 4 ⓦwww.cafeamadeus.at; U-Bahn Burggasse/Westbahnhof.** A genuine *Kaffeehaus*, just the other

Plenty of cafés have free wi-fi now, but if you want to find a wireless local area network (WLAN), probably the most congenial and central is in the MuseumsQuartier, where you can pick up free wi-fi in any of the bars or cafés and throughout the complex.

side of *Gürtel* from Neubau, with lovely old furnishings and a parquet floor. Open evenings only, with regular live music and literary readings. Mon–Fri 5pm–1am, Sat & Sun 6pm–1am.

**Europa 7, Zollergasse 8** ⓦ www.europa-lager.at; **U-Bahn Neubaugasse.** Lively, spacious café that attracts a trendy crowd, who love the posey window booths. DJs on the weekend; poker Mon at 8pm. Daily 9am–4am.

**Lux 7, Schrankgasse 4/Spittelberggasse 3** ⓦ www.lux-restaurant.at; **U-Bahn Volkstheater.** Rambling modern Spittelberg *Kaffeehaus*, with a friendly bistro feel and an eclectic menu featuring tofu-based dishes, pizzas and pancakes. Mon–Fri 11am–1am, Sat & Sun 10am–1am.

**Das Möbel 7, Burggasse 10** ⓦ www.dasmoebel .at; **U-Bahn Volkstheater.** Café-bar on the edge of Spittelberg, packed with minimalist furniture (which you can buy), a youngish crowd, weird toilets and reasonable sustenance on offer. Daily 10am–1am.

**Nil 7, Siebensterngasse 39; tram #49.** Simple, but stylish Egyptian café offering breakfast, falafel, hummus, kebabs and the like, all for under €10. Daily 10am–midnight.

**Café Weidinger 16, Lerchenfelder Gürtel; U-Bahn Burggasse.** One of the few surviving classic *Gürtel Kaffeehäuser*, with shabby upholstery, battered wood panelling and not a lick of paint for decades. Mon–Fri 7am–1am, Sat & Sun 8am–12.30am.

**Café Westend 7, Mariahilferstrasse 128; U-Bahn Westbahnhof.** Conveniently located directly opposite Westbahnhof, the faded grandeur of this traditional *Kaffeehaus* – once frequented by Hitler – is the best possible introduction to Vienna for those who've just arrived by train. Daily 7am–midnight.

**Wirr 1, Burggasse 70** ⓦ www.wirr.at; **tram #49.** Two-tone grey bubble camouflage makes up the décor of this *Nachtcafé* – breakfast is served until 4pm and happy hour (and DJs) kick off at 9pm. Mon–Wed 11am–2am, Thurs & Fri 11am–4am, Sat & Sun 10am–2am.

## Josefstadt (8th district)

Unless otherwise specified, the following places are marked on the map on p.141.

**Café Florianihof 8, Florianigasse 45** ⓦ www .florianihof.at; **U-Bahn Josefstädter Strasse.** Simple neighbourhood *Kaffeehaus* that has retained one or two Jugendstil touches, and yet has a light and airy, modern feel. Free wi-fi. Mon–Fri 8am–midnight, Sat & Sun 10am–8pm.

🏃 **Café Hummel 8, Josefstädter Strasse 66** ⓦ www.cafehummel.at; **U-Bahn Josef-städter Strasse.** Big, bustling local *Kaffeehaus*, with formica fittings and tables looking out on the nearby square – they do a brisk lunchtime trade. Free wi-fi. Mon–Sat 7am–midnight, Sun 8am–midnight.

**Café Merkur 8, Lammgasse 1** ⓦ www .cafemerkur.at; **U-Bahn Rathaus.** Laid-back, modern take on the local *Kaffeehaus*, with modern art on the walls and Viennese comfort food on the menu (breakfast until 5pm on the weekend). Daily 10am–2am.

**Café der Provinz 8, Maria-Treu-Gasse 3** ⓦ www .cafederprovinz.at; **U-Bahn Rathaus or tram #J.** Cute, cosy little neighbourhood café, with ad hoc wooden furnishings and delicious galettes, waffles and crêpes for under €10. No smoking. Daily 8am–11pm.

**Tunnel 8, Florianigasse 39** ⓦ www.tunnel -vienna-live.at; **U-Bahn Josefstädter Strasse.** Popular, unpretentious, L-shaped student café with cheap food, big helpings, self-service breakfasts until 11am; live music in the basement every night from 8pm. Daily 9am–2am.

**Vegi-Point 8, Florianigasse 18** ☎ 990 54 13, ⓦ www.tunnel-vienna-live.at/vegipoint; **U-Bahn Josefstädter Strasse.** Utilitarian, veggie fast-food: salads, soups, pasta, and a veggie burger with French fries for €3 – eat-in or take-away. Mon–Sat 11am–8pm.

**Die Wäscherei 8, Albertgasse 49/Laudongasse** ☎ 409 23 75-11, ⓦ www.die-waescherei.at; **U-Bahn Josefstädter Strasse.** Trendy, low-lit café-bar with a menu of studenty comfort food – very popular for weekend buffet brunch. Mon–Fri 5pm–2am, Sat 10am–2am, Sun 10am–midnight. Mains €8–12.

## Alsergrund (9th district)

The following places are marked on the map on p.145.

**Café Berg 9, Berggasse 8 ⓦ www.cafe-berg.at; U-Bahn Schottentor.** Relaxed, modern, mixed gay/straight café, attached to the city's chief gay bookshop, Löwenherz, with an attractive assortment of chairs and great breakfasts, light lunches and main meals. Daily 10am–1am.

**Blaustern 19, Döblinger Gürtel 2 ⓦ www .blaustern.at; U-Bahn Nussdorfer Strasse.** Popular, long-established neighbourhood *Kaffeehaus*, in the middle of the *Gürtel*, that's been given a modernist makeover. Mon–Fri 7am–1am, Sat & Sun 8am–1am.

**Statt-Beisl im WUK 9, Währingerstrasse 59 ⓦ www.statt-beisl.at; tram #40, #41 or #42.** Regular café-bar in the WUK cultural complex (to the left as you enter), offering lots of inexpensive veggie and vegan dishes. Daily 11am–2am.

**Café Stein 9, Währingerstrasse 6 ⓦ www .cafe-stein.com; U-Bahn Schottentor.** Posey designer café of long standing, on the corner of Kolingasse, with minimalist decor, funky music, trendy loos, baguettes, veggie food and breakfasts served until 8pm. Mon–Sat 7am–1am, Sun 9am–1am.

**Vegirant 9, Währingerstrasse 57 ☎407 82 87, ⓦ www.vegirant.at; U-Bahn Währingerstrasse-Volksoper.** The virtues of this modest place are cheap and plentiful veggie food – whether you go for the *Erdäpfelrahmsuppe* to *Waldpilzrisotto*, the portions are huge. Mon–Fri 11.30am–6pm.

**Café Weimar 9, Währingerstrasse 68 ⓦ www .cafeweimar.at; tram #40, #41 or #42.** L-shaped 1900 *Kaffeehaus* with a high ceiling, chandeliers, tuxedoed waiters and

snug booths. Good-value €8 lunchtime menu. Live piano Mon–Sat from 7.30pm, Sun from late afternoon. Free wi-fi. Mon–Sat 7.30am–midnight, Sun 9am–midnight.

**Café Wilder Mann 18, Währingerstrasse 85; tram #40, #41 or #42.** Established in 1897, this classic *Kaffeehaus* is characterized by its plain postwar decor – lino, booths and bentwood chairs. Mon–Fri 9am–9pm.

## Leopoldstadt (2nd district)

**Café Sperlhof 2, Grosse Sperlgasse 41; U-Bahn Taborstrasse; see map, p.158.** Backstreet café, with a colourful political history, that harbours hundreds of board games, playing cards, several billiard tables and other quirky artefacts. Mon–Sat 7.30am–midnight, Sun 8am–8pm.

**Gesundes 2, Lilienbrunngasse 3 ⓦ www .gesundess.at; U-Bahn Schwedenplatz; see map, p.158.** Organic health-food shop with just a few tables serving lunchtime-only veggie and vegan fare. Mon–Sat 9am–3pm.

## The suburbs

**Cobenzl 19, Am Cobenzl 94 ⓦ www.cobenzl.at; bus #38A from U-Bahn Heiligenstadt; see map, p.162–163.** Kaisergelb hilltop pavilion from 1809, now a Wienerwald institution, with great views over the city from the summer terrace. Daily 10am–11pm.

**Café Dommayer 13, Dommayergasse 1 ⓦ www.oberlaa-wien.at; U-Bahn Hietzing; see map, p.165.** Historic *Kaffeehaus* where Johann Strauss Junior made his premiere. Tuxedoed waiters, comfy alcoves, occasional live music and lots of coffee and cakes. A good rest stop after a hard day at Schönbrunn. Daily 7am–10pm. Live Strauss Sat 2–4pm.

**Gloriette 13, Schönbrunn Schlosspark ⓦ www .gartenhotel.com; U-Bahn Hietzing/Schönbrunn; see map, p.165.** Smart café in the dining hall of a grandiose monument with a spectac-

## Viennoiserie: origin of the pastries

According to some, Vienna is the home of the **bagel** and the **croissant**. The former is, of course, of Jewish origin, but is said to have been popularized here after a Jewish baker presented one to Jan Sobieski after the lifting of the 1683 siege of Vienna; its name is thought to come from *Bügel* (stirrup). The croissant also arose from this historical period, its shape said to represent the half-crescent moon on the Turkish flags. (Maria Theresia's daughter, Marie Antoinette, is responsible for exporting the croissant to France when she married the future Louis XVI.)

ular view over Schönbrunn from the hill in the Schlosspark. A lovely 20min walk from the U-Bahn. Daily 9am to dusk.

**Oktogon** 19, Am Himmel ⓦ www.himmel.at; bus #38A from U-Bahn Heiligenstadt; see map, p.162. Smart, modern, octagonal café-restaurant that makes a perfect lunch halt whilst out in the Wienerwald. Weekend brunch until 2pm. Live classical music on weekend afternoons. April–Oct Mon–Fri noon–10pm, Sat & Sun 11am–10pm; Nov–March Wed–Sun only.

**Saletti** 19, Hartäckerstrasse 80 ⓣ 479 22 22; bus #37A or #40A. A 1930s garden shelter (known as the Pavilion to its friends) near the Döblinger Friedhof, with outdoor seating overlooking the Wienerwald and a cosy interior for the winter. The breakfasts are varied and legendary. Daily 6.30am–1.30am.

CAFÉS

# Restaurants

V
ienna's restaurant scene is dominated by the legacy of the **Beisl** (Yiddish for "little house"), the city's chief traditional eating and drinking establishment. Essentially, the *Beisl* is an unpretentious, muzak-free, wood-panelled inn or *Gasthaus*, where you're expected to share a table with other customers; a family-run place, where folk of all social classes and ages come to drink, socialize, and eat hearty Viennese home cooking. On its last legs a decade or so ago, the *Beisl* has gained a new lease of life with the emergence of the neo-*Beisl*, a sort of pared-down, modern take on the old formula.

Most Viennese restaurants take great care over the preparation and presentation of their food, and nearly all offer highly **seasonal** fare: at Easter, you'll see dishes seasoned with *Bärlauch* (wild garlic); in May, freshly harvested *Spargel* (asparagus) appears almost everywhere; in summer, the puddings will feature summer fruits like *Ribiseln* (redcurrants); in autumn, wild mushrooms such as *Steinpilze* (porcini) and *Eierschwammerl* (chanterelles) feature on menus; *Kürbis* (pumpkins) are put to good use in October; special game (*Wild*) menus appear in late October; and around St Martin's Day (Nov 11), you'll see *Gans* (roast goose) on just about every menu.

The other specifically Viennese institution to sample is the **Heuriger** or wine tavern, which you can find all over the city's wine-growing suburbs. These come into their own in summer, when a night out at one is just about obligatory. *Heurigen* serve their own wine, and a traditional self-service cold buffet is usually on offer too. In case you can't make it out to the suburbs, or arrive in the wrong season, you can even sate yourself in one or two *Stadtheurigen* in the city centre.

The majority of our listings concentrate on typically Viennese establishments, although you can sample cuisines from all over the globe, from the Balkans to Japan. Note that while Vienna isn't a great city for **vegetarians**, most restaurants do serve one or two veggie dishes.

Remarkably, **prices** remain very reasonable compared to other European capitals, whether you eat in a traditional *Beisl*, a pizzeria or a more modern restaurant. All restaurants are marked on the relevant map throughout this guide – you'll find a page reference at each review or section introduction.

**Advance reservations** are advisable in most places, and bringing **cash** is a good idea – plenty of places don't take credit cards. **Tipping** in a *Beisl* usually consists of rounding up to the nearest euro; when the waiter gives you a bill for, say €7.50, you say €8 as you hand over the cash. In other restaurants, add fifteen percent to the bill unless it's already been done for you. To keep the price of meals to a minimum, look for the set **Tagesmenü** (predominantly at lunchtime and often known as a *Mittagsmenü*), which usually gives you two courses for well under €10. For **cafés**, which normally offer very good-value meals as well as coffee, cakes and snacks, see p.206.

## Viennese cuisine

**Viennese cuisine** (*Wiener Küche*) is more varied than in your average German-speaking city, reflecting the multiethnic origins of the old empire. In fact most of the city's signature dishes actually hail from elsewhere: the *Wiener Schnitzel* is from Milan, goulash is from Hungary, *Apfelstrudel* is from Turkey and the rest of the cuisine comes from Bohemia.

Soup (**Suppe**) is the starting point of most lunchtime menus. Be sure to ask for some of the delicious local **bread** (**Brot**) to go with it, and remember to count how many pieces you eat, as you'll be charged for each one at the end. The standard loaf or **Hausbrot** is a mixture of wheat and rye flour.

The capital's most famous **meat dish**, **Wiener Schnitzel**, is said to have originated from Milan. Traditionally deep-fried breaded veal, it can also be made from chicken or pork, and is normally accompanied by **Erdäpfelsalat**, a potato salad in a watery, sweet dill dressing. Emperor Franz-Josef's favourite dish (and that of many of his subjects) was **Tafelspitz**, thick slices of boiled beef, usually served with **G'röste** (grated fried potato or *rosti*). Another popular meat dish is **Backhendl**, a young chicken, breaded and deep-fried; and for the adventurous, there's the likes of **Beuschel** (veal-lung stew) to chew on.

The presence of **goulash** (**Gulasch**) on the menu is a Hungarian legacy, while the Italians are behind **Nockerl**, the Austrians' heavy version of pasta noodles; **Schinkenfleckerl**, flecks of ham baked in pasta, is especially popular. **Dumplings** (**Knödel**) are ubiquitous, and are more like English dumplings than the bread-like Czech version from which they derive. You'll also find **fish** on most menus, the most common being trout (**Forelle** or **Saibling**), pike (**Hecht**), carp (**Karpfen**) and pike-perch (**Fogosch**).

Obviously in a country with such a famously sweet tooth, there's no shortage of rich **desserts** (**Mehlspeisen**) on most menus. Apart from the ubiquitous **Apfelstrudel**, Bohemian **Palatschinken** (pancakes), filled with jam and/or curd cheese, are a regular feature. Look out, too, for **Marillenknödel**, sweet apricot dumplings, and the politically incorrect **Mohr im Hemd** – literally "Moor in a shirt" – a chocolate pudding with hot chocolate sauce and whipped cream.

Most of the city's **cafés** – covered in the previous chapter (see p.206) – serve traditional Viennese food. For a German food and drinks **glossary**, see p.278.

### Innere Stadt (1st district)

The following places are marked on the map on pp.40–41.

**Achilleus** 1, Köllnerhofgasse 3 ☎512 83 28; U-Bahn Schwedenplatz. Strangely Austrian-looking, but excellent, Greek restaurant. Mon–Sat 11am–midnight, Sun 11am–11pm. Mains €10–15.

**Augustinerkeller** 1, Augustinerstrasse 1 ☎533 10 26, ⓦwww.bitzinger.at; U-Bahn Karlsplatz. Vast *Stadtheuriger* with green- and black-striped booths in the cellars underneath the Albertina. Fast service and hearty Viennese food; a tad touristy, but fun. *Schrammelmusik* from 6.30pm. Daily 11am–midnight. Mains €10–20.

**Beim Czaak** 1, Postgasse 15 ☎513 72 15; U-Bahn Schwedenplatz. Lovely dark-green wood panelling and low lighting gives this well-established *Beisl* a cosy, but smart, feel. Mon–Sat 11am–midnight. Mains €8–16.

**Bio Bar** 1, Drahtgasse 3 ☎968 93 51, ⓦwww .biobar.at; U-Bahn Stephansplatz. Sparse, modern veggie/vegan restaurant, with long benches and tables; the menu changes daily and features soya versions of classic meat dishes, plus risotto, vegetable paella, bruschetta and lots of salad. Mon 11.30am–3pm, Tues–Fri 11.30am–3pm & 5.30–11pm, Sat & Sun noon–11pm. Mains €10–16.

**Bizi** 1, Rotenturmstrasse 4 ⓦwww.pizza-bizi .at; U-Bahn Stephansplatz. A reliable, functional filling station just off Stephansplatz. Devise your own pizza toppings, pasta dishes, assemble your own salad, or choose one of the main dishes and/or roasted vegetables. Takeaway or sit down.

Branches elsewhere in Vienna. Daily 10.30am–10.30pm. Mains €6–9.

**Brezlg'wölb 1, Ledererhof 9 ☏ 533 88 11; U-Bahn Herrengasse.** Lovely candlelit cave-like restaurant with deliberately olde worlde decor. Hidden in a cobbled street off Draht-gasse, it serves the usual Austrian favourites at knock-down prices. Daily 11.30am–1am. Mains €8–14.

**Esterházykeller 1, Haarhof 1 ☏ 533 34 82, Ⓦ www.esterhazykeller.at; U-Bahn Herrengasse.** Snug, brick-vaulted *Stadtheuriger* with very cheap wine and a limited range of hot and cold snacks. Situated off Naglergasse. Daily 11am–11pm. Mains €8–14.

**Expedit 1, Wiesingerstrasse 6; ☏ 512 33 13, Ⓦ www.expedit.net; U-Bahn Stubentor.** Bar, deli and cantina all rolled into one, this converted warehouse attracts a youthful crowd, who tuck into the antipasti and Ligurian specialities with gusto. Don't forget to check out the indoor *boccia*, an Italian version of *boules* in the basement (€5 for half an hour). Mon–Fri 11am–1am, Sat 6pm–1am. Mains €10–25.

**Figlmüller 1, Wollzeile 5 ☏ 512 61 77, Ⓦ www .figlmueller.at; U-Bahn Stephansplatz.** It's in every tourist guide to the city there is, but this is still *the* place to eat a giant *Wiener Schnitzel*, with a traditional potato salad, washed down with wine (there's no beer). Branches elsewhere in Vienna. Daily 11am–10.30pm. Closed Aug. Mains €8–16.

**Gigerl 1, Rauhensteingasse 3 ☏ 513 44 31; U-Bahn Stephansplatz.** A kind of neo-*Stadtheuriger*, a modern, stylish take on an old theme. Entrance at Blumenstockgasse 2. Daily 3pm–1am, Fri & Sat until 2am. Mains €8–12.

**Gösser Bierklinik 1, Steindlgasse 4 ☏ 533 75 98 12, Ⓦ goesser-bierklinik.at; U-Bahn Stephansplatz.** Ancient inn with wooden booths for drinking, and a more formal backroom restaurant serving traditional Austrian food. Mon–Sat 10am–11.30pm. Mains €15–23.

**Göttweiger Stiftskeller 1, Spiegelgasse 9 ☏ 512 78 17; U-Bahn Stephansplatz.** Ground-floor monastic wine cellars that feel more like a family *Beisl*. Utterly traditional food and a mixed clientele – very popular, especially at lunchtime. Mon–Fri 8am–10pm. Mains €7–12.

**Griechenbeisl 1, Fleischmarkt 11 ☏ 533 19 77, Ⓦ www.griechenbeisl.at; U-Bahn Schweden-platz.** Possibly the most ancient of all Vienna's inns (see p.65), frequented by the likes of Beethoven, Schubert and Brahms, a fact that it predictably milks in order to draw in the tourists. Daily 11am–12.30am. Mains €12–24.

**Hollmann Salon 1, Grashofgasse 3 ☏ 961 19 60 40, Ⓦ www.hollmann-salon.at; U-Bahn Schwe-denplatz.** A very classy (no-smoking) Viennese restaurant hidden away in the courtyard of the Heiligenkreuzhof, offering a good spread of immaculately presented meat, fish and veggie dishes. Mon–Fri noon–3pm & 6–10pm, Sat 10am–3pm & 6–10pm. Mains €13–18.

**Ilona-Stüberl 1, Bräunerstrasse 2 ☏ 533 90 29, Ⓦ www.ilonastueberl.at; U-Bahn Stephansplatz.** Long-standing Gypsy-music-free Hungarian restaurant with lashings of goulash on offer. Daily 11.30am–11.30pm; Oct–March closed Mon. Mains €8–15.

**Immervoll 1, Weihburggasse 17 ☏ 513 52 88; U-Bahn Stephansplatz.** Small, very popular lime- and pastel-green wood-panelled neo-*Beisl* designed by Hermann Czech, offering a short but excellent Viennese menu. Daily noon–11pm. Mains €8–15.

**Limes 1, Hoher Markt 10 ☏ 905 800, Ⓦ www .restaurant-limes.at; U-Bahn Stephansplatz/ Schwedenplatz.** Limes refers to the frontier of the Roman Empire, but this stark, minimalist eatery is indeed playfully decorated with a touch of lime; menu is Med-influenced. Mon–Sat 11am–midnight, Sat 10am–midnight. Mains €8–18.

**Meinl am Graben 1, Graben 19 ☏ 532 33 34, Ⓦ www.meinlamgraben.at; U-Bahn Stephans-platz.** The flagship store has an excellent seafood bar and a stand-up buffet on the ground floor, and an elegant first-floor restaurant, with a view straight down Graben. The cooking here is top notch, taking its inspiration from all over. Store: Mon–Fri 8am–7.30pm, Sat 9am–6pm. Restaurant: Mon–Fri 8am–midnight, Sat 9am–midnight. Restaurant mains €22–35.

**Melker Stiftskeller 1, Schottengasse 3 ☏ 533 55 30, Ⓦ melkerstiftskeller.at; U-Bahn Schot-tentor.** Vast, high-ceilinged *Stadtheuriger* owned by the famous Melk monks, serving traditional grub. Tues–Sat 5pm–midnight. Mains €8–16.

**Ofenloch 1, Kurrentgasse 8 ☏ 533 88 44, Ⓦ www.ofenloch.at; U-Bahn Stephansplatz.** Upmarket *Beisl*, just off Judengasse, with wood-panelled booths and a cosy, *gemütlich* atmosphere. Mon–Sat 11am–midnight. Mains €10–18.

**Palatschinkenkuchl** 1, Köllnerhofgasse 4 ☎512 31 05; **U-Bahn Schwedenplatz.** Informal restaurant popular with kids and adults alike for its savoury and sweet pancakes and milkshakes. Daily 10am–midnight. Inexpensive.

**Pfudl** 1, Bäckerstrasse 22 ☎512 67 05, ⓦwww .gasthauspfudl.com. Old-fashioned, *gemütlich Gasthaus* with chequered tablecloths and classic Viennese dishes on the menu. Daily 10am–midnight. Mains €10–24.

**Plachutta** 1, Wollzeile 38 ☎512 15 77, ⓦwww .plachutta.at; **U-Bahn Stubentor.** Smart green decor adorns this traditional family-run Viennese restaurant, specializing in Emperor Franz-Josef's favourite dish, *Tafelspitz*. Branches elsewhere in Vienna. Daily 11.30am–midnight. Mains €16–24.

**Regina Margherita** 1, Wallnerstrasse 4 ☎533 08 12, ⓦwww.barbaro.at; **U-Bahn Herrengasse.** Smart, bustling Neapolitan pizza-and-pasta joint in the inner court of the Palais Esterházy. Pizzas (€7–11) are cooked in a stupendous lava oven, and you can eat alfresco in summer. Mon–Fri noon–3pm & 6pm–midnight, Sat noon–midnight. Mains €10–20.

**Reinthaler** 1, Gluckgasse 5 ☎512 33 66; **U-Bahn Karlsplatz.** Dive down the steps to this genuine, no-nonsense Viennese *Beisl* that's busy with locals. No concessions to modern cooking (and none to veggies). Mon–Fri 9am–11pm. Mains €6–12.

**Zum finsteren Stern** 1, Schulhof 8 ☎535 21 00; **U-Bahn Schwedenplatz.** Vaulted wine bar in the side streets near Judenplatz with a lovely summer terrace, and home-made pasta and other Italian delights on the menu. Mon–Sat 6pm–1am. Mains €12–20.

**Zwölf-Apostelkeller** 1, Sonnenfelsgasse 3 ☎512 67 77, ⓦwww.zwoelf-apostelkeller.at; **U-Bahn Stephansplatz.** *Stadtheuriger* in an attractive seventeenth-century building with bars housed in three levels of cellars. *The* place to drink wine, but it's often difficult to find a space. *Schrammelmusik* from 7pm. Daily 11am–midnight. Mains €7–14.

## Ringstrasse

The following places are marked on the map on pp.88–89.

**Glacisbeisl** 7, Museumsplatz 1 (entrance Breite-gasse 4) ☎526 56 60, ⓦwww.glacisbeisl.at; **U-Bahn Volkstheater.** Hidden in the entrails of the MuseumsQuartier, *Glacisbeisl* has had a stark modern makeover; the food is still

good and the summer terrace as lovely as ever – be warned, though, it's very popular. Daily 11am–2am. Mains €8–14.

**Gmoa Keller** 3, Am Heumarkt 25 ☎712 53 10, ⓦwww.gmoakeller.at; **U-Bahn Stadtpark.** Pared-down old *Beisl* with a lovely vaulted ceiling and parquet flooring, and good Viennese cuisine. Mon–Sat 11am–midnight. Mains €7–13.

**Hansen** 1, Wipplingerstrasse 34 ☎532 05 42, ⓦwww.hansen.co.at; **U-Bahn Schottentor.** Attractive, smart restaurant located in the flower and gardening shop in the basement of the city's splendid former stock exchange. Mon–Fri 9am–11pm, Sat 9am–5pm. Mains €10–20.

**Steirereck** 1, Stadtpark ☎713 31 68, ⓦsteirereck.at; **U-Bahn Stadtpark or Stubentor.** Much hyped, pricey Styrian restaurant in the Stadtpark, which also runs the charming riverside *Meierei*, serving an incredible array of cheeses and less expensive meals from 9am. Mon–Fri 11.30am–2.30pm & 6.30–11pm. Mains €20–40.

**Vestibül** 1, Dr-Karl-Lueger-Ring 2 ☎532 49 99, ⓦwww.vestibuel.at; **U-Bahn Herrengasse.** Buzzing restaurant in one of the ornate wings of the Burgtheater, serving up classy dishes to a moneyed crowd. Mon–Fri 11am–midnight, Sat 6pm–midnight. Mains €15–30.

## Landstrasse (3rd district)

**Salm Bräu** 3, Rennweg 8 ☎799 59 92, ⓦwww .salmbraeu.com; see map, p.127. Conveniently located beer hall, which brews its own beer in an old monastic wine cellar, and serves filling pub food, right outside the Unteres Belvedere. Daily 11am–midnight. Mains €6–12.

**Stadtwirt** 3, Untere Viaduktgasse 45 ☎713 38 28, ⓦwww.stadtwirt.at; **U-Bahn Landstrasse/Wien-Mitte;** see map, p.127. Large, classic, wood-panelled family-run *Beisl*; the food is traditional Viennese, the wine sourced from their own vineyard. Mon–Fri 10am–midnight, Sat 4pm–1am, Sun 11am–4pm. Mains €13–19.

**Wild** 3, Radetzkyplatz 1 ☎920 94 77; tram #N from U-Bahn Schwedenplatz; see map, p.127. Stylish wood-panelled *Beisl* with lots of traditional dishes on the menu and a good selection of draught beers and wines. Kitchen closes 11.30pm. Daily 9am–1am. Mains €12–20.

## Wieden, Margareten and Mariahilf (4th, 5th & 6th districts)

**Aux Gazelles 6, Rahlgasse 5** ☎585 66 45, ⓦwww.auxgazelles.at; **U-Bahn Museums quartier; see map, p.102.** A converted brick factory with over-the-top North African decor, a café and deli, brasserie-restaurant, caviar and oyster bar, *salon de thé*, club bar and even a small *hammam*. Mon–Sat 11am–2am. Mains €14–24.

**Indian Pavilion 4, Naschmarkt Stand 74–75** ☎587 85 61; **U-Bahn Karlsplatz or Kettenbrück- engasse; see map, p.102.** Tiny Indian curry place in the heart of Naschmarkt, serving up inexpensive aromatic dishes from a menu that changes daily. Mon–Fri 11am–11pm, Sat 11am–5pm. Mains €5–9.

**Nice Rice 6, Mariahilferstrasse 45** ☎586 28 39; **U-Bahn Neubaugasse; see map, p.141.** Small vegetarian place, down a passageway off Mariahilferstrasse, serving inexpensive Eastern rice dishes. Mon–Fri 11am–11pm, Sat 11am–5pm. Mains €5–9.

**Ra'mien 6, Gumpendorferstrasse 9** ☎585 47 98, ⓦwww.ramien.at; **U-Bahn Museumsquartier; see map, p.102.** Very popular, clubby, designer noodle restaurant with a late-night bar (open until the early hours) attached. Tues–Sun 11am–midnight. Mains €8–14.

**Silberwirt 5, Schlossgasse 21** ☎544 49 07, ⓦwww.schlossquadr.at; **tram #62 or #65 and bus #13A; see map, p.102.** Neo-rustic *Beisl* on a lovely courtyard just south of the Naschmarkt, serving traditional Viennese cuisine. Daily noon–midnight. Mains €10–20.

**Steman 6, Otto-Bauer-Gasse 7** ☎597 85 09, ⓦwww.steman.at; **U-Bahn Zieglergasse; see map, p.141.** A classic wood-panelled *Beisl*, with a pared-down modern vibe, special- ising in Austrian wines and *Wiener Küche*, but with lots of choice for veggies and a two-course menu for just €7. Mon–Fri 11am–midnight. Mains €7–14.

**Strandhaus 4, Naschmarkt Stand 76–79** ☎587 04 56; **U-Bahn Karlsplatz; see map, p.102.** Fish restaurant at the beginning of the Naschmarkt; the stuff is as fresh as it gets in landlocked Vienna, and it's simply prepared. Mon–Fri 11am–10.30pm, Sat 10am–10.30pm. Mains €9–16.

**Tancredi 4, Grosse Neugasse 5/Rubensgasse 2** ☎941 00 48, ⓦwww.tancredi.at; **U-Bahn Taubstummengasse or tram #62 or #65; see map, p.102.** Simple, bright, whitewashed

restaurant with a lovely summer terrace that serves carefully prepared seasonal Viennese dishes. Mon 11.30am–2.30pm, Tues–Fri 11.30am–2.30pm & 6pm–midnight, Sat 6pm–midnight. Mains €12–20.

**Vapiano 6, Theobaldgasse 19** ⓦwww.vapiano .de; **U-Bahn Museumsquartier; see map, p.141.** Bright, spacious, modern self-service place with an open kitchen, where they'll make your pizza or pasta dish in front of you. Daily 11am–1am. Mains €7–10.

**Wieden Bräu 4, Waaggasse 5** ☎586 03 00, ⓦwww.wieden-braeu.at; **U-Bahn Taubstum- mengasse; see map, p.102.** Typical Austrian pub, with simple decor, fine beers brewed on the premises, and filling traditional food. Free wi-fi. Daily 11.30am–midnight; July & Aug Sat & Sun from 4pm. Mains €6–10.

## Neubau (7th district)

The following places appear on the map on p.141.

**Grünauer 7, Hermanngasse 32** ☎526 40 80; **tram #49.** Tiny local *Beisl*, in the backstreets of Neubau, which takes its traditional Viennese cooking and wine cellar seriously. Mon–Fri 6pm–midnight. Closed Aug. Mains €8–14.

**Plutzer Bräu 7, Schrankgasse 2** ☎526 12 15, ⓦwww.plutzerbraeu.at; **U-Bahn Volkstheater.** Spacious designer beer bar in Spittelberg, good for a quiet lunch or a much more boisterous evening drink. Regularly shows live TV sports. Daily 10.30am–2am. Mains €8–14.

**Schilling 7, Burggasse 103** ☎524 17 75, ⓦwww.schilling-wirt.at; **tram #5 or bus #48A.** A modish crowd frequents this *nouveau*, stripped-down *Beisl* on the corner of Halbgasse; the food is traditional but imagi- natively presented and freshly prepared. Daily 11am–midnight. Mains €7–14.

**Schnitzelwirt 7, Neubaugasse 52** ☎523 37 71, ⓦwww.schnitzelwirt.co.at; **tram #49.** Aside from *Figlmüller* (see p.217), this is the place to eat *Wiener Schnitzel* – here, they're just as huge, cheaper and served with chips. Mon–Sat 11am–10pm. Mains €6–10.

**Siebensternbräu 7, Siebensterngasse 19** ☎523 86 97, ⓦwww.7stern.at; **tram #49.** Popular, modern microbrewery, offering classic Viennese pub food, with lots of pan-fried dishes served with dark rye bread. Daily 10am–midnight. Mains €7–14.

**Spatzennest 7, Ulrichsplatz 1** ☎526 16 59, ⓦwww.gasthaus-spatzennest.at; **bus #13A or**

**#48A.** Much treasured, down-to-earth local Viennese *Beisl*, just off Burggasse. Daily except Fri & Sat 10am–10pm. Inexpensive.

**Una Abraham 7, Burggasse 76** ☎526 90 57; bus **#13A or #48A.** Old *Wirtshaus* that's been lovingly renovated and stylishly modernised – the cooking's great, too: fresh ingredients, delicious dishes such as artichokes in white wine, crayfish and avocado salad with a wasabi-lime vinagrette. Mon–Fri 5–11.30pm. Mains €8–14.

**Witwe Bolte 7, Gutenberggasse 13** ☎523 14 50, ⓦwww.witwebolte.at; U-Bahn Volkstheater. Long-established *Wiener Beisl* in the charming backstreets of Spittelberg, famous for having been visited by Josef II incognito in the eighteenth century. Lovely summer garden. Daily 11.45am–11.30pm. Mains €9–18.

**Zu den Zwei Lieserln 7, Burggasse 63** ☎523 32 82, ⓦwww.2lieserln.at; tram #49 or bus #48A. Very old-fashioned *Beisl*, with a nice summer garden, serving cheap and succulent *Wiener schnitzel*. Daily 11am–11pm. Mains €6–10.

## Josefstadt (8th district)

The following places are marked on the map on p.141.

**Il Sestante 8, Piaristengasse 50** ☎402 98 94, ⓦwww.sestante.at; U-Bahn Rathaus. Welcoming, L-shaped Sicilian restaurant decked out in warm apricot colours, with modern furnishings and wood panelling; tasty pizzas, fresh pasta and risotto. Daily 11.30am–11.30pm. Pizzas €7–12. Mains €10–20.

**¡más! 8, Laudongasse 36** ☎403 83 24, ⓦwww .restaurante-mas.at; tram #5, #43 or #44. Stylish, modern Latino joint serving filling enchiladas and tacos, nicely washed down with a margarita. Their Sunday all-you-can-eat Mexican brunch (10am–4pm; €18) is the perfect hangover cure. Mon–Sat 6pm–2am, Sun 10am–2am. Mains €8–12.

**Schnattl 8, Lange Gasse 40** ☎405 34 00 ⓦwww .schnattl.com; U-Bahn Rathaus. Very formal restaurant, where the local cuisine is cooked with a Styrian bent by Herr Schnattl himself; call to reserve a table in the courtyard. Mon–Fri 6pm–midnight. Mains €20–26.

## Alsergrund (9th district)

The following places are marked on the map on p.145.

**Flein 9, Boltzmanngasse 2** ☎319 76 89; tram **#37, #38, #40, #41 & #42.** Lovely, inventive changing menu served in a small informal setting. It's a perfect spot in fine weather, with a large terrace looking across Clam-Gallas Park. Mon–Fri 11.30am–3pm & 5.30–11.30pm. Mains €7–14.

**Kutschker 44 18, Kutschkergasse 44** ☎470 20 47, ⓦwww.kutschker44.at; tram #40 or #41. One tram stop north of Alsergrund, on the other side of the *Gürtel*, this very smart, modern neo-*Beisl* serves excellent Viennese food – try the duck breast. Tues–Sat 4pm–midnight. Mains €15–20.

🏃 **Stomach 9, Seegasse 26** ☎310 20 99; tram **#D.** Informal Styrian *Beisl*, with a lovely cobbled courtyard, specializing in creative beef dishes, but also catering well for veggies. Wed–Sat 4pm–midnight, Sun 10am–10pm. €10–15.

**Wickerl 9, Porzellangasse 24a** ☎317 74 89; tram **#D.** Unpretentious, popular neighbourhood *Beisl*; cheap, classic Viennese fillers, plus live TV sports. Mon–Fri 11am–11pm. Mains €8–12.

**Zum Reznicek 9, Reznicekgasse 10** ☎317 91 40; tram **#D.** Popular local *Beisl*, a short walk from Franz-Josefs Bahnhof, serving superb *Wiener Küche* with loads of beers on tap – ask for the offal specials. Daily noon–11pm. Mains €8–15.

## Leopoldstadt (2nd district)

The following places are marked on the map on p.158.

**Altes Jägerhaus 2, Aspernallee, Prater** ☎728 95 77, ⓦwww.altes-jaegerhaus.com; bus #77A. Typical old-fashioned *Beisl*, at the far end of the Hauptallee, little changed since 1899, with a large summer terrace. A nice place to enjoy hearty fare and a Budvar beer. April–Sept daily 9am–11pm; Oct–Dec & March Wed–Sun 9am–11pm; Jan & Feb Wed–Sun 9am–6pm. Mains €12–24.

**Gasthaus am Nordpol 3 2, Nordwestbahn-strasse 17/Nordpolstrasse** ☎333 58 54, ⓦwww.amnordpol3.at; tram #2 or #5. Ancient *Beisl* at the back of the Augarten, restored to new glory: lots of wood, friendly staff, and Bohemian bread, food and beer. Mon–Sat 5pm–midnight, Sun noon–midnight. Mains €7–13.

**Leopold 2, Grosser Pfarrgasse 11** ☎218 22 81, ⓦwww.restaurant-leopold.at; U-Bahn Taborstrasse. Chic, modern neo-*Beisl*, with high ceiling, pine furniture, classic local dishes and great Sunday brunches and a *Schanigarten*. Daily Mon–Sat 6pm–midnight, Sun 10am–3pm. Mains €6–16.

**Lusthaus** 2, Freudenau 254, Prater ☎728 95 65, ⓦwww.lusthaus-wien.at; bus #77A. This eighteenth-century rotunda, at the far end of Hauptallee, makes a perfect food halt while exploring the Prater. May–Sept Mon, Tues, Thurs & Fri noon–11pm, Sat & Sun noon–6pm; Oct–April daily except Wed noon–6pm. Mains €10–20.

**Schöne Perle** 2, Leopoldsgasse/Grosser Pfarrgasse ☎243 35 93, ⓦwww.schoene-perle.at; U-Bahn Taborstrasse. Smart but relaxed L-shaped local neo-*Beisl* serving typical Viennese dishes made with organic produce. Mon–Fri 11.30am–midnight, Sat & Sun 10am–midnight Mains €7–14.

**Schuppich** 2, Rotensterngasse 18 ☎212 43 40, ⓦwww.schuppich.at; U-Bahn Taborstrasse. A taste of Trieste (once the Habsburgs' main sea port), where goulash meets gnocchi; à la carte or a four-course menu for €25. Wed–Sat 6pm–midnight, Sun noon–4pm & 6–10pm. Mains €8–20.

**Schweizerhaus** 2, Strasse des 1 Mai 116, Prater ☎728 01 52, ⓦwww.schweizerhaus.at; U-Bahn Praterstern. Massive Czech-owned terrace restaurant in the Prater, known for its draught beer and Czech specialities such as tripe soup and grilled pigs' trotters (*Stelzen*). Mid-March to Oct Mon–Fri 11am–11pm, Sat & Sun 10am–11pm. Mains €6–20.

**Skopik & Lohn** 2, Leopoldsgasse 17 ☎219 89 77, ⓦwww.skopikundlohn.at; U-Bahn Taborstrasse. Mustard-coloured wood-panelled neighbourhood neo-*Beisl* with scribbly art on the ceiling, serving Med-influenced Viennese dishes; large and very nice summer terrace. Mon–Sat 6pm–1am. Mains €10–22.

## The suburbs

**Fischer Bräu** 19, Billrothstrasse 17 ☎369 59 49, ⓦwww.fischerbraeu.at; U-Bahn Nussdorferstrasse. Very civilized microbrewery pub, which produces a great, lemony, misty beer. Lots of tasty snacks and more substantial pub fare to be consumed in the bare-boards interior or the shady courtyard. Mon–Sat 4pm–1am, Sun 11am–1am. Mains €7–10.

**Schloss Concordia** 11, Simmeringer Hauptstrasse 283 ☎769 88 88; tram #6 or #71. Popular destination for a post-funeral knees-up, this candlelit mansion sits directly opposite the Zentralfriedhof and serves up a vast range of *Schnitzels* and other traditional food. Daily 10am–1am. Mains €6–12.

**Strandcafé** 22, Florian-Berndl-Gasse 20 ☎203 67 47, ⓦwww.strandcafe-wien.at; U-Bahn Alte Donau. This no-nonsense *Gasthaus* has a large riverside terrace overlooking the Alte Donau with UNO-City in the distance. Daily 11am–midnight. Mains €8–14.

**Villa Aurora** 16, Wilhelminenstrasse 237 ☎489 33 33; bus #146B from U-Bahn Ottakring. Beautiful bohemian ramshackle villa, out in the fields, overlooking the city, serving simple Viennese dishes. Daily 10am–midnight. Mains €8–16.

## Wine

Although Austrians tend to drink a lot more beer than wine, it's **wine** (*Wein*) that holds a special place in Vienna's history and geography. The capital is literally surrounded by vineyards, many of which lie within the city boundaries – there are even suggestions that the city's name derives from the word "wine".

The best place to try the local stuff is, of course, in a **Heuriger** or wine tavern. Wine is drunk by the **Viertel** (a 25cl mug) or the **Achterl** (a 12.5cl glass). The majority of wine produced in Austria is white, the dry, fruity **Grüner Veltliner** being the most popular. Most red wine hails from Burgenland, where **Blaufränkisch** is the ubiquitous grape type, producing a characteristically peppery wine with lots of blackcurrant flavour.

It's common practice to water down your white wine with soda water by ordering a **Gespritzer**. Look out, too, for **Sturm**, the half-fermented young wine that hits the streets and bars in autumn, and be sure to try a mug of **Glühwein** or mulled wine, available at Christmas markets all over the city in late November and December.

# Heurigen

**Heurigen** are the wine taverns found predominantly in the former villages of the city's outer suburbs, to the north and west of the centre on the slopes of the Wienerwald. The word *heurig* means "this year's": a vintner would encourage tastings in these taverns to try and sell a few bottles of his (exclusively white) **wine**. As an institution they are as old as the city itself, but they came into their own during the Biedermeier period (1815–48). In the good old days people used to bring their own picnics to consume, sat on wooden benches in the vintner's garden while drinking the wine, but nowadays, most *Heurigen* provide a **self-service buffet** of traditional Viennese dishes.

Traditionally a visit to a *Heuriger* is accompanied by *Schrammelmusik* – sentimental fiddle, guitar and accordion **music** – but nowadays this only features at the more touristy ventures, as the modern Viennese tend to prefer the experience without accompaniment. *Heurigen* are especially popular with locals in September and October, when the new wine – *Sturm* or *Most* – is available. In addition to the *Heurigen* in the outer suburbs, a handful of wine taverns known as **Stadtheurigen** are located nearer the centre, usually in the cellars of the city's monasteries. While these are not real *Heurigen* at all, they're still great places to drink wine and sample local cuisine – see the Innere Stadt restaurant listings.

With the exception of the *Stadtheurigen*, the **opening times** of most *Heurigen* are unpredictable (most don't open until mid-afternoon except on the weekend), but part of the fun is to simply set off to one of the districts and take pot luck. A display board at the centre of each village lists those *Heurigen* that are open. **Grinzing** is the most famous of Vienna's *Heuriger* village-suburbs, and consequently the most popular, followed by **Heiligenstadt** and **Nussdorf**. Less touristy alternatives include Sievering and Neustift am Walde, or Stammersdorf, and Strebersdorf across the Danube.

## Grinzing

**Reinprecht** 19, Cobenzlgasse 22 ☎ 320 14 71, ⓦ heuriger-reinprecht.at; tram #38 to the terminus. Huge, 300-year-old *Heuriger* housed in an old monastery, with live *Schrammelmusik*. Touristy but fun. March to mid-Dec daily 3.30pm–midnight.

**Zawodsky** 19, Reinischgasse 3 ☎ 320 79 78, ⓦ www.zawodsky.at; tram #38. Classic, simple *Heuriger*, with benches set out in a lovely apple orchard garden with fantastic views over Vienna. April–Nov Wed, Thurs & Fri 5pm–midnight, Sat & Sun 2pm–midnight.

## Heiligenstadt

**Mayer am Pfarrplatz** 19, Pfarrplatz 2 ☎ 370 33 61, ⓦ www.pfarrplatz.at; bus #38A from U-Bahn Heiligenstadt. One of Beethoven's many addresses in Vienna, now a cosy *Heuriger*, with live *Schrammelmusik* (daily from 7pm) and a large, shady patio garden out back. April–Nov Mon–Fri 4pm–midnight, Sat & Sun 11am–midnight.

## Kahlenbergerdorf

**Hirt/Klapf** 19, Eisernenhandgasse 165 ☎ 318 96 41, ⓦ www.kahlenbergerdorf.at; 15min walk from S-Bahn Kahlenbergerdorf. Lovely old-fashioned *Heuriger* tucked into the slopes below Leopoldsberg with fantastic views overlooking the Danube. April–Oct Wed–Fri 3–11pm, Sat & Sun noon–11pm; Nov–March Fri–Sun noon–11pm.

## Neustift am Walde

**Das Schreiberhaus** 19, Rathstrasse 54 ☎ 440 38 44, ⓦ www.dasschreiberhaus.at; bus #35A from U-Bahn Nussdorfer Strasse. Set amid Neustift's sloping vineyards, this friendly *Heuriger* is popular with parties, but is big enough to absorb them. Daily 11am–1am.

## Nussdorf

**Schübel-Auer** 19, Kahlenbergerstrasse 22 ☎ 370 22 22, ⓦ www.schuebel-auer.at; tram #D to the terminus. Good, century-old *Heuriger* right by the tram terminus, with a lovely leafy garden. A convenient staging post en route to *Sirbu* (below). Mid-Feb to mid-Nov Tues–Sat 4pm–midnight.

**Sirbu** 19, Kahlenbergerstrasse 210 ☎ 320 59 28; 15min walk from bus #38A terminus. Positioned amid the vineyards, with fabulous views from the hill above Nussdorf, and the usual self-service buffet and local wines. April–Oct Mon–Sat 3pm–midnight.

## Sievering

**Haslinger** 19, Agnesgasse 3 ☎ 440 13 47, ⓦ www.buschenschank-haslinger.at; bus #39A from U-Bahn Heiligenstadt to the terminus. *Heuriger* overlooking the rooftops of Sievering, offering warm and cold buffets, and boasting a lovely, sloping orchard garden. Tues–Fri 2pm–midnight, Sat & Sun 11.30am–midnight.

## Stammersdorf

**Göbel** 21, Stammersdorfer Kellergasse 131/Breitenweg ☎ 294 84 20, ⓦ www.weinbaugoebel.at; tram #31, then bus #228 or #233. Herr Göbel is an architect, and his *Heuriger* has a modern feel and a classy ambience, as well as prize-winning wines (red and white) and gourmet food. Phone to check opening times, which are usually Mid-March to Nov Mon 3–10pm, Sat & Sun 11am–10pm.

**Wieninger** 21, Stammersdorfer Strasse 78 ☎ 292 41 06, ⓦ www.heuriger-wieninger.at; tram #31 to the terminus from U-Bahn Floridsdorf. Lots of fresh, light, pine inside, a courtyard garden outside, and above-average buffet and wine. Thurs & Fri 3pm–midnight, Sat & Sun noon–midnight.

11

# Bars, clubs and live venues

The vast majority of the Viennese are safely tucked up in bed by as early as 10pm. Meanwhile, however, a hard core stay up until early in the morning – in fact it's quite possible to keep drinking round the clock.

Vienna's late-night **bars and clubs** are concentrated in two main areas. The first is around the **Naschmarkt**, where late-night licences abound, and from where it's easy enough to wander over into Mariahilferstrasse and Neubau to find further late-night distractions. The other burgeoning area is the *Gürtel* scene under the arches of the U6 U-Bahn, as it careers along from Thaliastrasse northwards. In warmer weather, during term time, it's also worth checking out the courtyards of the **Universitätscampus**, off Alserstrasse and the outdoor bars on the Copa Cagrana on the **Donauinsel** (see p.159).

Vienna's **club scene** is small for a city of 1.5 million, but dance, techno and electronica remain very popular. Nevertheless, the majority of Vienna's clubs are tiny affairs, little more than late-night DJ bars, which might host live bands, or resident DJs spinning discs (both danceable and non-danceable), while punters simply chill out and chat. As such, it's often difficult to differentiate between a bar, a club and a live venue, so we've simply organized the listings by area.

To find out what's on at Vienna's clubs, check out the "Party" section in the weekly listings tabloid *Falter* (see p.28). The two big annual popular music events are the **Jazz Fest Wien** (Ⓦ www.viennajazz.org), an international jazz festival that takes place in various venues around the city in June/early July, and the **Donauinselfest** (Ⓦ www.donauinselfest.at), the SPÖ-organized free summer pop festival on the Donauinsel.

Drink **prices** are pretty consistent – bars tend to charge either side of €5 for a *Krügerl* (half-litre) – except in the handful of pricier clubs where there's an admission charge. As for how to get home in the wee hours, the U-Bahn runs all nights on Fridays and Saturdays. And every night nightbuses leave from Schwedenplatz and usually do a circuit of the Ring before heading off to their destination – pick up a leaflet from or one of the transport offices (see p.23).

## The Innere Stadt

**American Bar (Loos Bar) 1**, Kärntner Durchgang 10 Ⓦ www.loosbar.at; U-Bahn Stephensplatz. The "Loos Bar" is a small, dark late-night cocktail bar off Kärntnerstrasse with a wonderfully luscious glass, marble and onyx 1908 interior by Adolf Loos. Mon–Wed & Sun noon–4am, Thurs–Sat noon–5am.

🏃 **Badeschiff 1**, Donaukanal Ⓦ www .badeschiff.at; U-Bahn Schwedenplatz.

Boat moored on the canal, with a floating outdoor swimming pool, restaurant, bar and club (below decks in the Laderaum). Laderaum: Tues–Sat 6pm–4am. Pool: May–Oct daily 8am–midnight.

**Club Habana 1, Mahlerstrasse 11; U-Bahn Karlsplatz.** Nightly Latin American/Caribbean-themed mayhem for salsa, merengue and zumba fiends, just off Kärntnerstrasse. Mon–Sat 7pm–4am.

**First Floor 1, Seitenstettengasse 1; U-Bahn Schwedenplatz.** A remake of a 1930s bar from Kärntnerstrasse, with a vast array of low-lit aquariums, courtesy of design team Eichinger oder Knechtl, and packed with a sophisticated crowd. Mon–Fri 5pm–3am, Sat & Sun 7pm–3am.

**Flanagan's 1, Schwarzenbergerstrasse 1–3 ⓦ www.flanagans.at; U-Bahn Karlsplatz.** The most central, and probably the best, of Vienna's rash of Irish pubs, with Guinness and Kilkenny, Irish/British food and big-screen sports. Mon–Thurs & Sun 10am–2am, Fri & Sat 10am–4am.

**Flex 1, Donaukanal/Augartenbrücke ⓦ www.flex.at; U-Bahn Schottenring.** The city's most serious dance-music club has a great sound system, and attracts the best DJs and a very young, enthusiastic crowd; it's situated at canal level, overlooking Wagner's Schützenhaus. Daily 8pm–4am.

**Jazzland 1, Franz-Josefs-Kai 29 ⓦ www .jazzland.at; U-Bahn Schwedenplatz.** Vienna's longest-running jazz venue is a cellar just below the Ruprechtskirche; music varies from trad and swing to blues and bebop; gigs start at around 9pm (no reservations taken). Mon–Sat 7pm–2am.

**Planters 1, Zelinkagasse 4 ⓦ www.plantersclub .at; U-Bahn Schottenring.** *Planters'* decadent, colonial cocktail-bar decor, and the unbelievable array of drinks on offer, attract a smart, dressed-up crowd. Mon–Wed & Sun 5pm–2am, Thurs–Sat 5pm–4am.

**Porgy & Bess 1, Riemergasse 11 ⓦ www .porgy.at; U-Bahn Stubentor.** This converted porn cinema is now the very stylish home of Vienna's best jazz venue, attracting top jazz and world music acts from all over the world; gigs start around 8.30pm. Daily 7.30pm until late.

**Strandbar Herrmann 3, Hermannpark 5 ⓦ www.strandbarherrmann.at; U-Bahn Schwedenplatz.** Another of Vienna's great summertime outdoor DJ venues: cocktails,

deckchairs and sand by the confluence of the River Wien (Wien-Fluss) and the Danube Canal (Donaukanal). April–Oct daily 10am–2am.

## Ringstrasse

**Ost 4, Schwindgasse 1 ⓦ www.ost-klub.at; U-Bahn Karlsplatz or tram #D.** As the name suggests, this place, off Schwarzenberg-platz, specializes in live acts from "east of Rennweg" – expect anything from Thracian clarinetists to women bands from St Petersburg. Thurs–Sat 6pm–4am, plus other occasional nights.

**Passage 1, Babenberger Passage, Burgring/ Babenbergerstrasse ⓦ www.sunshine.at; U-Bahn Museumsquartier/Volkstheater.** This funky futurist conversion of a pedestrian underpass at the back of the Kunsthistorisches Museum is the closest Vienna gets to a flashy, full-on club such as you'd find in Europe's bigger dance capitals. Daily 10pm–4am.

**Pavillon Volksgarten 1, Burgring 1 ⓦ volksgarten-pavillon.at; U-Bahn Volkstheater.** The *Pavillon* is the relaxed garden café above the *Volksgarten* club; entry is usually free (apart from Tuesday's popular techno night), there's *boules* to play and usually live music or DJs later on. In good weather April to mid-Sept daily 11am–2am.

**Rote Bar 7, Neustiftgasse 1 ⓦ www .volkstheater.at; U-Bahn Volkstheater.** Grandiose fin-de-siècle space in the Volkstheater that puts on a whole range of live acts from cabaret and political debates to DJs and world music. Daily 10pm–1am.

**Volksgarten 1, Burgring 1 ⓦ www.volksgarten .at; U-Bahn Volkstheater.** Vienna's longest-running club is a firm favourite with the party crowd. The curvy *Banane* bar is groovy and the outdoor dancefloor is a summertime treat. Daily 8pm–5am.

## Mariahilf, Neubau & Josefstadt

**B72 8, Hernalser Gürtel 72 ⓦ www.b72.at; U-Bahn Alserstrasse.** Dark, industrial, edgy designer club beneath the U-Bahn arches – features a mixture of DJs and live indie bands. Daily 8pm–4am.

**Blue Box 7, Richtergasse 8 ⓦ www.bluebox.at; U-Bahn Neubaugasse.** Long-standing café with resident DJs and a good snack menu, including excellent brunch buffet. Live music

## Lesbian and gay nightlife

If Vienna's club scene is pretty small, the city's **lesbian and gay scene** is even smaller, with only a handful of gay bars and clubs scattered across the city. The "gay district" is around the Naschmarkt, with the social and political soul of the gay community focused on the **Rosa-Lila Villa**, 6, Linke Wienzeile 102 (☎585 43 43, ⓦ www.villa.at; U-Bahn Pilgramgasse), the pink-and-purple HQ that proudly flies the rainbow flag and proclaims itself as a *Lesben und Schwulen Haus*. There's an annual pride event, **Regenbogenparade** (Rainbow Parade), held on the last Saturday in late June/early July, and an annual gay ball, **Regenbogenball**, in late January/early February. For news (in German) on other events, visit ⓦ www.hosiwien.at. For listings, consult the "lesbisch/schwul" section in *Falter*, pick up the monthly freebie *Xtra!* (ⓦ www.xtra-news.at), and check out the following places:

**Café Berg** 9, Berggasse 8; U-Bahn Schottentor (also reviewed on p.213). Cool café attached to the city's main gay bookshop, with mixed gay/straight clientele, especially during the day. The food's good, and you can pick up flyers about up-and-coming gay events. Daily 10am–1am.

**Felixx** 6, Gumpendorferstrasse 5; ⓦ www.felixx-bar.at; U-Bahn Museumsquartier. Sophisticated but friendly late-night gay/lesbian bar-restaurant that hosts occasional live music/drag acts. Daily 6pm–3am.

**Frauencafé** 8, Lange Gasse 11; ⓦ www.frauencafe.com; U-Bahn Lerchenfelder-strasse. Vienna's only permanent women-only space is a small, friendly café next door to a feminist bookshop. Thurs & Fri 6pm–midnight, plus other occasional nights.

**Kaiserbründl** 1, Weihburggasse 18–20; ⓦ www.kaiserbruendl.at; U-Bahn Stephansplatz. Wonderfully ornate nineteenth-century *hammam* with additional, more recent, camp-it-up frescoes, popular with gay men of all ages. Daily 2pm–midnight, Fri & Sat until 2am.

**Mango Bar** 6, Laimgrubengasse 3; ⓦ www.mangobar.at; U-Bahn Kettenbrücken-gasse. Smart, stylish and rather cruisey bar, packed with young guys. Daily 9pm–4am.

**Café Savoy** 6, Linke Wienzeile 36; U-Bahn Kettenbrückengasse. Other than during Saturday's flea market, when a mixed crowd descends on the place, this high-camp fin-de-siècle café is predominantly populated with gay men. Mon–Fri 5pm–2am, Sat 9am–2am.

**Village** 6, Stiegengasse 8; ⓦ www.village-bar.at; U-Bahn Kettenbrückengasse. Swish, Americana-style cocktail bar that pulls in a crowd of smart young folk for its regular theme nights. Daily 8pm–3am.

**Why Not?** 1, Tiefergraben 22; ⓦ www.why-not.at; U-Bahn Herrengasse. Late-night gay/lesbian cellar bar and disco, popular with young gay men and women. Fri & Sat 10pm–4am.

**Café Willendorf** 6, Linke Wienzeile 102; ⓦ www.cafe-willendorf.at; U-Bahn Pilgram-gasse. Popular café-restaurant inside the Rosa-Lila Villa, with a nice leafy courtyard. Another good place to pick up information about events. Mon–Wed & Sun 6pm–1am, Thurs–Sat 6pm–2am.

---

from 8pm. Mon–Thurs 10am–2am, Fri & Sat 10am–4am.

**Camera** 8, Neubaugasse 2 ⓦ www.camera-club.at; U-Bahn Neubaugasse. Popular little dance club where the DJs keep the crowd happy with everything from Detroit Jazz to the local Icke Micke posse. Thurs–Sat 10pm–6am.

**Chelsea** 8, Lerchenfelder Gürtel 29–31 ⓦ www.chelsea.co.at; U-Bahn Thaliastrasse. Favourite anglophile venue with up-and-coming indie guitar bands, techno DJs and live Premier-ship matches on a Sunday afternoon. Mon–Sat 6pm–4am.

**Donau** 7, Karl Schweighofergasse 10 ⓦ www.donautechno.com; U-Bahn Volkstheater. Chill-out sounds from the in-house techno DJs, and strange projections on the vaulted ceiling and walls. Mon–Thurs

8pm–4am, Fri & Sat 8pm–6am, Sun 8pm–2am.

**futuregarden** 6, Schadekgasse 6; U-Bahn Neubau. Spartan, minimalist club-bar near the Esterházypark Flakturm, where DJs play electro beats; popular with the local art-student crowd. Mon–Thurs 6pm–2am, Fri & Sat 6pm–4am, Sun 7pm–2am.

**Loop** 8, Lerchenfelder Gürtel 26–27 ⓦloop .co.at; U-Bahn Thaliastrasse. Another well-established stop on the *Gürtel* crawl, *Loop* is like a studenty version of a cocktail lounge, with DJs at the weekends. Mon–Thurs 7pm–2am, Fri & Sat 7pm–4am, Sun 7pm–2am.

**rhiz** 8, Lerchenfelder Gürtel 37–38 ⓦrhiz.org; U-Bahn Lerchenfelder Strasse. A modish cross between a bar, a café and a techno club, with several DJs spinning everything from dance to trance from 9pm. Mon–Sat 6pm–4am, Sun 6pm–2am.

**Roxy** 4, Operngasse 24 ⓦwww.roxyclub.at; U-Bahn Karlsplatz. Plush club, run by the slick Sunshine Enterprises posse who own *Passage* (see p.225), and attracting an eclectic mix of local and international DJ talent. Mon–Sat 10pm–4am.

**Shiraz** 9, Döblinger Gürtel 185 ⓦwww.shiraz .at; U-Bahn Nussdorfer Strasse. Split-level wine bar under the U-Bahn arches, decked out in sophisticated Middle Eastern style and serving the eponymous wine, plus shisha pipes.

**Stadthalle** 15, Vogelweidplatz 14, ⓦwww .stadthalle.at; U-Bahn Burggasse. Vienna's chief large-scale music venue, with two halls, attracting the usual roster of big-name acts. Gig times vary.

**Tanzcafé Jenseits** 6, Nelkengasse 3 ⓦwww .tanzcafe-jenseits.com; U-Bahn Neubaugasse. Tiny, discreet bohemian bar with a plush fin-de-siècle feel, and retro dance tunes from every decade on the jukebox. Tues–Sat 9pm–4am.

**Tunnel** 8, Florianigasse 39 ⓦwww.tunnel -vienna-live.at; tram #5. Large, L-shaped student café-pub with daily live bands down in the cellar from 8pm. Daily 9am–2am.

## Alsergrund

**WUK** 9, Währingerstrasse 59 ⓦwww.wuk.at; tram #40, #41 or #42. Red-brick arts venue

with a great café and a wide programme of events, including live music and DJ nights; check the *Falter* listings. Daily 11am–2am.

## Leopoldstadt

**Fluc** 2, Praterstern 5 ⓦwww.fluc.at; U-Bahn Praterstern. Anything (weird) goes at this industrial-style underground venue near the Prater, which features experimental live acts and DJs. Daily 6pm–2am.

## The suburbs

**Arena** 3, Baumgasse 80 ⓦwww.arena.co.at; U-Bahn Erdberg. It's a long trek out to this former slaughterhouse on the corner of Französengraben, but there's a real variety of stuff going on here – all-night raves, outdoor concerts, open-air cinema. Check the listings before setting out. Daily 4pm–2am.

**Gasometer Halle** 11, Guglgasse 8 ⓦwww .gasometer.at; U-Bahn Gasometer. The best medium-sized venue to catch imported acts, located in the Gasometer complex. Gig times vary.

**Reigen** 14, Hadikgasse 62 ⓦwww.reigen.at; U-Bahn Hietzing. Unpretentious café, restaurant and live venue that's great for jazz, blues, reggae, Latin and, in fact, music from all over the world. Daily 6pm–2am.

**Szene Wien** 11, Hauffgasse 26 ⓦwww .szenewien.com; U-Bahn Enkplatz. Regularly good live music venue, with a café (and garden) serving great food, run by a radical bunch from Simmering. Doors open 8pm. Closed mid-July to Aug.

**U4** 12, Schönbrunnerstrasse 222 ⓦwww .clubnet.at; U-Bahn Meidling-Hauptstrasse. Legendary cavernous disco, with frequent and varied gigs and themed nights and the city's best-known bouncer. Mon–Sat 10pm–late.

**Vorstadt** 16, Herbststrasse 37; U-Bahn Burggasse. Ottakring *Beisl* just beyond the *Gürtel*, with a lovely *Schanigarten* and a lively and varied programme of live European folk and roots music. Mon–Sat 5pm–2am, Sun 10am–2am. Closed July & Aug.

⑫

# The arts

V ienna prides itself on its **musical** associations, and classical music and opera, in particular, are heavily subsidized by the Austrian state. The chief cultural **festival** – featuring opera, music and theatre – is the **Wiener Festwochen**, which lasts from mid-May until mid-June. At Easter, there's the **Osterklang** festival of ecclesiastical music, while the **Frühlingsfestival** in April and May is a music festival focusing on Austrian composers. The city's film festival or **Viennale** is held at the end of October, followed closely by the **Wien Modern** festival of contemporary classical music in November, but by far the busiest time of the year is **Fasching**, Vienna's ball season (Nov–Feb). Last and least, there's the **International Accordion Festival**, held over the course of four weeks from late February to the middle of March. For more on the cultural calendar, see p.29.

To find out **what's on**, pick up the tourist board's free monthly listings booklet *Wien-Programm*, which gives the schedules of the big opera and concert houses and theatres, plus a day-by-day concert guide, ball calendar and details of current art exhibitions. The weekly listings tabloid *Falter* also has a pullout "Programm" section, which catalogues all theatre, dance, cabaret and classical music concerts (look for "Musik-E") as well as listing all films.

## Tickets

Ticket **prices** vary enormously in Vienna: the Staatsoper is a case in point, with seats ranging from €10 to €250. For some events – most notably the Vienna

### Waltz and schmaltz

It's easy enough to hear a bit of classic Strauss or light Mozart at any time of the year in Vienna, though tickets don't come cheap: €40–55 is the average price range. The **Salonorchester Alt Wien** (Ⓦwww.soundofvienna.at) play daily in period costumes at the Kursalon in the Stadtpark (see p.110), and at other good-looking venues across the city. The **Vienna Walzer Concerts** (Ⓦwww.strauss-concerts.com) perform Strauss and the like decked out in Biedermeier costume every week at the Palais Palffy on Josefsplatz. The **Wiener Residenzorchester** (Ⓦwww.wro.at) perform Mozart and Strauss in period costume in the Palais Auersperg behind Parlament and other venues. The Mozart Ensemble puts on chamber concert performances of Mozart and his contemporaries all year in the ornate *sala terrena* at Singerstrasse 7 (Ⓦwww.mozarthaus.at). There are also regular concerts of Mozart, Strauss and the like in the Hofburg's Redoutensaal (May–Oct; Ⓦwww.hofburgorchester.at) and in parts of Schönbrunn (Ⓦwww.imagevienna.com). Finally, if you yearn to hear schmaltzy Viennese songs sung live in a more informal setting, check out **Café Schmid Hansl**, 18, Schulgasse 31 (Ⓣ406 36 58; tram #40 or #41 from U-Bahn Volksoper; Tues–Sat 8pm–4am).

## Stehplätze

Vienna may be an expensive place, but its top opera houses and concert halls are open to even the poorest music student thanks to the system of *Stehplätze* or **standing-room tickets**, which can cost as little as €2 each. *Stehplätze* are limited to one per person and usually go on sale around an hour before the performance (exact timings vary, so check first). It's standard practice, once you've got into the auditorium, to tie a scarf to the railings to reserve your standing place. Bags and coats, though, should be put into the cloakroom.

Boys' Choir and the New Year's Day Concert – it's not so much price as availability that's a problem. However, the big state venues offer cheap *Stehplätze* on the day of the performance (see box above), and some offer unsold tickets at a discount to students, around an hour or thirty minutes before the show starts.

The cheapest way to **buy tickets** is to go to the venue's own box office. With the Staatsoper, Volksoper, Burgtheater and Akademietheater, you can either buy direct or from their shared central box office, the Bundestheaterkassen, not far from the Staatsoper at 1, Goethegasse 1 (Mon–Fri 8am–6pm, Sat & Sun 9am–noon; ☎514 44-7880, ⓦ www.bundestheater.at; U-Bahn Karlsplatz). There's also a ticket booth, Wien-Ticket Pavillon, next to the Staatsoper (daily 10am–7pm), which sells tickets for all venues, and occasionally has half-price tickets for musicals and for other events.

## Opera and classical music

Vienna has a musical pedigree second to none. Haydn, Mozart and Ludwig spent much of their time in Vienna, as did local-born Franz Schubert. Brahms and Bruckner followed in their wake, and coincided with the great waltz fever generated by the Strauss family and Josef Lanner. In the early twentieth century, the Vienna opera house was under the baton of Gustav Mahler, while its concert halls resounded to the atonal music of Arnold Schönberg, Anton Webern and Alban Berg.

Though Vienna hasn't produced any world-class composers for some time, it does still boast one of Europe's top opera houses in the **Staatsoper**, served by one of its finest orchestras, the **Wiener Philharmoniker** (ⓦ www.wienerphilharmoniker.at). The orchestra's New Year's Day Concert in the Musikverein is broadcast across the globe; to obtain tickets you must contact the box office on January 2 for the following year's concert (ⓦ www.musikverein.at). If you don't have a ticket, don't despair; the concert is broadcast live on Austrian TV, and relayed live on an enormous screen in front of the Rathaus at noon and again at 5pm. When the big state theatres are closed in July and August, opera and classical music concerts are also shown for free every evening outside the Rathaus.

The most famous musical institution in the city is, of course, the **Wiener Sängerknaben** (ⓦ www.wsk.at), or Vienna Boys' Choir, which performs Mass at the Hofburgkapelle (ⓦ www.hofburgkapelle.at) every Sunday at 9.15am (Jan–June & mid-Sept to Dec). Tickets for the Mass (€5–30) can be booked online, although some are held over each week and go on sale on Fridays at the chapel box office (Fri 11am–1pm & 3–5pm). The other option is to settle for one of the free *Stehplätze*, which are distributed before Mass; get there for 8.15am to be sure of a place (although some people leave early having got bored). Be warned, however, that the choir remains out of sight up in the organ loft until right at the end.

## Mostly opera and operetta

**Kammeroper** 1, Fleischmarkt 24 ☎512 01 00, ⓦwww.wienerkammeroper.at; U-Bahn Schwedenplatz. Vienna's smallest opera house is a Jugendstil theatre hidden in the backstreets of the Innere Stadt. Little-known works prevail – anything from Rossini to Britten – and the immediacy of the venue is a boon. Box office Mon–Fri noon–6pm.

**Staatsoper** 1, Opernring 2 ☎513 15 13, ⓦwww.wiener-staatsoper.at; U-Bahn Karlsplatz. Vienna's largest opera house (see also p.107) stages a staggering forty operas a season played in rep. It's a conservative place, but attracts the top names, and has the benefit of the Wiener Philharmoniker in the pit. Ticket prices range from around €10 to €200, but with over 500 *Stehplätze* (€3–4) going on sale every night from the west side of the foyer, eighty minutes before the curtain goes up, it is among the most accessible opera houses in the world. Closed July & Aug.

**Theater-an-der-Wien** 6, Linke Wienzeile 6 ☎588 85, ⓦwww.theater-wien.at; U-Bahn Karlsplatz. Famous as the venue where Beethoven's *Fidelio* and Strauss's *Die Fledermaus* premiered (see p.107), this theatre has returned to its roots and now concentrates on opera; tickets range from around €10 to €160 with *Stehplätze* for €7.

**Volksoper** 9, Währingerstrasse 78 ☎514 44-3670, ⓦwww.volksoper.at; U-Bahn Währingerstrasse-Volksoper or tram #40, #41 or #42. Vienna's number-two opera house, situated in the ninth district, near the *Gürtel*, specializes in operetta, plus the occasional, more adventurous musical and opera production; tickets range from around €5 to €80, with seventy or so *Stehplätze* a night (€2–4).

## Mostly classical music

**Bösendorfer-Saal** 1, Domgasse 5 ☎504 6651-310 ⓦwww.boesendorfer.com; U-Bahn Taubstummengasse. Intimate, newly renovated vaulted cellar in the basement of the Mozarthaus, where Austrian piano-manufacturers Bösendorfer put their models through their paces in recitals and chamber music concerts (often free entry).

**Konzerthaus** 3, Lothringerstrasse 20 ☎242 002, ⓦkonzerthaus.at; U-Bahn Karlsplatz. Early twentieth-century concert hall designed by Viennese duo Fellner & Helmer. Three main halls: the Grosser Saal, Mozart-Saal and Schubert-Saal, plus the new Berio-Saal. The classical music programme here tends to be a bit more adventurous and varied than the Musikverein's, with the odd nod to world music, jazz and even pop.

**Musikverein** 1, Bösendorferstrasse 12 ☎505 81 90, ⓦwww.musikverein.at; U-Bahn Karlsplatz. Two ornate concert halls in one building, gilded from top to bottom inside. The larger of the two, the Grosser Saal, has the best acoustics in the country, and is the unofficial home of the Wiener Philharmoniker, while the smaller hall, the Brahms Saal, is used mainly for chamber concerts. *Stehplätze* available for the Grosser Saal (€5–7).

# Theatre

Obviously, for non-German-speakers, most of Vienna's **theatres** and satirical **cabarets** have limited appeal. However, there are a couple of English-speaking theatre groups; a few theatres that specialize in musicals; one dedicated dance venue; several puppet theatres, where language is less of a problem; and the Burgtheater, whose interior alone is worth the price of a ticket.

## Straight theatres

**Akademietheater** 3, Lisztstrasse 1 ☎514 44-41400, ⓦwww.burgtheater.at; U-Bahn Karlsplatz. Number two to the Burgtheater, using the same pool of actors, but specializing in more contemporary chamber works.

**Burgtheater** 1, Dr-Karl-Lueger-Ring 2 ☎513 1 513, ⓦwww.burgtheater.at; U-Bahn Herrengasse. Vienna's most prestigious theatrical stage puts on innovative and serious drama in rep. The foyer and staircases are spectacular; the auditorium was modernized after bomb damage in 1945. Tickets cost from around €5 to €50, with 150 *Stehplätze* (€2.50) going on sale every night, an hour before the curtain goes up. Closed July & Aug.

## Fasching

Though clearly analogous with Mardi Gras and Carnival, Vienna's **Fasching** lasts much longer, with the first balls taking place on **November 11**, and continuing – mostly on Saturdays and Sundays – until **Ash Wednesday** the following year and beyond.

Under the Habsburgs, the most famous ball was the Kaiserball, held in the Hofburg on New Year's Eve, and presided over by the emperor himself. Nowadays, it's the **Opernball**, held on the Thursday before Ash Wednesday in the Staatsoper, that gets all the attention, with the debutantes parading all in white, and an array of B-list celebrities in attendance.

The other three hundred or so balls are a hotchpotch held by various associations – everything from the gay and lesbian **Regenbogenball** to the **Ball der Burgenländischen Kroaten** – in Vienna's top hotels and palaces; those followed by the word **Gschnas** are masked.

To find out what's on, pick up a **Wiener Ballkalender** (ⓦ www.ballkalender.com) from the tourist office. If you're worried about your dancing ability, numerous dance classes are on offer; ask the tourist board for details.

**Theater-in-der-Josefstadt** 8, Josefstädterstrasse 24–26 ☎ 427 00-300, ⓦ www .josefstadt.org; U-Bahn Rathaus or tram #2. Beautiful, early nineteenth-century theatre, with boxes galore, staging serious popular German-language drama from classics to contemporary. Tickets from €5 to €50, with *Stehplätze* €4.

**Volkstheater** 7, Neustiftgasse 1 ☎ 521 11-400, ⓦ www.volkstheater.at; U-Bahn Volkstheater. Late nineteenth-century theatre designed by Fellner & Helmer, with the groovy *Rote Bar* to hang out in (see p.225). Modern plays, foreign works and classics, plus the odd operetta.

### Dance

**TanzQuartierWien (TQW)** 7, Museumsplatz 1 ☎ 581 35 91, ⓦ www.tqw.at; U-Bahn Museumsquartier. Experimental dance performance space, in the Kunsthalle building in the MuseumsQuartier complex.

### English-speaking theatres

**International Theatre** 9, Porzellangasse 8 ☎ 319 62 72, ⓦ www.internationaltheatre.at; tram #D. Local-based, expat (mostly American) company with a small, 68-seat venue on the corner of Müllnergasse and Porzellangasse. Closed July & Aug.

**Vienna's English Theatre** 8, Josefsgasse 12 ☎ 402 12 60, ⓦ www.englishtheatre.at; U-Bahn Lerchenfelderstrasse. Larger, professionally-run venue, with interesting productions flown in from abroad (mostly London and New York).

### Miscellaneous

**RadioKulturhaus** 4, Argentinierstrasse 30a ☎ 501 70-377, ⓦ radiokulturhaus.orf.at; U-Bahn Taubstummengasse. The Grosser Sendesaal is the main performance space of Austrian state radio, and home of the Vienna Radio Symphony Orchestra. However, it hosts a whole range of events and gigs from straight theatre to jazz concerts.

### Puppet theatre

**Figurentheater Lilarum** 3, Göllnergasse 8 ☎ 710 26 66, ⓦ lilarum.at; U-Bahn Kardinal-Nagl-Platz. Puppet theatre out in Landstrasse, with several performances a day. Wed–Sun and during school holidays.

**Märchenbühne der Apfelbaum** 7, Kirchengasse 41 ☎ 523 17 29-20, ⓦ maerchenbuehne.at; U-Bahn Volkstheater. This puppet theatre specializes in classic fairy tales, so even without any German you can at least follow the plot. Fri–Sun 4pm.

**Schönbrunner Schlossmarionettentheater** 13, Schloss Schönbrunn, Hofratsktrakt ☎ 817 32 47; ⓦ www.marionettentheater.at; U-Bahn Hietzing. String-puppet theatre in Schönbrunn specializing in Viennese operas: performances aimed at children last just over an hour, while the full-length versions are over two hours. Performances Wed–Sun.

# Cinema

Austrian **cinema** is not really up there with the greats, and unless your German is up to scratch, you're best off sticking to British and American films. One film that's fun to see, and is shown every weekend at the Burg-Kino, is **The Third Man** (*Der Dritte Mann*), made in 1949, set amid the rubble of postwar Vienna and starring Orson Welles (see p.106).

Check out the week's cinema **listings** online at Ⓦ www.film.at, or in *Falter*, the city's weekly listings tabloid. *OF* means it's in the original language without subtitles; *OmengU* means it's in the original with English subtitles; *OmU* means it's in the original with German subtitles, but should not be confused with *OmÜ*, which means it's in the original, but has a live voice-over German translation. And finally, *dF* means it's dubbed into German.

Cinema **tickets** cost €8 or less; Monday (*Kino-Montag*) is cheap-ticket day. Vienna's international film festival, the **Viennale**, takes place in the middle of October and is definitely worth catching. In July and August, you can watch **open-air films** in Karlsplatz (see below) and various other locations around the city – look out for *Sommerkino*.

**Artis International** 1, Schultergasse/Jordangasse ⓣ 535 65 70; U-Bahn Stephansplatz. Central multiplex cinema showing films in English in six different salons.

**Bellaria** 7, Museumstrasse 3 ⓣ 523 75 91; U-Bahn Volkstheater. Old Neubau cinema that specializes in German and Austrian black-and-white movies.

**Breitenseer Lichtspiele** 14, Breitenseerstrasse 21 ⓣ 982 21 73, Ⓦ www.bsl-wien.at; U-Bahn Hütteldorferstrasse. Vienna's oldest cinema, which opened in 1909, is still going strong, with much the same fittings.

**Burg Kino** 1, Opernring 19 ⓣ 587 84 06, Ⓦ www .burgkino.at; U-Bahn Museumsquartier. Two-screen cinema on the Ringstrasse that shows films in the original, without subtitles. *The Third Man* has a regular spot (Fri 10.45pm & Sun 3.15pm).

**English Cinema Haydn** 6, Mariahilferstrasse 57 ⓣ 587 22 62, Ⓦ www.haydnkino.at; U-Bahn Neubaugasse. As the name suggests, this is a cinema that shows the latest films in English, without subtitles.

**Filmmuseum** 1, Augustinerstrasse 1 ⓣ 533 70 54, Ⓦ www.filmmuseum.at; U-Bahn Karlsplatz.

Vienna's main art-house cinema, on the ground floor of the Albertina, with a very esoteric programme, all in the original, generally without subtitles.

**Gartenbau Kino** 1, Parkring 12 ⓣ 512 23 54, Ⓦ www.gartenbaukino.at; U-Bahn Stubentor. 1960s Ringstrasse cinema – the largest in Vienna – owned by the Viennale, showing a mixture of classics and recent releases, usually in the original language.

**Kino unter Sternen** 1, Resselpark, Karlsplatz ⓣ 585 23 24, Ⓦ www.afterimage.at; U-Bahn Karlsplatz. Open-air showings of classics in their original language "underneath the stars" in the park on Karlsplatz. July only.

**Metro Kino** 1, Johannesgasse 4 ⓣ 512 18 03, Ⓦ www.filmarchiv.at; U-Bahn Stephansplatz. Amazing, ornate, centrally located cinema run by Filmarchiv Austria (Austrian Film Archives), showing classics and mini-festivals.

**Stadtkino Wien** 3, Schwarzenbergplatz 7 ⓣ 712 62 76, Ⓦ www.stadtkinowien.at; U-Bahn Karlsplatz. Art-house cinema with disabled access, just a short distance from the Innere Stadt. Closed Aug.

# Visual arts

In addition to its vast permanent collections of art (detailed in the main text of the Guide), Vienna has a large number of galleries that host temporary exhibitions. Check out the latest shows and opening times in the tourist board's free monthly booklet *Programm*.

**Architekturzentrum Wien** 7, **Museumsplatz 1;** Ⓦ www.azw.at; **U-Bahn Volkstheater.** In the courtyard of the MuseumsQuartier (see p.96), and specializing in contemporary architectural exhibitions. Daily 10am–7pm; €7.

**Bank Austria Kunstforum** 1, **Freyung 8;** Ⓦ www.bankaustria-kunstforum.at; **U-Bahn Herrengasse.** Major venue for visiting foreign exhibitions of big-name contemporary art, sponsored by one of Austria's high-street banks. Daily 10am–7pm, Fri until 9pm.

**BAWAG Contemporary** 1, **Franz-Josefs-Kai 3;** Ⓦ www.bawag-foundation.at; **U-Bahn Schwedenplatz.** Former tile factory transformed by one of the country's leading banks into an exhibition space showcasing Austrian artists. Daily 2–8pm.

**Generali Foundation** 4, **Wiedner Hauptstrasse 15;** Ⓦ foundation.generali.at; **U-Bahn Karlsplatz.** Funky modern space owned by the eponymous insurance company and hidden away off Karlsplatz, serving up interesting contemporary sculpture and mixed-media work. Tues–Sun 11am–6pm, Thurs 11am–8pm; €6.

**Kunsthalle Wien** 7, **Museumsplatz 1;** Ⓦ kunsthallewien.at; **U-Bahn Volkstheater.** The city's official space for big contemporary art exhibitions is a bit lost in the bowels of the old Winter Riding School in the MuseumsQuartier; see p.96. Daily 11am–7pm, Thurs until 9pm.

**Kunsthalle Wien – project space** 4, **Karlsplatz, Treitlstrasse 2;** Ⓦ kunsthallewien.at; **U-Bahn Karlsplatz.** Glassy box in the centre of Karlsplatz used for international visiting exhibitions and frequented by Vienna's artiest crowd. Mon & Sun 1–7pm, Tues–Sat 4pm–midnight.

**Künstlerhaus** 1, **Karlsplatz 5;** Ⓦ www.k-haus.at; **U-Bahn Karlsplatz.** The Kunstverein (Artists' Society), next door to the Musikverein, puts on major retrospectives in painting, sculpture and photography. Daily 10am–6pm, Thurs until 9pm; €8.50.

**Momentum** 7, **Karl-Schweighofer-Gasse 12;** Ⓦ www.momentum.co,at; **U-Bahn Volkstheater.** Photography gallery that promotes Austrian photography – from reportage to abstract – and has lots of prints for sale. Tues–Fri 11am–7pm, Sat 11am–3pm.

**Secession** 1, **Friedrichstrasse 12;** Ⓦ www.secession.at; **U-Bahn Karlsplatz.** The famous Jugendstil exhibition space, with Klimt's *Beethoven Frieze* in the basement (see p.103), continues to host provocative modern art shows and installations. Tues–Sun 10am–6pm.

**Thyssen-Bornemisza Art Contemporary** 1, **Himmelpfortgasse 13;** Ⓦ www.tba21.org; **U-Bahn Stephansplatz.** Contemporary art gallery run by Francesca Habsburg, daughter of collector Thyssen-Bornemisza, who lives on the top floor. Tues–Sun noon–6pm

**WestLicht** 7, **Westbahnstrasse 40;** Ⓦ www.westlicht.at; **tram #5 or #49.** The city's most innovative photography gallery. Tues, Wed & Fri 2–7pm, Thurs 2–9pm, Sat & Sun 11am–7pm.

**13**

# Shopping

F ew people come to Vienna exclusively to shop, though, in fact, the city boasts quite a lot of quirky independent stores, while prices belie its reputation as one of Europe's most expensive. Window shopping along **Graben** and **Kohlmarkt** can be fun, as, in among the international designers, you can still find shops sporting the "K. K." or "k.u.k." emblem – *kaiserlich und königlich* (Imperial and Royal) – of the last Empire. In the backstreets of the **Innere Stadt**, you'll also find numerous excellent bookstalls and some serious antique shops clustered around the Dorotheum (see opposite). The streets of **Neubau**, to the north of Mariahilferstrasse, are also good for browsing, and of course, the city boasts a great Saturday **Flohmarkt** (flea market) at the back end of the Naschmarkt.

For a capital, Vienna has very few large supermarkets, with just the small Billa and Julius Meinl stores scattered across the city. **Mariahilferstrasse** remains the main shopping drag for department stores and mainstream shops, along with **Kärntnerstrasse**.

## Arts, crafts and antiques

**Antique shops** (*Antiquitäten*) are clustered in the streets around the Dorotheum (see opposite), though there are few bargains to be had. Shops specializing in Art Nouveau and early twentieth-century gear can be found in Neubau, particularly around the Spittelberg area, off Siebensterngasse. For bric-a-brac, secondhand goods (*Altwaren*), and possibly a bargain or two, head for the streets around the Naschmarkt, and, of course, for the Naschmarkt flea market itself (see p.236), where you'll have to haggle.

**Adil Besim 1**, Graben 30 ⓦwww.adil-besim.at; U-Bahn Stephansplatz. The king of Vienna's carpet shops, in business since 1946, selling kilims, rugs and tapestries at serious

prices. Mon–Fri 9.30am–6pm, Sat 10am–5pm.
**Augarten 1**, Stock-im-Eisen-Platz 3–4 ⓦwww .augarten.at; U-Bahn Stephansplatz. Vienna's

very own hand-painted china manufacturers have an outlet here, though you can also visit and buy direct (including some seconds) from the factory (see p.158). Mon–Sat 10am–6pm.

**Backhausen 1, Schwarzenbergstrasse 10** ⓦwww.backhausen.at; U-Bahn Karlsplatz. Backhausen reproduce beautiful Wiener Werkstätte textiles, ceramics and furniture, as well as housing a museum in the basement. Mon–Fri 10am–6pm, Sat 10am–5pm.

**Bananas 5, Kettenbrückengasse 15** ⓦwww .bananas.at; U-Bahn Kettenbrückengasse; branch at 6, Gumpendorferstrasse 10–12. A stone's throw from the Naschmarkt (and flea market), Bananas specializes in furniture and accessories from the 1950s through to the 1980s. Mon–Fri 1–6pm, Sat 11am–4pm.

**Dorotheum 1, Dorotheergasse 17** ⓦwww .dorotheum.com; U-Bahn Stephansplatz. "Aunt Dorothy's", as it's known, is one of the world's leading auction houses, with daily sales and a fixed-price shop; there's even a café for posing in. Mon–Fri 10am–6pm, Sat 9am–5pm.

**J. & L. Lobmeyr 1, Kärntnerstrasse 26;** ⓦwww .lobmeyr.at; U-Bahn Stephansplatz. Famous

glass manufacturers, and a lovely shop, with a museum on the top floor (see p.48). You can buy glass designed by Adolf Loos and Josef Hoffmann as well as more modern pieces. Mon–Fri 10am–7pm, Sat 10am–6pm.

**Das Kunstwerk 4, Operngasse 20 & 6, Laimgrubengasse 24** ⓦwww.daskunstwerk.at; U-Bahn Karlsplatz & Museumsquartier. Jugendstil and Art Deco furniture, glassware and lamps by the likes of Wagner, Lötz, Loos and Thonet. Mon–Fri 1–7pm, Sat 10am–2pm.

**MAK-Shop 1, Weiskirchnerstrasse 3** ⓦwww .makdesignshop.at; U-Bahn Stubentor. Museum shop selling wacky modern furniture and accoutrements by the designers of the School of Applied Arts. Tues 10am–midnight, Wed–Sun 10am–6pm.

**Thonet 9, Berggasse 31** ⓦwww.thonet.com; tram #D. Furniture company, famed for its bentwood chairs, and still producing Adolf Loos and Wiener Werkstätte designs. Mon–Fri 10am–6pm, Sat 9am–5pm.

**Woka 1, Palais Breuner, Singerstrasse 16** ⓦwww.woka.com; U-Bahn Stephansplatz. Shop selling reproduction lamps and the like, designed by Adolf Loos and other Wiener Werkstätte artists. Mon–Fri 10am–6pm, Sat 10am–5pm.

## Bookshops

Though Vienna has a staggering number of **bookshops** (*Buchhandlungen*), most of them in the Innere Stadt, only a handful are English-language. Nevertheless, many of the stores below stock a wide choice of English-language volumes. Be warned, however, that the Austrians slap tax on books, so prices are much higher than elsewhere in Europe.

**Babette's 4, Schleifmühlgasse 17** ⓦwww .babettes.at; U-Bahn Karlsplatz. Smart little cookery specialist, with lots of books (and plenty in English) and even a daily lunchtime menu to sample. Mon–Fri 10am–7pm, Sat 10am–5pm.

**British Bookshop 1, Weihburggasse 24–26** ⓦwww.britishbookshop.at; U-Bahn Stephans-platz. A fair selection of novels and biogra-phies in English; half the shop is given over to EFL teaching materials. Mon–Fri 9.30am–6.30pm, Sat 9.30am–6pm.

**Freytag & Berndt 1, Kohlmarkt 9** ⓦwww .freytagberndt.at; U-Bahn Stephansplatz. Flagship store of Austria's most prestigious map-makers, with loads of maps, as well as guides to Vienna and the rest of the world in

English, including a large selection of Rough Guides. Mon–Fri 9am–7pm, Sat 9am–6pm.

**Löwenherz 9, Berggasse 8** ⓦwww.loewenherz .at; U-Bahn Schottenring. Gay bookstore attached to the wonderful *Café Berg* (see p.213). Mon–Thurs 10am–7pm, Fri 10am–8pm, Sat 10am–6pm.

**Morawa 1, Wollzeile 11** ⓦwww.morawa.at; U-Bahn Stubentor. Huge bookshop stretching right back to Bäckerstrasse; the English section is on the first floor, guides and a vast range of English magazines and newspapers are at the back. Mon–Fri 9am–7pm, Sat 9am–6pm.

**Mord & Musik 7, Lindengasse 22** ⓦwww .mordundmusik.at; U-Bahn Neubaugasse. Unusual shop specializing in crime fiction and experimental electronic music. Mon–Fri 2–6.45pm, Sat 11am–4.45pm. **Satyr-Filmwelt** 1, Marc-Aurel-Strasse 5; U-Bahn Schwedenplatz. Loads of books in German, French and (mostly) English on movies and music. Good selection of art house videos and posters, and CD soundtracks, too. Entrance is at Vorlaufstrasse 2. Mon–Fri 10am–7.30pm, Sat 9am–5pm. **Shakespeare & Co** 1, Sterngasse 2 ⓦwww .shakespeare.co.at; U-Bahn Schwedenplatz.

Floor-to-ceiling English-language bookstore, with friendly staff and a great selection of novels, art books and magazines. Mon–Sat 9am–9pm. **Thalia** 6, Mariahilferstrasse 99 ⓦwww.thalia.at; U-Bahn Neubaugasse; plus several other branches. Vienna's biggest bookstore, with a well-stocked English section, lots of media on sale and a music department. Mon–Wed 9.30am–7pm, Thurs & Fri 9.30am–8pm, Sat 9.30am–6pm.

## Department stores

Vienna is still the land of the small shop, and has remarkably few **department stores**. The main two are listed below.

**Gerngross** 7, Mariahilferstrasse 38–48 ⓦwww .gerngross.at; U-Bahn Neubaugasse. Vienna's largest department store is actually just several floors of franchises, but it does sell everything from toys to clothes. Good sushi bar on the top floor. Mon–Wed & Fri 9.30am–7pm, Thurs 9.30am–8pm, Sat 9.30am–6pm. **Steffl** 1, Kärntnerstrasse 19 ⓦwww.kaufhaus -steffl.at; U-Bahn Stephansplatz. Classic

department store – the only one in the Innere Stadt – with perfume and jewellery on the ground floor, free internet access, a café and bookstore on the fourth floor, and the *Sky* café/restaurant/bar, with great views, on the top. Mon–Wed 9.30am–7pm, Thurs & Fri 9.30am–8pm, Sat 9.30am–6pm.

### Markets

**Bio-Bauernmarkt** 1, Freyung ⓦwww.biobauernmarkt-freyung.at; U-Bahn Schottentor/Herrengasse. Organic fruit, veg and other edibles from the neighbouring *Länder*, plus a fair few arts and crafts stalls. Every other Sat & Sun 9am–6pm.

**Brunnenmarkt** 16, Brunnengasse; U-Bahn Thaliastrasse. Multicultural fruit and veg market in Ottakring that stretches for something like a kilometre along Brunnengasse. Mon–Fri 6am–7.30pm, Sat 6am–5pm.

**Christkindlmarkt** 1, Rathausplatz ⓦwww.christkindlmarkt.at; U-Bahn Rathaus or tram #1 or #2. The Christmas market held in front of the Rathaus, selling gifts and food, is the biggest, though there are smaller ones in Spittelberg, Freyung and outside the Mariahilferkirche. Daily mid-Nov to Christmas Eve 9am–9pm.

**Flohmarkt** 6 & 7, Linke & Rechte Wienzeile; U-Bahn Kettenbrückengasse. Vienna's Saturday flea market is fascinating and worth checking out just for the vibe. East Europeans flock to it to sell off everything from old rags to old riches. Sat 6.30am–4pm.

**Flohmarkt im Autokino** Autokinostrasse 2, Gross Enzersdorf; bus #26A from U-Bahn Kagran; ⓦwww.autokino.at. A totally different experience from the Naschmarkt, and only really for the intrepid, this is a sprawling, chaotic fleamarket in the city's drive-in cinema. Sun 6am–1pm.

**Naschmarkt** 6 & 7, Linke & Rechte Wienzeile; U-Bahn Karlsplatz/Kettenbrückengasse. Vienna's most exotic fruit and veg market, with Turkish, Balkan, Chinese, Middle Eastern and Austrian produce, takeaway stalls plus clothes and sundries. On Saturday mornings, there's a *Flöhmarkt* (flea market) extension west of Kettenbrückengasse U-Bahn. Mon–Fri 6am–7.30pm, Sat 6am–5pm.

# Fashion

Vienna's Innere Stadt has branches of all the usual international **fashion** stores you'd find in most European capitals. The shops listed below concentrate on retro clothes and clubbing gear. There are also a few places listed where you can buy **Trachten**, the traditional Alpine costume of *Dirndl* dresses and blouses for women and *Walker* (jackets) or *Loden* (capes) for men, which is still alarmingly popular throughout the country.

**Derby Handschuhe 1**, Plankengasse 5 ⓦwww .derby-gloves-vienna.com; U-Bahn Stephansplatz. A veritable quality *Handschuh* (glove) fest in suede and leather. Mon–Fri 10am–6pm.

**Eselmist 7**, Burggasse 89 ⓦwww.eselmist.at; U-Bahn Burggasse or bus #49A. Eselmist (donkey shit) is a wonderful vintage clothing store in the backstreets of Neubau. Mon–Fri 10am–7pm, Sat 10am–5pm.

**EWA 7**, Lindengasse 37; U-Bahn Neubaugasse. Vast emporium of secondhand and retro gear with live DJs from 2pm daily and original fashions designed by the owners. Mon–Fri 10am–7pm, Sat 10am–6pm.

**Helford Jersey 1**, Franz-Josefs-Kai 19; U-Bahn Schwedenplatz. Model cars, baseball caps, Vienna T-shirts, and reasonably priced *Trachten* clothes for the kids. Mon–Fri 10am–7pm, Sat 10am–5pm.

**Love Saves the Day 7**, Siebensterngasse 28 ⓦwww.lstd-wear.com; U-Bahn Volkstheater. LSD, as it's known to its friends, sells brightly coloured, groovy 1960s retro clothing and accessories. Mon–Fri 11am–7pm, Sat 11am–5pm.

**Mühlbauer 1**, Seilergasse 10 ⓦwww.muehlbauer .at; U-Bahn Stephansplatz. *Hutmanufaktur* since 1903, this is the colourful hat company's white, minimalist showpiece; other branches – such as the one at no. 5 – sell clothes. Mon–Sat 10am–6.30pm, Sat 10am–6pm.

**Nachbarin 6**, Gumpendorferstrasse 17 ⓦwww .nachbarin.co.at; U-Bahn Museumsquartier. Super-stylish women's clothing, shoes and jewellery from contemporary European designers. Mon noon–6pm, Tues–Fri 11am–6pm, Sat 11am–2pm.

**Rag 7**, Mariahilferstrasse 20 ⓦwww.rag.co.at; U-Bahn Museumsquartier. Baggy trousers and other slack accoutrements for the skateboarding posse. Mon–Fri 10am–7pm, Sat 10am–6pm.

**Shu! 7**, Neubaugasse 14 ⓦwww.shu.at. Shu is no ordinary shoe shop – this is a place packed with adventurous, unique, unusual avant-garde footwear. Tues–Fri noon–7pm, Sat noon–5pm.

**Tostmann 1**, Schottengasse 3a ⓦwww .tostmann.at; U-Bahn Schottentor. The Vienna branch of this Salzkammergut firm is *the* place to fix yourself up head to toe in *Trachten* – there's even a museum on the stuff in the basement. Mon–Sat 10am–6pm.

**Vintage Mode 4**, Schliefmühlgasse 15a; U-Bahn Karlsplatz. Really quite glamorous vintage dresses, shoes, hats and gloves from 1940s onwards. Mon–Fri 10am–6.30pm, Sat 10am–5.30pm.

# Food and wine

For cheap fruit and veg, you really have to go to the **Naschmarkt** (see box opposite). With such small supermarkets, the gap is filled, in part, by the city's flash, quality **delis**.

**Anker 15**, Westbahnhof; U-Bahn Westbahnhof; hundreds of branches across Vienna. The largest bakery chain in the country, producing excellent bread, rolls and pastries; most branches also serve coffee. Mon–Fri 7am–6pm, Sat 7.30am–5pm, Sun 9am–5pm.

**Arthur Grimm 1**, Kurrentgasse 10 ⓦwww .grimm.at; U-Bahn Stephansplatz; branches at 2, Untere Augartenstrasse 39, & 4, Wiedner Haupstrasse 82. Most bakeries in Vienna are wonderful, but *Grimm's* is particularly wonderful, with a vast range of fresh bread and pastries. Serves coffee, too. Mon–Fri 6.30am–6.30pm, Sat 6.30am–noon.

**Billa 1**, Singerstrasse 6 ⓦwww.billa.at; U-Bahn Stephansplatz; branches all over the city. The most central of the ubiquitous supermarket chain, with a very groovy trolley escalator to take you into the basement. Handy for gathering picnic fodder – Ja! Natürlich is their organic range. Mon–Thurs 8am–7pm, Fri 8am–7.30pm, Sat 7.30am–6pm.

**Biomaran 7, Kaiserstrasse 57–59** ⓦwww .biomarkt.co.at; **U-Bahn Burggasse or tram #5.** The city's biggest organic supermarket chain with everything from fruit and veg to alcohol. Mon–Wed 7.30am–7pm, Sat 8am–5pm.

**Biowelt am Naschmarkt 4, Stand 330, Naschmarkt** ⓦwww.bio-welt.at; **U-Bahn Karlsplatz/Kettenbrückengasse.** Organic health food shop, deli, bakery and grocery, all rolled into one in the heart of the Naschmarkt. Mon–Fri 9am–6.30pm, Sat 8am–6pm.

**Bobby's Food Store 4, Schleifmühlgasse 8** ⓦwww.bobbys.at; **U-Bahn Karlsplatz/Taubstummengasse.** All those things from home (UK or North America) you think you need, from Cadbury's chocolate and Weetabix to Colman's mustard and Marmite/Vegemite. Mon–Fri 10am–6.30pm, Sat 10am–6pm.

**Böhle 1, Wollzeile 30** ⓦwww.boehle.at; **U-Bahn Stubentor.** Top-notch Austrian deli with a huge range of beer, wine, vinegar, fruit and salads, plus a daily takeaway menu. Mon–Fri 8.30am–7pm, Sat 9.30am–5pm.

**Demmer's Teehaus 1, Mölkerbastei 5** ⓦwww .demmer.at; **U-Bahn Herrengasse.** Tea addicts' paradise, with Indian and Chinese teas sold loose, and a café upstairs. Mon–Fri 9am–6.30pm, Sat 9.30am–1.30pm.

**Gegenbauer 4, Stand 111–114, Naschmarkt** ⓦwww.gegenbauer.at; **U-Bahn Karlsplatz.** Family-owned company selling a vast array of vinegar, flavoured oils and mustards in bottles, flagons and barrels. Mon–Fri 9am–6pm, Sat 8am–5pm.

**Manner 1, Rotenturmstrasse 2** ⓦwww.manner .at; **U-Bahn Stephansplatz.** Manner wafers have been going since 1890 and remain the country's most popular snack. This flagship store on the corner of Stephansplatz stocks a vast range. Daily 10am–9pm.

**Meinl am Graben 1, Am Graben 19** ⓦwww .meinlamgraben.at; **U-Bahn Stephansplatz.** The flagship Julius Meinl store has an incredible choice of luxury goodies to buy, eat and drink on two floors. Mon–Fri 8am–7.30pm, Sat 9am–6pm.

**Schönbichler 1, Wollzeile 4** ⓦwww .schoenbichler.at; **U-Bahn Stephansplatz.** Amazing selection of more than 100 teas, plus china teapots, coffee, brandies, Kirsch and a staggering collection of malt whiskies. Mon–Fri 9am–6pm, Sat 9am–5pm.

**Unger & Klein 1, Gölsdorfgasse 2** ⓦwww .ungerundklein.at; **U-Bahn Schwedenplatz/ Schottenring.** Trendy Eichinger oder Knecht–designed wine shop where you can buy a glass to drink or a bottle to take away. Mon–Fri 3pm–midnight, Sat 5pm–midnight.

**Wein & Co 6, Getreidemarkt 1** ⓦwww.weinco .at; **U-Bahn Karlsplatz.** Big wine emporium and deli, near the Naschmarkt, where you can eat, quaff or simply buy to take away. Mon–Fri 10am–midnight, Sat 9am–midnight, Sun 11am–midnight.

**Xocolat 1, Freyung 2** ⓦwww.xocolat.at; **U-Bahn Karlsplatz.** Shop in the Freyung arcade selling bars, hot chocolate, chocolate spreads, Hülle mir Fülle, Zotter from Austria and other choco delights from all over Europe. Mon–Fri 10am–6pm, Sat 10am–5pm, Sun noon–5pm.

**Zum schwarzen Kameel 1, Bognergasse 5; U-Bahn Herrengasse;** ⓦwww.kameel.at. Terribly smart deli that's yet another Viennese institution, eat-in or takeaway food and lots of very fancy wine too. Mon–Sat 9am–9pm.

**Zum süssen Eck 9, Währingerstrasse 65** ⓦwww.suesseseck.at; **U-Bahn Währinger Strasse/Volksoper.** Retro candy store selling every type of boiled sweet from days of yore – worth a look just for the high-camp humour of the window display. Mon & Sun 2–7.30pm, Tues–Sat 10am–7.30pm.

# Music

**Arcadia 1, Kärntnerstrasse 40; U-Bahn Karlsplatz.** Bookshop beneath the arcades of the Staatsoper and full of things to do with opera. A great place to mug up on the plot before you go and see a show. Daily 10am–7pm.

**Audio Center 1, Judenplatz 9; U-Bahn Stephansplatz;** ⓦwww.audiocenter.at. The best selection of jazz CDs and records in the city (plus some world music), and lots of info on the local jazz scene. Mon–Fri 10am–7pm, Sat 10am–5pm.

⑬

**Black Market** 1, Gonzagagasse 9 ⓦ www
.soulseduction.com; U-Bahn Schwedenplatz.
Record store that's Vienna's unofficial dance
music HQ – the bar is something of a
clubbers' hangout. Mon–Fri noon–7pm,
Sat 11am–6pm.

**Gramola** 1, Graben 16 ⓦ www.gramola.at;
U-Bahn Stephansplatz. Excellent selection of
cheap classical CDs in this tiny stuccoed
store. Mon–Wed 9.30am–6.30pm, Thurs &
Fri 9.30am–7pm, Sat 9.30am–6pm.

**Rave Up** 6, Hofmühlgasse 1; U-Bahn Pilgram-
gasse; ⓦ www.rave-up.at. Great record store
with everything from indie music to hip hop,
reggae and techno – and lots of Viennese
electronica, Mon–Fri 10am–6.30pm, Sat
10am–5pm.

**Teuchtler Alt & Neu** 6, Windmühlgasse 10;
U-Bahn Museumsquartier. Secondhand CDs
and records, with a particularly good
selection of jazz and classical, and low
prices. Mon–Fri 1–6pm, Sat 10am–noon.

## Toys and accessories

**Hobby-Sommer** 7, Neubaugasse 26 ⓦ www
.hobby-sommer-austria.at; U-Bahn Neubaugasse. Model railways from around the
world, and models of the Airfix variety.
Mon–Fri 9.30am–6pm, Sat 10am–5pm.

**Huber & Lerner** 1, Weihburggasse 4 ⓦ www
.huber-lerner.at; U-Bahn Stephansplatz. This
former imperial stationers is the place to
get your bespoke headed notepaper
(at a price). Mon–Fri 9.30am–6pm, Sat
10am–5pm.

**Imaginarium** 1, Neuer Markt 8a ⓦ www
.imaginarium.info; U-Bahn Karlsplatz. Brilliant
range of imaginative toys from this Catalan
toy chain, and a separate miniature
entrance for kids. Mon–Fri 10am–7pm,
Sat 10am–6pm.

**Lorenzi** 7, Siebensterngasse 41; tram #49;
ⓦ www.lorenzi.co.at. Amazing selection of
*Stahlwaren* – pricey knives, scissors,
daggers and swords – by top manufac-

turers from a shop that's been here since
1885. Mon–Fri 9am–12.30pm & 2–6pm,
Sat 10am–2pm.

**Piatnik** 7, Schottenfeldgasse 19 ⓦ www.piatnik
.com; U-Bahn Zieglergasse/Westbahnhof.
Famous Austrian firm, founded in 1824,
which makes playing cards and also sells
Zippo lighters, pipes, kids' toys and board
games. Mon–Fri 9am–6pm, Sat 9am–1pm.

**Rudolf Waniek** 1, Hoher Markt 5; U-Bahn
Schwedenplatz. Former court suppliers of
glassware and metalware, now peddling salt
cellars, decanters, coffee-making machines
and quality domestic utensils. Mon–Fri
9.30am–6pm, Sat 10am–5pm.

**Spielzeugschachtel** 1, Rauhensteingasse 5
ⓦ www.spielzeugschachtel.com; U-Bahn
Stephansplatz. The "Toy Box" contains a
feast of jigsaws, games, wooden toys and
children's books. Mon–Fri 10am–6.30pm,
Sat 10am–5pm.

So now we've told you about the things not to miss, the best places to stay, the top restaurants, the liveliest bars and the most spectacular sights, it only seems fair to tell you about the best travel insurance around

WorldNomads.com
keep travelling safely

Recommended by Rough Guides

# Contexts

# Contexts

# History

## The Romans

People have lived in the area of modern-day Vienna for many thousands of years, due to its geographical position at the point where the ancient trade route or amber route crossed the Danube. Following on from early Bronze and Iron Age settlements, a Celtic tribe known as the Boii occupied the hills above Vienna, probably from as early as 500 BC, but were driven from the area around 50 BC by the short-lived Dacian kingdom. Vienna was then swallowed up by the neighbouring Celtic kingdom of **Noricum**.

In 15 BC the **Romans**, under Emperor Augustus, advanced into Noricum as far as the Danube, and the area was absorbed into the Roman province of Pannonia. For the next four centuries, the river was used as a natural military border or *limes* by the Romans, further strengthened by a series of forts along its banks. The main Roman camp along this stretch of the Danube was at Carnuntum, to the east, with Vienna – or **Vindobona** as it was then called – as a subsidiary military fortress built for a single legion of around six thousand soldiers.

The Roman Forum is thought to have been somewhere around the Hoher Markt (see p.63) in today's Innere Stadt. In the first century AD, Vindobona became the base for the Tenth legion, whose job it was to fend off attacks from the neighbouring Germanic tribes to the north and east, particularly the Marcomanni and the Quadi. These two tribes crashed through the Danubian frontier in 169 AD only to be beaten back by Emperor Marcus Aurelius, who died in Vindobona in 180 AD.

## The Babenbergs

After the Romans finally abandoned Vindobona to the **Huns** in 433 AD, the city, like the rest of Europe, entered the **Dark Ages**. However, it's interesting to note that even at this early stage in its history, during the great migrations that followed the collapse of Roman power, the area of modern-day Vienna stood on one of the main ethnic crossroads of Europe: pressed from the east by first the Huns, later the Avars, from the north and south by the Slavs, and from the west by Germanic tribes.

The coronation of **Charlemagne** as Holy Roman Emperor in 800 marked the end of the Dark Ages in Europe. Parts of modern-day Austria, meanwhile, became a military colony – referred to by nineteenth-century historians as the "Ostmark" – of Charlemagne's Frankish Empire. With the collapse of the empire in 888, it was the Saxon king, Otto the Great, who succeeded in subduing the German lands. His successor, Otto II, went on to hand the "Ostmark" to the **Babenberg dynasty** in 976, whose job it was to protect the empire's eastern frontiers, once more formed by the Danube. The Babenberg dynasty ruled the territory for the next 270 years, first as margraves and later as dukes.

In their search for some kind of official birthday for their country, many Austrian scholars have latched on to the first known mention of the name Ostarrîchi, which appears in a Latin parchment from around 996. However, throughout the Middle Ages, the region was mostly referred to either simply as *provincia orientalis* or else named after its first ruler, the **Margrave Leopold I** (976–94). To begin with, the Babenberg Margravate was confined to a small stretch of the Danube centred most probably on Melk, but gradually it expanded eastwards as far as the River Leitha and northwards as far as the River Thaya. Successive Babenbergs founded a number of monasteries in the region, in particular Leopold III (1095–1136), who was later canonized for his good works and became the country's patron saint.

In 1156, during the reign of **Heinrich II Jasomirgott** (1141–77), the Babenbergs' Margravate was at last elevated to a Duchy, with its new capital at Vienna and the ducal palace situated in Am Hof (see p.59). However, in 1246 the Babenberg male line came to an end with the death of Duke Friedrich II (1230–46) on the battlefield. The dispute over who should rule over the Duchy of Austria and Styria, as it was now known, dragged on for the next thirty years. In 1251, the future Bohemian king, **Otakar II**, took up residence in Vienna and claimed the duchy for himself, shoring up his claim by marrying Friedrich II's widow.

# The early Habsburgs

While Otakar was laying claim to the Babenbergs' inheritance, he was also putting himself forward as a candidate for the throne of the Holy Roman Empire. In the end, though, the throne was handed in 1273 to **Rudolf of Habsburg**, a little-known count whose ancestral home was Habsburg Castle in modern-day Switzerland. In 1278 Rudolf's forces defeated (and killed) Otakar at the **Battle of Marchfeld**, east of Vienna, allowing Rudolf to lay claim to the Duchy of Austria. The Viennese, who had backed Otakar, were less than pleased about the outcome of the battle, and weren't easily placated by Rudolf's son, Albrecht, who had been given the duchy by his father.

The Habsburgs, though, were here to stay, their dynasty destined to rule over Austria for the next 640 years. Initially, however, Vienna only sporadically served as the dynastic capital. **Rudolf IV** (1356–65) was one of the few to treat it as such, founding the university and laying the foundation stone of what is now the Stephansdom, before dying at the age of just 26. Rudolf's endeavours earned him the nickname "The Founder", but he failed to secure a bishopric for Vienna.

For that the city had to wait until the reign of **Friedrich III** (1440–93). Despite numerous setbacks – he was besieged in the Hofburg by one of his own family in 1462, and briefly lost control of Vienna to the Hungarian king Matthias Corvinus in 1485 – Friedrich was responsible for consolidating the Habsburgs' power base. In 1452, he became the last Holy Roman Emperor to be crowned in Rome, and the following year elevated the family's dukedom to an archdukedom. Famously dismissed by Matthias Corvinus as "neither holy, Roman, nor an empire", the Holy Roman Empire was something of a fantasy, whose emperor, theoretically at least, ruled over all the German-speaking lands. Though the reality was somewhat different, the Habsburgs persisted with their imperial pretensions, passing the title down the male line until its eventual dissolution in 1806.

In the meantime, the Habsburgs continued to add to their dynastic inheritance through a series of judicious marriages by **Maximilian I** (1493–1519) and his offspring, prompting the oft-quoted maxim, adapted from Ovid: "Let others wage war; you, happy Austria, marry." By the time Emperor Karl V came to the throne in 1519, the Habsburgs ruled an empire on which, it was said, the sun never set, with lands stretching from its Spanish possessions in South America to Vienna itself – bolstered in 1526 by the addition of the kingdoms of Bohemia and Hungary. Vienna remained just one of several imperial residences, its development constantly hampered by the threat posed by the Ottoman army of Süleyman the Magnificent, who had been advancing steadily westwards across Europe.

# The Turkish sieges

In 1526, the Turks scored a decisive victory against the Hungarians at the **Battle of Mohács,** and began to advance into Habsburg territory. In the summer of 1529 they captured Budapest, and by September the Sultan's vast army was camped outside Vienna, the "city of the golden apple" as they called it. Although it is the later siege of 1683 (see below) that captured the imagination of historians, the **Siege of 1529** was a much closer-run thing. The Ottoman Empire was at its zenith and Vienna was defended only by a small garrison of around fifteen thousand troops under Count Salm. However, having shelled the city and killed some 1500 Viennese, in October the Turkish army of at least 120,000 men suddenly withdrew – whether because of bad weather or some other reason, no one knows – back to Hungary. It seems almost as if Vienna simply wasn't worth the effort, despite the fact that the city was there for the taking.

In a defiant gesture, **Ferdinand I** (1556–64) subsequently established Vienna as his permanent base, building the zigzag fortifications that were to surround the city for the next three hundred years or more. With the retreat of the Turks, Ferdinand's troubles were by no means over, however, for **Lutheranism** was spreading at an alarming rate among the German-speaking lands. By the middle of the century it's estimated that Vienna was eighty percent Protestant. To combat this new plague, Ferdinand called in the fiercely proselytizing Jesuits in 1556. Nevertheless, the new creed flourished under the relatively liberal reign of **Maximilian II** (1564–76), and only after Rudolf II (1576–1612) moved the capital to Prague, leaving Archduke Ernst in charge of Vienna, did repressive measures force a turning of the tide.

When the **Thirty Years' War** broke out in 1618, Vienna was well on the way to becoming a Catholic city again, thanks partly to the Jesuits' stranglehold on the education system. By the time of the Peace of Westphalia in 1648, the city, which had emerged from the war relatively unscathed, was firmly under the grip of the Counter-Reformation, and those Viennese who would not renounce their Protestantism were forced into exile.

## The Siege of 1683

That the city managed to survive the **Siege of 1683** was no thanks to Emperor **Leopold I** (1657–1705), a profligate, bigoted man whose reign marked the beginning of the **Baroque era** in Vienna. Under Leopold, a whole new wing of the Hofburg was built, but the emperor is best known for his operatic extravaganzas – he himself was a keen composer – in particular the four-hour-long equestrian ballet he staged, just one of some four hundred theatrical events put on during his reign.

While Leopold was busy working out ways to spend more from the state's coffers, the priest Abraham à Santa Clara was busy preaching against such indulgences, not to mention against the Protestant, the Jew and the Turk – "an Epicurean piece of excrement" as he put it in one of his fiery sermons. In 1679, a plague claimed the lives of an estimated seventy thousand Viennese, and four years later, Vienna was to face the worst crisis in its history as the town was forced to endure its second siege by the Ottoman army. Naturally enough, at the approach of the Turks, Leopold, and anyone else who had the money, fled to the safety of Linz and Passau.

If anything, Vienna had more chance of surviving the Siege of 1683 than it had in 1529. The Turks were no longer at the zenith of their power and the city was properly fortified this time – in addition, a relief force of around eighty thousand was on its way, albeit rather slowly. Nevertheless, by mid-July, the city was confronted with an army of more than 150,000, including a harem of over 1500 concubines guarded by seven hundred black eunuchs, a contingent of clowns, and numerous poets trained in bawdy songs. The Viennese, protected by a garrison of just ten thousand men, were understandably ready to make peace with the grand vizier, **Kara Mustafa Pasha**.

The grand vizier's fatal flaw was overconfidence. Convinced that the city was his for the taking, and loath to share the booty among his army if he took the city by force, he orchestrated a two-month siege of Vienna. By September, however, a relief force of Poles, under their king, **Jan Sobieski**, and sundry German troops under the Duke of Lorraine, finally came to the aid of the city. On September 12, the papal legate Marco d'Aviano conducted a Mass on the hills above the city and, though outnumbered, the imperial forces managed to rout the Turks, in the process capturing 20,000 buffaloes, bullocks, camels and mules, 10,000 sheep, corn and flour, sugar, oil and most famously, coffee. Diamonds, rubies, sapphires and pearls, silver and gold, and "the most beautiful sable furs in the world", belonging to Kara Mustafa, fell into the grateful hands of King Sobieski. The grand vizier was discovered to have decapitated his favourite wife and his pet ostrich, rather than have them fall into the hands of the infidels, and, as was the custom in humiliating cases of defeat, he effected his own execution by allowing an emissary to strangle him with a silken cord in Belgrade on Christmas Day later that year.

# The eighteenth century

After the siege of 1683, Vienna could finally establish itself as the Habsburgs' permanent *Residenzstadt* or *Kaiserstadt*. Over the following years, **Baroque art and architecture** really took off, as extensive rebuilding of damaged churches, monasteries and palaces took place within the Innere Stadt. The Viennese aristocracy could also now at last build in the suburbs without fear of attack. Most famously the palace of **Schönbrunn** began to evolve, while Prince Eugène of Savoy (see p.133), who took command of the imperial forces and drove the Turks out of Hungary, built the Belvedere.

In keeping with the spirit of the age, **Emperor Karl VI** (1711–40) proved as spendthrift as his father Leopold, adding the magnificent Prunksaal library and the Winterreitschule to the Hofburg, and erecting Vienna's finest Baroque church, the Karlskirche (see p.104). The one area in which Karl VI singularly failed was in producing a male heir to the throne. In the end, the emperor had to accept the fact that his eldest daughter, Maria Theresia, was going to have to take over when he died. In an attempt to smooth her accession, Karl introduced the so-called Pragmatic Sanction in 1713, which allowed for female succession, and got all the states nominally within the Holy Roman Empire to promise to recognize his daughter's right to the Habsburgs' hereditary lands. Naturally enough, everyone agreed with the emperor while he was alive, and as soon as he died immediately went back on their word.

## Maria Theresia (1740–80)

So it was that **Maria Theresia** (see p.167) found herself forced to fight the **War of the Austrian Succession** (1740–48) as soon as she took over from her father.

For a while, she was even forced to hand over the imperial title to Karl of Bavaria in an attempt to pacify him, though it was eventually regained and handed to her husband, Franz Stephan of Lorraine (she herself, as a woman, could not become Holy Roman Emperor). At the end of the war in 1748, Maria Theresia was forced to cede Silesia to Prussia, and despite an attempt to win it back during the **Seven Years' War** (1756–63), it remained, for the most part, in Prussian hands.

On the domestic front, Maria Theresia's reign signalled the start of the **era of reform**, influenced by the ideas of the Enlightenment. To push through her reforms the empress created a formidable centralized bureaucracy, taking power away from the provincial Diets. When the pope abolished the Jesuit order in 1773, Maria Theresia took the opportunity to introduce a state education system. In 1776 she abolished torture, and passed de facto abolition of the death penalty (though hard labour usually killed the convict within a year in any case). Despite her reforms, it would be wrong to get the impression that the empress was some free-thinking democrat. She believed wholeheartedly in absolutism, and, as a devout Catholic, ensured Catholic supremacy within the empire with yet more anti-Protestant edicts.

## Josef II (1780–90)

With the death of her husband in 1765, Maria Theresia appointed her eldest son, Josef, as co-regent. But it wasn't until after the empress's death in 1780 that Josef's reforming zeal could come into its own (see p.77). His most significant edict was the 1781 **Toleranzpatent**, which allowed freedom of worship to Lutherans, Calvinists and the Greek Orthodox. Like his mother, he was himself a devout Catholic, but was even more determined to curtail Church – and particularly papal – power. To this end, he dissolved four hundred contemplative or "idle" monasteries, and, as many saw it, was bent on "nationalizing" the Church.

Under Josef II all religious processions (previously a daily occurrence on the streets of Vienna) were banned except the annual Corpus Christi procession. Pope Pius VI was so concerned he came to Vienna in person in 1782 to try to change the emperor's mind, but to no avail. With the best of intentions, Josef interfered in every aspect of his citizens' lives, causing widespread resentment. For – again like his mother – despite his enlightened policies, Josef was still very much the despot. He was, above all, responsible for creating the Habsburgs' secret police force, which was to become so infamous in the nineteenth century.

# The Napoleonic era

Emperor Leopold II, who unenthusiastically succeeded Josef II in 1790, died suddenly of a stroke after a reign of less than two years. As a result, Leopold's eldest son became **Emperor Franz II** (1792–1835). No great military man – his troops had been fighting the French for two years before he bothered to show himself at the front line – Franz was an unlikely candidate to become one of Napoleon's great adversaries.

In 1797, during his first Italian campaign, **Napoleon** succeeded in humiliating the Habsburg forces at Mantua, and was within a hundred miles of Vienna when the Habsburg emperor sued for peace. The scenario was repeated in 1800 when Napoleon's forces once more marched on Vienna. By 1803, the Habsburgs had lost the Netherlands and parts of northern Italy to the French. Napoleon added insult to injury by declaring himself emperor the following year, in an attempt to reestablish the Holy Roman Empire under French hegemony. In retaliation, Franz declared himself Emperor Franz I of Austria (a hitherto nonexistent title), though the gesture looked more like an admission of defeat, since Franz was already Holy Roman Emperor.

## The 1805 occupation of Vienna

In 1805, in alliance with Russia and Britain, Austria decided to take on Napoleon again, only to suffer a crushing defeat at Ulm. Unable to stop the advance of the *Grande Armée*, the allies decided to regroup further east, leaving Napoleon free to march on Vienna, where he arrived on November 13, 1805. The imperial family had already taken flight to Hungary, carrying the contents of the Hofburg with them. Though there was no fighting, the billeting of 34,000 French troops put an enormous strain on the city, and supplies quickly ran short. The French stayed until January 12, 1806, exacting taxes, war reparations and appropriating many works of art, including four hundred paintings from the Belvedere. Four days later, Franz returned to Vienna amid much rejoicing, though in political terms there was little to rejoice about.

During the French occupation, the Allies had lost the Battle of Austerlitz to Napoleon, and concluded the **Treaty of Pressburg**, leaving the Habsburgs without their Italian possessions, the Tyrol and the Vorarlberg. Further humiliation followed in 1806 when Napoleon established the Confederation of the Rhine, and Franz was forced to relinquish his title of Holy Roman Emperor.

## The 1809 occupation of Vienna

For the next few years, the Austrians had no hope of exacting revenge. But in the spring of 1809, with Napoleon encountering problems fighting Wellington in Spain, they seized the moment to reopen hostilities. Despite being once more defeated at Ratisbon, the Austrian forces under the emperor's brother, Archduke Karl, managed to regroup east of Vienna. Once more Napoleon was free to march on Vienna. As usual, the imperial family had taken flight to Hungary, but this time the city tried to defend itself. Napoleon reached the outskirts on May 10, 1809, and sent two emissaries to negotiate. They were promptly lynched by the Viennese; the French bombardment started the following evening. It was an uneven battle – "Our batteries shot off a few shots; they were ineffective," as one eyewitness stated; the French, for their part, fired some 1600 shells, and killed 23 civilians. The next day the city capitulated, its 16,000-strong garrison no match for the 100,000 French troops.

Despite taking Vienna, Napoleon's *Grande Armée* went on to suffer its first major defeat ten days later at the **Battle of Aspern**, just east of Vienna, at the hands of Archduke Karl. However, Karl failed to press home his advantage, and Napoleon held on to Vienna, going on to defeat the Austrians decisively six weeks later at the **Battle of Wagram**, when the Austrians threw in the towel. The city was forced to celebrate the new emperor's birthday on August 13, and in the peace, signed on October 14, the Austrians were obliged to give up Galicia and Croatia. Two days later Napoleon left Vienna, and on October 29, the French held a farewell ball. Towards the end of the following month, Emperor Franz crept back incognito into the Hofburg.

**Clemenz Metternich** became the chief minister of Austria, and began to pursue a policy of rapprochement. His greatest coup in this direction was getting Napoleon to marry Emperor Franz's 18-year-old daughter, Marie Louise, in March 1810. By 1813, with the tide turning against Napoleon, Metternich even managed to persuade his reluctant emperor to join the latest anti-French grand alliance.

# The 1815 Congress of Vienna

Vienna missed out on the rest of the Napoleonic wars, but was centre stage when it came to the peace. Following the defeat of Napoleon at Leipzig and his exile to Elba, the victorious powers met for the **Congress of Vienna** in the autumn of 1814. If nothing else, the congress was a great social success. The most public celebration took place on the anniversary of the Battle of Leipzig, when some twenty thousand war veterans were wined and dined alfresco in the Prater. All of Vienna was agog at the spectacle, but by New Year, most of the foreigners had outstayed their welcome. The congress was costing the emperor a fortune that even he could not afford, forcing him to raise taxes, while many of the participants

## The Congress of Vienna

The one time that Vienna truly occupied centre stage in European history was during the **Congress of Vienna**. In October 1814, two emperors, three kings, eleven princes, ninety ambassadors and fifty-three uninvited representatives congregated in Vienna under the chairmanship of Prince Metternich, to try to thrash out a balance of power following the collapse of the Napoleonic Empire. In addition to the "Big Four" of **Austria, Prussia, Britain and Russia**, there were innumerable smaller delegations, including thirty-two minor German royals, with their wives, mistresses and secretaries of state – there was even an unofficial deputation from the Jews of Frankfurt. Lord Castlereagh, Britain's chief emissary, thought the Congress would last four weeks at the most – in the end, it dragged on for nearly nine months. The Final Act of the Congress wasn't signed until June 1815, long after Napoleon's escape from Elba – "The Congress is dissolved," he announced on landing at Cannes – and just twelve days before the final showdown of Waterloo.

The Congress has gone down in history as the largest and longest party the city has ever seen, encapsulated in the famous quote by the Prince de Ligne*: "*Le congrès danse, mais il ne marche pas*" ("The Congress dances, but it doesn't work"). Empress Maria Ludovica, Franz I's wife, said the Congress cost her ten years of her life – and indeed she died within a year of its conclusion. In order to distract the lesser participants from the futility of the Congress, a vast programme of **entertainment** had to be organized. Ironically, the Austrian Emperor Franz I, who ultimately footed the bill, was no great party animal himself. Nevertheless, every night dinner was served in the Hofburg at forty tables; 1400 horses were required to transport the royal guests to the palace. There were tombolas, fireworks, tournaments, ballooning, theatre performances, sleighing expeditions in the Wienerwald, concerts – including the premiere of *Fidelio* conducted by Beethoven himself – and lots of dancing.

The Tsar, it was said, danced forty nights on the trot, his amorous adventures compounding his political rivalry with Metternich; the Russian Princess Bagration, nicknamed "the naked angel" for her habit of displaying her décolletage publicly, was voted the most beautiful; and Lord Castlereagh was deemed the most ridiculous. He was later joined by the Duke of Wellington, who hated the whole charade: "The hot rooms here have almost killed me," he wrote home. At one ball in the Hofburg, six thousand guests turned up instead of the three thousand invited, as the imperial bouncers had resold the tickets. Appropriately enough, the Congress's most lasting contribution to posterity was the popularization of **the waltz**. It was also during the Congress that **Brie de Meaux** was officially declared "*le roi des fromages*" by the Prince de Talleyrand during a cheese competition.

*The prince, who was in his eighties at the time, actually coined the epigram even before the Congress had begun, repeating it on every possible occasion until his death in December, brought on by a cold contracted while waiting outside his house for his latest mistress.

were living on credit notes. Nevertheless, it dragged on until after Napoleon escaped from Elba, finally winding itself up in May 1815.

Despite the shenanigans, the congress did, in fact, manage fairly successfully to establish a status quo in Europe. Many of the borders agreed upon in Vienna were to endure for over a century. In the peace deal, Austria won back much of North Italy and Galicia, Croatia, Salzburg, the Tyrol and the Vorarlberg, although on Metternich's advice, claims over the Netherlands and other far-flung territories that would be hard to defend, were relinquished. The congress also pledged itself to further regular meetings between the heads of the victorious states – meetings at which it was agreed that in order to maintain international peace, they would combine to suppress any further revolutionary uprisings within Europe.

# Biedermeier Vienna

Following the congress, Vienna enjoyed more than thirty years of peace and stability, a period known retrospectively as the *Vormärz* – literally "pre-March", because it preceded the March 1848 revolution. The same stretch of time is also known throughout the German-speaking lands as the **Biedermeier era** (for more on the origin of the term, see p.282). In later years, the Viennese would look back on this period through rose-tinted spectacles as a time of introspective domesticity, played out to the tunes of Johann Strauss the Elder and the melodies of Franz Schubert.

As ever, there is more than a grain of truth in the myth, as in the counter-myth that this was one of the most oppressive regimes in the history of the Habsburgs. The man most closely associated with the conservative and reactionary politics of the Biedermeier era was **Metternich**. Under him, and his "poodle" – the chief of police Count Josef Sedlnitzky – the vast machinery of the Josephine civil service, which had been designed to help push through reforms, was now used to thwart any further change. Censorship and the activities of the secret police and its informers did so much to stifle intellectual life that by 1848 the playwright Franz Grillparzer reflected miserably, "Despotism has destroyed my life, at least my literary life."

With the death of the emperor Franz I in 1835, the Habsburgs faced something of a crisis, as the heir to the throne, **Ferdinand I** – a victim of Habsburg inbreeding – was, in the vocabulary of the day, an "imbecile", nicknamed *Nandl der Trottel* ("Ferdy the Dotty"). He was, in fact, nothing of the sort: he could be perfectly coherent, but suffered badly from epilepsy, which affected his short-term memory. To combat the latter's deficiencies, a Regency Council was established, with Ferdinand as chair – or in his absence his brother, Archduke Ludwig – and his brother Franz Karl, Count Kolowrat and Metternich as permanent members. Within the council Metternich had to struggle to maintain his influence.

# The 1848 revolution

With the deposition of the French king and the outbreak of revolution in Paris in late February **1848**, it was only a question of time before matters came to a head in the other European capitals. Vienna, now a city of 400,000, suffered from chronic overcrowding (though this was nothing new), and sporadic food shortages, yet it still came as some surprise when it became the first city to follow in the footsteps of the French. On **March 13**, the Estates of Lower Austria, consisting of nobles and senior clergy, were due to meet in the Landhaus on Herrengasse. They were pressing for various reforms, including the freedom of the press, but top of the agenda was the removal of Metternich. In the morning a crowd gathered outside the Landhaus, and, after listening to a German translation of the inflammatory speech given recently by the Hungarian revolutionary Lajos Kossuth in the Hungarian Diet, forced their way into the building. At around 1pm, a detachment of Italian grenadiers fired into the crowd, killing around thirty unarmed protesters, mostly students, and sparking off a revolution.

That evening, after playing for time, Metternich finally resigned and fled from the capital (disguised as a washerwoman, according to popular legend). The emperor – who when told of the outbreak of revolution had apparently said "But do they have permission?" – immediately made a rapid retreat, declaring "Tell the people I agree to everything." A **National Guard** was formed by the revolutionaries – with Johann Strauss the Younger as *Kapellmeister* – augmented by an academic legion of armed students, with whom they were to man the city in place of the despised imperial troops. Meanwhile, the imperial court promised a constitution, and a "Responsible Ministry" of bureaucrats was formed to produce it. On April 25, the court proposed a constitutional monarchy, with two chambers elected by limited franchise based on property, and with the emperor permitted to veto any laws. Not surprisingly, the idea was out of kilter with the popular revolutionary mood and rioting, in favour of a single-chamber parliament elected by universal suffrage, ensued on May 15. The National Guard erected barricades around the city, and the emperor and his entourage quickly fled to Innsbruck in a stagecoach.

Elections were duly held throughout the empire (with the exception of Italy and Hungary, each busy with its own revolution) and the first **parliament** in Habsburg history met in the unlikely surroundings of the Hofburg's Winterreitschule on July 22. The deputies were by no means revolutionaries, the majority coming from the educated middle classes, with close to a third of peasant origin. Hampered throughout by disputes between the various nationalities, the assembly did manage to pass one lasting piece of legislation: the emancipation of the peasantry. By August, the court felt secure enough to return to Vienna, bolstered by General Radetzky's military victory over the rebels in Italy and the recapture of Prague by General Windischgrätz.

The spark that lit the final fuse of the Viennese revolution took place on **October 6**. A battalion, due to be sent to fight against Kossuth's Hungarian revolutionaries, mutinied and joined forces with radicals in the National Guard. Civil war then broke out as some within the National Guard fired on the radicals. In the confusion, the war minister, General Latour, was lynched by the mob (see p.60), and the imperial family removed themselves once more, this time to Olomouc in Moravia. As Windischgrätz marched his troops towards the capital, the radicals among the academic legion and the National Guard erected barricades and awaited the final showdown. Their only hope lay in the possibility of a Hungarian relief force, which in the event arrived too late. After several days' bombardment and around two thousand casualties, Windischgrätz flushed out the last of the rebels on October 31.

# The reign of Franz-Josef I

Meanwhile, back in Olomouc, the emperor Ferdinand (and his brother Franz Karl) was coerced by the imperial family into renouncing the throne in favour of the latter's 18-year-old nephew, **Franz-Josef** (see p.72). A new government was formed under the leadership of the arch-conservative Prince Felix Schwarzenberg, while the assembly continued to meet in the nearby Moravian town of Kremsier (Kroměříž to try to thrash out a new constitution. Then, to the astonishment of the assembly, Schwarzenberg announced on February 28, 1849, that as the emperor had himself formulated a new constitution, their services were no longer required. Although the new constitution granted equal rights to all, it was anything but liberal, granting the emperor the power of veto over all legislation, the power to dissolve parliament and rule by decree, and the power to dismiss and appoint ministers as he saw fit. Meanwhile in Hungary, the Austrians were forced to swallow their pride and enlist the help of the Russians in order to defeat Kossuth's Hungarian revolutionaries once and for all.

In the immediate aftermath of the revolution, it was decided to strengthen the fortifications of the city. Eventually, though, the tide of opinion in the government shifted in favour of tearing down the walls, to prevent a repeat of October 1848 when the revolutionaries had managed to resist the forces of law and order. Finally, in 1857, the emperor decreed that the walls were to come down, and a **Ringstrasse** constructed in their place, lined with noble institutions (see p.86). This wide boulevard remains Franz-Josef's most significant architectural legacy, though its final sections were not completed until the last decade of his reign.

## 1866 and all that

After some ten years of relative peace, Franz-Josef suffered his first of many embarrassing military setbacks at the Battle of Solferino in 1859. It was not so much the resultant loss of Lombardy that was the problem, but the opportunity it gave the Hungarians to demand their independence once more. In an attempt to placate them, Franz-Josef agreed in 1861 to establish a two-chamber parliament in Vienna. The Hungarians remained unimpressed and failed to send delegates to fill any of their 85 allotted seats in the lower house.

Five years later, the empire was rocked by an even greater crisis with its army's humiliating defeat at the **Battle of Königgrätz** in the Austro-Prussian War. Not only did the Habsburgs lose forever the battle for hegemony over the rest of Germany, but they were finally forced to strike a deal with the Hungarians (while studiously ignoring the demands of the empire's other nationalities).

With the 1867 **Ausgleich** or Compromise, the so-called Dual Monarchy of Austria-Hungary was established. According to this new arrangement, Franz-Josef was to be crowned king of Hungary (he was already emperor of Austria), and the Hungarians were to get their own parliament in Budapest, with autonomy over everything except defence, foreign affairs and the overall imperial budget. Everything within Hungary was to be prefaced with a "k." for *königlich*, everything in the rest of the empire was to be prefaced with the initials "k.k." or *kaiserlich-königlich* (imperial-royal), while everything Austro-Hungarian was prefaced with "k.u.k." or *kaiserlich-und-königlich*.

Meanwhile, delegates from the "Austrian" half of the empire met in Vienna's **parliament** (see p.93). Among the delegates were Czechs, Poles, Croats, Slovenes, Italians and German-speakers from every corner of the empire, who spent most of their time arguing over language issues and abusing each other both verbally and physically. The number of people eligible to vote increased gradually until universal male suffrage was finally introduced in 1907, but in reality, the emperor still ruled supreme since he and his ministers could pass any laws they wanted as "emergency measures", not to mention dissolve parliament and rule by decree (which they did on numerous occasions).

To make matters worse, the economy suffered its worst financial crisis ever in the crash of May 1873, shortly after Vienna's **Weltausstellung** or World Exhibition opened in the Prater (see p.151). The 72 banks in Vienna were reduced to eight in the ensuing decade; construction of the Ring was halted and the big projects – the Parliament, Rathaus, Burgtheater and Universität – were only completed in the 1880s. The empire's industrialization was also affected; railway construction reached an annual low of 75km of new track in 1880, with a severe knock-on effect on other heavy industries.

# Fin-de-siècle Vienna

Between 1860 and the turn of the century, Vienna more than trebled in size, its population topping two million. Like most industrialized cities of the period, it was a city of enormous contrasts. Wealth and power were in the hands of the upper aristocracy, who alone had an entrée into court society, and exercised enormous influence over the careers of individuals through the system of *Protektion* or patronage. Meanwhile, the bulk of the population, many of them recently arrived immigrants from other parts of the empire, were packed like sardines in the *Mietkaserne* (rent barracks) of the newly built suburbs. At the bottom of the heap were the nocturnal *Bettgeher*, the five percent of the population who could afford only to rent someone else's bed from them during the day.

A significant proportion of the new immigrants were Jews from the empire's rural *shtetls* (small, predominantly Jewish towns). By the turn of the century they made up nearly ten percent of the population. In some walks of life, they comprised an even greater percentage: more than half of all the city's doctors and lawyers were Jews, as were most of its journalists and bankers. The Jew had long been a stock Viennese scapegoat (see p.61). Now with the 1873 crash – the fault, it was said, of Jewish financiers – and the continuing influx of Orthodox Jews into the city, **anti-Semitism** began to flourish. It found a spokesman in the pan-German nationalist **Georg von Schönerer**, whose fanatical followers used to wear the effigy of a hanged Jew on their watch chains. Schönerer's political career faltered, however, after 1888 when he was sent to prison for breaking into the offices of the Jewish-owned newspaper, the *Neues Wiener Tagblatt*.

Anti-Semitism was given a more respectable, populist twist by **Karl Lueger** (see p.92). This Vienna-born politician became leader of the Christian Social Party, whose combination of Catholicism, anti-Semitism and municipal socialism went down alarmingly well with the Viennese electorate. In 1897, Lueger became mayor of Vienna, and the crowd that turned out for his funeral in 1910 was the largest the city had ever seen – among the mourners was the young **Adolf Hitler** (see p.101).

Most middle-class Jews, understandably, gravitated towards the other side of the political spectrum, dominating the upper echelons of the **Social Democratic Workers' Party** (SDAP), after it was founded in 1889. The party's chief ideologue before World War I was the Prague-born Jew Viktor Adler, whose peculiar ideology of **Austro-Marxism** was to dominate the party's thinking for the next half-century. As far as Adler was concerned capitalism was doomed to failure, so the party could afford to adopt a peaceful approach to politics until the time was right for revolution.

Amid all the tensions between Right and Left, Jew and Gentile, rich and poor, **fin-de-siècle Vienna** also succeeded in nurturing intellectual and artistic creativity such as the city had never known, much of it inspired by the assimilated Jews. **Arnold Schönberg**, and his followers **Alban Berg** and **Anton Webern**, changed the face of classical music with their atonal – or as Schönberg preferred,

253

"pantonal" – revolution (see p.104). **Gustav Mahler**, meanwhile, turned heads both as a composer and as boss of the Staatsoper. In medicine, **Sigmund Freud** (see p.146) coined the term "psychoanalysis", and expounded on the new discipline in his seminal *Interpretation of Dreams*. In 1897 **Gustav Klimt** led a revolt against the artistic establishment, known as the Secession; following in his footsteps were the likes of **Egon Schiele** and **Oskar Kokoschka**. Otto Wagner left the most visible legacy of this period, in the **Jugendstil** and early modernist buildings still to be seen on the streets of Vienna today. For more on the Secession, see the colour section in this book.

# World War I

On June 28, 1914, the heir to the throne, **Archduke Franz Ferdinand** and his wife, Sophie, were assassinated in Sarajevo by Bosnian Serbs, with weapons supplied by the chief of Serbia's army intelligence. There was little genuine sadness in court circles, for as Stefan Zweig bluntly put it, "The archduke Franz Ferdinand lacked everything that counts for real popularity in Austria: amiability, personal charm and easy-goingness." Even his uncle, Emperor Franz-Josef, was more relieved than anything else, as the two got on famously badly.

To begin with, there was also very little action by Austria on the diplomatic front, but eventually, on July 28, Franz-Josef and his ministers sent an ultimatum to Serbia, with an impossible set of conditions and a 48-hour time limit. As Serbia could not agree to all the conditions, Austria-Hungary declared war on her. The Russians immediately mobilized to defend their Slav brothers, with Britain and France, Russia's allies, following suit. By August 4, the major European powers were at war.

Perhaps surprisingly, the outbreak of war brought patriotic crowds on to the streets of Vienna, and other cities around the empire, with Left and Right alike rallying round the Habsburg cause. Of course, everyone thought the affair would be over by Christmas; only after years of military defeats, huge casualties and food shortages did the population begin to turn against the war. On October 21, 1916, Viktor Adler's son Friedrich took matters into his own hands and assassinated the Austrian prime minister, **Count Karl Stürgkh** (see p.48). At his trial in May the following year, Friedrich Adler gave such a damning indictment of the war that his execution was postponed so as not to boost the antiwar cause further. On November 21, 1916, Franz-Josef finally died at the age of 86, leaving the throne to his 29-year-old great-nephew Karl.

**Emperor Karl I** is perhaps best known for his bungled attempt to negotiate a separate peace for his empire with the western allies in March 1917. The approach was rebuffed at the time and a year later became public knowledge, causing huge embarrassment to all concerned. Only victory on the battlefield could now save the dynasty, but it was not to come.

In October 1918, the empire began to crumble from within, with national committees taking over the regional capitals. In Vienna, the Social Democrats, who were in favour of self-determination for the empire's various nationalities, set up a provisional government under Karl Renner. On November 2, 1918, with the end of the war in sight, the Hungarian battalion guarding Schönbrunn upped and left, leaving the imperial family and their servants unguarded. The next day an armistice was signed, and eight days later, Emperor Karl I agreed to sign away his powers, withdrawing first to Eckartsau outside Vienna, and eventually, in 1919, going into exile in Switzerland.

# The First Republic

The Austrian Republic – or more correctly **Deutsch-Österreich** or "German Austria" – was proclaimed from the steps of Vienna's parliament on November 12, 1918 (see p.94). The colours chosen for the national flag – red, white, red – were those of the Babenbergs. At first, however, there was precious little enthusiasm for the new country among its people. The Christian Socials wanted a constitutional monarchy, the Pan-Germans wanted Anschluss with Germany, while the Socialists wanted Anschluss with a Socialist Germany. In the proclamation of November 12, the country was even described as "a constituent part of the German Republic". In the regions, both the Tyrol and Salzburg voted overwhelmingly in favour of Anschluss with Germany (requests that were denied by the international community), while the Vorarlberg voted to join the Swiss.

In February 1919, the first national elections took place, creating a coalition government of the SDAP and the Christian Socials under the chancellorship of Social Democrat **Karl Renner**. Nevertheless a political vacuum continued until the end of the year, with soldiers' and workers' councils threatening to follow the revolutionary soviet example of neighbouring Bavaria and Hungary. There were even two unsuccessful attempts by the newly formed Austrian Communist Party (KPÖ) to stage a putsch, in April and June 1919.

The new government's foremost task was to feed the population, particularly that of Vienna. Deprived of its former territories, and hampered by a bad harvest, they managed it only with the help of the Allied Famine Relief programme. The government's next most arduous job was to negotiate the **Treaty of St-Germain**

THE BREAK-UP OF THE AUSTRO-HUNGARIAN EMPIRE 1918

with the victorious allies. Many in the delegation still hoped for Anschluss with Germany, but it was not to be. The Austrians (along with the Hungarians) were branded an "enemy state", while the rest of the so-called "successor states" like Czechoslovakia were not, and were expressly forbidden ever to undertake Anschluss with Germany. With his oft-quoted remark, Georges Clemenceau summed up the Austrians' lack of a bargaining position when he pointed to the map and said, "What's left is Austria."

## Red Vienna

Vienna began the war with an ethnically diverse population of 2.1 million, as imperial capital of a multinational empire of 52 million; by the end of the war, the city's population was down to 1.8 million, and it was head of a country of just 6.4 million. Only two significant minorities remained: Czechs and Jews, who together made up around twenty percent of the total population. The Czechs, who now had their own independent motherland, enjoyed the status of a protected minority, leaving the Jews to serve once more as chief scapegoat.

This situation was exacerbated by the very visible presence of around 25,000 Jewish refugees from Galicia, poverty-stricken pedlars whose Orthodox garb made them all the more conspicuous. At the same time, the much larger assimilated Jewish population, who were prominent in the arts, the media and the SDAP, became the target of vicious **anti-Semitism** from the Christian Social and Pan-German parties. The cleric Ignaz Seipel, head of the Christian Socials and among the most vociferous anti-Semites, flirted with the idea of re-ghettoizing the Jews. This sort of rhetoric was a permanent feature of the First Republic, which the SDAP consistently failed to tackle head-on.

In the municipal elections of May 1919, the Social Democrats won 54 percent of the vote, and Vienna got its first Socialist mayor, **Jakob Reumann**. The party held power in the capital for nearly fifteen years, a period which has gone down in history as **Rotes Wien** or "Red Vienna" (see p.185). Their social reforms have since become legendary, but their most visible legacy is the huge housing estates like the Karl-Marx-Hof (see p.184) that ring the city.

Meanwhile, in the national elections of June 1920, the SDAP–Christian Social coalition broke down, and in fresh elections in October that year, the latter came out as the biggest single party. The two parties remained at loggerheads throughout the 1920s, with the extremist Pan-German Greater German People's Party a further destabilizing element.

## Paramilitary politics

For most of the First Republic, then, the country remained split between the heavily industrialized Social Democrat capital of Vienna, where some thirty percent of the population lived, and the deeply conservative, Catholic, rural *Länder* where the Christian Socials dominated. What made this political polarization all the more dangerous was that by the mid-1920s both sides were backed up by **paramilitary organizations**, as if the country were at civil war.

On the one hand, the right-wing **Heimwehr** had their origins in armed groups that defended Austria's borders in the chaotic early days of the republic. Based on individual *Länder* and each with their own leader, the Heimwehr organizations didn't share a political platform but were united in their opposition to the Left. On the other hand, the Social Democrats had created the republic's first ad hoc army, the Volkswehr, in the last weeks of the war. They continued to dominate the Volkswehr until it was replaced by the establishment of the official Austrian army or Bundeswehr. As a result, the SDAP eventually formed its own armed division, the **Schutzbund**, in 1923. Throughout the 1920s the party mouthed the rhetoric of class war, while pursuing moderate, social democratic policies. In 1926, the party went even further and declared itself ready to use force if necessary to protect the interests of the workers. The bourgeois press interpreted this as a call for revolution, though the slogan coined by Otto Bauer was "Democratic as long as we can be; dictatorship only if we are forced to it, and insofar as we are forced." To the dismay of many on the left, the SDAP proved itself much less willing to resort to violence than its right-wing foes.

On July 14, 1927, three right-wing activists were acquitted of murdering a socialist man and boy. The next day several thousand workers spontaneously descended on the **Justizpalast** (see p.94) and set fire to it. Taken by surprise by the size of the demonstration, the mounted police panicked and fired point-blank into the crowd. In the ensuing chaos, 89 people were killed, and up to a thousand wounded, and the Justizpalast burned to the ground. The SDAP called an indefinite national strike, but refused to call out the Schutzbund. With the heavily armed Heimwehr acting as strike-breakers, the general strike was easily crushed and civil war was postponed for a few more years.

## Austro-fascism

The onset of the Great Depression further destabilized what was already a fragile democracy. In the elections of November 1930, the Heimwehr, under Prince Starhemberg, won its first parliamentary seats for its newly formed political wing, the Heimatblock. The Social Democrats, meanwhile, emerged for the first time since 1919 as the largest single party, with 41 percent of the vote, but once more it was the Christian Socials who went on to form a series of weak coalition governments. The last of these was formed in May 1932 under the chancellorship of **Engelbert Dollfuss**, with a parliamentary majority of just one.

On March 4, 1933, in an attempt to break a tied vote in parliament, the Social Democrat Karl Renner resigned as Speaker in order to free himself to vote. When Renner's two deputy speakers from the Christian Social and Pan-German parties both followed suit, Dollfuss seized the opportunity to dissolve parliament, claiming it could no longer function properly. The same weekend, Adolf Hitler won an absolute majority in the German parliament. The onset of **Nazism** had a sobering effect on the majority of Austrians, particularly the SDAP, which immediately dropped their call for Anschluss.

On March 15, Dollfuss sent the police in to prevent parliament from reconvening. In response, the SDAP leadership procrastinated and held back from calling in the Schutzbund; two weeks later the latter was outlawed. Dollfuss was determined to combat the threat from Nazi Germany, but instead of agreeing to an anti-Nazi alliance with the SDAP, the chancellor threw in his lot with Mussolini, holding the first of many meetings with the Italian dictator in April. On May 21, no doubt prompted by Mussolini, Dollfuss established the Austro-fascist **Fatherland Front** (Vaterländische Front or VF), under the slogan "Austria Awake!"

In May the Communist Party was banned and in July the Austrian Nazi Party was outlawed. A violent showdown with the Social Democrats, who still controlled the Vienna city council, followed in **February 1934** (Februaraufstand). The first incident took place in Linz, where the local Schutzbund, on their own initiative, opened fire on the police. A three-day battle ensued, with the bloodiest set-to in Vienna's **Karl-Marx-Hof** housing estate, which Dollfuss eventually ordered the army to bomb into submission. The SDAP had stumbled into civil war and it was soundly beaten. The party was swiftly outlawed, and its leaders fled abroad or were imprisoned.

Just as it appeared he had successfully established an Austro-fascist state, Dollfuss was assassinated on July 25, 1934 (see p.58), during the **Juliputsch**, an abortive coup d'état staged by Austrian Nazis, apparently without the knowledge of Hitler. His successor, **Kurt Schuschnigg**, was forced to rely ever more heavily on Mussolini for support. As a foreign policy this proved disastrous, for in 1935 Hitler and Mussolini began to patch up their differences, and suddenly Schuschnigg found himself being urged by Mussolini to come to an agreement with Hitler. Schuschnigg did just that in the Austro-German agreement of July 11, 1936. In return for Hitler's recognition of Austria's "full sovereignty", Schuschnigg agreed to an amnesty of all Nazi prisoners, and the appointment of various "prominent nationalists" – not Nazis, but fellow travellers – to his government.

In January 1938, the Austrian police raided the apartment of Leopold Tavs, one of Schuschnigg's deputies, and discovered a plan to overthrow the government with German help. As tension between the two countries mounted, the Nazi ambassador, Franz von Papen, suggested Schuschnigg should visit Hitler at his mountain retreat at Berchtesgaden near the Austrian border. At this meeting, Schuschnigg was given one of Hitler's command performances in which he ranted and raved and eventually demanded, among other things, that Schuschnigg hand over yet more key governmental posts to the Austrian Nazi Party. Schuschnigg acquiesced and agreed to appoint the Nazi **Dr Arthur Seyss-Inquart** interior minister.

As the Austrian Nazis increased their activities, Schuschnigg decided to chance his arm with a **plebiscite** to decide the country's future, reckoning (probably correctly) that the majority would vote against the Anschluss. Hitler was certainly not prepared to risk electoral defeat and swiftly demanded the resignation of Schuschnigg and his entire government. Schuschnigg announced his resignation over the radio, in order to avoid "spilling German blood", and Seyss-Inquart took over the chancellorship. President Wilhelm Miklas refused to agree to the latter's appointment and resigned, and Seyss-Inquart wasted no time in inviting the German army into the country on the pretext of preventing civil war.

# Anschluss and World War II

In the event, there was no bloodshed: **German troops invaded Austria** on March 12, 1938, and encountered no resistance whatsoever. Hitler himself began his slow and triumphant journey to the capital in the wake of his troops. First he visited his birthplace of Braunau-am-Inn, then he moved on to his "home town" of Linz, where he was received with such enthusiasm by the locals that he decided there and then to immediately incorporate Austria into the Greater German Reich, rather than pursue the more conciliatory path of preserving Austrian autonomy. Eventually, on March 15, Hitler appeared on the balcony of the Hofburg before thousands of jubilant Viennese.

As a propaganda exercise, Hitler also decided to go ahead with Schuschnigg's plebiscite, which took place on April 10. The 99 percent "Yes" vote in favour of the **Anschluss** came as no surprise, with less than two thousand Viennese voting "No". To be fair, those known to be opposed to the Nazis, including Schuschnigg and his followers, had already been arrested – some 76,000 by the time Hitler arrived in Vienna – while Jews and other "undesirables" were barred from voting. On the other hand, many whom one would expect to have opposed the Anschluss publicly declared themselves in favour, including the archbishop of Vienna, Cardinal Theodor Innitzer, and the Social Democrat, Karl Renner.

Although the Treaty of St-Germain precluded any Anschluss with Germany, only the Soviet Union and Mexico lodged any formal international protest against the invasion. Meanwhile, the very name of Austria was wiped off the map, initially replaced by the term "**Ostmark**", but eventually simply divided into seven *Gaue* or districts, ruled by Nazi *Gauleiter*.

## The fate of Vienna's Jews

In the words of eyewitness George Clare, the Anschluss unleashed a "volcanic outburst of popular anti-Semitism". Jews were dragged out into the street, physically assaulted and humiliated, and then forced to scrub Schuschnigg slogans off the walls. In one instance in the well-to-do suburb of Währing, a group of Nazis urinated on local Jewish women as they forced them to scrub the streets in front of cheering onlookers. A large number of the city's most prominent Jews were arrested immediately, and either sent to concentration camps, or released with orders to leave the country.

In May, the Nuremberg Laws were introduced. Without warning, two thousand Jews were arrested and shipped off to Dachau, primarily to encourage still more Jews to emigrate. On the night of November 10–11 – dubbed **Kristallnacht** or "Crystal Night" – the majority of synagogues in the Reich were torched, and numerous Jewish premises ransacked. Another 6500 Jews were arrested that night, 4600 of whom were sent to Dachau. By the outbreak of World War II, more than half of Vienna's Jews had emigrated.

Once the Nazis had invaded Poland, their policy towards the Jews changed, favouring deportation to the death camps, via ghettos, over forced emigration. Deportations began in earnest in February 1941, while emigration came to a complete standstill in November 1941. Of the 65,000 Jews now left in Austria, more than half had been sent to the death camps by June 1942. By the end of the war, around two hundred or so Austrian Jews had managed to survive in hiding, with just over two thousand returning from the camps after the war.

## Collaboration and resistance

Seyss-Inquart was initially appointed *Reichsstatthalter* (Governor) of Vienna, but was transferred to Poland after the outbreak of the war, and eventually ended up in control of the Netherlands, where as *Reichskommissar* he oversaw countless atrocities for which he was hanged at the Nuremberg war trials. Control of Vienna was eventually handed over to the dashing young German lieutenant, **Baldur von Schirach**, whose artistic pretensions – he wrote poetry – were considered highly suitable for Viennese sensibilities. Schirach made the most of his position, moving into the sumptuous governmental offices on Ballhausplatz, employing no fewer than seventeen chambermaids, and entertaining official visitors in lavish style in the Hofburg.

Although Hitler preferred to import German Nazis to fill many positions within the Austrian Nazi hierarchy, party membership was higher in Austria than in Germany, and Austrians themselves provided more than their ten percent population ratio of concentration-camp guards. The Linz-born Nazi **Adolf Eichmann**, who ran Vienna's "Central Office for Jewish Emigration" (see p.137) and was one of the architects of the "Final Solution", is probably the most infamous, though *Schindler's List* also increased the notoriety of the Vienna-born camp commandant Amon Goeth. Another Linz-born Nazi, Ernst Kaltenbrunner, rose to Heinrich Himmler's number two in the SS, while the Carinthian Odilo Globocnik – one-time *Gauleiter* of Vienna – with ninety fellow Austrians on his staff, supervised the deaths of some two million Jews in the extermination camps of Sobibor, Treblinka and Belzec.

Organized **resistance** to Hitler was, it has to be said, extraordinarily difficult for anti-Nazi Austrians, given the level of collaboration among their fellow citizens, and the efficiency with which the Nazis had wiped out the potential leadership. Aside from individual acts of heroism, there was very little significant non-Communist resistance within Austria. Partisan activity was restricted to a few remote alpine areas, and not until the spring of 1944 did an organized home resistance, code-named **O5**, begin to emerge.

Unlike every other Nazi-occupied country, however, the Austrians had no official government-in-exile. Exiled Austrian politicians spent their time bickering, split between an unlikely alliance between the son of the last emperor, Otto von Habsburg, and the Communists, and the two mainstream political parties. The most significant diplomatic step took place in November 1943, when the Allied powers published the **Moscow Declaration** stating that Austria was a "victim" of Nazi aggression and that it should be re-established as a "free and democratic state".

## The liberation of Vienna

Vienna itself remained relatively free from direct contact with the war until 1944, when **Allied bombing raids** intensified. Over the next fourteen months, they were responsible for the deaths of nine thousand Viennese civilians. Important buildings hit included the Staatsoper, the Belvedere, the Burgtheater, Schönbrunn, the Rathaus, Parlament and the Universität; Stephansdom fell victim to Soviet artillery in the last few days of liberation.

By April 5, 1945, the Red Army was nearing the outskirts of the city. The O5 leadership under Major Szokoll had planned to initiate an uprising against the Nazis the very next day, but were betrayed by a junior officer, Lieutenant Walter Hanslick. Several O5 leaders were arrested, tortured and publicly hanged. The revolt had failed and it took the Russians another three days to reach the *Gürtel*, and another five days' street fighting to finally win control of the city.

The commander-in-chief of Russian troops in Austria, **Marshal Tolbukhin**, gave his assurances that the Soviets would liberate the country, respect the social order and refrain from appropriating any territory. In reality, Soviet troops spent much of the next few months raping Austrian women and stealing anything they could find. The actions of the Red Army during this period gave rise to the grim Viennese joke that Austria could probably survive a third world war, but it could never endure a second liberation.

# Allied Occupation (1945–55)

On April 27, the Soviets sponsored the formation of a provisional government under the veteran Social Democrat **Karl Renner**, causing widespread alarm about Soviet intentions among the western Allies. Although Renner's cabinet was made up, for the most part, of Socialists and members of the newly founded right-wing People's Party or ÖVP, the Communists were given three posts, including the key positions of interior minister and education and information minister. As a form of protest at this unilateral action, the western Allies refused to recognize the Renner government.

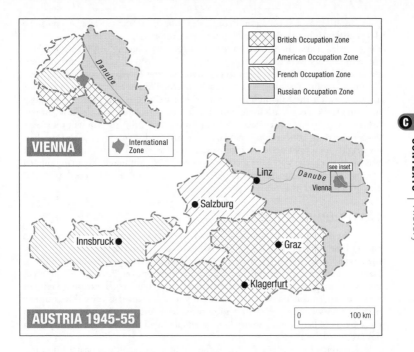

British Occupation Zone
American Occupation Zone
French Occupation Zone
Russian Occupation Zone

*Danube*

VIENNA    International Zone

see inset

Linz    *Danube*
Vienna

● Salzburg

Innsbruck ●    ● Graz

● Klagenfurt

AUSTRIA 1945-55    0    100 km

Meanwhile, there was continuing confusion over the occupation zones. Although the Moscow Declaration had stated that Austria was a victim of Nazi aggression, the country was nevertheless to be divided just like Germany, with Vienna, as Berlin, lying deep within the Russian sector. However, controversy over the exact zoning of Vienna helped delay the arrival of Western troops in the capital until late August. The Russians took the opportunity to fleece the capital and eastern Austria of all they could. Vienna, it was agreed, was to be divided between the four Allies, with the Innere Stadt preserved as an international sector, patrolled by one representative of each of the occupying powers. This comical sight on the streets of Vienna became the hallmark of the so-called **"four-in-a-jeep" period**, and the setting for *The Third Man*. As Karl Renner put it, Vienna was like a small rowing boat in which four elephants sat at the oars pulling in various directions.

## Elections and de-Nazification

In October the western Allies finally recognized the Renner government, and the Russians, for their part, agreed to free elections. However, whatever hopes they might have had of the Communists gaining power in Austria were dashed by the results of the **November 1945 elections**. The Communists won a derisory 5.4 percent of the vote, up from their previous high of 1.9 percent in 1932, but earning them just four seats in the 165-seat parliament, and the consolation prize of the Ministry of Electrification. In an almost exact repeat of the election results of the 1920s, the country remained split down the middle between Left and Right. Although the ÖVP won almost fifty percent of the vote, it was Renner who headed the new coalition government of the Socialist Party (SPÖ) and the ÖVP.

One of the most pressing and controversial tasks of the postwar era was the **de-Nazification** process. Initially, this was the responsibility of the Allied powers: the Americans and the British busied themselves by handing out forms in which the respondents were invited to confess; the French, with collaborators of their own back home, were less keen to get involved; the Russians, predictably, were the most assiduous, though they were as concerned to remove political opponents as ex-Nazis. Of the half-million Austrians who were Nazi Party members, only a handful were executed at Nuremberg (for crimes committed outside Austria); von Schirach was given twenty years. Back in Austria itself, the government took over de-Nazification, condemning 38 Nazis to death, and depriving the rest of their civil rights for a brief period before an amnesty was agreed in 1948. Some attempt was made to rid the state bureaucracy of its ex-Nazis, but inevitably many slipped through the net, Eichmann among them, though he was later kidnapped, tried and executed in Israel in 1962.

## Communist agitation

When the Red Army liberated Vienna in April 1945, few people expected the city and the country to remain under **Allied occupation** for ten years. However, the Soviets were keen to pay back the Austrians for their mass participation in the Nazi armed forces. At the postwar Potsdam conference, the Soviets were granted, instead of cash reparations for war damage, the right to all external German assets in eastern Austria. Over the next ten years, the Russians took this as a carte blanche to asset-strip the entire region of eastern Austria, transporting factories piece by piece back to the Soviet Union, and all in all reaping some half a billion dollars' worth of assets.

Soviet control of eastern Austria – the country's agricultural heartland – also gave them considerable political leverage. With the entire country suffering chronic **food shortages**, the Soviets deliberately hoarded supplies from their sector, supplying them direct to workers in Soviet-run industries. This won them considerable support in the eastern zone, and increased unrest in the western zones. For despite the Communists' electoral setback, the Russians still had hopes of taking control of Austria. The winter of 1946–47 was particularly harsh, and the Communists took advantage by fomenting food riots in May 1947. Rioters besieged the Austrian chancellery and called for a national strike. In the end the putsch failed, because the Socialist trade-union leaders refused to support the strike, and the Russians held back from using military force.

While **Marshall Plan** aid from the west helped ease conditions throughout Austria from the summer of 1947 onwards, the Communist coup in Czechoslovakia in February 1948 and the Berlin blockade (June 1948–May 1949) only increased political tensions. Despite their recent setbacks, the Communists had high hopes for the national elections of October 1949. However, though the ruling coalition lost ground, it wasn't to the Communists, who remained on a derisory five percent, but to the newly formed, extreme right-wing **Union of Independents** (VdU), who scored 11.6 percent of the vote, attracting the support of the majority of ex-Nazi Party members, who had recently been given back their voting rights.

In the autumn of 1950, Marshall Plan aid was cut back drastically. With the Austrian government forced to increase sharply the price of food, coal and electricity, strikes broke out among workers in cities across Austria. Seizing the moment, the Communists staged their second and most serious coup attempt. Once again, it began with a Communist-inspired mass demonstration outside the chancellery, after which barricades were erected, roads blocked, tram tracks cemented up and bus windows broken. The Russians stopped police reinforcements in their sector from being called up, and only with great difficulty was the situation kept under control. In the end, however, the Socialist trade unions and the government took sufficient steps to stem the tide, and the general strike held on October 4, though heeded by large numbers of workers in the Russian sectors of Vienna and eastern Austria, was called off the following day.

## The Austrian State Treaty of 1955

The **withdrawal of Allied troops** from Austria in 1955 – or more specifically the Soviet withdrawal – was something of a unique event in the otherwise grim history of the Cold War. And something of a surprise, given the previously unscrupulous behaviour of the Soviets in Austria (and elsewhere in Europe).

For nearly ten years, negotiations over a peace treaty with Austria had been at a stalemate, with the Soviets insisting that a German peace treaty be prerequisite to an Austrian treaty. The Soviet threat over the future of Austria was used by them to try and forestall German rearmament. However, with the establishment of the Federal Republic of Germany in 1949, it was clear that this policy had failed. A struggle within the Kremlin then ensued over Soviet policy towards Austria. Following the death of Stalin, this struggle intensified and was eventually won by Khrushchev, who decided to use the **Austrian State Treaty** as a way of initiating a period of détente.

Other factors influenced Soviet policy. Hopes of creating a Communist Austria had died with the failure of the 1950 putsch. The Soviet sector meanwhile had been bled dry and was no longer of any great economic benefit. A neutral Austria, on the other hand, created a convenient buffer that split NATO's northern and southern flanks. And so on May 15, 1955, the Austrian State Treaty or Staatsvertrag was signed by the four powers in Vienna's Belvedere. The Austrian chancellor, **Leopold Figl**, waved the treaty triumphantly from the balcony and over half a million Austrians celebrated in the streets of the capital.

# 1955–83: consensus politics

With the popular vote split between Left and Right, the two main parties of the ÖVP and the SPÖ formed a succession of coalitions which lasted until 1966. To avoid repeating the mistakes of the past, and to placate the occupying powers, a system of **Proporz** was established, whereby each party shared equally every governmental and state post. In some ways institutionalized political corruption, this process began at the top among the ministries, and continued right down to the local post office. At the same time, special bodies or chambers representing the various interest groups – the Chamber of Trade, the Chamber of Labour and so on – were established. Like *Proporz*, these new institutions ensured that the country enjoyed an unprecedented period of political and social stability, but left the parliament without an effective opposition and created a system open to widespread abuse. Like the Germans, though, the Austrians enjoyed a period of economic growth and prosperity, and there were few voices of complaint.

In the elections of 1966, the People's Party at last achieved an absolute majority and formed the first one-party government of the postwar era. Many Austrians feared a repeat of the 1920s, but in practice little changed. The system of *Proporz* and the institutions of the corporate state continued to hand out "jobs for the boys", and only at the very top level of government were the Socialists excluded

## Simon Wiesenthal (1908–2005)

The Holocaust survivor and Nazi-hunter, **Simon Wiesenthal**, was one of the most controversial figures in Austria's postwar political scene.

Wiesenthal was born in Buczacz, a Yiddish-speaking *shtetl* in the Austro-Hungarian province of Galicia (later part of Poland and now Ukraine). His father, a well-to-do sugar merchant, was killed fighting for the Habsburgs on the eastern front during World War I. As a young man, Wiesenthal **studied architecture in Prague**, since Polish architecture faculties were closed to Jews, and in 1936 returned home to marry **Cyla Müller**, an old schoolmate. The newlyweds moved to Lvov, where Wiesenthal worked as an architectural engineer until the Nazi–Soviet Pact of September 1939, when the Red Army marched into town and Wiesenthal was forced to forgo his "bourgeois" profession in a bedding factory.

The Nazi invasion of Soviet territory in June 1941 was celebrated with an **anti-Semitic pogrom** led by Ukrainian auxiliaries, during which Wiesenthal was lined up in front of a firing squad. He was saved by the timely ringing of the church bells calling the faithful (including the soldiers about to execute him) to Mass. That night a Ukrainian friend helped him by accusing him of being a Soviet spy – this meant he was beaten up and interrogated but not killed. He was then put to work in the OAW, a **forced-labour** railway-repair works, first as a sign-painter, and later as a draughtsman. He and his wife were comparatively well treated by the Nazi in charge, who even helped Cyla to escape, first to Lublin, and later to Warsaw. He also saved Wiesenthal from imminent execution in April 1943 – he was naked and lined up ready to be shot – and, in September of that year, encouraged him to go into hiding.

After concealing himself in an attic and hanging out with partisans, Wiesenthal was eventually discovered hiding under the floorboards of a flat in June 1944. Transferred to the Gestapo headquarters in Lvov and fearing torture, he tried to commit suicide three times without success. As German troops fled from the advancing Soviets, he was sent westwards via Plaszow, Auschwitz, Gross-Rosen and Buchenwald, before ending up in **Mauthausen** in Austria, where he was left for dead in the "death block". On this occasion, he was saved by a Polish Kapo, who needed someone to design birthday cards for the guards. This meant that he was one of the lucky few still alive on May 5, 1945, when Mauthausen was liberated by the US Army.

Just three weeks after the liberation of Mauthausen, Wiesenthal began to work for the **US War Crimes Unit**, helping them track down SS officers. He was soon

from power. Their turn came in 1970, when a slight economic downturn gave the SPÖ a narrow victory, followed by an outright majority in elections the following year. Under the chancellorship of **Bruno Kreisky**, the Socialists enjoyed thirteen years of power, during which Kreisky carried the SPÖ further from their radical Marxist past than ever before. The end came in the elections of 1983 when the SPÖ lost its overall majority and was forced into a coalition government with the far-right Freedom Party (FPÖ), successor to the postwar VdU (see p.283).

# The Waldheim affair

Having struggled to make headlines in the international press in the 1960s and 1970s, Austria was catapulted onto the world media stage in 1986 during the campaign for the Austrian presidency. The ÖVP candidate, **Kurt Waldheim**, was a figure of some international stature who had been UN Secretary-General for ten years (1972–82). However, during the campaign, Waldheim's war record was called into question. From the summer of 1942 until the end of the war, he transferred to the OSS, the American wartime intelligence group, in nearby Linz, where he was reunited with his wife, who had also, remarkably, survived, spending the last year of the war working as a slave labourer in Germany. In 1947, frustrated with the Allies' waning interest in Nazi-hunting, Wiesenthal eventually founded the **Dokumentationszentrum** (Documentation Centre), for which he is best known. During this period he helped track down some two thousand former Nazis, including **Adolf Eichmann** and other leading figures. In 1953, he gave up his full-time pursuit of ex-Nazis and took a job helping with the rehabilitation and retraining of refugees. In 1961, Eichmann was kidnapped in Argentina by Mossad, the Israeli secret service, and spirited away to Israel to face prosecution. Wiesenthal was invited to attend the trial, and, with Mossad denying any involvement in the kidnapping, was only too happy to give press conferences on his early role in the pursuit of Eichmann. With the publication of *I Hunted Eichmann*, Wiesenthal's fame became widespread, and he decided to move to Vienna and reopen his Dokumentationszentrum to "work against Holocaust amnesia".

In Austria, Wiesenthal is probably best known for his **public feud with Bruno Kreisky**, the Austrian chancellor (1970–83) and fellow Jew, which began in 1970 when Wiesenthal exposed four of Kreisky's first cabinet as ex-Nazis. Kreisky called Wiesenthal a "Jewish fascist", and accused him of being a Nazi collaborator during his time at the OAW in Lvov. Legal battles between the two dragged on for years, and Wiesenthal was eventually awarded damages for slander, but Kreisky remained more popular with the public throughout the 1970s. Wiesenthal made even more enemies during the Waldheim affair, when he refused to back the line of the World Jewish Congress (WJC) and the US government, who together accused the Austrian president of being a war criminal. Wiesenthal maintained that there wasn't enough evidence to make such claims, and would only go so far as to brand Waldheim a liar and call for his resignation on those grounds.

The 1990s saw Wiesenthal's stature rise both globally and within Austria. Poland and Austria both bestowed their highest decorations on him, and shortly before his 87th birthday, the Vienna City Council voted to make him an *Ehrenbürger* (honorary citizen). Wiesenthal died aged 96 in the city in 2005, but the Simon Wiesenthal Center in Los Angeles (ⓦwww.wiesenthal.com) continues his work to this day.

had served as a lieutenant in the Balkans with the German Army. Waldheim was never a member of the Nazi Party (one initial allegation) and there was never any clear evidence that he was directly involved in the atrocities committed by the army in the Balkans, though he was formally charged with (but never tried for) war crimes by the Yugoslavs after the war. What was more difficult to believe, however, was his claim that he had no knowledge of the deportation of Greek Jews to the death camps, despite being an interpreter for the Italian Army in Greece for much of the war.

To the dismay of many around the world, these charges, albeit unproven, did Waldheim's candidacy no harm at all domestically, and he was duly elected **President of Austria** with 54 percent of the vote. The international campaign against Waldheim began with the boycott of his swearing-in ceremony by the US ambassador, and culminated in his being put on the US Department of Justice's "Watch List" of undesirable aliens. Waldheim – and by association Austria – became an international pariah, restricted in his state visits to Arab countries. At Waldheim's suggestion, a commission was set up to investigate the charges against him; far from exonerating him, however, its report found him guilty of "proximity to legally incriminating acts and orders", a somewhat woolly phrase that could be applied to just about any Austrian who'd served in the German Army. The British government, meanwhile, followed up the Yugoslav charge that Waldheim had been involved in war crimes against British commandos in the Balkans. The British enquiry concluded that Waldheim's rank was too junior to have had any influence over the fate of the commandos, adding that "knowledge is not itself a crime".

# The rise and fall of the FPÖ

As if the Waldheim affair in the 1980s were not bad enough, the country had to contend with the rise of the FPÖ in the 1990s, under charismatic leader **Jörg Haider**. A strange grouping of free-market liberals and ultraconservatives, the FPÖ was very much a fringe player in Austrian politics until 1983, when it became junior coalition partner with the SPÖ. In 1986, Haider became party chairman, causing the collapse of the SPÖ–FPÖ coalition and prompting elections. In his first stab at the polls, Haider won nearly ten percent of the vote, frightening the two main parties back into the grand SPÖ–ÖVP coalition of the postwar years. Unfortunately, this only served to play into Haider's hands, increasing popular resentment against the system of *Proporz* and thus boosting support for the FPÖ.

Haider presented himself as something new in national politics, free from the cynical power-sharing manoeuvres of the two main parties. Both of his parents were Nazi Party members who had felt sidelined by postwar Austrian society, and Haider himself deliberately courted far-right support. Elected **Governor of Carinthia** in 1989, Haider expressed enthusiasm for Nazi employment policy in a speech two years later – precipitating his fall from office, but not his fall from popularity.

Haider's main electoral plank was to exploit the fears shared by many Austrians over the country's new wave of **immigrants**, who arrived from the former eastern bloc and war-torn Yugoslavia during the 1990s. Although in a 1995 referendum sixty percent voted in favour of joining **European Union**, the austerity measures the country needed to implement in order to meet the criteria necessary to join a single European currency convinced many that it had been the wrong decision.

Haider's FPÖ gradually increased its share of the vote throughout the 1990s, taking 22 percent of the vote in the general elections of 1994 and 1995. The biggest shock, though, was in Vienna, in 1996, when the SPÖ lost its overall majority for the first time in the city's history, with the FPÖ becoming the main opposition in the Rathaus, ahead of the ÖVP.

## 1999: the ÖVP-FPÖ coalition

In **1999**, campaigning on an openly xenophobic platform – with posters reading "Stop der Überfremdung. Österreich zuerst" ("Stop the foreign tide. Put Austria first") setting the tone – the FPÖ surpassed even their own wildest dreams by getting 27 percent of the vote, beating the ÖVP into third place by a margin of 415 votes (both the FPÖ and the ÖVP were awarded 52 seats in parliament). The SPÖ received 33 percent, their worst result since 1945. Talks between the SPÖ and ÖVP broke down and President Klestil had no choice but to invite the ÖVP to enter talks with the FPÖ in the hope of forming a government.

In the end, ÖVP leader **Wolfgang Schüssel** became chancellor, with several top posts going to the FPÖ. Haider refused to take part in the government, to the relief of many Austrians, instead becoming Governor of Carinthia once more. He quit the FPÖ leadership and was replaced by the less openly extremist Susanne Riess-Passer. The **ÖVP-FPÖ government** was sworn in by an unenthusiastic Klestil in February 2000. All other EU states immediately froze bilateral relations with Austria in protest at the FPÖ's inclusion in government. The new government's programme – centred on promises to cut government spending and pave the way for tax cuts – carefully avoided any reference to the FPÖ's pre-election rhetoric, and the EU withdrew their sanctions after six months. Many Austrians were deeply shamed by the FPÖ's accession to power, and launched the **Widerstand** (Resistance), a massive Heldenplatz demo followed by a rolling campaign of weekly demonstrations and cultural events designed to show that the liberal, tolerant values of centre-left Austria were still very much alive.

Paradoxically, the ÖVP profited more from the new situation than the FPÖ. Chancellor Schüssel, together with ÖVP foreign minister **Benita Ferrero-Waldner**, won popular support for the way in which they appeared to defend Austria's dignity against a hostile EU. Meanwhile, the FPÖ began to unravel, with Haider increasingly at odds with the rest of the party, eventually forcing the resignation of the FPÖ ministers and prompting new elections.

In the **2002 elections**, the **FPÖ vote collapsed** to a mere ten percent, while the ÖVP surged to 42 percent – the biggest swing in postwar Austrian politics – and the SPÖ got a fairly respectable 37 percent. The **2006 elections** simply confirmed the demise of the far-right vote with the FPÖ taking eleven percent, just behind the Greens. The postwar status quo was re-established, with the SPÖ and ÖVP receiving 35 and 34 percent of the vote respectively and entering once more into a grand coalition. Haider himself formed his own party, the Alliance or BZÖ, but polled a mere four percent. Then, in a dramatic turn of events, in 2008, Haider died in a car crash, while over the alcohol limit, in his beloved Carinthia.

The Waldheim affair and the rise of the FPÖ were a **PR disaster** for Austria, and there's a continuing sense of bewilderment in the country that a nation that promoted itself so successfully as the home of Lipizzaner horses and happy alpine holidays should be internationally notorious for something entirely different. Despite this, Vienna continues to buck the trend, just as it did between the wars. The SPÖ regained an overall majority in the city council in 2001 and thankfully they continue to run the city – in coalition with the Greens since 2010 – along solid social democratic principles, ploughing money into public services that make Vienna's education, health and public transport systems the envy of the world.

# Books

Books on the Habsburgs and the various artistic figures from Vienna's glorious past are easy to come by. However, remarkably little has been written in English in the twentieth century about Austria and its capital, and not much fiction is available in translation.

## History and society

Steven Beller *Vienna and the Jews, 1867–1938*. Beller shows how the Jews played a central role in the vibrant cultural life of Vienna at the start of the last century. Thorough, if rather dry.

Gordon Brook-Shepherd *The Austrians*. Readable, a little over-earnest, history that attempts to trace the Austrian-ness (or lack of it) in the country's history from the Babenbergs to entry into the EU in 1994.

William M. Johnston *The Austrian Mind: An Intellectual and Social History 1848–1938*. Johnston knows his stuff; though this is a pretty academic approach, it provides a fascinating insight into fin-de-siècle Vienna.

Robert Knight *Contemporary Austria and the Legacy of the Third Reich 1945–95*. Highlights the failure of de-Nazification and the subsequent rise of Haider's FPÖ, the consequences of which were partly obscured by the country's postwar prosperity.

Frederic Morton *A Nervous Splendor: Vienna 1888/1889*; *Thunder at Twilight: Vienna 1913–1914*; *The Forever Street: A Novel*. Morton (whose real name is Fritz Mandelbaum) has trawled through the newspapers of the time to produce two very readable dramatized accounts of two critical years in the city's history. The first centres on the Mayerling tragedy, the second on the Sarajevo assassination. *Forever Street* follows a Jewish family's fortunes from 1873 to the Holocaust.

Robin Okey *The Habsburg Monarchy c.1765–1918*. A comprehensive and up-to-date account of the empire.

Hella Pick *Guilty Victim: Austria from the Holocaust to Haider*. Probably the best book on postwar Austria, both as a political history and a meditation on the country's (often half-hearted) attempts to come to terms with the darker elements of its past.

Carl E. Schorske *Fin-de-Siècle Vienna*. Fascinating scholarly essays on, among other things, the impact of the building of the Ringstrasse, and of Freud, Klimt, Kokoschka and Schönberg on the city's culture.

John Stoye *The Siege of Vienna*. Account of the remarkable Siege of 1683 when the Turks were only prevented from taking the city by the timely intervention of the Polish king, and during which the croissant was born.

A. J. P. Taylor *The Habsburg Monarchy 1809–1918*. Readable, forthright as ever and thought-provoking account of the demise of the Habsburgs.

Andrew Wheatcroft *The Habsburgs: Embodying Empire*. Wheatcroft's intriguing history traces the rise and fall of the Habsburgs from their modest origins in Switzerland to their demise at the head of the Austro-Hungarian empire, looking closely at individual family members, and the promotion of its dynastic image.

# Memoirs and travel

**Elias Canetti** *The Tongue Set Free.* The Bulgarian-born Nobel Prize-winning Canetti was a Sephardic Jew who lived in Vienna during the 1930s; his fragmentary memoirs of the period are superb.

**George Clare** *Last Waltz in Vienna: The Destruction of a Family 1842–1942.* Incredibly moving – and far from bitter – autobiographical account of a Jewish upbringing in interwar Vienna that ended with the Anschluss.

**Edward Crankshaw** *Vienna: The Image of a Culture in Decline.* Part travel journal, part history, and first published in 1938, this is a nostalgic, but by no means rose-tinted, look at the city. The same author's *Fall of the House of Habsburg* is an accessible popular history of the empire's last days.

**Patrick Leigh Fermor** *A Time of Gifts.* The first volume of Leigh Fermor's trilogy based on his epic walk along the Rhine and Danube rivers in 1933–34. Written forty years later in dense, luscious and highly crafted prose, it's an evocative and poignant insight into the culture of *Mitteleuropa* between the wars.

**Peter Singer** *Pushing Time Away.* A biography of the author's grandfather, David Oppenheim, giving insight into the wrangles in Freud's circle and Red Vienna, through the rise of fascism to the horrors of life and death in Theresienstadt.

**Reinhard Spitzy** *How We Squandered the Reich.* Chilling and frank autobiographical account of a young Austrian idealist who became a member of the SS.

**Simon Wiesenthal** *The Sunflower.* Wiesenthal relates an instance from his time at Mauthausen when an ailing SS guard called him to his bedside and asked for forgiveness. In the second half of the book, Wiesenthal asks leading intellectuals to respond to the dilemma of forgiveness.

**Stefan Zweig** *The World of Yesterday.* Seminal account of fin-de-siècle Vienna written just before Zweig was forced by the Nazis into exile in South America, where he and his wife committed suicide.

# Biography

**Steven Beller** *Franz Joseph.* Shortest and most portable of the books on Franz-Josef; more of a political than a biographical account, it's a bit lacking in personal history.

**T.C.W. Blanning** *Joseph II.* Aimed at the general reader, this tells the story of Joseph and his attempts at reform against the background of the Austrian enlightenment.

**Jean-Paul Bled** *Franz Joseph.* Well-rounded account of the old duffer, with a smattering of the sort of scurrilous gossip missing in some other biographies.

**Edward Crankshaw** *Maria Theresa.* Readable account of the "Virgin Empress", though disappointingly short on light touches.

**Charles Drazin** *In Search of The Third Man.* Background story full of anecdotes about the writing, filming and cult success of *The Third Man.*

**Peter Gay** *Mozart.* A slim, easy-to-read volume which nevertheless includes a good deal of stimulating analysis. Easily the best compact Mozart biography you can get.

**Brigitte Hamann** *The Reluctant Empress*; *Hitler's Vienna*. The former is a surprisingly even-handed account of Empress Elisabeth's extraordinary life, warts and all. *Hitler's Vienna* is an account of Hitler's early youth in Vienna, which played an important part in helping form the prejudices of the Nazi leader.

**Malcolm Hayes** *Anton von Webern*. Not as well known as Schönberg, or as successful as Berg, Webern is seen by some as a progressive, and accused by others of being a Nazi sympathizer. Hayes, understandably, sits on the fence.

**Michael Jacobs** *Sigmund Freud*. Brief biography of the bearded one: a quick trot through his ideas and the subsequent criticisms thereof.

**Allan Janik & Stephen Toulmin** *Wittgenstein's Vienna*. Not a biography of the philosopher so much as a fascinating book on the cultural life of the Habsburg capital in the first half of the twentieth century.

**Alma Mahler-Werfel** *Diaries 1896–1902*. Gushingly frank diaries of a supremely attractive young woman, courted by the likes of Klimt and Zemlinsky. The period covered follows Alma until shortly after her marriage to the composer Gustav Mahler.

**David Nelson** *Vienna for the Music Lover: The Complete Guide to Vienna's Musical Sites and Performances Today*. Notwithstanding its cumbersome title, this is an interesting book that takes you in the footsteps of the composers, aided by maps and illustrations.

**Hella Pick** *Simon Wiesenthal: A Life in Search of Justice*. Written with the subject's cooperation shortly before his death, this biography tracks his wartime sufferings and catalogues his postwar activities. Pick is sympathetic yet objective, and gives a rare glimpse into the Nazi-hunter's personal life.

**Brigitte Timmerman** *The Third Man's Vienna*. A paperback coffee-table book full of stills of *The Third Man* and contemporary news archives, with text by the woman who started the city's *Third Man* tours.

**John Van der Kiste** *Emperor Francis Joseph*. If the Steven Beller (see p.269) is too dry, then this slightly racier read about the bewhiskered ruler should do the trick.

**Alexander Waugh** *The House of Wittgenstein: A Family at War*. The archetypal dysfunctional family: tyrannical father, cold mother, eight warring siblings of whom two or three committed suicide. Their personal problems are exacerbated by the Nazi occupation and their being categorised as full Jews (which horrified the patriotic Paul).

# Austrian fiction

**Ingeborg Bachmann** *Songs in Flight*; *The Thirtieth Year*; *The Complete Poetry of Ingeborg Bachmann*. An acclaimed poet, novelist and short-story writer from the 1950s, Bachmann was fascinated by the impotence of language and developed a voice of her own. For a flavour of her work, try the bilingual edition of her poems, *Songs in Flight*.

**Thomas Bernhard** *Cutting Timber*; *An Irritation*; *Wittgenstein's Nephew*; *Extinction*; *Concrete*; *The Voice Imitator*. Dense, stream-of-consciousness ruminations from one of the leading critics of the hypocrisy and mediocrity of postwar Austria. Any of the above will prove to be a good introduction to his inimitable style.

**Hermann Broch** *The Death of Virgil*; *The Guiltless*. With the Anschluss, Broch, who was of Jewish parentage, was briefly interned in a camp, where he began *The Death of Virgil*, which focuses on the last hours of Virgil's life and his questioning of the role his art has given him in society. *The Guiltless* is a more direct and readable examination of the dark side of mid-twentieth-century German culture.

**Lilian Faschinger** *Vienna Passion*. A complex tale, whose black New Yorker heroine, researching into Anna Freud in Vienna, comes across the fascinating story of Rosa Havelka, servant to the empress and mistress to the heir to the throne at the end of the nineteenth century.

**Peter Handke** *Plays 1*; *A Sorrow Beyond Dreams*. Handke is Austria's most provocative contemporary playwright, whose partnership with filmmaker Wim Wenders has brought him international recognition. *Plays 1* gives you six of his best from the 1960s and 1970s, including *Kaspar* and *Offending the Audience*, Handke's favourite pastime. *A Sorrow Beyond Dreams* is a short, painful and moving prose elegy to his mother, following her suicide.

**Elfriede Jelinek** *Wonderful, Wonderful Times*; *The Piano Teacher*; *Lust*; *Greed*. The works of the Nobel Prize-winning Jelinek are often an uncomfortable read: *The Piano Teacher* (made into a film in 2001) delves into the world of masochism and voyeurism; *Wonderful, Wonderful Times*, which takes place in the late 1950s, digs up the city's murky past.

**Mike Mitchell** *The Dedalus Book of Austrian Fantasy*. Everything from Kafka to modern surreal for those whose taste is on the wild side.

**Robert Musil** *The Man Without Qualities*; *Diaries 1899–1941*. Often compared with Joyce and Proust, Musil's 1000-page unfinished novel, *The Man Without Qualities*, takes place at the twilight of the Habsburg Empire. Those addicted to Musil's irony-drenched, essayistic prose should also dip into his diaries.

**Josef Roth** *Radetsky March*. Pitifully underrated, this is Roth's finest work – a nostalgic and melancholic portrait of the moribund Vienna of Franz-Josef. Of Roth's masterful short novels *Job* deals with Judaism and *Flight Without End* is a heartbreaking tale of dislocation and world-weariness.

**Arthur Schnitzler** *Hands Around*; *Dream Story*. A classic portrayal of decadent Viennese fin-de-siècle society, *Hands Around* came back to prominence in the 1950s after being filmed as *La Ronde* by Max Ophüls, and enjoyed a comeback in the late 1990s on the stage in an adaptation called *The Blue Room* by David Hare. *Dream Story* was the inspiration for Stanley Kubrick's last film, *Eyes Wide Shut*.

**Harold B. Segel** (ed) *The Vienna Coffeehouse Wits 1890–1938*. A rare opportunity to read translated snippets of work by *Kaffeehaus* regulars such as Karl Kraus, Peter Altenberg and Felix Salten (the little-known author of *Bambi* and *The Story of a Vienna Whore*, one of which was made into a Disney cartoon).

**Stefan Zweig** *The Burning Secret and Other Stories*. Exquisitely wrought tales from fin-de-siècle Vienna, including *Letter from an Unknown Woman*, the best and most poignant of Zweig's tales, and another story adapted into a movie by Ophüls.

# Literature by foreign writers

**Phil Andrews** *Goodnight Vienna.* A light read for football fans as the English soccer coach is under threat, a key player is murdered and the trail leads beneath the streets of Vienna.

**Richard Bassett and John Lehmann** *Vienna: a traveller's companion.* An anthology of travellers' impressions of the city through the centuries.

**Elias Canetti** *Auto-da-Fé; Crowds and Power.* The first novel of the Nobel Prize-winning Canetti, a Bulgarian-born Sephardic Jew who wrote in German, revolves around the life of a miserable scholar living in fin-de-siècle Vienna. *Crowds and Power* is a nonfiction work about mob mentality inspired by Canetti's participation in the torching of Vienna's Justizpalast in 1934.

**Eva Ibbotson** *The Star of Kazan.* Any 9- to 12-year-old who has fallen in love

with the Lipizzaner stallions will enjoy this old-fashioned adventure story.

**John Irving** *Setting Free the Bears.* Stream-of-verbiage novel centred (vaguely) on Vienna's zoo after the war.

**Philip Kerr** *A German Requiem.* Final volume of a gripping spy trilogy set in postwar Vienna.

**Robert Löhr** *The Chess Machine.* Enjoyable novel set in 1770 in Vienna, based around the true story of the world's first chess computer.

**Mary Stewart** *Airs Above the Ground.* Murder mystery written in the 1960s and set in and around Vienna's Spanish Riding School.

**Frank Tallis** *Mortal Mischief; Vienna Blood.* Intriguing murder mysteries set in Vienna at the turn of the century starring a disciple of Freud. Strong on detail and atmosphere.

# Art and architecture

**Laurenc Bonet** *Otto Wagner/Gustav Klimt.* A good selection of coloured illustrations in this two-for-the-price-of-one book.

**Christian Brandstätter** *Wonderful Wiener Werkstätte 1903–1932.* You couldn't wish for a more exhaustively illustrated book on the early twentieth-century designers.

**Alessandra Comini** *Egon Schiele; Gustav Klimt.* The former contains a good selection of full-colour reproductions, as well as an account of Schiele's life set into its cultural context; the latter deals with all facets of Klimt's art and traces connections with the work of his contemporaries and the theories of Freud.

**Harry Rand** *Hundertwasser.* This illustrated account of his work is

illuminated by conversations between author and artist.

**Aldo Rossi, B. Gravagnuolo** *Adolf Loos.* A wonderfully illustrated book for the general reader, covering the life and works of the "father of modernism".

**Rolf Toman** (ed) *Vienna Art and Architecture.* A huge coffee-table volume covering the city from the Middle Ages to the present day, with numerous colour illustrations, accompanied by lots of informative text.

**Alfred Weidinger** *Kokoschka and Alma Mahler: Testimony to a Passionate Relationship.* Detailed account of the artist's doomed relationship with Mahler's widow, illustrated with lots of Kokoschka's drawings and paintings from the period.

# Language

# Language

# German

Although a high proportion of Austrians speak some English, any of your attempts to converse in a few phrases of **German** will be heartily appreciated. That said, German is a highly complex language that you can't hope to master quickly. The biggest problem for English-speakers is that German words can be one of three genders: masculine, feminine or neuter. Each has its own ending and corresponding ending for attached adjectives, plus its own definite article. If in doubt, it's safest to use either the neuter or male forms.

Pronunciation (and spelling) is less of a problem, as individual syllables are generally pronounced as they're printed – the trick is learning how to place the stresses in the notoriously lengthy German words. Though Austrians speak German with a distinct accent, and the Viennese have their own dialect, when speaking to a foreigner most folk will switch to standard German.

The following is a rundown of the basics you'll need on a city break to Vienna. For more detail, check out the *Rough Guide German Phrasebook*, set out dictionary-style for easy access, with English–German and German–English sections, cultural tips for tricky situations and a menu reader.

## Vowels and umlauts

a as in r**a**ther

e as in g**ay**

i as in f**ee**t

o as in n**o**se

u as in b**oo**t

ä is a combination of a and e, sometimes

pronounced like **e** in b**e**t (eg L**ä**nder) and sometimes like **ai** in p**ai**d (eg sp**ä**t).

ö is a combination of o and e, which has no real English equivalent, but is similar to the French *eu*.

ü is a combination of u and e, like bl**ue**.

## Vowel combinations

ai as in wh**y**

au as in m**ou**se

ie as in tr**ee**

ei as in tr**i**al

eu as in b**oi**l

## Consonants

Consonants are pronounced as they are written, with no silent letters. The differences from English are:

j pronounced similar to an English y

r is given a dry throaty sound, similar to French

s pronounced similar to, but slightly softer than an English z

v pronounced somewhere between f and v

w pronounced like an English v

z pronounced ts

The German letter ß usually replaces ss in a word: pronunciation is identical.

ch is a strong back-of-the-throat sound as in the Scottish lo**ch**.

sp (at the start of a word) pronounced shp

st (at the start of a word) pronounced sht

# German words and phrases

## Basics

| | |
|---|---|
| Yes, No | Ja, Nein |
| Please/You're welcome | Bitte |
| A more polite form of Bitte | Bitte schön |
| Thank you, Thank you very much | Danke, Danke schön |
| Where, when, why? | Wo, Wann, Warum? |
| How much? | Wieviel? |
| Here, there | Hier, Da |
| All mean "open" | Geöffnet, Offen, Auf |
| Both mean "closed" | Geschlossen, Zu |
| Over there | Da drüben |
| This one | Dieses |
| That one | Jenes |
| Large, small | Gross, Klein |
| More, less | Mehr, Weniger |
| A little | Wenig |
| A lot | Viel |
| Cheap, expensive | Billig, Teuer |
| Good, bad | Gut, Schlecht |
| Hot, cold | Heiss, Kalt |
| With, without | Mit, Ohne |
| Right | Rechts |
| Left | Links |
| Straight ahead | Gerade aus |
| Go away | Geh weg |

## Greetings and times

| | |
|---|---|
| Good day | Grüss Gott |
| Good morning | Guten Morgen |
| Good evening | Guten Abend |
| Good night | Gute Nacht |
| Goodbye | Auf Wiedersehen |
| Goodbye (on the telephone) | Auf Wiederhören |
| Goodbye (informal) | Tschüs |
| Hello/Goodbye | Servus |
| How are you? (polite) | Wie geht es Ihnen? |
| How are you? (informal) | Wie geht es dir? |
| Today | Heute |
| Yesterday | Gestern |
| Tomorrow | Morgen |
| The day before yesterday | Vorgestern |
| The day after tomorrow | Übermorgen |
| Day | Tag |
| Night | Nacht |
| Midday | Mittag |
| Midnight | Mitternacht |
| Week | Woche |
| Weekend | Wochenende |
| Month | Monat |
| Year | Jahr |
| In the morning | Am Vormittag /Vormittags |
| In the afternoon | Am Nachmittag /Nachmittags |
| In the evening | Am Abend |

## Days, months and dates

| | |
|---|---|
| Monday | Montag |
| Tuesday | Dienstag |
| Wednesday | Mittwoch |
| Thursday | Donnerstag |
| Friday | Freitag |
| Saturday | Samstag |
| Sunday | Sonntag |
| January | Jänner |
| February | Februar |
| March | März |
| April | April |
| May | Mai |
| June | Juni |
| July | Juli |
| August | August |
| September | September |

| | | | |
|---|---|---|---|
| October | Oktober | Holidays | Ferien |
| November | November | Bank holiday | Feiertag |
| December | Dezember | Monday, the first of April | Montag, der erste April |
| Spring | Frühling | | |
| Summer | Sommer | The second of April | Der zweite April |
| Autumn | Herbst | The third of April | Der dritte April |
| Winter | Winter | | |

## Some signs

| | | | |
|---|---|---|---|
| Women's toilets | Damen/Frauen | Emergency | Not |
| Men's toilets | Herren/Männer | Emergency exit | Notausgang |
| Entrance | Eingang | Hospital | Krankenhaus |
| Exit | Ausgang | Police | Polizei |
| Arrival | Ankunft | No smoking | Nicht rauchen |
| Departure | Abfahrt | No entrance | Kein Eingang |
| Exhibition | Ausstellung | Push | Drücken |
| Motorway | Autobahn | Pull | Ziehen |
| Diversion | Umleitung | Vacant | Frei |
| Attention! | Achtung! | Occupied | Besetzt |
| Beware! | Vorsicht! | Prohibited | Verboten |

## Questions and requests

All enquiries should start with the phrase *Entschuldigen Sie bitte* (Excuse me, please). Though strictly you should use *Sie*, the polite form of address, with everyone except close friends, young people often don't bother with it. However, the older generation and anyone official will certainly be offended if you address them with the familiar *Du*.

| | | | |
|---|---|---|---|
| Do you speak English? | Sprechen Sie Englisch? | What time is it? | Wieviel Uhr ist es? |
| I don't speak German | Ich spreche kein Deutsch | Are these seats taken? | Sind die Plätze noch frei? |
| Please speak more slowly | Sprechen Sie bitte langsamer | The bill please | Die Rechnung bitte |
| | | Is that table free? | Ist der Tisch frei? |
| I don't understand | Ich verstehe nicht | The menu please | Die Speisekarte bitte |
| I understand | Ich verstehe | Waitress . . . ! (for attention) | Fräulein . . . ! |
| How do you say that in German? | Wie sagt mann das auf Deutsch? | Waiter . . . ! (for attention) | Herr Ober . . . ! |
| Can you tell me where . . . is? | Können Sie mir sagen wo . . . ist? | Have you got something cheaper? | Haben Sie etwas billigeres? |
| Where is . . . ? | Wo ist . . . ? | Are there rooms available? | Haben Sie Zimmer frei? |
| How much does that cost? | Wieviel kostet das? | Where are the toilets please? | Wo sind die Toiletten bitte? |
| When does the next train leave? | Wann fährt der nächste Zug? | I'd like that one | Ich hätte gern dieses |
| At what time? | Um wieviel Uhr? | I'd like a room for two | Ich hätte gern ein Zimmer für zwei |

| I'd like a single room | Ich hätte gern ein Einzelzimmer | Does it have a shower, bath, toilet? | Hat es Dusche, Bad, Toilette? |
|---|---|---|---|

## Numbers

| | | | |
|---|---|---|---|
| 0 | null | 18 | achtzehn |
| 1 | eins | 19 | neunzehn |
| 2 | zwei | 20 | zwanzig |
| 3 | drei | 21 | ein-und-zwanzig |
| 4 | vier | 22 | zwei-und-zwanzig |
| 5 | fünf | 30 | dreissig |
| 6 | sechs | 40 | vierzig |
| 7 | sieben | 50 | fünfzig |
| 8 | acht | 60 | sechzig |
| 9 | neun | 70 | siebzig |
| 10 | zehn | 80 | achtzig |
| 11 | elf | 90 | neunzig |
| 12 | zwölf | 100 | hundert |
| 13 | dreizehn | 1000 | tausend |
| 14 | vierzehn | 2000 | zweitausand |
| 15 | fünfzehn | 2012 | zweitausand-und-zwölf |
| 16 | sechszehn | 2013 | zweitausand -und-dreizehn |
| 17 | siebzehn | | |

# Food and drink

## Basics

| | | | |
|---|---|---|---|
| Abendessen | supper/dinner | Mittagessen | lunch |
| Auflauf | omelette | Nachspeise | dessert |
| Beilagen | side dishes | Öl | oil |
| Brot | bread | Pfeffer | pepper |
| Butter | butter | Reis | rice |
| Ei | egg | Salat | salad |
| Frühstuck | breakfast | Salz | salt |
| Gabel | fork | Semmel | bread roll |
| Gebäck | pastries | Senf | mustard |
| Hauptgericht | main course | Spätzle/Nocker | pasta/noodles |
| Honig | honey | Speisekarte | menu |
| Käse | cheese | Suppe | soup |
| Knödel | dumplings | Tasse | cup |
| Kren | horseradish | Teller | plate |
| Löffel | spoon | Vorspeise | starter |
| Messer | knife | Zucker | sugar |

## Vegetables (Gemüse)

| | | | |
|---|---|---|---|
| Blaukraut | red cabbage | Kohlsprossen | Brussels sprouts |
| Bohnen | beans | Lauch | leek |
| Champignons | button mushrooms | Maiskolben | corn on the cob |
| Erbsen | peas | Paprika | green or red peppers |
| Erdäpfel | potatoes | Paradeiser | tomatoes |
| Fisolen | green beans | Pilze | mushrooms |
| G'röste | fried grated potatoes | Pommes Frites | chips/French fries |
| Gurke | gherkin/cucumber | Rote Rübe | beetroot |
| Karfiol | cauliflower | Sauerkraut | pickled cabbage |
| Karotten | carrots | Spargel | asparagus |
| Knoblauch | garlic | Spinat | spinach |
| Kohl | cabbage | Zwiebeln | onions |

## Meat (Fleisch) and poultry (Geflügel)

| | | | |
|---|---|---|---|
| Eisbein | pig's trotters | Kuttelfleck | tripe |
| Ente | duck | Lamm | lamb |
| Fasan | pheasant | Leber | liver |
| Gans | goose | Nieren | kidneys |
| Hackfleisch | mincemeat | Puter | turkey |
| Hammelfleisch | mutton | Rindfleisch | beef |
| Hase | hare | Schinken | ham |
| Hirn | brains | Schweinefleisch | pork |
| Hirsch | venison | Speck | bacon |
| Huhn | chicken | Taube | pigeon |
| Innereien | innards | Zunge | tongue |
| Kalbfleisch | veal | | |

## Fish (Fisch)

| | | | |
|---|---|---|---|
| Aal | eel | Matjes | herring |
| Forelle | trout | Meeresfrüchte | seafood |
| Hecht | pike | Muscheln | mussels |
| Hummer | lobster | Scholle | plaice |
| Karpfen | carp | Seezunge | sole |
| Krabben | prawns | Thunfisch | tuna |
| Krebs | crab | Tintenfisch | squid |
| Lachs | salmon | Zander | pike-perch |
| Makrele | mackerel | | |

## Common food terms

| | | | |
|---|---|---|---|
| Am Spiess | on the spit | Frisch | fresh |
| Blau | rare | Gebacken | fried in breadcrumbs |
| Eingelegte | pickled | Gebraten | roasted |

| | | | |
|---|---|---|---|
| Gedämpft | steamed | Heiss | hot |
| Gefüllt | stuffed | Kalt | cold |
| Gegrillt | grilled | Kümmelbraten | roasted with caraway |
| Gekocht | cooked | | seeds |
| Geräucht | smoked | Powidl | plum sauce |
| Hausgemacht | home-made | | |

## Fruit (Obst)

| | | | |
|---|---|---|---|
| Ananas | pineapple | Himbeeren | raspberries |
| Apfel | apple | Kirschen | cherries |
| Banane | banana | Marillen | apricots |
| Birne | pear | Pflaumen | plums |
| Brombeeren | blackberries | Ribisel | redcurrants |
| Erdbeeren | strawberries | Rosinen | raisins |
| Grapefruit | grapefruit | Trauben | grapes |
| Heidelbeeren | bilberries | Zwetschgen | plums |

## Desserts

See also the "Coffee and cakes" colour section.

| | | | |
|---|---|---|---|
| Baiser | meringue | Marillenknödel | sweet apricot |
| Bienenstich | honey and almond tart | | dumplings |
| Buchteln | sweet dumplings | Mohr im Hemd | chocolate steamed |
| Kaiserschmarren | pancake and stewed | | pudding with cream |
| | fruit | Palatschinken | pancakes |
| Käsekuchen | cheesecake | | |

## Austrian specialities

| | | | |
|---|---|---|---|
| Backhendl | chicken fried in breadcrumbs | Schlipfkrapfen | ravioli-like pasta parcels with a meat and/or potato filling |
| Bauernschmaus | plate of cold sausage, pork and ham | Schweinshaxe | pork knuckle |
| Beuschel | chopped lung | Stelze | leg of veal or pork |
| Brettljause | platter of cold meats and bread | Tafelspitz | boiled beef, potatoes and horseradish |
| Debreziner | paprika-spiced sausage | | sauce |
| Grammelknödel | pork dumplings | Tiroler Gröstl | potatoes, onions and flecks of meat fried in a pan |
| Kärntner Käsnudl | large parcel of pasta dough filled with cheese | Tiroler Knödel | dumplings with pieces of ham, often eaten in a soup |
| Kasspätzln | pasta noodles with cheese | Wiener Schnitzel | breaded veal cutlet |
| Schinkenfleckern | ham with noodles | Zwiebelrostbraten | slices of roast beef topped with fried onions |

## Drinks (Getränke)

| | | | |
|---|---|---|---|
| Apfelsaft | apple juice | Obstler | fruit schnapps |
| Bier | beer | Orangensaft | orange juice |
| Flasche | bottle | Roséwein | rosé wine |
| Gespritzer | white wine with soda | Rotwein | red wine |
| Glühwein | mulled wine | Sauermilch | sour milk |
| Grog | hot water with rum and sugar | Schnapps | spirit |
| | | Sekt | sparkling wine |
| Kaffee | coffee | Sturm | new wine |
| Kakao | cocoa | Tee | tea |
| Kir | white wine with blackcurrant liqueur | Traubensaft | grape juice |
| | | Trocken | dry |
| Korn | rye spirit | Wasser | water |
| Kräutertee | herbal tea | Weisswein | white wine |
| Milch | milk | Zitronentee | tea with lemon |
| Mineralwasser | mineral water | | |

# Glossary

## German terms

**Ausstellung** Exhibition

**Bahnhof** Station

**Bau** Building

**Beisl** Pub

**Berg** Mountain, hill

**Bezirk** City district

**Brücke** Bridge

**Brunnen** Fountain

**Burg** Castle

**Denkmal** Memorial

**Dom** Cathedral

**Donau** River Danube

**Dorf** Village

**Durchgang** Passageway

**Durchhaus** Literally a "through-house" – a house whose ground floor is open, allowing access to a street or courtyard

**Einbahnstrasse** One-way street

**Erdegeschoss** Ground floor

**Erzherzog** Archduke

**Fasching** Carnival

**Feiertag** Holiday

**Flughafen** Airport

**Friedhof** Cemetery

**Fussgängerzone** Pedestrian zone

**Gasse** Alley

**Gemälde** Painting

**Gemütlich** Snug or cosy

**Grab** Grave

**Gürtel** The city's outer ring road

**Haltestelle** Bus/tram stop

**Haus** House

**Herzog** Duke

**Heuriger** Wine tavern

**Hof** Court, courtyard, mansion, housing complex

**Innere Stadt** Vienna's first district, the "Inner City"

Jugendherberge Youth hostel

Kaffeehaus Café

Kaiser Emperor

Kapelle Chapel

Kärnten Carinthia

Kaserne Barracks

Kino Cinema

Kirche Church

Kloster Monastery, convent

König King

Kunst Art

Kunstkammer Cabinet of curios

Land (pl. Länder) Name given to each of the nine federal provinces of Austria

Niederösterreich Lower Austria

Not Emergency

Oberösterreich Upper Austria

Palast Palace

Platz Square

Prinz Prince

Rathaus Town hall

Reich Empire

Residenz Palace

Ring The Ringstrasse, built on the old fortifications in 1857

Ritter Knight

Saal Hall

Sammlung Collection

Säule Column

Schanigarten Summer terrace/backyard

Schatzkammer Treasury

Schloss Castle

Stadt Town

Stiege Steps

Stift Collegiate church

Stock Floor

Strasse Street

Tor Gate

Trakt Wing (of a building)

Turm Tower

Viertel Quarter, district

Volk People, folk

Vororte The outer suburbs which lie beyond the Gürtel: Vienna's tenth to twenty-second districts

Vorstädte The inner suburbs which lie between the Ring and the Gürtel: Vienna's third to ninth districts

Wald Forest

Wien Vienna

Zimmer Room

## Political terms and acronyms

Anschluss Literally a "joining together" or "union" – the euphemism coined by the Nazis for the invasion and annexation of Austria in March 1938.

Austro-fascism Term to describe the one-party state set up by Engelbert Dollfuss in 1933. Dollfuss headed the Fatherland Front, a non-Nazi clerical-fascist movement which lasted until the Anschluss in 1938.

Austro-Marxism Philosophy expounded by SDAP theorists such as Otto Bauer in the early twentieth century. While still adhering to the language of class war, its programme was essentially revisionist, arguing that the downfall of capitalism was inevitable, and didn't have to be brought about by violence.

Babenburg Dynasty who ruled over Austria from 976 to 1246.

Biedermeier The term (Bieder means "upright") derives from the satiric figure of Gottlieb Biedermeier, a pious, law-abiding Swabian schoolmaster created in 1850 by Ludwig Eichrocht. It has come to be applied retrospectively to the period between 1815 and 1848 when Austria was under the sway of Prince Metternich. The era came to symbolize a safe, bourgeois, cosy lifestyle, and the label applied to its history, art and culture.

BZÖ (Bündis Zukunft Österreich). The rather ominous-sounding Alliance for the Future of Austria is a far-right party founded in 2005 by the late Jörg Haider and other leading members of the FPÖ.

CSP (Christlichsoziale Partei). The Christian Social Party was founded in the 1890s by Karl Lueger, who later became mayor of Vienna. The Christian Socials' combination of Catholicism, municipal socialism and anti-Semitism proved very popular with the Austrians. They were the main party of government in the 1920s and from their ranks rose Engelbert Dollfuss, who later introduced Austro-fascism in 1933.

FPÖ (Freiheitliche Partei Österreichs). The Austrian Freedom Party was the successor to the postwar VdU (see below). A far-right party that rose to prominence in the 1990s and scored spectacular electoral success under the charismatic and controversial leadership of Jörg Haider.

Habsburg Royal dynasty whose power base was Vienna from 1273 to 1918. They also held the office of Holy Roman Emperor from 1452 to 1806, and by marriage, war and diplomacy acquired territories all over Europe.

Heimwehr Right-wing militia whose origins lay in the local armed groups formed after the collapse of the empire in 1918. After 1927, these regional militias joined together and created a political wing, the Heimatblock, which supported the onset of Austro-fascism in 1933.

Holy Roman Empire Revived title of the Roman Empire, first bestowed by the pope on Charlemagne in 800. The emperor was chosen by the seven electors and passed around between the Hohenstaufen, Luxembourg and Habsburg families until 1438, when the Habsburgs made the title hereditary. It was dissolved on the orders of Napoleon in 1806.

Josephine Of or pertaining to the reign of Emperor Josef II (1780–90).

KPÖ (Kommunistische Partei Österreichs). Austrian Communist Party.

Kristallnacht Literally "Crystal Night", after the broken glass that was strewn across the streets during the pogrom of November 9–10, 1938. On this one night the majority of Jewish shops and institutions in the Third Reich – and all but one of the synagogues in Vienna – were destroyed by the Nazis.

k.u.k. kaiserlich und königlich (Imperial and Royal) – a title used after 1867 to refer to

everything in the Austro-Hungarian empire. Everything within Hungary was prefaced with a k. for königlich, everything in the rest of the empire k. k. (kaiserlich-königlich; Imperial-Royal).

NSDAP (National Sozialistiche Deutsche Arbeiterpartei). National Socialist German Workers' Party, the official name for the German Nazi Party.

ÖVP (Österreichische Volkspartei). Austrian People's Party, the postwar descendant of the Christian Socials, and the principal postwar centre-right party.

Pan-German This adjective covers a whole range of far-right political parties that advocated Anschluss with Germany, many of whom came together in the 1920s under the banner of the Greater German People's Party (Grossdeutsche Volkspartei, GDVP).

Red Vienna The period of Socialist municipal government in Vienna which lasted from 1919 to 1934.

Schutzbund SDAP militia founded in 1923.

SDAP (Sozial-Demokratische Arbeiterpartei). Social Democratic Workers' Party, the name given to the Socialist Party prior to World War II.

SPÖ (Sozialistische Partei Österreichs). The postwar Austrian Socialist Party, later changed to the Sozialdemokratische Partei Österreichs, but keeping the same acronym.

Staatsvertrag The Austrian State Treaty of 1955, which signalled the withdrawal of Allied troops – American, British, French and Soviet – from Austria, in return for Austrian neutrality.

Toleranzpatent The Patent of Tolerance decreed by Josef II in 1782, which allowed freedom of religious observance to Lutherans, Jews and, to a lesser extent, Protestants.

VdU (Verband der Unabhängigen). Union of Independents. Extreme nationalist party formed in 1949 and precursor of the FPÖ.

VF (Vaterländische Front). The Fatherland Front was founded in 1933 by Engelbert Dollfuss, the Christian Social Austrian chancellor who dissolved parliament and introduced Austro-fascism in 1933. The Front was a patriotic, clerical-fascist organization aimed at preventing the Nazis from seizing power.

## Architectural terms

**Ambulatory** Passage round the back of a church altar, in continuation of the aisles.

**Art Nouveau** Sinuous and stylized form of architecture and decorative arts, known as Secession or Jugendstil in Austria.

**Atlantes** Pillars in the shape of musclemen, named after the Greek god Atlas whose job it was to hold up the world.

**Baldachin** A canopy over an altar, tomb, throne or otherwise.

**Baroque** Expansive, exuberant architectural style of the seventeenth and eighteenth centuries, characterized by ornate decoration, complex spatial arrangement and grand vistas.

**Biedermeier** Simple, often Neoclassical, style of art and architecture popular from 1815 to 1848 and in part a reaction against the excesses of the Baroque period.

**Caryatid** Sculptured female figure used as a column. Similar to Atlantes (see above).

**Chancel** Part of the church where the main altar is placed, usually at the east end.

**Diapers** Ornamental patterning in brickwork.

**Empire** Neoclassical style of architecture and decorative arts practised in the first half of the nineteenth century.

**Filigree** Fanciful, delicate ornamental decoration in stone or metal.

**Fresco** Mural painting applied to wet plaster, so that the colours immediately soak into the wall.

**Glacis** Sloping ground between walls of Vienna's Innere Stadt and the suburbs prior to 1857.

**Gothic** Architectural style prevalent from the twelfth to the sixteenth centuries, characterized by pointed arches and ribbed vaulting.

**Historicism** Style of architecture which apes previous styles – ie neo-Baroque, neo-Renaissance, neo-Gothic – also known as Ringstrasse style.

**Jugendstil** German/Austrian version of Art Nouveau, literally "youthful style" – see also Secession, below.

**Loggia** Covered area on the side of a building, usually arcaded.

**Lunette** An oval or semicircular opening to admit light into a dome.

**Nave** Main body of a church, usually the western end.

**Neoclassicism** Late eighteenth- and early nineteenth-century style of architecture and design returning to classical Greek and Roman models as a reaction against the excesses of Baroque and Rococo.

**Oriel** A bay window, usually projecting from an upper floor.

**Quoins** External corner stones of a wall.

**Ringstrasse** Pompous historicist style of architecture which aped Gothic, Renaissance, Baroque and Classical architecture, and which was very popular during the construction of Vienna's Ringstrasse.

**Rococo** Highly florid style of architecture and design, forming the last phase of Baroque.

**Romanesque** Solid architectural style of the late tenth to thirteenth centuries, characterized by round-headed arches and geometrical precision.

**Secession** Movement of artists who split (seceded – hence the term) from the city's Academy of Arts in 1897. Also used more generally as a term synonymous with Jugendstil.

**Sgraffito** Monochrome plaster decoration effected by means of scraping back the first white layer to reveal the black underneath.

**Spandrel** The surface area between two adjacent arches.

**Stucco** Plaster used for decorative effects.

**Transepts** The wings of a cruciform church, placed at right angles to the nave and chancel.

**Trompe l'oeil** Painting designed to fool the onlooker into thinking that it is three-dimensional.

**Wiener Werkstätte** (Vienna Workshops). A group of Secession artists founded in 1903.

# Small print and
# Index

# A Rough Guide to Rough Guides

SMALL PRINT

Published in 1982, the first Rough Guide – to Greece – was a student scheme that became a publishing phenomenon. Mark Ellingham, a recent graduate in English from Bristol University, had been travelling in Greece the previous summer and couldn't find the right guidebook. With a small group of friends he wrote his own guide, combining a highly contemporary, journalistic style with a thoroughly practical approach to travellers' needs.

The immediate success of the book spawned a series that rapidly covered dozens of destinations. And, in addition to impecunious backpackers, Rough Guides soon acquired a much broader and older readership that relished the guides' wit and inquisitiveness as much as their enthusiastic, critical approach and value-for-money ethos.

These days, Rough Guides include recommendations from shoestring to luxury and cover more than 200 destinations around the globe, including almost every country in the Americas and Europe, more than half of Africa and most of Asia and Australasia. Our ever-growing team of authors and photographers is spread all over the world, particularly in Europe, the US and Australia.

In the early 1990s, Rough Guides branched out of travel, with the publication of Rough Guides to World Music, Classical Music and the Internet. All three have become benchmark titles in their fields, spearheading the publication of a wide range of books under the Rough Guide name.

Including the travel series, Rough Guides now number more than 350 titles, covering: phrasebooks, waterproof maps, music guides from Opera to Heavy Metal, reference works as diverse as Conspiracy Theories and Shakespeare, and popular culture books from iPods to Poker. Rough Guides also produce a series of more than 120 World Music CDs in partnership with World Music Network.

Visit www.roughguides.com to see our latest publications.

## Rough Guide credits

**Text editor**: Greg Ward
**Layout**: Sachin Tanwar
**Cartography**: Lokamata Sahu
**Picture editor**: Rhiannon Furbear
**Production**: Rebecca Short
**Proofreader**: Stewart Wild
**Cover design**: Nicole Newman, Dan May, Jess Carter
**Photographer**: Natascha Sturny
**Editorial**: **London** Andy Turner, Keith Drew, Edward Aves, Alice Park, Lucy White, Jo Kirby, James Smart, Natasha Foges, James Rice, Emma Beatson, Emma Gibbs, Kathryn Lane, Monica Woods, Mani Ramaswamy, Harry Wilson, Lucy Cowie, Alison Roberts, Lara Kavanagh, Eleanor Aldridge, Ian Blenkinsop, Charlotte Melville, Joe Staines, Matthew Milton, Tracy Hopkins; **Delhi** Madhavi Singh, Jalpreen Kaur Chhatwal, Jubbi Francis
**Design & Pictures**: **London** Scott Stickland,

Dan May, Diana Jarvis, Mark Thomas, Nicole Newman, Sarah Cummins; **Delhi** Umesh Aggarwal, Ajay Verma, Jessica Subramanian, Ankur Guha, Pradeep Thapliyal, Anita Singh, Nikhil Agarwal, Sachin Gupta
**Production**: Liz Cherry, Louise Minihane, Erika Pepe
**Cartography**: **London** Ed Wright, Katie Lloyd-Jones; **Delhi** Rajesh Chhibber, Ashutosh Bharti, Rajesh Mishra, Animesh Pathak, Jasbir Sandhu, Swati Handoo, Deshpal Dabas
**Marketing, Publicity & roughguides.com**: Liz Statham
**Digital Travel Publisher**: Peter Buckley
**Reference Director**: Andrew Lockett
**Operations Coordinator**: Becky Doyle
**Operations Assistant**: Johanna Wurm
**Publishing Director (Travel)**: Clare Currie
**Commercial Manager**: Gino Magnotta
**Managing Director**: John Duhigg

## Publishing information

This sixth edition published July 2011 by
**Rough Guides Ltd**,
80 Strand, London WC2R 0RL
11, Community Centre, Panchsheel Park, New Delhi 110017, India

**Distributed by the Penguin Group**

Penguin Books Ltd,
80 Strand, London WC2R 0RL

Penguin Group (USA)
375 Hudson Street, NY 10014, USA

Penguin Group (Australia)
250 Camberwell Road, Camberwell, Victoria 3124, Australia

Penguin Group (NZ)
67 Apollo Drive, Mairangi Bay, Auckland 1310, New Zealand

Rough Guides is represented in Canada by Tourmaline Editions Inc. 662 King Street West, Suite 304, Toronto, Ontario M5V 1M7

Cover concept by Peter Dyer.

Typeset in Bembo and Helvetica to an original design by Henry Iles.

Printed in Singapore
296pp includes index
A catalogue record for this book is available from the British Library
ISBN: 978-1-84836-681-7
The publishers and authors have done their best to ensure the accuracy and currency of all the information in **The Rough Guide to Vienna**, however, they can accept no responsibility for any loss, injury, or inconvenience sustained by any traveller as a result of information or advice contained in the guide.

3   5   7   9   8   6   4   2

MIX
Paper from responsible sources
FSC™ C018179

## Help us update

We've gone to a lot of effort to ensure that the sixth edition of **The Rough Guide to Vienna** is accurate and up-to-date. However, things change – places get "discovered", opening hours are notoriously fickle, restaurants and rooms raise prices or lower standards. If you feel we've got it wrong or left something out, we'd like to know, and if you can remember the address, the price, the hours, the phone number, so much the better.

Please send your comments with the subject line "**Rough Guide Vienna Update**" to ©mail @uk.roughguides.com. We'll credit all contributions and send a copy of the next edition (or any other Rough Guide if you prefer) for the very best emails.

Find more travel information, connect with fellow travellers and book your trip on ®www .roughguides.com

## Acknowledgements

**Rob Humphreys** would like to thank Kate for testing out the day bed again, to the Sachers for their *gemütlichkeit*, and to Jo, Lara and, in particular, Greg, for their forbearance and understanding.

## Photo credits

All photography by Natascha Sturny © Rough Guides except the following

Introduction
The Hofburg © Latitudestock/Getty Images
Roof of Stephansdom © Chris Coe/Axiom
Mozart ceramic souvenirs © Steve Outram/Aurora Photos/Corbis
Haus der Musik © age fotostock/SuperStock
Fiaker in front of Michaelerkirche © imagebroker .net/SuperStock
MuseumsQuartier © age fotostock/SuperStock

Things not to miss
01 Tram © Charles Bowman/Robert Harding World Imagery/Corbis
03 Staatsoper © Massimo Borchi/Atlantide Phototravel/Corbis
05 Schatzkammer © Hans Vermeyen/Austrian Archives/Corbis
06 Trześniewski © allOver photography/Alamy
08 Haus der Musik © Haus der Musik
09 Karlskirche © imagebroker.net/SuperStock
10 Fiaker © Grant Faint/Getty Images
11 Café Central © René Mattes/Hemis/Corbis
12 *The Third Man* © Haywood Magee/Hulton-Deutsch Collection/Corbis

18 Kunsthistorisches Museum © Prisma/ SuperStock
19 *The Kiss*, Gustav Klimt © The Gallery Collection/Corbis
20 Stephansdom and Vienna skyline © Ellen Rooney/Axiom

The Secession colour section
Knight detail *Beethoven Frieze*, Gustav Klimt © Osterreichische Galerie Belvedere/The Bridgeman Art Library
Illustration from *Ver Sacrum* by Kolo Moser © Imagno/Austrian Archives
Here's a Kiss to the Whole World *Beethoven Frieze*, Gustav Klimt © SuperStock
Detail of Stadtbahn Pavilion, Karlsplatz © Rudy Sulgan/Corbis

Coffee and cakes colour section
Café Central © Ben Mangor/SuperStock
Cappuccino, Café Sperl © Hemis.fr/SuperStock
*Sachertorte* © Herwig Prammer/Reuters/Corbis
Demel © Herwig Prammer/Reuters/Corbis

# Index

Map entries are in colour.

293

# Map symbols

maps are listed in the full index using coloured text

| | | | |
|---|---|---|---|
| – – – – | Chapter Boundary | ✈ | International airport |
| – – – – | International boundary | Ⓤ | U-Bahn |
| ▬▬▬ | Motorway | Ⓢ | S-Bahn |
| ═══ | Main road | ✡ | Synagogue |
| — | Minor road | 🕌 | Mosque |
| ⅏ | Steps | ⓘ | Information office |
| ]= = =[ | Underpass tunnel | ⊠ | Post office |
| —•— | Railway | ▬ | Building |
| — | Tram line | ✚ | Church |
| ▬▬▬ | River/canal | ⬭ | Stadium |
| — | Wall | ▦ | Park |
| ⊠—⊠ | Gate | ⌐+⌐ | Christian cemetery |
| ▲ | Mountain peak | ⌐-⌐ | Jewish cemetery |

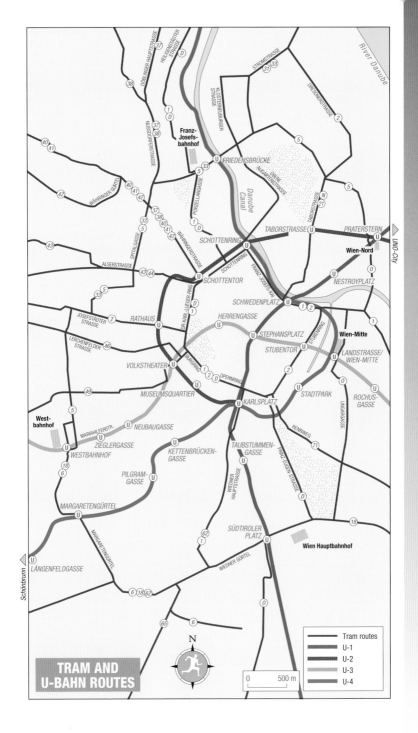

**TRAM AND
U-BAHN ROUTES**

Tram routes
U-1
U-2
U-3
U-4

0       500 m

N

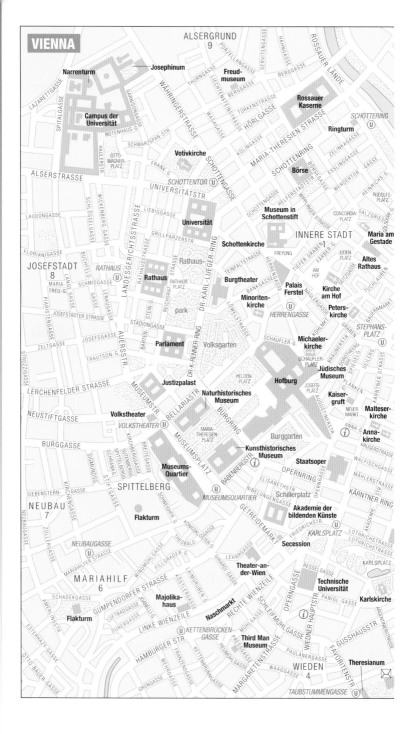

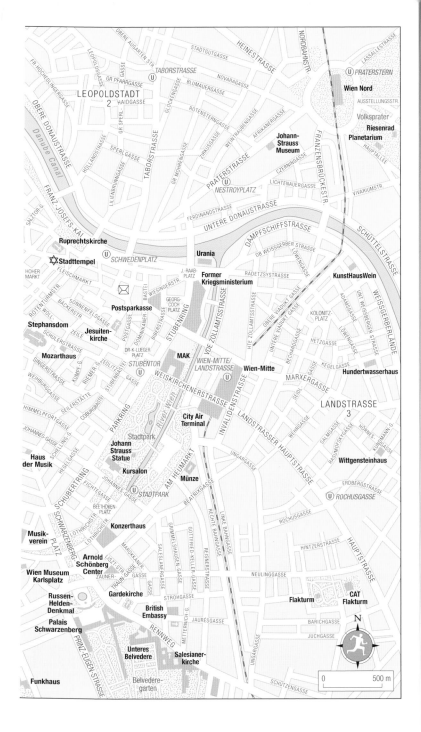

# U-BAHN AND S-BAHN LINES

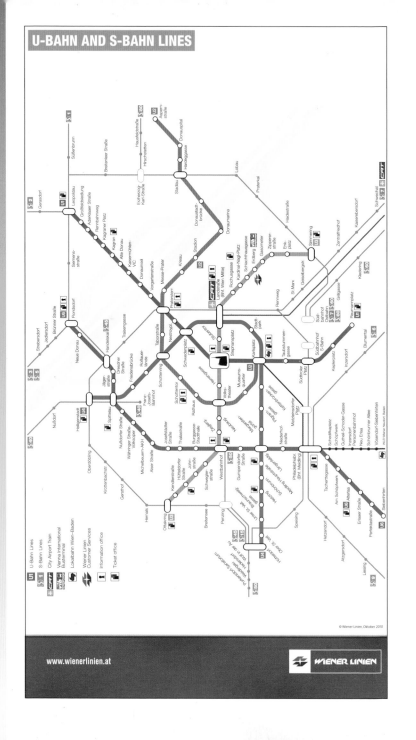

www.wienerlinien.at

© Wiener Linien, Oktober 2010

WIENER LINIEN